THE ARDEN SHAKESPEARE

GENERAL EDITORS:
RICHARD PROUDFOOT, ANN THOMPSON
and DAVID SCOTT KASTAN

THE TAMING OF THE SHREW

The Arden Shakespeare

All's Well That Ends Well: edited by G. K. Hunter*
Antony and Cleopatra: edited by John Wilders
As You Like It: edited by Agnes Latham*
The Comedy of Errors: edited by R. A. Foakes*
Coriolanus: edited by Philip Brockbank*
Cymbeline: edited by J. M. Nosworthy*
Hamlet : edited by Harold Jenkins*
Julius Caesar: edited by David Daniell
King Henry IV parts 1 and 2: edited by A. R. Humphreys*
King Henry V: edited by T. W. Craik
King Henry VI part 1: edited by Edward Burns
King Henry VI part 2: edited by Ronald Knowles
King Henry VI part 3: edited by A. S. Cairncross*
King Henry VIII: edited by R. A. Foakes*
King John: edited by E. A. J. Honigmann*
King Lear: edited by R. A. Foakes
King Richard II : edited by Peter Ure*
King Richard III: edited by Anthony Hammond*
Love's Labour's Lost: edited by H. R. Woudhuysen
Macbeth: edited by Kenneth Muir*
Measure for Measure: edited by J. W. Lever*
The Merchant of Venice: edited by John Russell Brown*
The Merry Wives of Windsor: edited by Giorgio Melchiori
A Midsummer Night's Dream: edited by Harold F. Brooks*
Much Ado About Nothing: edited by A. R. Humphreys*
Othello: edited by E. A. J. Honigmann
Pericles : edited by F. D. Hoeniger*
The Poems: edited by F. T. Prince*
Romeo and Juliet: edited by Brian Gibbons*
Shakespeare's Sonnets: edited by Katherine Duncan-Jones
The Taming of the Shrew: edited by Brian Morris*
The Tempest:: edited by Virginia Mason Vaughan and Alden T. Vaughan
Timon of Athens: edited by H. J. Oliver*
Titus Andronicus: edited by Jonathan Bate
Troilus and Cressida: edited by David Bevington
Twelfth Night: edited by J. M. Lothian and T. W. Craik*
The Two Gentlemen of Verona: edited by Clifford Leech*
The Two Noble Kinsmen: edited by Lois Potter
The Winter's Tale: edited by J. H. Pafford*

*Second Series

THE ARDEN EDITION OF THE
WORKS OF WILLIAM SHAKESPEARE

THE TAMING
OF THE SHREW

Edited by
BRIAN MORRIS

The Arden website is at
http://www.ardenshakespeare.com

The general editors of the Arden Shakespeare have been
W. J. Craig and R. H. Case (first series 1899-1944)
Una Ellis-Fermor, Harold F. Brooks, Harold Jenkins and
Brian Morris (second series 1946-82)

Present general editors (third series)
Richard Proudfoot, Ann Thompson and David Scott Kastan

This edition of *The Taming of the Shrew* by Brian Morris
first published 1981 by Methuen & Co. Ltd

Published by the Arden Shakespeare
Reprinted 2000

Editorial matter © 1962 Methuen & Co. Ltd

Arden Shakespeare is an imprint of Thomson Learning

Thomson Learning
Berkshire House
168-173 High Holborn
London WC1V 7AA

Printed in Singapore

British Library Cataloguing in Publication Data
A catalogue record for this book is available from the British Library
Library of Congress Cataloguing in Publication Data
A catalogue record has been applied for

ISBN 0-17-443588-6(hbk)
ISBN 1-903436-10-9 (pbk)
NPN 9 8 7 6

FOR
JEAN ROBERTSON

Tu nihil invita dices faciesve Minerva
(HORACE, *Ars Poetica*, 385)

CONTENTS

PREFACE

'Grammatici certant', said Horace, 'et adhuc sub iudice lis est': scholars dispute, and the case is still before the court. No edition of a Shakespeare play can hope to be definitive, and the present one owes much to its predecessors while offering 'things old and new' to those which shall succeed it. The text is set up from a re-examination of F (1623), in the light of Charlton Hinman's work, and is not based on R. Warwick Bond's Arden edition of 1904, since Bond believed that *The Taming of A Shrew* was a source for *The Taming of the Shrew*, a view which I am unable to accept. The introduction and commentary are new, though I have naturally made extensive use of the work of previous editors and commentators, especially the editions by Bond, Dover Wilson, Hosley, Sisson and Hibbard.

Many debts are incurred in a work of this kind, and it is a pleasure to thank the libraries which have afforded me notable courtesies, and the many colleagues and other scholars who have patiently answered my many questions, read drafts, and offered suggestions. I am particularly grateful for help of various kinds to Anne Bantoft, Gordon Corbet, Michael J. Day, Brian Gibbons, Roma Gill, Ernst Honigmann, E. D. Mackerness, the late Allardyce Nicoll, Frank Pierce, Robin Robbins, Philip Roberts, Niall Rudd, Marvin Spevack, F. W. Sternfeld and Anne Thompson.

Like all other Arden editors I am especially grateful to the General Editors, Professor Harold Brooks and Professor Harold Jenkins; this series is their mighty monument. In my case, the indebtedness is both deep and long, since for ten years they have coaxed, cajoled, encouraged and stimulated a tardy son whose purpose must all too often have seemed almost blunted. Their vigilance has preserved me from many errors, their suggestions have enriched the book at every point, and their charity is above all their works. Like Sebastian, 'I can no other answer make, but thanks, / And thanks, and ever thanks'—and they will not fail to note, I hope with approval, that in this quotation from *Twelfth Night* I have preferred the Arden text, with Theobald's emendation, to the metrically defective version in F.

ix

An even longer debt of admiration and gratitude, extending far beyond the present work, is acknowledged in the dedication.

Coleg Prifysgol Dewi Sant   BRIAN MORRIS
Llanbedr Pont Steffan
June 1981

ACKNOWLEDGEMENTS

Extracts from Gascoigne's *Supposes* and Grimeston's translation of Goulart's *Thrésor d'histoires admirables et mémorables* are taken from *Narrative and Dramatic Sources of Shakespeare*, ed. G. Bullough, vol. 1 (3rd impression, 1964), and are printed here by permission of Routledge and Kegan Paul Ltd.

ABBREVIATIONS AND REFERENCES

The abbreviated titles of Shakespeare's works are as in C. T. Onions, *A Shakespeare Glossary*, 2nd edn (1919). Passages quoted or cited are from the complete *Tudor Shakespeare*, ed. Peter Alexander (Collins, 1951).

I. EDITIONS

Alexander	*William Shakespeare, The Complete Works*, ed. Peter Alexander, 1951.
Bantam	*The Taming of the Shrew*, ed. Campbell, Rothschild and Vaughan, New York/Toronto/London, 1967.
Bond	*The Taming of the Shrew*, ed. R. Warwick Bond, 1904 (Arden Shakespeare).
Camb.	*The Works of William Shakespeare*, ed. William George Clark and John Glover, 1863–6 (Cambridge Shakespeare).
Capell	*Mr. William Shakespeare his Comedies, Histories, and Tragedies*, ed. Edward Capell, 1768.
Collier	*The Works of William Shakespeare . . . with the various readings, and notes . . . by J. Payne Collier*, 1842–4; 2nd edn, 1853; 3rd edn, 1858.
Dyce	*The Works of William Shakespeare. The Text revised by the Rev. Alexander Dyce*, 1857; 2nd edn, 1864–7; 3rd edn, 1875–6.
F	*Mr. William Shakespeares Comedies, Histories, & Tragedies*, 1623.
F2	*Mr. William Shakespeares Comedies, Histories, & Tragedies*, 1632.
F3	*Mr. William Shakespear's Comedies, Histories, and Tragedies . . . The Third Impression*, 1664.
F4	*Mr. William Shakespear's Comedies, Histories, and Tragedies . . . The fourth Edition*, 1685.
Frey	*The Taming of the Shrew*, ed. Albert R. Frey, New York, 1888 (Bankside Shakespeare).
Globe	*The Works of William Shakespeare*, ed. W. G. Clark and W. Aldis Wright, Cambridge and London, 1864.
Grant White	*The Works of William Shakespeare*, ed. Richard Grant White, Boston, 1857.
Halliwell	*The Complete Works of Shakspere*, revised by J. O. Halliwell, London and New York, 1852; 2nd edn, revised, 1856.
Hanmer	*The Works of Shakespear . . . Carefully Revised and Corrected by the former Editions*, ed. Thomas Hanmer, Oxford, 1744.
Heilman	*The Taming of the Shrew*, ed. Robert B. Heilman, New York/Toronto/London, 1966 (Signet Edition).

Hibbard	*The Taming of the Shrew*, ed. G. R. Hibbard, 1968 (New Penguin Shakespeare).
Hood	*The Taming of the Shrew*, ed. R. C. Hood, 1975 (Macmillan Shakespeare).
Hosley	*The Taming of the Shrew*, ed. Richard Hosley, in *William Shakespeare: The Complete Works*, New York, 1969 (Pelican Shakespeare).
Johnson	*The Plays of William Shakespeare . . . To which are added Notes by Sam. Johnson*, 1765.
Keightley	*The Plays of William Shakespeare. Carefully edited by Thomas Keightley*, 1864.
Malone	*The Plays and Poems of William Shakespeare . . . with . . . notes by Edmond Malone*, 1790.
NCS	*The Taming of the Shrew*, ed. Sir Arthur Quiller-Couch and John Dover Wilson, Cambridge, 1928 (New [Cambridge] Shakespeare).
Perry	*The Taming of the Shrew*, ed. H. T. E. Perry, Yale, 1921; revised, T. G. Bergin, 1954.
Pope	*The Works of Shakespear . . . Collected and Corrected . . . by Mr. Pope*, 1723.
Q	*A Wittie and Pleasant Comedie Called The Taming of the Shrew . . . Written by Will. Shakespeare*. London, Printed by *W.S.* for *Iohn Smethwicke* . . . 1631.
Rann	*The Dramatic Works of Shakespeare . . . with notes by Joseph Rann*, Oxford, 1787.
Reed	*The Plays of William Shakespeare . . . Revised and augmented by Isaac Reed*, 1813.
Riverside	*The Riverside Shakespeare*, textual ed. G. Blakemore Evans, 1974.
Rowe	*The Works of Mr. William Shakespear . . . Revis'd and Corrected by N. Rowe Esq.*, 1709; 2nd edn, 1709; 3rd edn, 1714.
Singer	*The Dramatic Works of William Shakespeare with Notes . . . by Samuel Weller Singer*, 1826; revised edn, 1856.
Sisson	*William Shakespeare, The Complete Works*, ed. C. J. Sisson, 1954.
Steevens	*The Plays of William Shakespeare . . . To which are added notes by Samuel Johnson and George Steevens*, 1773; 2nd edn, revised and augmented, 1778.
Theobald	*The Works of Shakespeare . . . Collated with the Oldest Copies, and Corrected; with Notes . . . By Mr. Theobald*, 1733; 2nd edn, 1740.
Warburton	*The Works of Shakespear. The Genuine Text . . . settled . . . By Mr. Pope and Mr. Warburton*, 1747.

2. TEXTUAL COMMENTARIES

Sisson, *New Readings*	C. J. Sisson, *New Readings in Shakespeare*, Cambridge, 1956 (reprinted 1961).
Thirlby	Styan Thirlby, conjectures adopted by Theobald, 1733; others published in J. Nichols, *Literary Illustrations of the Eighteenth Century*, 1817.

| Tyrwhitt | [Thomas Tyrwhitt,] *Observations and Conjectures upon some Passages of Shakespeare*, Oxford, 1766. |
| Walker | W. S. Walker, *A Critical Examination of the Text of Shakespeare* [ed. W. N. Lettsom], 1860. |

3. OTHER WORKS

Abbott	E. A. Abbott, *A Shakespearean Grammar*, 1869.
Arber	*The Stationers' Registers*, 1554–1640, ed. Edward Arber, 1875.
AV	Authorised Version of the Bible, 1611.
Bullough	Geoffrey Bullough (ed.), *Narrative and Dramatic Sources of Shakespeare*, vol. i, 1957.
Chambers, *ES*	E. K. Chambers, *The Elizabethan Stage*, 1923.
Chambers, *WS*	E. K. Chambers, *William Shakespeare: A Study of Facts and Problems*, 1930.
Cotgrave	Randall Cotgrave, *A dictionarie of the French and English tongues*, 1611; 2nd edn (ed. Robert Sherwood), 1632.
Golding	*Shakespeare's Ovid: being Arthur Golding's Translation of the Metamorphoses*, ed. W. H. D. Rouse, 1961.
Greg, *EPS*	W. W. Greg, *The Editorial Problem in Shakespeare*, Oxford, 1942; 3rd edn, 1954.
Greg, *SFF*	W. W. Greg, *The Shakespeare First Folio*, 1955.
H. & S.	*Ben Jonson*, ed. C. H. Herford and Percy and Evelyn Simpson, Oxford, 1925–52.
Hulme	Hilda M. Hulme, *Explorations in Shakespeare's Language*, 1962.
Kökeritz	Helge Kökeritz, *Shakespeare's Pronunciation*, 1953.
Madden	D. H. Madden, *The Diary of Master William Silence*, 1907.
Muir	Kenneth Muir, *The Sources of Shakespeare's Plays*, 1977.
OED	*Oxford English Dictionary.*
Onions	C. T. Onions, *A Shakespeare Glossary*, 2nd edn, revised, 1919.
Shakespeare's England	*Shakespeare's England. An Account of the Life and Manners of his Age*, ed. Sidney Lee and C. T. Onions, 1916.
Smith and Wilson	*The Oxford Dictionary of English Proverbs*, compiled by William George Smith; 3rd edn, ed. F. P. Wilson, Oxford, 1970.
Spenser, *FQ*	*Spenser's Faerie Queene*, ed. J. C. Smith, Oxford, 1909.
Sugden	E. H. Sugden, *A Topographical Dictionary to the Works of Shakespeare and his Fellow-Dramatists*, 1925.
Tilley	M. P. Tilley, *A Dictionary of the Proverbs in England in the Sixteenth and Seventeenth Centuries*, Ann Arbor, Michigan, 1950.

4. PERIODICALS

E&S	*Essays and Studies.*
ES	*English Studies.*
HLQ	*Huntington Library Quarterly.*
JEGP	*Journal of English and Germanic Philology.*
MLN	*Modern Language Notes.*
MLQ	*Modern Language Quarterly.*

MLR	Modern Language Review.
N&Q	Notes and Queries.
PMLA	Publications of the Modern Language Association of America.
PQ	Philological Quarterly.
RES	Review of English Studies.
SAB	Shakespeare Association Bulletin.
SEL	Studies in English Literature.
SJ	Shakespeare Jahrbuch.
SQ	Shakespeare Quarterly.
Sh.S.	Shakespeare Survey.
TLS	The Times Literary Supplement.

References to periodicals normally cite author, periodical and year of publication, but volume and page numbers are sometimes added to aid identification.

INTRODUCTION

I. THE TEXT

The Taming of the Shrew was first published in the Folio of 1623, and this is the only text which has authority. It appears among the Comedies as the eleventh play in the volume, and occupies twenty-two pages from sig. S2^v to sig. V1. Charlton Hinman has established that printing followed normal procedures for the Folio, with the exception of a considerable delay before the setting of the last half-page (V1), and he identifies three compositors, working recognizable stints.[1] The following table, based on Hinman, identifies each compositor's share of the text, though, since the setting was by formes, the pages were composed in an order different from that in which they appear in print.

Sig. S2^v–S6^v	Compositor B	Folio pp. 208–16
Sig. T1–T2^v	Compositor C	Folio pp. 217–20
Sig. T3–T4^v	Compositor B	Folio pp. 221–4
Sig. T5–T6^v	Compositor A	Folio pp. 225–8
Sig. V1	Compositor B	Folio p. 229

The establishment of each compositor's work is important because each had personal preferences and habits in matters like spelling, punctuation, and abbreviation of speech-prefixes, and they were not all equally likely to follow copy. They combined, in this instance, to produce a reasonably clean text with no more than the average scatter of misprints. Hinman notes evidence of proof correction in quires S and V (there are no variants which imply proof-reading in quire T), and the following relate to the text of *The Taming of the Shrew*:

	Sig.	Column and line	Uncorrected	Corrected
1.	S5^v	page no.	212	214
2.	S5^v	a3	dowric	dowrie
3.	S5^v	a47	fir	fir
4.	S5^v	b14	Tne	The

1. Charlton Hinman, *The Printing and Proof-Reading of the First Folio of Shakespeare* (Oxford, 1963), vol. II, pp. 446–62.

Sig.	*Column and line*	*Uncorrected*	*Corrected*
5. S5^v	b23	firſt	firſt
6. S5^v	b55	I neuer	I neuer
7. V1	sig.	Vv	V

S5^v exists in three states, since the correction in variants 2–5 was made fairly promptly, but the page-number error (variant 1) was not corrected until much later since about half the Folger copies show '212' instead of '214'. Similarly, about half the Folger copies show the uncorrected state of V1. There is a relative paucity of press variants in the Comedies after page C4, and Hinman concludes that, in general, the proof-reader appears to have been perfectly content to trust the compositors to reproduce the essential substance of the copy they used.[1] He points out, however, that 'a tolerably sharp eye' was needed to catch some of the variants on S5^v, and says, 'The text was certainly read, and read with some care; but reference to copy is by no means implied'.[2]

THE COPY

The compositors of F1 must have had before them a manuscript of some sort. The possibilities to be considered are: Shakespeare's foul papers,[3] as he delivered them to the theatre; those foul papers annotated by the theatre's book-keeper in the course of reading and casting; a transcript of the foul papers (made by the author or by someone else), or such a transcript annotated by the book-keeper; the theatre's prompt-copy, properly prepared for performance.[4]

We may be reasonably certain that it was not prompt-copy. Greg summarizes the features of such a manuscript as follows:

Characteristic of prompt-copy are the appearance of actors' names duplicating those of (usually minor) characters, possibly the general appearance of directions a few lines too early, and warnings for actors or properties to be in readiness.[5]

1. Hinman, *First Folio*, vol. 1, p. 333.

2. Ibid., vol. 1, p. 263.

3. Critics define 'foul papers' variously: some call them the author's 'original drafts'; Bowers defined them as 'the author's last complete draft in a shape satisfactory to him for transfer to fair copy', and Greg agreed. The matter is discussed in Honigmann, *The Stability of Shakespeare's Text* (1965), esp. pp. 17–18, where he prefers 'any kind of draft preceding the first fair copy'.

4. Honigmann notes that Shakespeare may have written on loose sheets of paper, and several states of composition might co-exist in one manuscript (ibid., p. 18).

5. Greg, *SFF*, p. 142.

Apart from the complex case of 'Sincklo' (discussed below) there are four places where what may well be actors' names appear in the text. At IV.ii.67–72 F1 reads:

> *Tra.* If he be credulous, and trust my tale,
> Ile make him glad to seeme *Vincentio*,
> And giue assurance to *Baptista Minola*.
> As if he were the right *Vincentio*.
> *Par.* Take me your loue, and then let me alone.
> > *Enter a Pedant.*
> *Ped.* God saue you sir.

The first 'me' in line 71 must be a misprint for 'inne', and Dover Wilson points out[1] that 'Par' probably stands for a player's name which was written in the margin of the manuscript opposite the stage-direction to indicate the actor of the Pedant's part, and was then mistaken for a prefix to the previous line. He identifies him as William Parr, who first appears in the plot of 1 *Tamar Cam*, performed in 1602 by the Admiral's Men.[2] At III.i.80 the name 'Nicke' appears as the speech-prefix for a Messenger, and commentators have suggested that this is Nicholas Tooley, who figures in the list of 'Principal Actors' at the beginning of F1. The single line that is given to Katherina's Haberdasher at IV.iii.63 has the speech-prefix 'Fel.', and this may be William Felle, who is not known as an actor but appears in Henslowe's *Diary* in 1599 as William Bird's 'man'. The list of Petruchio's servants in IV.i has been suspected of concealing actors' names, and one of them, Peter, appears again (but as Tranio's servant) as a 'mute' at IV.iv.68. Of the four, 'Par' and 'Nicke' certainly look like actors' names, but 'Fel' and 'Peter' are less certain, since 'Fel' might well be an abbreviation of 'Fellow' and 'Peter' no more than a character's name. The evidence from actors' names, however, is by no means indisputable evidence of prompt-copy, since such names could have been inserted into the manuscript by the book-keeper at any time after its delivery to the theatre. They may equally well, as we shall see below, originate with the author.

Almost all the stage-directions for entry occur on time. The principal exception is at II.i.271 where Baptista, Gremio and

---

1. NCS, 113–20, where Dover Wilson gives an exhaustive account of the actors' names in *Shr.*; Allison Gaw, 'Actors' Names in Basic Shakespearean Texts', *PMLA* (1925); Karl P. Wentersdorf, 'Actors' Names in Shakespearean Texts', *Theatre Studies* (1976–7).

2. The identification may well be correct, but it rests on a single (and very late) piece of evidence.

Tranio enter in the middle of Petruchio's speech, three lines before he says, 'Heere comes your father'. This is hardly significant, and might even be explained by the need for Baptista to overhear what Petruchio is saying. None of the stage-directions gives any warning for actors or properties to be in readiness. Indeed, the evidence of the stage-directions works decisively against any theory of prompt-copy. However careless an author may be in this matter, a prompter requires all entries and most exits to be correct and clearly indicated.[1] They are not so in the F text. In Induction i there is no exit for the Hostess at line 10, or for the Servingman at 72, and in each succeeding scene of the play, with the exception of I.ii and IV.v, there are unmarked exits which have to be supplied by the editor in a modern edition. More important, there are several examples of unmarked entries. At II.i.38 there is no entry for Hortensio, and Biondello is not named; we have simply '*Tranio, with his boy*'. At the beginning of III.ii there is no entry for Lucentio, and at line 181 Grumio is omitted from the list of those who enter after the wedding, though he is clearly among them and has lines to speak. At IV.ii.5 we have '*Enter Bianca*', though the following dialogue shows she must be accompanied by Lucentio. The opening of IV.v gives an entry for Petruchio, Katherina and Hortensio, but no mention is made of the servants to whom Petruchio speaks. At V.i.83 Tranio says 'Call forth an officer', but there is no stage-direction for his entry, though he obviously does appear on stage since Gremio addresses him directly a little later. But the most glaring example is the opening direction to V.ii, where, among the large number of people who enter, Tranio is mentioned twice, and Petruchio and Katherina, the main characters in the scene, are not mentioned at all. And neither is Hortensio. Such a stage-direction would be worse than useless in the theatre, and it cannot be the work of the prompter.

A prompter also needs to be quite clear about who says what. There are two passages in the F text where speech-prefixes are wrongly assigned and the result is nonsense (III.i.46–56 and IV.ii.4–8). In each case Hortensio, disguised as Litio, is involved, and the correct reattribution of the speeches is not difficult (see Commentary and, especially for the reading 'Litio', II.i.38n.). It is unlikely that a compositor would have made the several changes which produce F's text at these points, and it is

1. Exits are less important to a prompter than entrances. As Agnes Latham says (*AYL*, Arden edn (1975), p. xv), 'An actor can be trusted to get himself off the stage when he is no longer required.'

probable that some confusion was present in his copy—precisely the kind of confusion that a prompter would be obliged to clear up.

It is also unlikely that the compositors had before them Shakespeare's foul papers as he delivered them to the theatre, though this is less easy to demonstrate. Behind whatever served as copy for F must lie an authorial manuscript of some sort, and its characteristics will persist to a greater or lesser extent through any process of annotation or transcription. Similarly, a playwright's papers, be they ne'er so foul, will be likely to show (in stage-directions at least) some traces of the theatrical performance for which they are intended. In Greg's view the most common features betraying the foul-paper origin of a printed text include the following:

> loose ends and false starts and unresolved confusions in the text, which sometimes reveal themselves as duplications in print: next, inconsistency in the designation of characters in directions and prefixes alike, and occasionally the substitution of the name of an actor, when the part is written with a particular performer in view: lastly, the appearance of indefinite and permissive stage-directions, and occasionally of explanatory glosses on the text.[1]

Apart from the confusion over speech-prefixes at III.i and IV.ii, discussed above, there is nothing in the text of *The Shrew* which would qualify as a 'loose end'; certainly there is no such obvious false start as is found, for example, in *Romeo and Juliet*, V.iii. 102–3, where F reads (with Q2–4): 'I will beleeue, / Shall I beleeue, that vnsubstantiall death is amorous?' This is a clear example of an undeleted first attempt at the phrase, surviving through several printed texts; the reading takes us back close to Shakespeare's pen.[2] Such confusions and problems as there are in *The Shrew* (like the role of Hortensio) have no such manifest presence. An analysis of the speech-prefixes and the designation of characters in stage-directions reveals little that is instructive. In 1935 McKerrow drew attention to the fact that in the original editions of some plays the designation of characters is erratic and various, whereas in others it is almost completely regular.[3] He lists *The Shrew* in this second class, and Greg agrees, although he points

1. Greg, *SFF*, p. 142.

2. See the discussion of this and other similar readings in *Romeo and Juliet*, ed. Brian Gibbons (Arden edn, 1979), pp. 15ff.

3. R. B. McKerrow, 'A Suggestion regarding Shakespeare's Manuscripts', *RES* (1935).

out that we must except the Induction. In the two scenes of the Induction there is minor variation in the use of speech-prefixes, though Sly is referred to as 'Beg.' throughout. The Huntsmen are 'Hunts.', '2. Hun.', '1.Hun.', '2.H.', '1. Hunts.'; the Players are 'Players', '2. Player.', 'Plai.'; the Servants are '1. Ser.', '2. Ser.', '3. Ser.', '3. Man.', '2. Man.', '1 Man', '2 M'; and the Lady is 'Lady.', or 'La.'. Thereafter, the speech-prefixes are remarkably regular, with only such minor variations as 'Petr.' or 'Pet.' for Petruchio and 'Kate.' or 'Ka.' for Katherina. The variations in the Induction may lend some support to Honigmann's suggestion that an author's manuscript may have been written on loose sheets and represent more than one stage of composition, but it is not sufficient to establish foul-paper origin for the whole of the text. There is one point, however, at which we can almost certainly detect Shakespeare's hand. At Induction i. 86 the F text assigns a speech not to '2. Player' or 'Plai.' but to 'Sincklo'. This is the name of a known actor (see p. 49 and Commentary), and the text refers to his performing in an identifiable play. It is very unlikely that a book-keeper or prompter could be responsible for this, and highly probable that Shakespeare is here indicating the actor he has in mind for this particular role, just as he specifies Kemp and Cowley for the parts of Dogberry and Verges in *Much Ado about Nothing*, iv.ii (Q and F). But, in general, the regularity of the text, the consistency in character designation, and the absence of duplications, second thoughts and confusions argue against any theory that foul papers, as delivered to the theatre, formed the copy for F.

A few of the stage-directions suggest the book-keeper's rather than the author's hand. At the opening of Induction i, F reads '*Enter Begger and Hostes, Christopher Sly*'. The Beggar is nowhere called Sly in the speech-prefixes; he refers to the Slys at Induction i. 3, but it is not until ii. 5 that he calls himself 'Christophero Sly'. The most likely explanation is that the book-keeper added the name to Shakespeare's original stage-direction. At the end of i. i the Sly episode is introduced by the direction '*The Presenters aboue speakes*', and concludes with the instruction '*They sit and marke*'. These might be authorial, but they look more like an intervention in the theatre indicating how the end of i. i is to be played. Shakespeare would be less likely than a book-keeper to describe Sly and his entourage as 'Presenters'. A theatre origin may also be suspected for '*Pedant lookes out of the window*' at v.i. 13. The problematical phrase '*Gremio is out before*' in the stage-direction which opens v.i is patient of more than one interpretation (see

Commentary) but coming as it does after '*Enter Biondello, Lucentio and Bianca*' it looks very much like someone's afterthought. It is difficult to believe that a dramatist, in the process of composition, would realize that he had a character on stage who had not 'entered' via the appropriate stage-direction and would then emend that direction with so unusual a phrase. As we have seen, Shakespeare was not hyper-fastidious about providing entries for all his characters. But it is reasonable to surmise that a book-keeper, reading through the play, might notice that Gremio has lines to speak and add a phrase to the author's imperfect stage-direction, indicating in however strange a way that Gremio was not part of the Biondello–Lucentio–Bianca group. It is generally agreed amongst critics that the vast majority of stage-directions offer very little assistance in distinguishing between foul papers and prompt-copy, but this small group seems to originate in the theatre rather than in the author's study, and there may, of course, be many more of the same sort which do not betray their origin.

It can be demonstrated, however, that if the book-keeper did go through this manuscript he did not do a thorough job of preparing it for stage performance. Many of the stage-directions contain reference to indefinite numbers, and these would have to be regularized in rehearsal and production. Examples occur regularly throughout the play. At Induction i.13 we have '*Winde hornes. Enter a Lord from hunting, with his traine*' and at line 77 '*Enter Players*'. In Induction ii we twice find the phrase 'with attendants' though the number is not specified. iii.ii opens with '*Enter Baptista, Gremio, Tranio, Katherine, Bianca, and others, attendants*'. At iv.i.95 we find '*Enter foure or fiue seruingmen*', though a few lines earlier Grumio has been more specific—'Call forth *Nathaniel, Ioseph, Nicholas, Phillip, Walter, Sugersop* and the rest'. It may be Shakespeare who is being specific but extravagant in the text, and the book-keeper, realizing the limited resources of the company, who settles for the imprecise number in the stage-direction. But we might equally assume that the author did not make up his mind. In the same scene we have '*Enter seruants with supper*', and '*Enter Seruants seuerally*', where again no numbers are specified. '*With Attendants*' and '*with seruants*' occur again in v.i. All these directions are probably authorial, but a vigilant preparation of the manuscript in the theatre would probably have made them much more definite.

A number of stage-directions clearly derive from the author and from no one else. They are permissive, or descriptive, or indicative of action, properties or dress. There is a nice example at the opening of Induction ii: '*Enter aloft the drunkard with attendants, some with apparel, Bason and Ewer, & other appurtenances, & Lord.*' There are two in 1.i which indicate relationships between characters: '*Flourish. Enter Lucentio, and his man Triano*' [*sic*], and '*Enter Baptista with his two daughters, Katerina & Bianca, Gremio a Pantelowne, Hortensio sister* [read suitor] *to Bianca. Lucen. Tranio, stand by*'. No prompter would need to know that Tranio is Lucentio's man, that Katherina and Bianca are Baptista's daughters, or that Gremio is a pantaloon character, but this is precisely the kind of information an author would supply to himself and to the theatre company reading his play. Similarly, Petruchio's first entrance, in 1.ii, is signalled by '*Enter Petruchio, and his man Grumio*'. In the same scene there are references to disguise and to dress: '*Enter Gremio and Lucentio disguised*', '*Enter Tranio braue, and Biondello*', and in the following scene the description is even more particular, '*Enter Gremio, Lucentio, in the habit of a meane man, Petruchio with Tranio, with his boy bearing a Lute and Bookes*'. The stage appearance of a character is sometimes indicated, as in '*Enter Hortensio with his head broke*' (II.i.141) or '*Enter Baptista and Lucentio: Pedant booted and bare headed*' (IV.iv.18),[1] and so is stage action, as in '*Exit Biondello, Tranio and Pedant as fast as may be*' (V.i.102).[2] All this contrasts sharply with the kind of stage-directions one would expect to encounter in a text set up from prompt-copy. In *As You Like It*, for example, the stage-directions 'are very few and are expressed in the briefest imperatives',[3] providing only what a prompter needs. The prevalence in *The Shrew* of such full, varied and sometimes non-theatrical directions suggests that we are much closer to the author's original papers.

This impression may be deepened by noticing the presence in F's text of a number of Shakespearean spellings.[4] Compositors usually regularize the spellings of their copy to accord with their

1. Some caution is necessary here, since the Pedant is already on stage and has been described as '*drest like Vincentio*' in an earlier stage-direction. I suspect some dislocation of the text at this point.

2. Cf. *The Comedy of Errors*, IV.iv.144, ed. R. A. Foakes (Arden edn, 1962), where F reads '*Exeunt omnes, as fast as may be, frighted*', and Foakes's comments, pp. xiii and 86. Again, caution is necessary in interpretation, since Q1 *Romeo and Juliet*, II.vi.15, reads '*Enter Juliet somewhat fast*' and this can hardly be authorial. See Gibbons, edn cit., p. 11.

3. *AYL*, ed. Agnes Latham (Arden edn, 1975), p. xii.

4. The evidence for Shakespeare's orthography is principally derived from the three pages believed to be in his hand (Hand D) in the MS. play of *Sir Thomas More*. See A. W. Pollard and others, *Shakespeare's Hand in the Play of Sir Thomas More* (Cambridge, 1923), esp. pp. 113–41, and A. C. Partridge, *Orthography in Shakespeare and Elizabethan Drama* (1964).

own habits and preferences, and this process is complicated by the need to justify lines. But some authorial spellings will survive, and their frequency or infrequency has been held to indicate proximity, or lack of it, to his foul papers. There can, of course, be no certainty that any spelling is peculiar to Shakespeare, or that he always spelt any word in the same way. But when a word occurs in the three pages in Hand D in the *More* manuscript and in F's text of *The Shrew* with the same spelling, that spelling is probably Shakespeare's; the probability is higher if F's text also has instances of the same word with a different spelling. On fol. 8ᵇ of the *More* manuscript we find 'ruff' and the word occurs in F as 'Ruffes' at IV.iii.56. Hand D's 'dogges' is matched by F's 'dogge' (Ind. i.19 and 23), 'dogges' (IV.i.149) and 'dogge-wearie' (IV.ii.60). 'Warrs' appears in Hand D, and 'warre' three times in F (IV.v.30; v.ii.2; v.ii.163). 'Come', spelt with final e, occurs 84 times in F, but at IV.iv.24 we have 'com', as it is spelt ('com', 'Coms') in Hand D. Dover Wilson quotes Hand D's 'howskeeper' (with omission of medial e) as Shakespearean, and this may be reflected in F's 'houshold' (Ind. ii.140; II.i.271) and 'houshold-stuffe' (III.ii.229), where the more usual spelling 'house' is found 26 times. Shakespeare's fondness for 'oo' spellings may link 'afoord' in Hand D with 'affoords' at Ind. i.102, which elsewhere occurs twice as 'affords'.[1] The spelling 'obay' is found three times in Hand D, and F has 'obay' (v.ii.165) and 'Obey' (III.ii.221). 'Waight' is in Hand D, and 'waight' (II.i.205) and 'waighty' (I.i.247; IV.iv.26) in F, which does not record a 'weight' spelling at all. 'Countrey' is the spelling in Hand D, and we find 'Countreyman' twice in F (I.ii.188; IV.ii.77), and 'Countrimen' at I.i.197. Finally, 'bin' (for been) is the spelling of Hand D, and 'bin' occurs eight times in F, equalled by the eight appearances of 'beene'.[2] The total of ten Shakespearean spellings is only half the number recorded in Q1 of *A Midsummer Night's Dream*, which the editor suggests is close to Shakespeare's foul papers.[3] So it may be reasonable to suppose that F's text of *The Shrew* is further removed than that, but the evidence of the ten spellings, taken with those stage-directions which obviously betray the author's hand, might lead us to conjecture that the distance is not very great.

1. Cf. *MND*, ed. Harold F. Brooks (Arden edn, 1979), p. xxvi.

2. Other 'Shakespearean spellings' have been identified on different criteria. In NCS *Much Ado* Dover Wilson suggests 'maruailes' (cf. 'maruaile' at v.i.6); Honigmann, op. cit., p. 118, includes 'Sybell' (cf. 'Sibell' at I.ii.69).

3. *MND*, ed. Harold F. Brooks (Arden edn, 1979), p. xxvi.

The evidence so far adduced suggests that the copy for F was either Shakespeare's foul papers, annotated, fairly lightly, by the book-keeper, or a transcript of those papers, made by their author or by another hand, to which the book-keeper has made additions. It is impossible, in the end, to discriminate with certainty between foul papers and transcript,[1] but there is one characteristic of the F text which favours the idea of transcript. Dover Wilson argues[2] that the most obvious and irritating feature of F's text is 'the presence of a number of lines which have been metrically ruined by the omission, or less often by the addition, of some small word or words'. He finds evidence of this in more than forty lines, which he illustrates in the following list:

Will't please your lord*ship* drink a cup of sack	Ind. ii. 2[3]
And her witholds from me *and* other more	I. ii. 120
Of all thy suitors, here I charge *thee*, tell	II. i. 8
Much more a shrew of *thy* impatient humour	III. ii. 29
As *I* before imparted to your worship	III. ii. 128
Why, thou say'st true—it is *a* paltry cap	IV. iii. 81
What's this? a sleeve? 'tis like *a* demi-cannon	IV. iii. 88
Have to my widow! and if she *be* froward	IV. v. 77

Realizing that such omissions might derive from a compositor, Dover Wilson checked other texts, including the F text of *A Midsummer Night's Dream* which, he argued (correctly), was printed from Q2 (1619), so that the compositor's accuracy could be tested. In the case of *The Dream* he found that 'in the course of the reprinting the F compositors added no more than ten misprints of the type we are considering', and concluded, 'It would seem then that the number of misprints in *The Shrew* is quite abnormal for a verse-play'. He conceded that this might be explained by 'an unusually incompetent couple of compositors', but clearly preferred to believe that 'the trouble sprang from the copy itself, and . . . must be attributed to careless transcription'. At this later date, with Hinman's analyses to hand, we may feel

1. See Honigmann, op. cit., pp. 19–21, on 'Intermediate Fair Copies', and Appendix C, '*The Captives*: Foul Papers or Copy?'.

2. *The Shrew*, NCS edition, pp. 97–104. I am much indebted to Dover Wilson's assessment of the evidence here, though I do not agree with him on all points—for example, on 'auditory misprints' (pp. 99–100). It had not been realized, when he wrote, that copyists were liable to this kind of error, 'hearing' the words in their heads as they transcribed them.

3. The text here is quoted from Dover Wilson's (modernized) edition, and the italicized words are those omitted in F. Act, scene and line references are keyed to the present edition.

more confident in rejecting the unusually incompetent compositors, since there is no evidence that Compositors A, B and C
were prone to produce misprints of omission on this remarkable
scale elsewhere in the Folio. They must derive from the copy, and
they are best explained by supposing that, for some reason, the
foul papers were transcribed by Shakespeare or by someone else.
At this point we must take into account Dover Wilson's other
proposal that dictation entered into the process of transmission of
The Shrew, and that two hands were involved, one responsible for
the dialogue and the other for inserting the stage-directions. As
evidence of dictation he cites F's 'goods' for 'gauds' at II.i.3,
'Bots, Waid', for 'bots, swayed' (III.ii.53), 'But sir' for 'But to her'
(III.ii.126), 'come' for 'done' (v.ii.2), and 'too' twice for 'two'
(v.ii.62 and 186). I find these unconvincing: 'gauds' could easily
be misread as 'goods', especially if Hand D is characteristic of
Shakespeare's handwriting;[1] 'But to her' is by no means an
obvious correction, and several modern editors prefer F at this
point; 'done' seems more likely to be misread than misheard as
'come', and 'too' for 'two' is the kind of homophonic error anyone
can make by carrying words in his head. One cannot hang a
hypothesis about the transmission on 'Bots, Waid', the one remaining reading, which, in any case, could well be a compositor's
attempt to make sense of two unfamiliar words. The evidence for
an annotator who confined his work to the stage-directions is less
flimsy, but not compelling. Dover Wilson quotes the confusions
over speech-prefixes and attributions at III.i.46–56 and IV.ii.1–8.
At IV.ii.5 a stage-direction is affected, for F reads '*Enter Bianca*'
where 'Enter Bianca and Lucentio' is required, and Dover Wilson
argues that the creator of that direction was misled by the mis-
attribution of the previous line to 'Luc' and simply dropped the
second name. But, as we have seen, the omission of entries for
characters is common enough in F. He also points out that while
the name 'Tranio' is always spelt correctly in the dialogue it
sometimes appears as 'Trayno' or even 'Triano' in the stage-
directions.[2] This is a stronger piece of evidence, but it could
equally well be explained by assuming that a transcriber who was
careless enough to drop small words from over forty lines was also
none too fussy about the spelling of this particular name. Our

1. See the detailed analysis of Hand D contributed by Sir E. Maunde
Thompson to A. W. Pollard and others, *Shakespeare's Hand in the Play of Sir
Thomas More* (Cambridge, 1923), pp. 57–112.
2. This is not strictly true. He is 'Tronio' in the dialogue at v.i.75, but this
may be no more than a misprint.

examination of the stage-directions has already established that the book-keeper probably had a hand in such things as 'Gremio is out before' (opening of v.i), and either he or a transcriber might have been faced with an abbreviation like 'Tra.' in the stage-directions, and expanded it now one way, now another.

We may reject Dover Wilson's conjectures about dictated text and a separate hand responsible for the stage-directions without in any way weakening his case for a transcription as the copy for F. The evidence of the many omitted small words is strong. The question remains whether the transcriber was Shakespeare himself or someone else. Scribal copies were certainly not uncommon, and the work of Ralph Crane and others has been well documented.[1] On the other hand, as Honigmann has reminded us, authors did sometimes make copies of their own plays. We cannot even conjecture whether Shakespeare would have been an accurate or a careless transcriber of his own work, but the omission of so many small words, which spoils the metre of a line, seems to me to tilt the balance of probability in favour of an independent transcriber rather than the poet who wrote those lines and who would have had their rhythm running so strongly in his head.

The question of the copy for F is not unconnected with others about the date of the play and its relation to *The Taming of A Shrew* (discussed below), but the evidence from the text itself may conveniently be summarized at this point. Greg concludes that 'F was printed from a manuscript that had been annotated for the stage but not itself used in performance. . . . The simplest thing is to suppose that fresh foul papers of the whole were produced in 1594.'[2] My own view is broadly the same. I believe that F was set up from a scribal transcript of Shakespeare's foul papers, which had been annotated by the book-keeper, possibly at the reading and casting stage, but which had not served as the basis of a performance. The date of that transcript, and the reason for making it, are another matter.

2. 'THE SHREW' AND 'A SHREW'

A Pleasant Conceited Historie called The taming of a Shrew. As it was sundry times acted by the Right honorable the Earle of Pembrook his servants was entered on the Stationers' Register on 2 May 1594,

1. See F. P. Wilson, 'Ralph Crane, Scrivener to the King's Players', *The Library* (1926), and Greg, *EPS*, pp. 25 ff.
2. Greg, *SFF*, p. 215.

printed by Peter Short for Cuthbert Burbie, and published in the same year. Shakespeare's *The Taming of the Shrew* first appeared in print twenty-nine years later in F (1623). The two plays are clearly related in some way, and the similarity in their titles makes it difficult to be confident which play is being referred to in the handful of contemporary references which have survived. They seem to have been treated as identical for purposes of copyright. The colophon of F records that it was 'Printed at the Charges of W. Jaggard, Ed. Blount, I. Smithweeke, and W. Aspley', and Smithweeke (or Smethwick) and Aspley seem to have been included in the syndicate because they held effective rights in plays of Shakespeare already published.[1] Greg traces the descent of copyright in this play from 1594 to 1623.[2] *A Shrew* was printed in 1594 by virtue of its Stationers' Register entry, and reprinted in 1596 and 1607.[3] Peter Short died in 1603 and was succeeded by his widow, Emma, who married Humphrey Lownes in 1604, but no assignment of copies is recorded. On 22 January 1607 the play is entered to Nicholas Ling by order of a court and with Burby's consent, and the 1607 edition was printed for Ling by Valentine Simmes. On 19 November 1607 it was entered to John Smethwick as a copy 'Whiche dyd belonge to Nicholas Lynge', and Greg notes that Ling would appear to have been already dead, though his will was not proved until 1610. He concludes, 'Ling's title to the copy was evidently valid, and so presumably was Smethwick's.' Thus *The Taming of the Shrew* was published in F on the strength of Smethwick's ownership of the copyright of a quite different play with an almost identical title.

The two plays agree in many respects. The main 'taming' plot is the same in both, and both have a sub-plot of romantic intrigue; Christopher Sly appears in both plays; the shrew is tamed in both by the same means. In both plays the husband behaves scandalously at the wedding, starves his wife afterwards, rejects the work of a Haberdasher and a Tailor, and misuses his servants. In both the wife is brought to submission, asserts that the sun is the moon and pretends an old man is a young girl. Each play culminates in a feast at which men wager on their wives' obedience. In some places the dialogue corresponds closely, occasionally

1. Greg, *SFF*, p. 5. It was not considered necessary to include *The Shrew* in the list of copies 'not formerly entred to other men' entered on the Stationers' Register (8:11:1623) for the First Folio.

2. Ibid., p. 62.

3. For variants between these editions see *The Taming of a Shrew*, ed. F. S. Boas (1908).

and briefly word for word; in others, and for long stretches, there is no connection. With the exception of Katherina (Kate) the characters have different names, and one play is set in Padua, the other in Athens. The precise nature of the relationship has been the subject of critical speculation from Pope to the present day, and it is the most difficult and intractable problem that any editor of *The Shrew* faces. Three hypotheses have been proposed:

(*i*) that *A Shrew* is the principal source for *The Shrew*;
(*ii*) that *A Shrew* derives from *The Shrew* (the 'Bad Quarto' theory);
(*iii*) that both plays derive independently from a common source, a lost play on the 'Shrew' theme (the *Ur-Shrew*).[1]

The term 'Bad Quarto' ((*ii*) above) requires a little clarification. Honigmann points out to me (privately) that, since Alexander and others first used it, the phrase has hardened into meaning 'a text in which a close reconstruction of the original has been attempted by one or more actors from a cast that had performed the original version'. In this sense (as we shall see later) *A Shrew* is not well described as a Bad Quarto, and Honigmann (following Alexander in *A Shakespeare Primer*, p. 148) prefers to call it a 'stolen and garbled' version.

The idea that *A Shrew* is the source of *The Shrew* is less an argument than an assumption based on a late dating for *The Shrew*. The traditional view was that it was written in the second half of the 1590s. Bond probably represents the opinion of early-twentieth-century scholars when he says, 'on the whole, I see no reason to attempt a more precise date than Professor Dowden's ?1597'.[2] Only J. W. Shroeder, among recent critics, has offered a defence of this traditional view, but the main weight of his argument is directed towards showing that the analysis of parallel passages (used by Duthie) and the chronological difficulties in

1. The principal proponents of each hypothesis in the past century have been: (*i*) F. S. Boas, *Shakespeare and his Predecessors* (1896), *The Taming of a Shrew*, ed. (1908); R. Warwick Bond, *The Taming of the Shrew* (Arden edn, 1904); E. K. Chambers, *William Shakespeare* (1930); J. W. Shroeder, *JEGP* (1958). (*ii*) Wilhelm Creizenach, *Geschichte des neueren Dramas*, vol. IV (1909); J. S. Smart, *Shakespeare, Truth and Tradition* (1928); Peter Alexander, *TLS* (16 September 1926), *Shakespeare* (1964), *TLS* (8 July 1965), *SQ* (1969); J. Dover Wilson, *The Taming of the Shrew*, NCS edn (1928); B. A. P. Van Dam, *ES* (1928); E. A. J. Honigmann, *MLR* (1954); Richard Hosley, *HLQ* (1963–4), *SEL* (1961); J. C. Maxwell, *N&Q* (April 1968). (*iii*) A. H. Tolman, *PMLA* (1890); Hardin Craig, *Shakespeare* (1935); R. A. Houk, *PMLA* (1942); G. I. Duthie. *RES* (1943); W. W. Greg, *The Shakespeare First Folio* (1955).
2. Bond, pp. xlv–xlvi.

both *A Shrew* and *The Shrew* (on which Houk relies) do not require us to postulate an *Ur-Shrew*; they can be explained by other means, and do not preclude the possibility that *A Shrew* is a source-play. Shroeder does not claim to solve the problem, stating only that 'there is still something to be said for the old-fashioned notion that *A Shrew* is simply a text, admittedly imperfect, of an old play which Shakespeare used as one of the sources for his own comedy' (p. 425), and that 'the long debate about their relationship ought in fairness to be kept open and alive' (p. 443). He offers two pieces of evidence not adduced before. In three places[1] (i. 75-7, vi. 28-31, xv. 52-5) *A Shrew* promises humorous business which does not occur, 'business of precisely the low-comedy sort that a pirate ought logically to preserve'. All three do take place in *The Shrew*: Sly does attempt to take his 'wife' to bed, Kate breaks the lute on Hortensio's head, and Petruchio and Kate do disabuse Vincentio. Shroeder argues that it is less likely that a piratical reconstructor, recalling such pieces of business, carefully foreshadowed them in speech but omitted them in action, than that Shakespeare developed verbal hints in his source into full stage business. Secondly, he contends that those 'Marlovian' passages in *The Shrew* which are paralleled in *A Shrew* are best explained as Shakespeare working 'with a dim recollection of both Marlowe and *A Shrew* in his head'.[2] Both pieces of evidence require explanation by opponents of Shroeder's view, but his general hypothesis of *A Shrew* as a source-play has not won wide acceptance since 1958, and its basic weakness is that it does not fully confront Alexander's view of *A Shrew* as, essentially, a Bad Quarto.

The Bad Quarto hypothesis, as Alexander proposed it in 1926, depends on three claims:

(*i*) that the sub-plot of *A Shrew* and *The Shrew* is substantially the same as the main plot of Ariosto's *I Suppositi*, and that *The Shrew*'s handling of it is closer to Ariosto's than *A Shrew*'s;

(*ii*) that certain scenes connected with the sub-plot, common to *A Shrew* and *The Shrew* but not derived from Ariosto, are coherent in *The Shrew* but incoherent in *A Shrew*;

1. I quote *A Shrew* from the text in *Narrative and Dramatic Sources of Shakespeare*, ed. Bullough, vol. 1, 3rd impression (1964) and *The Shrew* from the present edn.

2. All the parallels between Marlowe and *A Shrew* are listed in Boas's edition, Appendix 1, pp. 91-8.

(*iii*) that the seven parallel passages in the main plot first
adduced by Hickson in 1850 demonstrate the dependence
of *A Shrew* on *The Shrew*.[1]

These are all arguments suggesting 'the direction of change', and,
between them, cover the whole play with the exception of the
Induction and the Sly interludes peculiar to *A Shrew*.[2] The first
claim is illustrated by considering the location of the action in
each case. Ariosto's play is set in Ferrara, *The Shrew* in Padua,
A Shrew in Athens. If *The Shrew* followed Ariosto it is easy to see
why Shakespeare transferred the scene, since for his audience
Padua was the typical Italian university town. The sequence
Ferrara–Padua–Athens is more probable than Ferrara–Athens–
Padua.[3] In support of the second claim Alexander argues that the
scene between Kate and Valeria in *A Shrew* (scene vi) is 'no more
than an imperfect improvisation on Shakespeare's theme'. But
Hickson's seven parallels, since they involve close textual comparison, are crucial to any consideration of the relationship
between these two texts. Alexander quotes one of them and
considers it enough to prove the case; Shroeder takes the same
one and one other and suggests that they are not parallel at all.
The passages need to be presented in full and as a group, to do
justice to Hickson's proposal.[4] Taken separately, each one
amounts to no more than a probability that the direction of
change is from *The Shrew* to *A Shrew*. Taken together, they have a
cumulative power, which is the greater because no one has produced a comparable list of examples arguing the reverse direction
of change.

    Two articles published in the 1940s powerfully sum up the case
for postulating an *Ur-Shrew* from which *The Shrew* and *A Shrew*
derive independently. R. A. Houk, in one of the most exhaustive
and meticulous accounts of the problem, proposed an *Ur-Shrew*
which might have been a complete manuscript play or might
have been no more than a set of notes, from which the text of
A Shrew derived by some Bad Quarto process of reporting or
reconstruction, and which Shakespeare later either adapted or
completed as *The Shrew*.[5] The evidence is deployed in two sections,

    1. Samuel Hickson, *N&Q* (30 March 1850).
    2. But see also Peter Alexander, *SQ* (1969).
    3. Alexander also considers in detail those characters whose transformations
are common to *I Suppositi*, *The Shrew* and *A Shrew*.
    4. See Appendix 1.
    5. Raymond A. Houk, 'The Evolution of *The Taming of the Shrew*', *PMLA*
(1942), pp. 1009–38.

the first of which is concerned with the order of scenes and the chronology in the first part of *A Shrew*, and the second with the chronology and inconsistencies in the latter part of *The Shrew*. His first hypothesis is that 'The deranged order of certain scenes in *A Shrew* suggests that *A Shrew* is a corruption of an earlier form of the play in which the order of the scenes corresponded to that of *The Shrew*'.[1] This is supported by examination of three of the interludes, and the strongest case is presented by the interlude at *A Shrew*, v. 187–94, which ends:

> LORD   My Lord heere comes the plaiers againe,
> SLIE   O brave, heers two fine gentlewomen.

Then Valeria enters with Kate (scene vi), and gives her a lute lesson. This does not answer to Sly's announcement, and Houk argues that the 'lute scene' is misplaced. He repositions it after v. 12, that is after the 'dowry' scene and before the 'betrothal' scene. A consequence of this is that the scene in which Aurelius and Polidor send Valeria to Alfonso's house as a music teacher must be repositioned immediately before the opening of scene v, the 'dowry' scene. This order of scenes satisfies the requirements of the interlude at v. 187ff., which begins with Sly's question '*Sim*, when will the foole come againe?', referring to Sander who has recently left the stage, and ends with the reference to 'two fine gentlewomen', which is then immediately followed by the entry of Alfonso's two daughters, Emelia and Philema, accompanied by Aurelius and Polidor. The rearrangement of scenes also gives a sequence from the opening of scene v (The Tamer, Introduction of Teacher, Dowry arranged, Lute scene, Betrothal, First interlude, The Wooing) which is exactly the same as that of the corresponding scenes in *The Shrew*. Two other interludes involve repositioning of a lesser importance, and Houk concludes that the 'original form' of the play presented these scenes in the order in which they occur in *The Shrew*.

The second hypothesis, that the obscured chronology of the first part of *A Shrew* points to an earlier form of the play which indicated the chronology more clearly (as *The Shrew* does), depends upon a complete analysis of the time-scheme in each text. Houk suggests five days for *The Shrew*, whereas in *A Shrew* 'there is much obscurity, and no more than two days are certainly involved'. This suggests that the 'original form' presented a clear and extended chronology, which *The Shrew* retains and *A Shrew* corrupts. Houk's evidence for the first hypothesis is strongly

1. Ibid., p. 1014.

challenged by Shroeder,[1] on the grounds that the interludes might be repositioned quite differently in the text, but, in any case, Houk's first two hypotheses do not establish the case for an *Ur-Shrew*, as he himself admits when he says: 'The conclusions of this section would seem to be in harmony with the theory of Hickson, Alexander, and Wilson that *A Shrew* is a corruption of *The Shrew*, revised or unrevised.'[2]

The evidence that *The Shrew* is a revision of an earlier form of the play which was similar, in some respects, to *A Shrew* is arranged around two proposals. First, that 'The element of rivalry in *The Shrew*, culminating in an elopement, involves a shortening of the chronology of the latter part of the play—a shortening which seems to have been the result of a revision which introduced the element of rivalry into an earlier form of the play', and second, 'that interludes of an earlier form of the play were eliminated during the revision, made under the influence of *I Suppositi*, which introduced into *The Shrew* the elements of rivalry, elopement, and shortened chronology'. A key example in support of the first proposal is the 'early arrival' of the Pedant in IV.iv. He accounts for it as follows:

> Sir, by your leave, having come to Padua
> To gather in some debts, my son Lucentio
> Made me acquainted with a weighty cause
> Of love between your daughter and himself.
> (IV.iv. 24–7)

Houk argues that Shakespeare uses coincidence to explain this early arrival of the supposed father of the supposed Lucentio—'if time had to be allowed in *The Shrew*, as in *A Shrew*, for the Pedant to come as if in response to a message, the forgery scene could not have been placed so early in the week. While Baptista is busy about the assurances of dowry, Lucentio and Bianca steal their marriage. Not only does the marriage, accordingly, take place before the day appointed, but it occurs also before the arrival of Katherine and Petruchio.'[3] All this depends upon 'Vincentio's' coming in response to a message, but, as Honigmann points out,[4] Shakespeare never mentions the sending of a message because he assumes the same state of affairs as obtains in his acknowledged source, Gascoigne's translation of Ariosto's *I Suppositi* as *Supposes*. There (to quote Honigmann),

1. Shroeder, *JEGP* (1958), pp. 431–6.   2. Houk, op. cit., p. 1023.
3. Ibid., pp. 1027–8.   4. Honigmann, *MLR* (1954), p. 302.

Phylogano (=Vincentio) is reported to be expected in Ferrara (=Padua) before Damon (=Baptista) has fixed a date-limit for the appearance of Erostrato's (=Lucentio's) father to guarantee the dowry.... If Shakespeare assumed that 'Vincentio' was going to Padua in any case 'To gather in some debts' (*The Shrew*, IV.iv.25), as *Supposes* suggested, then Houk's idea of a message to 'Vincentio' can be dropped, as also Houk's inferences that 'Vincentio' came unexpectedly early to Padua, that Bianca's marriage therefore took place before the appointed day, and that Petruchio and Kate therefore came late because the wedding was early.

If this explanation is accepted, the most important of Houk's 'inconsistencies' can be dismissed, and the need to postulate an *Ur-Shrew* reduced.

Another, seemingly strong, chronological inconsistency, which both Houk and Duthie adduce, occurs at IV.v.61–2. Petruchio tells Vincentio of Bianca's marriage:

> The sister to my wife, this gentlewoman,
> Thy son by this hath married.

Petruchio cannot possibly know this, and Hortensio, who supports him, speaks contrary to the knowledge he has that both he and Lucentio (Tranio) have forsworn Bianca (IV.ii.25–9). Again, Honigmann points out that the *audience* already knew about the marriage from the events in IV.iv, and that to assume 'that the characters were informed of the affairs that affected them was only to make use of one of the common privileges of the dramatist'.[1] Honigmann does not disprove Houk's hypotheses, but in each case he offers a simpler and more plausible alternative, weakening the case for an *Ur-Shrew*.

Houk's final claim, that the interludes of an earlier form of the play were eliminated during the revision but have left certain relics or parallels in *The Shrew*, is in some ways his strongest, but since it involves consideration of the whole 'Sly framework' question it may usefully be deferred until later (see below, pp. 39–45). This apart, it may fairly be said that Houk's arguments for an *Ur-Shrew* have been challenged rather than supported by later critics, with one exception: G. I. Duthie.[2]

1. Ibid., p. 303.
2. G. I. Duthie, *RES* (1943), pp. 337–56. Duthie states in a postscript that his article was complete before he had the opportunity to read Houk's, but 'As regards the relationship between *A Shrew* and *The Shrew* Mr. Houk and I support the same hypothesis'.

Duthie's presentation of the case for an *Ur-Shrew* is probably the most lucid and has certainly been the most influential.[1] It has also been the focus of most of the critical opposition to the *Ur-Shrew* theory since 1943. For that reason I shall present his arguments and the attempts to refute them together, since together they summarize the position before Richard Hosley approached the question from an entirely new angle in 1964. Duthie's general proposal may be stated in his own words:

> *A Shrew* is substantially a memorially constructed text, and is dependent upon an early *Shrew* play now lost. *The Shrew* is a re-working of this lost play. In the early play the Sly material and the main plot were at least largely Shakespearian, and were in or near their final state. . . . There is no reason to believe that *A Shrew* does not give us the main outlines of the sub-plot of the early play.[2]

He accepts Hickson's seven parallels and adds new ones. The most powerful compares Petruchio's soliloquy at iv.i.175–98 with Ferando's at *A Shrew*, ix.42–52. Ferando's lines convey the general sense of Petruchio's, and show some verbal parallels; they arrange in new combinations words the author remembers from the original, and eke them out with invention and reminiscences of passages from other plays—precisely the characteristics of the Bad Quarto texts of *Romeo and Juliet* and *Hamlet*. At ix.46–7 Ferando says:

> Ile mew her up as men do mew their hawkes,
> And make her gentlie come unto the lure.

Duthie quotes Madden[3] to show that Shakespeare has used the correct falconer's terms to describe how he is 'to man my haggard', while the compiler of *A Shrew* has confused 'mewing' with 'manning' to produce sporting nonsense. The direction of change is strongly indicated. Duthie also contributes eight other examples of passages where *A Shrew* combines phrases and fragments from various parts of *The Shrew*. For example, Ferando, at *A Shrew*, v.19–20, says:

1. It seems to have influenced Greg; see *SFF*, pp. 211–12.

2. Duthie, op. cit., p. 356.

3. 'Hawks are mewed up for moulting and not to teach them to come to the lure. It is in the manning of the haggard falcon, by watching and by hunger, and not in her mewing or in her training to the lure, that Shakespeare saw a true analogue to the taming of the shrew' (Madden, p. 325).

> My mind sweet *Kate* doth say I am the man,
> Must wed, and bed, and marrie bonnie *Kate*.

This seems to combine Gremio's 'woo her, wed her, and bed her, and rid the house of her' (I.i.144–5) with Petruchio's 'bonny Kate' (II.i.186, III.ii.225) and his lines in the corresponding scene:

> Thou must be married to no man but me.
> For I am he am born to tame you, Kate.
>
> (II.i.268–9)

The thought of this passage is mixed with the construction of I.ii.263–4 where Tranio says:

> If it be so, sir, that you are the man
> Must stead us all and me amongst the rest.

Duthie concludes, 'It appears to me very much more probable that a memorial reconstructor combined various fragments which he happened to remember from different points in *The Shrew* than that Shakespeare separated out commonplace words and phrases from two contiguous lines in a source play and re-distributed them at wide intervals in a re-working' (p. 343). The evidence of these eight parallels, together with the considerable number of verbal contacts which occur in certain scenes, led Duthie to believe that in the Sly material and the main plot at least '*A Shrew* depends upon *The Shrew* or upon a text very close indeed to that of *The Shrew*'. Subsequent critics, with the exception of Shroeder, have accepted this evidence as conclusive. So no *Ur-Shrew* is needed for these parts of the play.

Duthie's case for an *Ur-Shrew* rests on his explanation of the relationship between the sub-plots of *A Shrew* and *The Shrew*. *A Shrew* has three sisters, three suitors and no rivalry. *The Shrew* has two sisters, and rivalry between three suitors (Lucentio, Hortensio and Gremio) for the younger of them. Duthie finds it easier to account for this difference 'by supposing that *A Shrew* represents a version of the story anterior to that given in *The Shrew* than by supposing that here it embodies a modification of the latter' (p. 346). The supporting evidence relies on 'inconsistencies' in *The Shrew*'s sub-plot, each of which involves Hortensio:

(i) III.ii.1–125. Here Tranio (posing as Lucentio) displays an intimacy with Petruchio inappropriate in him but appropriate in Hortensio. In *A Shrew* the corresponding speeches are given to Polidor (=Hortensio). Therefore in the 'earlier play' these speeches were assigned to Hortensio, and in the revision to Tranio because Hortensio is, at this point, masquerading as Litio.

Honigmann allows that this is 'a loose end', but explains it through the complexity of the plot, where Shakespeare is without a model for this part of the action and may have had second thoughts about the man who could be most useful as Petruchio's intimate; or he may simply have forgotten. Jean Robertson (in a letter to me) points out that Duthie sees the 'Litio disguise' as a late change made by Shakespeare for the sake of the comic scene in III. i, but fails to note the garbled remains of the head-breaking lute scene in *A Shrew* (vi. 1–46) which he supposes to represent the pre-revision *Shrew*. She accounts for Tranio's familiarity with Petruchio in III. ii by reminding us that an Elizabethan audience would recognize in Tranio the stock character of the valet assuming his master's garb. He is pretending to be Lucentio, who wants to marry Bianca, who must wait until her elder sister is married. It is his job to expedite Petruchio's marriage to Katherina, he is afraid Petruchio's outlandish attire will deter Baptista, and therefore offers to lend him more suitable clothes. She adds that Valeria's weakly and differently motivated impersonation of his master, in *A Shrew*, and his being sent off disguised as a music tutor to the sisters, look like recollections of Tranio's disguise as Lucentio and Hortensio's as Litio. I find this a convincing explanation of Duthie's strongest 'inconsistency'.

(*ii*) IV. ii. 54. Tranio says that Hortensio has gone to Petruchio's house: 'Faith, he is gone unto the taming-school', though Hortensio has never stated his intention to do so. In *A Shrew* Aurelius (=Lucentio) tells his servant that Polidor has gone to the taming-school (x. 25) and is justified in doing so because he has heard Polidor say so (viii. 113–14). At the corresponding point in *The Shrew* Hortensio is disguised as Litio (III. ii) and could not state his intention. Therefore, *A Shrew* follows the earlier play and *The Shrew*, disguising Hortensio, retained the anomaly.

Honigmann simply asks 'why on earth Hortensio should have stated his intention', and finds this insufficient evidence for postulating an *Ur-Shrew*. Alexander[1] points out that the real inconsistency lies in *A Shrew*. Polidor, from the beginning of the

1. *TLS* (8 July 1965), p. 588.

action, has been shown as in love with Emilia, and his love is requited. The pair exchange high-flown declarations of undying love at vi. 56–70 and xiv. 1–12. Polidor has no need of such lessons as Petruchio gives; he has never suffered such treatment as Hortensio received from Katherina. The report of Polidor's visit to the taming-school is therefore simply a survival from the original situation presented in *The Shrew*. As it stands in *A Shrew* it has no meaning whatever. Taken together, Honigmann and Alexander offer a fair refutation of Duthie's point.

(*iii*) In ii. i Hortensio (a known suitor for Bianca) is absent, because disguised as Litio, from Baptista's auction of Bianca between Tranio and Gremio, and no one shows any awareness of his genuine claim. Similarly, in iii. i the thought of Hortensio's suit never enters Lucentio's head. In iv. ii, when Hortensio reveals his identity to Tranio, Tranio says, 'I have often heard / Of your entire affection to Bianca', though he has known about it since i. ii. Shakespeare's only motive for Hortensio as a suitor is to motivate his disguise as Litio for comic purposes. Thereafter he is dropped as a suitor. This is best explained by *A Shrew* preserving the three-sister *Ur-Shrew*, which Shakespeare revised by dropping one sister and introducing rivalry for Bianca, with comic effect produced by the rivals disguised. Hortensio is then dropped as an official suitor, with consequent inconsistency.[1]

Honigmann accounts for these anomalies by reminding us of the existence of the acknowledged source-play, *Supposes*. The reason for ignoring Hortensio's claim in ii. i is that Shakespeare is, at this point, rewriting the material in *Supposes*, where there is no Hortensio, and the choice lies between Cleander (=Gremio) and Dulippo (=Tranio). The same is true in iii. i. At the corresponding point in *Supposes* there is no Hortensio, and Shakespeare is transcribing Lucentio's (=Erostrato's) explanation:

I hoped to have caste a blocke in his waie, by the meanes that my servaunt . . . should proffer himself a suter, at the least to countervaile the doctors proffers.[2]

No one has taken up the alleged inconsistency in iv. ii, probably

1. Duthie also quotes Petruchio's lines about Lucentio's marriage at iv. v. 61–2. They form part of Houk's case, and are discussed above; see p. 19.

2. i. iii. I quote *Supposes* from Bullough's text in *Narrative and Dramatic Sources of Shakespeare*, vol. i.

because it does not seem like an inconsistency at all. It is a long way from I.ii to IV.ii, Tranio *has* often heard of Hortensio's affection, and, above all, the audience need reminding of the salient facts after such a plethora of disguising and supposing. Thus, cogent explanations have been provided for all the inconsistencies Duthie avers, and the case for an *Ur-Shrew*, based upon them, is consequently vitiated.[1]

Duthie finally acknowledged Alexander's claim that *The Shrew* and *Supposes* agree against *A Shrew* in certain features (p. 353). He explains it thus:

> I see nothing incredible about the assumption that the sub-plot of the lost *Shrew* play was indebted to *Supposes* in certain respects and that Shakespeare, re-working it, reverted to *Supposes* for other elements.

The consequences of such an assumption are followed through by J. C. Maxwell[2] in the particular matter of the number of sisters and the number of suitors. The Bad Quarto theory implies a sequence *Supposes–The Shrew–A Shrew*; Duthie's theory implies *Supposes–Ur-Shrew* (with which, in the matter of sisters and suitors, *A Shrew* agrees)–*The Shrew*. Filling in the figures, we find that *Supposes* has two rivals for Polynesta, an old man and a young man. *The Shrew* has, in addition to these, a third rival for Bianca (Hortensio) who is also a young man. There is no rivalry in *A Shrew* for the hand of Emilia, but there is a third sister with whom Aurelius (who corresponds to Lucentio)[3] falls in love. Maxwell offers the two possibilities:

> Either (1) Shakespeare complicated *Supposes* by adding a third rival, and the compiler of *A Shrew* then dropped the theme of rivalry and, left with a spare young man on his hands, paired him off with a newly invented sister.
>
> Or (2) the author of the *Ur-Shrew* dropped the theme of rivalry, and with it the old man as suitor, and introduced, for no obvious reason, a new pair of lovers. Shakespeare then reverted to *Supposes* for the old man as a rival to Lucentio, eliminated the third sister, and transformed her lover into a third rival for Bianca.

1. The question of Hortensio's role and the alleged inconsistencies in it is fully discussed below; see pp. 37–9.

2. *N&Q* (April 1968), pp. 130–1.

3. Maxwell's article (which I follow very closely here) misprints 'Hortensio' for 'Lucentio' at this point. He must have meant 'Lucentio', and I make the obvious correction.

Maxwell rejects this second possibility, since whether or not we attribute the *Ur-Shrew* to Shakespeare the second alternative is so implausible as to be untenable unless there were overwhelming independent evidence for a 'three sister, three suitor' *Ur-Shrew*. And there is not. If we anticipate a little, we may add a further piece of evidence to Maxwell's case. Richard Hosley has argued by parallels of situation and language that the ballad of a *Shrewde and Curste Wyfe* is the immediate source of the main plot of *The Shrew* (see below, p. 70). Here is a story of *two* daughters, the elder of whom is a shrew. The adoption of this story leads the way quite naturally to Shakespeare's use of *Supposes*, also with *two* daughters, for his sub-plot; and it makes an earlier version of *The Shrew* with *three* daughters, and then a return to the two daughters given in both sources, even more unlikely.[1]

In his last contribution to the debate[2] Alexander proposed an explanation of the sub-plot of *A Shrew*. It is, he says, not an original production at all, but begins as an attempt to reproduce the Bianca plot as we find it in *The Shrew*. There, Baptista directly informs the suitors of his resolution

> not to bestow my youngest daughter
> Before I have a husband for the elder.
> (i. i. 50–1)

In *A Shrew* it is Polidor who informs Aurelius that Alfonso has sworn

> His eldest daughter first shall be espowsde,
> Before he grauntes his yoongest leave to love.
> (iv. 17–18)

In *The Shrew* Hortensio tells Petruchio

> That none shall have access unto Bianca
> Till Katherine the curst have got a husband.
> (i. ii. 126–7)

In *A Shrew* Polidor suggests to Aurelius that they persuade Ferando to marry Kate:

> And if he compasse hir to be his wife,
> Then may we freelie visite both our loves.
> (iv. 50–1)

In *The Shrew* Baptista's ban is the cause of the disguises which

---

1. I am grateful to Jean Robertson for drawing my attention to this point.
2. Alexander, *SQ* (1969).

Lucentio and Hortensio adopt to visit Bianca secretly. But in *A Shrew* no further notice is taken of Alfonso's oath. So Polidor and Aurelius have free access to the two sisters while still unaware of the date of Katherina's marriage. The compiler of *A Shrew*, trying to reproduce the sub-plot of *The Shrew*, gave it up as too complicated to reproduce, and fell back on love scenes in which the manoeuvres of the disguised Lucentio and Hortensio are replaced by extracts from *Tamburlaine* and *Faustus*. Alexander's suggestion offers a hint of how the compiler of *A Shrew* set to work. And this is a step in a new direction.

The central concern of Richard Hosley's examination of the sources and analogues of *The Shrew* is to establish links between Shakespeare's text and other documents which may have contributed to it.[1] But he offers three considerations which incline him to reject the *Ur-Shrew* theory in favour of the Bad Quarto. Firstly, economy of hypothesis. He points out that there is no external evidence for the existence of a lost *Shrew* play; it is merely a postulate to explain differences between two extant texts. Secondly, the differences between *A Shrew* and *The Shrew*. These, though great, are not so great that they exceed all precedent in the comparison of 'good' and 'bad' texts; he cites examples from *Romeo and Juliet, Henry V, The Merry Wives of Windsor* and *Hamlet*.[2] Even the almost complete difference in the nomenclature of the characters can be accounted for if we assume that this was, for some reason, a deliberate act on the part of the compiler of *A Shrew*. Thirdly, the brilliant threefold structure of *The Shrew*, with its induction, main plot and sub-plot unified by the 'Supposes' theme. He argues that 'if we postulate that *The Shrew* had a source in a lost Shrew play of which *A Shrew* is a bad quarto, we are assuming that Shakespeare was not responsible for the basic tripartite conception, for the essential threefold structure would have been present in the supposed *Ur-Shrew*'. And he challenges us to find another dramatist, around 1593, capable of writing such a play. This effectively disposes of a non-Shakespearean *Ur-Shrew*, but that was not what Duthie (at least) had in mind. Duthie is less than transpicuously clear about what he calls the 'early play', but he argues that since 'the main plot of *The Shrew*

---

1. Richard Hosley, 'Sources and Analogues of *The Taming of the Shrew*', *HLQ* (1963–4).

2. Hosley is in error when he says (p. 292) that there is no character in *A Shrew* corresponding to Tranio; he is called Valeria. And *A Shrew* does not *provide* a page for Polidor; it *transfers* Lucentio's boy Biondello to Polidor, together with some of his badinage.

is for the most part, I think, unmistakably Shakespearian' (p. 353) it follows that 'the postulated earlier play was Shakespearian, as regards the main plot at least'. He adds, in a footnote, 'The material concerning Sly was doubtless also Shakespearian in the earlier play', but he believes that Shakespeare excised the material concerning Sly after the end of I. i, and that the 'revision' of the early play involved principally the sub-plot. But we are not told whether it was Shakespeare or someone else who created that sub-plot, diverging from *Suppofes*, though Duthie seems to lean toward the likelihood that '*A Shrew* can be described as a reported version of a Shakespearian "first sketch"'. The full *Ur-Shrew* theory, therefore, can offer any point along the spectrum from a complete lost play on the Shrew theme by someone other than Shakespeare to a late draft of *The Shrew*, differing only in its Sly material and sub-plot from the text of F, to explain any variation between *A Shrew* and *The Shrew*. This lacks both elegance and rigour. It is what mathematicians would call 'too strong a proof', in that it would account for almost any possible variation or coincidence between the two texts. One of the stronger points about Hosley's argument from the sources of *The Shrew* is that by abandoning the idea of an *Ur-Shrew* we are freed from the necessity of searching for a source or analogue involving three sisters (as in *A Shrew*). As he shows, there are close analogues for the two-sisters story, and verbal links between two of them and Shakespeare's play. The nearest three-sisters version is no closer than Jutland.[1]

None of the published contributions to the debate takes much account of the verbal texture of *A Shrew*'s sub-plot, except to point out the manifest debt to Marlowe in many places. Supporters of the *Ur-Shrew* theory would not look for verbal correspondence between the sub-plots of *A Shrew* and *The Shrew* because the sub-plot is precisely what Shakespeare is thought to have revised from the lost original. Harold Brooks, however, has made an extensive (unpublished) comparison between *A Shrew* and the 'non-Katherina/Petruchio scenes' of *The Shrew*, which he has very kindly allowed me to use, and his analysis establishes significant links.

From the beginning there are parallels and echoes. The first

1. See Hosley, op. cit., p. 295; Duthie, op. cit., p. 352; Reinhold Köhler, 'Zu Shakespeare's *The Taming of the Shrew*', *SJ*, III (1868); Karl Simrock, *Die Quellen des Shakespeare in Novellen, Märchen, und Sagen* (1870), vol. I, p. 345; A. H. Tolman, *PMLA* (1890); John W. Shroeder, 'A New Analogue and Possible Source for *The Taming of A Shrew*', *SQ* (1959).

two scenes in *A Shrew* correspond to *The Shrew*'s Induction scenes, and the sub-plot starts at scene iii (=1.i). At iii.6–7 *A Shrew* reads:

> I cannot as I would
> Give entertainment to my deerest friend.

Compare *The Shrew*, 1.i.44–5:

> a lodging fit to entertain
> Such friends as time in Padua shall beget.

The 'lodging' is echoed in *A Shrew*'s 'where shal we lodge' (iii.16). A more complex example occurs at iii.22–6:

> But staie; what dames are these so bright of hew
> Whose eies are brighter then the lampes of heaven,
> Fairer then rocks of pearle and pretious stone,
> More lovelie farre then is the morning sunne,
> When first she opes hir orientall gates.[1]

The first line is paralleled in the corresponding position by 'But stay awhile, what company is this?' (1.i.46), while the next two lines recall Petruchio's at iv.v.31–2:

> What stars do spangle heaven with such beauty
> As those two eyes become that heavenly face?

while the last two are like 11.i.172–3:

> I'll say she looks as clear
> As morning roses newly wash'd with dew.

This 'collection' of allusions from separated parts of *The Shrew* into one place suggests memorial reconstruction on the part of *A Shrew*'s compiler, as Duthie demonstrated in his examination of the main plot.[2]

There are several points of comparison in scene iv. Polidor reports that Alfonso has sworn

> His eldest daughter first shall be espowsde,
> Before he grauntes his yoongest leave to love.
>
> (ll. 17–18)

which makes neither provision nor condition for the middle daughter of the three, but sounds very like Baptista's resolve

---

1. Further complicated by the fact that the second and third lines are directly quoted from Marlowe, *1 Tamburlaine*, iii.iii.118 and 120, in reverse order.

2. See Duthie, op. cit., pp. 338–46, especially the analysis of the Petruchio/Ferando soliloquies.

> not to bestow my youngest daughter
> Before I have a husband for the elder.
>
> (I.i.50–1)

Polidor claims that anyone married to Kate had 'As good be wedded to the divell himselfe' (iv.22) which echoes Gremio's words at I.i.121–5: 'A husband? A devil . . . Thinkest thou, Hortensio . . . any man is so very a fool to be married to hell?' Aurelius' reference to 'Grecian *Helena*'

> For whose sweet sake so many princes dide,
> That came with thousand shippes to *Tenedos*,[1]

may be compared with Tranio's 'Fair Leda's daughter had a thousand wooers' (I.ii.242). This is the more impressive because it is not, like 'scold', 'devilish' or 'humour', part of the staple vocabulary for a scene on this subject.

Another collection of allusions occurs in the Aurelius/Polidor/Valeria section of scene v (ll. 139–58). Polidor says:

> he spoke to me,
> To helpe him to some cunning Musition.

Hortensio, at I.ii.171–2, speaks of having met a gentleman

> Hath promis'd me to help me to another,
> A fine musician to instruct our mistress.

Lucentio mentions cunning schoolmasters at I.i.187, and Hortensio/Litio is described as 'Cunning in music and the mathematics' at II.i.56. Polidor, two lines after the ones quoted above, tells Valeria, 'thou I know will fit his turne', which echoes Gremio's 'Fit for her turn' at I.ii.168, and he begins his next speech (v.149–58) with the words

> Now sweete *Aurelius* by this devise
> Shall we have leisure for to courte our loves.

We may compare this with what Hortensio says at I.ii.134–6:

> That so I may by this device at least
> Have leave and leisure to make love to her,
> And unsuspected court her by herself.

Such close linkage is not what we would expect to find if *The Shrew* had revised the sub-plot of an *Ur-Shrew*, which was faithfully followed in *A Shrew*.

1. Complicated by the reference to Marlowe, *2 Tamburlaine*, II.iv.83–9.

The evidence is even stronger in scene vi. Duthie argues (p. 349) that 'at certain points the sub-plot of *The Shrew* gives evidence of being a revision of an earlier version agreeing with *A Shrew*. In this earlier version Hortensio did not disguise himself.' Yet, as we have noticed above (p. 22), scene vi of *A Shrew* contains a garbled version of the head-breaking scene which Hortensio reports in *The Shrew*, ii.i. Again, the verbal links are strong. Lines 28–34 in *A Shrew* show the sequence 'jack . . . pate . . . breake . . . lute . . . on thy head . . . fiddle'. Hortensio's speech in ii.i contains 'broke . . . lute . . . on the head . . . pate . . . fiddler . . . Jack'. At *A Shrew*, vi.39, Valeria says: 'For I was neare so fraid in all my life.' Hortensio, at ii.i.143, confesses to Baptista the cause of his pallor: 'For fear, I promise you, if I look pale.' The verbal coincidence in this scene is not confined to the head-breaking episode. At lines 63–4 Polidor's

> Oh faire *Emelia* I pine for thee,
> And either must enjoy thy love, or die

echoes Lucentio's words at *The Shrew*, i.i.155–6:

> Tranio, I burn, I pine, I perish, Tranio,
> If I achieve not this young modest girl.

Later scenes continue to exhibit the same pattern of occasional verbal contact between the two sub-plots. In scene viii, after the exit of Ferando and Kate, there is the following exchange between Alfonso and Emelia:

> ALFON.   So mad a cupple did I never see.
> EMEL.   They're even as well matcht as I would wish.
> (ll. 99–100)

In the corresponding scene of *The Shrew* (iii.ii) the same phrases are used in the conversation between Tranio, Lucentio and Bianca:

> *Tra.* Of all mad matches never was the like.
> *Luc.* Mistress, what's your opinion of your sister?
> *Bian.* That being mad herself, she's madly mated.
> (ll. 240–2)

The word 'couple' occurs in Baptista's 'Nay, let them go, a couple of quiet ones', only two lines earlier. In scene x there is the 'taming-school' reference already discussed (see above, pp. 22–3), where one line is almost exactly the same in both texts: 'Faith he's gon unto the taming schoole' (*A Shrew*); 'Faith, he is gone unto the taming-school' (*The Shrew*). In scene xii Aurelius asks Phylotus to impersonate his father, 'For you doo very much resemble him', and in the corresponding passage (IV.ii) Tranio tells the Pedant that his father 'In countenance somewhat doth resemble you'. There is a significant coincidence and progression of phrase in scene xiv, where Phylema, about to be united with Aurelius, says:

> Let *Neptune* swell, be *Aurelius* calme and pleased,
> I care not I, betide what may betide. (ll. 57–8)

At the end of IV.iv Lucentio, about to elope with Bianca, says:

> She will be pleas'd, then wherefore should I doubt?
> Hap what hap may, I'll roundly go about her.
> (ll. 102–3)

In *Supposes*, v.i the 'Fayned Erostrato' uses a similar phrase: 'hap what hap can, I can never hap well in favour with him againe'.[1] If we assume that *Supposes* is the source of *The Shrew*, of which *A Shrew* is a memorial reconstruction, the progression of phraseology is natural. If we adhere to the *Ur-Shrew* theory we must either argue that Shakespeare reconsulted *Supposes* or accept a considerable coincidence.

I have by no means exhausted Brooks's list of parallel passages, but those I have selected cover the whole conduct of the sub-plots and strongly suggest that here, as in the main plot and the Sly material, *A Shrew* is relying on the text of *The Shrew* and not on some earlier, unrevised exemplar. Nor is *A Shrew*'s dependence for its sub-plot material limited to the sub-plot scenes of *The Shrew*. Brooks's analysis includes a list of parallels between the non-Kate/Petruchio scenes of *A Shrew* and the Kate/Petruchio scenes of *The Shrew*, and these lend support to the theory that the compiler of *A Shrew* remembered phrases promiscuously and at random when writing his text. The list is long, but I select two examples to make the point. At *A Shrew*, iv.85 (in a passage which has no analogue in *The Shrew*) Ferando says: 'To bonie *Kate*, the patientst wench alive.' This coupling of 'bonny' and 'patient' recalls three lines at least in *The Shrew*: 'And bonny Kate, and sometimes Kate the curst' (II.i.186); 'For patience she will prove a second Grissel' (II.i.288); 'this most patient, sweet, and virtuous wife' (III.ii.193). *A Shrew*'s compiler seems to be combining phrases from separated parts of *The Shrew*. Then, at x.4 (in a 'sub-plot' context), Aurelius has the line 'As chast as Phoebe

1. Bullough, p. 146.

in her sommer sportes'. This recalls Petruchio's words to Katherina at II.i.254–5:

> O be thou Dian, and let her be Kate,
> And then let Kate be chaste and Dian sportful.

Katherina's 'chastity' has been transferred to Phylema, and the reference to Phoebe/Diana has gone with it.

The manifest dependence of *A Shrew* upon *The Shrew*, in phrase, reference and allusion, not only in the main plot but in the subplot as well, together with the compiler's random recollection of material from anywhere and everywhere in *The Shrew*, weakens still further the case for postulating an *Ur-Shrew* of any kind. The inconsistencies alleged by Houk and by Duthie can be explained, and the overwhelming weight of verbal parallels right through the texts makes the relationship of *A Shrew* and *The Shrew* quite comparable with that of the Good and Bad Quartos of plays like *Romeo and Juliet* and *Hamlet*.[1] In the light of all the evidence, and of the way in which that evidence has built up through the past fifty years, we may reasonably discard both the 'source-play' theory and the '*Ur-Shrew*' theory, and conclude that *A Shrew* is a memorial reconstruction of *The Shrew*, though (as we may later come to see) not an attempt perfectly to re-create its original. It is a Bad Quarto but, as Hosley says, 'of rather a different type from the bad quartos of other Shakespearean plays—an "abnormal" type, that is to say, which involves a good deal more conscious originality on the part of its author or authors than is usually to be observed in bad-quarto texts'.[2]

Acceptance of the Bad Quarto theory does, however, bring with it certain consequences. The 'source-play' theory could account for almost any feature of either text by saying that the 'old play' was relatively crude and that Shakespeare was adapting or improving his original. Similarly, the *Ur-Shrew* theory could solve any problem which arose, and more, by postulating that amorphous, shifting and unexaminable entity from which each text derived independently. The Bad Quarto theory is more stringent, more rigorous, and demands a higher standard of evidence. The close verbal analyses of Duthie and Brooks have shown that this can be sustained, but four other matters remain to be accounted for: (*i*) the promised stage business in *A Shrew*; (*ii*) the Marlovian passages in *A Shrew*, and the other material peculiar to it; (*iii*) the role of Hortensio, and (*iv*) the Sly framework and interludes.

1. See Duthie, op. cit., pp. 338–9.   2. Hosley, op. cit., p. 293.

The first of these need not detain us long. Shroeder argues that in three places *A Shrew* promises humorous business which does not occur, though it takes place in *The Shrew*, and that no piratical reconstructor would have omitted this. It is almost the only positive argument in his defence of the 'source-play' theory, but it does not stand up to close examination. In describing all three episodes as 'the low-comedy sort that a pirate ought logically to preserve', he makes two unwarranted assumptions: first, that they *are* low comedy and, second, that every pirate preserves low comedy. Neither is true. In *A Shrew*'s Induction the boy who plays Sly's 'wife' is instructed to 'Dally with him', but feign some excuse not to go to bed with him. Shroeder maintains that in *A Shrew* this is not fulfilled in action, but in *The Shrew* it is. Yet in *A Shrew* the boy does 'dally', wishing that he were 'but halfe so eloquent, / To paint in words what ile performe in deeds', Sly does say that 'she and I will go to bed anon', and his intention is only frustrated by the arrival of the Players. The corresponding passage in *The Shrew* is somewhat more explicit, but in no way substantially different. Similarly, in *A Shrew*'s lesson scene Kate threatens to break Valeria's lute over his head (vi. 28–31) but does not do so. Neither is it part of the action in *The Shrew*. Katherina does it off-stage, and the event is reported by Hortensio (ii. i. 142–59). Thirdly, at the end of scene xv of *A Shrew* Ferando states his intention to disabuse the Duke of Cestus, but he fails to carry it out. We cannot say that in Act V of *The Shrew* Petruchio disabuses Vincentio; if anyone does, it is Lucentio. Shroeder is making distinction where there is no difference, and he mistakes the whole tone of *A Shrew* if he thinks it is inclined towards low comedy. With its wealth of Marlovian bombast and magnificence it makes every effort to strain towards the high style whenever the material permits. On the Bad Quarto hypothesis Shroeder's three episodes are easily explained as the compiler's efforts to avoid knockabout action and maintain the unity of his chosen tone.

The Marlovian passages in *A Shrew* are important. They offer support to the Bad Quarto theory, and they help with the dating of the play. Boas lists sixteen points of correspondence between *A Shrew* and Marlowe, pointing out (p. xxxi) that though they occur chiefly in the sub-plot they are by no means confined to it. There are two in the Induction, several are found in speeches by Ferando, and one in a speech by Sander. They crop up sporadically, in quite diverse contexts, and, as Boas says, 'they have every appearance of being the work, not of a collaborator, but of the original writer attempting at intervals to soar on borrowed plumes'. In some cases he shows himself oddly ignorant of mythology, as at ii. 19–20 where he has Pegasus running over the Persian plains, or at vi. 68 where he seems not to know his Phoebus from his Phoebe. The correspondences themselves range from direct, accurate quotation through paraphrase and patchwork to quite light allusion. One of the strongest links is Boas's first example. At i. 10–13 the Lord, returning from hunting, quotes *Doctor Faustus*, iii. 1–4:[1]

> *Fau.* Now that the gloomy shadow of the earth,
>   Longing to view *Orions* drisling looke,
>   Leapes from th' antartike world vnto the skie,
>   And dimmes the welkin with her pitchy breath. . . .

The 1616 text has one variant, 'night' for 'earth' in the first line. Apart from reading 'lookes' for 'looke' in the second line *A Shrew* follows Marlowe word for word, but follows 1616 in reading 'night'. This suggests that before 1594 there was a version of *Doctor Faustus* which was (in this respect at least) closer to 1616 than to 1604. This is confirmed by Boas's sixteenth example, where *A Shrew* alludes to a passage (B text, iv. iii. 1449–50; Greg, p. 253) which is not in the 1604 text at all. But the pattern is complicated by the loose quotation from *Faustus* at *A Shrew* viii. 1–5 (Boas's example number thirteen), where *A Shrew* reproduces more or less the verbal order of 1616, but reads 'Pickadevantes' with 1604, against 1616's 'beards'. The textual problems of *Doctor Faustus* are a well-known quagmire for editors, but the evidence from *A Shrew* suggests that its compiler was familiar with a text different in some respects from either of those which eventually appeared in print. Opinions differ as to the date of composition of Marlowe's play, but most critics now stress the importance of its source, *The Historie of the damnable life, and deserved death of Doctor John Faustus*, published in Frankfurt in 1587. An English translation by 'P.F.' appeared in 1592, which added some details to the German original, and these details are found in the play.[2] Unless new evidence appears, it is not unreasonable

1. *Marlowe's Doctor Faustus 1604–1616: Parallel Texts*, ed. Greg (Oxford, 1950), p. 176. I quote from the A text (1604).
2. See *The Plays of Christopher Marlowe*, ed. Roma Gill (Oxford, 1971), p. 332, and her edn of *Doctor Faustus* (New Mermaids, 1965), pp. xii–xiii. See also Greg, *Marlowe's Doctor Faustus 1604–1616*, pp. 1–6, where he argues that the extant text of P.F.'s translation is the second edition, but that the first preceded it by a matter of months only, and Harold Jenkins, in *MLR* (1951), pp. 85–6, who proposes that the first edition may have been as early as 1589.

to believe that *Faustus* was written in or after 1592. This would mean that *A Shrew* was compiled at some time after 1592 and before 1594, when it appeared in print.

The other Marlovian passages are all related to the two parts of *Tamburlaine* (published 1590). They are usually found when the compiler needs a ringing phrase or a dazzling image. The most important, for our purposes, is spoken by Ferando at vii. 71–4 (Boas, number twelve):

> Thou shalt have garments wrought of Median silke,
> Enchast with pretious Jewells fecht from far,
> By Italian Marchants that with Russian stemes,
> Plous up huge forrowes in the *Terren Maine*.

This is a patchwork of passages from Marlowe, half-remembered and stitched together:

> (*i*) Thy garments shall be made of Median silk,
> Enchas'd with precious jewels of mine own.
>
> (*1 Tamburlaine*, 1.ii. 95–6)[1]
>
> (*ii*) And Christian merchants, that with Russian stems
> Plough up huge furrows in the Caspian Sea.
>
> (*1 Tamburlaine*, 1.ii. 194–5)
>
> (*iii*) The Terrene main wherein Danubius falls.
>
> (*2 Tamburlaine*, 1.i. 37)

Ferando's lines are very like 'the patch-work blank verse passages manufactured by the reporters of the "bad" texts of *Romeo and Juliet* and *Hamlet*',[2] and the compiler's practice here is precisely what, according to the Bad Quarto hypothesis, he does with *The Shrew*.

Boas's other examples show the compiler remembering two or three lines at a time but quoting them in the wrong order, or paraphrasing a brief passage, or simply recalling a phrase like 'snowie Apenis' (vii.64) from *2 Tamburlaine*, 1.i. 111 (the snowy Appenines). Twice, as we have seen (pp. 28–9), he mingles his recollection of Marlowe with phrases from separated parts of *The Shrew*, 'arranging in new combinations the words which he does recollect from the original, and eking out these recollections with his invention and sometimes with reminiscences of passages in other plays'.[3]

These direct borrowings from Marlowe are only part of a more general Marlovian flavour found in many parts of *A Shrew*, which

---

1. I quote *Tamburlaine* from Gill, op. cit.
2. Duthie, op. cit., p. 339.   3. Ibid.

have no known source and seem to be the compiler's original work.[1] Some of it is quite good pastiche, contributing to the high-flown tone of the play. For example, at xiv. 21–7, Phylema says:

> Not for great *Neptune*, no nor *Jove* himselfe,
> Will *Phylema* leave *Aurelius* love,
> Could he install me *Empres* of the world,
> Or make me Queene and guidres of the heavens,
> Yet would I not exchange thy love for his,
> Thy company is poore *Philemas* heaven,
> And without thee, heaven were hell to me.

There is much of this kind of writing in the Polidor–Emelia–Aurelius–Phylema scenes and it contrasts strongly with the broken-backed, pedestrian verse found elsewhere in the play, when the compiler apparently has no model, and is simply concerned with advancing the plot without adequate recollection of the words in *The Shrew*. Scene xii opens thus:

> Now Senior *Phylotus*, we will go
> Unto *Alfonsos* house, and be sure you say
> As I did tell you, concerning the man
> That dwells in *Cestus*, whose son I said I was,
> For you doo very much resemble him.

1. Since Boas compiled his list (1908) additions have been made to it by others. In *PMLA* (1947) the unbated industry of Raymond Houk discovered a correspondence between *A Shrew*, vi. 10, 'I take no great delight in it' and *Faustus*, A 1232, 'you take no delight in this', with fainter parallels in the surrounding lines. Robert A. H. Smith (*N&Q* (April 1979), p. 116) offers two persuasive examples, comparing *A Shrew*, ii. 32, 34,

> Long time hath moorned for your absence heere …
> To gratulate your honours safe returne.

with *Faustus*, A 934, 936 (not present in the B text),

> Where such as beare his absence, but with griefe …
> Did gratulate his safetie with kinde words …

and *A Shrew*, xiv. 7–8,

> Should thou assay to scale the seate of Jove,
> Mounting the suttle ayrie regions …

with *Faustus*, B 779–80, 794–5,

> Grauen in the booke of *Ioues* high firmament,
> Did mount him vp to scale *Olimpus* top …
> And mounted then vpon a Dragons backe,
> That with his wings did part the subtle aire.

Lines 779–80 occur with one variant ('himselfe' for 'him vp') in the A text; lines 794–5 do not. Smith's examples lend support to the idea that *A Shrew*'s compiler knew a text of *Faustus* different from both A and B. Further borrowings from other sources may, of course, turn up.

Were it not for the last line this might have been intended as prose, but in this and other scenes the interspersing of regular blank verse lines among these limping rhythms suggests that the compiler had the iambic pentameter distantly in mind throughout. A third stylistic 'layer' is found in the comic scenes, often in prose, which are added to the plot. These usually concern the minor characters, like the exchange between Sander and Polidor's Boy in scene v, lines 111–14:

> BOY My name sirha, I tell thee sirha, is cald Catapie.
> SAN. Cake and pie, O my teeth waters to have a peece of thee.
> BOY Why slave wouldst thou eate me?
> SAN. Eate thee, who would not eate Cake and pie?

This is sorry stuff, and the existence of so many various and strongly distinguished styles in this anonymous text might give rise to suspicion of multiple authorship. And the Bad Quarto theory does not rule out the possibility of collaboration between several people in a memorially reconstructed text.

Hortensio's role in *The Shrew* has raised certain problems for some critics. Proponents of the *Ur-Shrew* theory have drawn attention to some temporal inconsistencies and dramatic implausibilities which, they argue, are best explained by assuming that Shakespeare rewrote the earlier play in which Hortensio was either not present, or, if he was, did not disguise himself. First among these is the fact that Hortensio, a known suitor for Bianca, is absent from, and totally ignored in, Baptista's 'auction' of Bianca between Gremio and Tranio in II.i. Hortensio cannot be present because he is disguised as Litio, and this is thought to show how the 'new' material disrupts the 'old' plot. It seems to me that it does not. In I.i Hortensio and Gremio agree a truce until they can find someone to marry Katherina, when they will be able to resume their rivalry. In I.ii Hortensio does a deal with Petruchio: he will help Petruchio to a wife, and Petruchio will present him 'disguis'd in sober robes' to Baptista as a music master, which will allow him to court Bianca covertly. Hortensio thus breaks the truce, but all is fair in love and war. Gremio bends the rules slightly in using Lucentio/Cambio to woo by proxy. At the end of the scene the wooing is complicated when Tranio/Lucentio declares himself a third suitor for Bianca. All three suitors are present at the beginning of II.i, though Hortensio and Lucentio are in disguise. The 'tutors' go off to their pupils, and Hortensio comes back after Katherina has broken his lute over

his head. Baptista, as compensation, sends Hortensio/Litio to
teach the less violent Bianca. This places him exactly where he
wants to be, and he can begin his courtship undisturbed. The
audience is fully aware that Hortensio has surreptitiously achieved
the greatest possible advantage; they do not feel he is being
unfairly treated. When Petruchio 'wins' Katherina, and Baptista
tells him ''tis a match', the terms of Baptista's embargo have been
fulfilled, and Bianca's hand is once more 'open to offer'. Gremio
and Tranio are on the spot, tricksters both. It is inconceivable
that they should request an adjournment until, in fairness,
Hortensio can be sought and brought to bid against them. So far
as they are concerned it is his bad luck that he is not there, and
they naturally seize the advantage. And Baptista is as mercantile
as they are. He knows he has gambled in matching Katherina
with Petruchio: 'now I play a merchant's part, / And venture
madly on a desperate mart' (II. i. 319–20). He needs to ensure a
quick and safe return on Bianca. He has no reason to believe that
Hortensio could possibly outbid either Gremio or Tranio/
Lucentio—the play gives no indication that Hortensio is a wealthy
man—and so, with simple commercial instinct, he ignores him
and sells to the higher bidder. This is perfectly in accord with the
play's attitude toward marriage in the first two acts. Petruchio
has 'come to wive it wealthily in Padua', where marriage contracts are money matters and success in love goes to the rich and
quick-witted. We do not need any earlier play to explain Hortensio's absence from this scene; we are being shown how he is
outwitted.

Duthie's objection that in III. ii the speeches assigned to Tranio
would come more appropriately from Hortensio has already been
dealt with (see p. 21), and the other 'inconsistencies' are discussed
on the following pages. I find no implausibility whatever in
Hortensio's role. He is a nice young man, who is gently mocked
for not being clever enough, and who loses in the battle of wits.
He takes lessons at Petruchio's 'taming-school', and by the end of
the play we see him slowly learning how to cope with his widow.
The role of his opposite number, Polidor, in *A Shrew* is quite
different, and Alexander (defending the Bad Quarto theory)
explains how this could come about.[1] Although Shakespeare's
plot has only two sisters the final scene of the play presents us with
three married couples, necessary for the full dramatic impact of
the Wager to be felt. Shakespeare has kept the third bridegroom,
Hortensio, in reserve, employing him in comic business and to

1. *TLS* (8 July 1965), p. 588.

complicate the intrigue around Bianca, until he is required, with his widow, 'to provide the indispensable third party in the final test'. The compiler of *A Shrew* remembered the three couples in the last scene, but forgot most of the rest of Hortensio's part. So Kate is given a third sister with whom Polidor is paired from the very beginning of the action. He is therefore not available to be the victim of the Shrew's temper, as Hortensio is in the head-breaking scene, but that scene was too vivid to forget and too good to leave out and so Valeria is recruited to reproduce it. This seems to me a very reasonable explanation of a problem which has caused critics more trouble than it should.

The problem of the Sly framework and interludes is more intransigent. The central question is did Shakespeare intend his play to have Sly interludes and a dramatic epilogue to match the Induction, or not? The evidence of the texts themselves is simple and inconclusive. Both *The Shrew* and *A Shrew* have two induction scenes, which tell the story of the drunken beggar who falls asleep and is tricked by a lord and his retinue into believing that he is a lord; he accepts the deception, and when a troupe of players arrives he settles down to watch their play. Thereafter, *The Shrew* has only one interlude, at the end of I.i, where Sly is dozing and is enjoined to wake up and watch the play. This episode ends with the stage-direction '*They sit and mark*'; the text never refers to him again, and there is no epilogue. *A Shrew* has four interludes (v. 187–94, xiv. 78–9 plus xv. 1, xvi. 45–54, xvi. 127–33) in which Sly comments on the action until he falls asleep, when the Lord orders him to be removed and replaced under the alehouse wall dressed in his old rags. There is then a twenty-three-line Epilogue (scene xix) in which the Tapster wakes Sly, who says he has had 'the bravest dreame' and goes off home to encounter his wife. *A Shrew*'s interludes have no close verbal correspondence with anything in *The Shrew* except that the third (xvi. 45–54, where Sly says, 'I say wele have no sending to prison') recalls the situation and phraseology of v.i.87, where Gremio says, 'Stay, officer. He shall not go to prison.' As Hibbard points out,[1] *A Shrew*'s interludes could be inserted into Shakespeare's play (as Pope did insert them), at the end of II.i, at the end of IV.iv, after v.i.102, and at the end of v.i, respectively. But nothing in *The Shrew* calls for them.

Since the facts are few and plain (and scholarly debate has added interpretation and analogue rather than information) the

1. Hibbard, pp. 157–60. For the text of the interludes and Epilogue see Appendix II.

critical positions adopted may be summarized without doing violence to their proponents. Four principal solutions have been suggested to the Sly problem:[1]

(*i*) Shakespeare did write a closing scene for Sly, but our text of the play is defective. The last pages of the book may have been accidentally lost before it went to the printers, or perhaps the original ending fell into disuse because of an actor shortage.[2]

(*ii*) Shakespeare did intend that the play should close by reverting to the Sly story, as in *A Shrew*, but he did not write out the closing scene because he intended that it be played *ex tempore*.[3]

(*iii*) Shakespeare deliberately dropped Sly after 1.i for artistic reasons; e.g. because it would have been anticlimactic to return to it after the resounding conclusion of the play about Kate and Bianca.[4]

(*iv*) Shakespeare dropped Sly because it was conventional for a play to have an induction without any corresponding dramatic epilogue.[5]

For clarity of exposition it seems best to consider these four hypotheses in reverse order.[6]

Hosley defends the view that the F text of *The Shrew* is 'substantially complete as we have it' by a study of the whole 'induction tradition' in Elizabethan and Jacobean drama, pointing out that over half (26 out of 45) of the plays which have an induction lack a dramatic epilogue. He places *The Shrew* in this category,

1. I quote these categories from Sears Jayne, 'The Dreaming of *The Shrew*', *SQ* (1966), pp. 41–56. Jayne does not take into account such earlier views as Schelling's, that Shakespeare 'wearied' and left the play unfinished, or Fleay's (*Shakespeare Manual*, pp. 175–86) that doubted Shakespeare's authorship, but they have not commanded support.

2. See NCS, pp. 142–3; T. W. Baldwin, *The Organization and Personnel of the Shakespearean Company* (Princeton, 1927), Table II.

3. See Hardin Craig, '*The Shrew* and *A Shrew*: Possible Settlement of an Old Debate', *Elizabethan Studies in Honor of George F. Reynolds* (Boulder, 1945), pp. 150–4. Greenfield (see below) quotes others in support of this theory, but rejects it, along with Quiller-Couch (NCS, p. xviii), who says of it, 'But this we allow to be merest conjecture'.

4. See E. P. Kuhl, 'Shakespeare's Purpose in Dropping Sly', *MLN* (1921), pp. 321–9; Thelma N. Greenfield, 'The Transformation of Christopher Sly', *PQ* (1954), pp. 34–42.

5. See Richard Hosley, 'Was there a "Dramatic Epilogue" to *The Taming of the Shrew*?', *SEL* (1961), pp. 17–34.

6. We may add to this list Jayne's own theory, which he summarizes in a sentence: '(*v*) The inner play should be played as though it were Sly's dream, with Sly playing Petruchio; at the end of the inner play, Sly should wake up as Sly again, and try to puzzle out his dream in a comic pantomime' (Jayne, p. 43). I know of no critic who has supported Jayne's theory in print.

adding that the limitations of personnel in an Elizabethan theatrical company made it usual for the actors of an induction to double in roles of the play proper, and that since most of the principal actors were usually on stage in the final scene it was frequently inconvenient to stage a dramatic epilogue. The basic weakness of his case is his definition of an induction: 'a short dramatic action introducing a full-length play, normally performed by two or more actors and creating a fictional situation different from that of the play itself.' Such a formula permits the inclusion of such plays as *The Malcontent, Bartholomew Fair* and *A Game at Chess* in the same bracket as Greene's *Alphonsus*. But in each of the first three plays the induction is complete in itself; it requires no 'working out' in a dramatic epilogue. The induction to *The Shrew*, by contrast, offers an unfinished story and leaves questions unanswered: what happens when Sly wakes up? is he still 'a lord'? how does he get back to being a beggar? Without some epilogue, at least, the dramatic experience, from the audience's point of view, is incomplete and unresolved. *The Shrew*, surely, should be considered not with all other plays which have an induction of any sort, but with those framework plays where the inductions arouse certain audience expectations, plays like *The Spanish Tragedy, The Old Wives' Tale*, or *The Knight of the Burning Pestle*, which feature in Hosley's list but whose importance is submerged by the weight of irrelevant numbers. Hosley's statistical analysis rests upon too inchoate a base of categorization to justify any conclusion that there exists a tradition of induction plays without dramatic epilogues within which *The Shrew* rightly belongs.

In claiming that *The Shrew* was originally designed without a dramatic epilogue Hosley seeks support from the view that such an epilogue would be an anticlimax after the events of v.ii, culminating in Katherina's great speech. Both Bond (p. 33n.) and Kuhl also make this point, though Kuhl believes that the disappearance of Sly after 1.i was part of Shakespeare's deliberate strategy. I find this whole line of argument unacceptable. The charge of anticlimax is never brought against *A Midsummer Night's Dream*, or *As You Like It*, or *Twelfth Night*, where conditions are similar to those at the end of *The Shrew*. If there is any anticlimax it is in the dialogue immediately following the exit of Petruchio and Katherina in v.ii, where Hortensio and Lucentio moralize the tale. And one cannot argue that because an epilogue *ought* not to be there, it *was* not there.

The idea that there is no written epilogue to *The Shrew* because the scene was meant to be played *ex tempore* (which is important in Jayne's theory) receives some support from the 'jig' tradition, and from the fact that clowns frequently speak 'more than is set down for them'. But it is difficult to believe that after such careful writing in the Induction Shakespeare would have left it to the actors to speak the epilogue *ex tempore*. And it fails to account for the presence of the interludes in *A Shrew* and implies that its written epilogue is the compiler's own work. It would also be, so far as we know, without precedent or successor in Shakespeare. I think we may safely relegate it to the realm of conjecture, and unlikely conjecture at that.

It is therefore in the first of the 'four principal solutions' that an explanation of the Sly problem must be sought. The 'missing last page' idea is too simple to account fully for the difficulties, since even if the last page of the manuscript fell off on the way to the printer the Sly interludes, scattered through the play (to which *A Shrew* is witness), would remain. So we must consider the possibility that the F text of *The Shrew* is in some way defective, and that this may be linked to a shortage of actors necessary for a performance of the full play.

This is the view favoured by Alexander in the last of his contributions to the debate.[1] He summarizes his proposition as follows:

> Shakespeare, some time before the closing of the theaters in 1592, wrote *The Shrew* for Pembroke's men. He had then at his disposal a company of considerable size that would allow the tinker and his aristocratic attendants to sit and watch the Shrew piece. The Quarto is a piracy that reports however imperfectly the conclusion that was originally played in these pre-1592 years. Later the Sly business was cut down as too demanding in personnel.

Alexander brings little evidence to support his hypothesis, but it accords broadly with the conclusions of the far more detailed analysis undertaken by Wentersdorf.[2] His casting analysis (p. 203), based on the premise that the text originally included two or three final Sly episodes, shows that sixteen actors with speaking parts (plus at least five supernumeraries) would be required to stage v. i–ii; there are eleven roles for adult actors and five boys' roles.

1. Peter Alexander, 'The Original Ending of *The Taming of the Shrew*', *SQ* (1969), pp. 111–16.

2. Karl P. Wentersdorf, 'The Original Ending of *The Taming of the Shrew*: A Reconsideration', *SEL* (1978), pp. 201–15.

And he states that 'Without excision, doubling is impossible for the sixteen major roles'.[1] If the Sly episodes were cut in Acts IV and V the actors of Sly and the Lord could double as the Pedant and Vincentio, and the boy who played Sly's Lady could double as Hortensio's widow. During the plague years 1592–4 there is considerable evidence of the abridgement of plays for performance by smaller companies,[2] and so Wentersdorf argues that there is at least a *prima facie* case for the abridgement theory.

Supporting evidence is found in the text. *The Shrew*'s one interlude, at the end of I.i, ends with the stage-direction '*They sit and mark*', which both Wentersdorf and Alexander stress as an unmistakable indication of the author's intention that the Presenters were to remain and watch the whole process of the action about to begin. Nothing in *A Shrew* corresponds to this, but its first interlude (at a point equivalent to the end of I.ii in *The Shrew*) ends with Sly's observation 'O brave, heers two fine gentlewomen', which is followed by the entry of Kate and Valeria (male). Act II of *The Shrew*, however, opens with the first entry of the two principal female characters, Katherina and Bianca. So it may be that Sly's cue-line is remembered from an interlude that was once in *The Shrew* at this point but has not survived. *A Shrew*'s second and third interludes offer no such points of comparison with *The Shrew*. The fourth, occurring at a point corresponding to the end of V.i and the beginning of V.ii, is crucial. Sly is asleep, having fallen asleep at the end of the third interlude, and the Lord orders him to be taken up, dressed 'in his one apparell againe' and replaced 'underneath the alehouse side below'. This in itself guarantees the necessity of an epilogue, since the action must be seen to be completed, but it does more. The absence of a Sly interlude after V.i in *The Shrew* creates a problem. Act V, scene i takes place out of doors, and Petruchio and Katherina bring Vincentio to the door of Lucentio's house, though they are going further:

> My father's bears more toward the market-place.
> Thither must I, and here I leave you, sir.
>
> (v.i.8–9)

Later, at the end of the scene, the audience is reminded that they have not quite completed their trip to Baptista's, and they leave to do so. In v.ii, which takes place in Lucentio's house, they

---

1. Wentersdorf corrects Hosley (*SEL*, 1961) on this point.

2. Chambers, *WS*, I, pp. 214–15, 229–32; Greg, *EPS*, pp. 55–6; Greg, *Two Elizabethan Stage Abridgements* (1922).

immediately re-enter (together with others) for the celebration *subsequent* to the nuptial feast at Baptista's. There is nothing in the text to indicate any time lapse, and so this is a clear breach of what has come to be known as the 'Law of Re-entry'.[1] Wentersdorf points out that the anomaly 'strongly suggests that there has been some dislocation of the text at this point' and the simplest way to account for it is 'to posit the original existence of an intervening episode, however brief, that would cover ... the supposed passage of several hours of real time'. The Sly episode, as reported in *A Shrew*, provides exactly what is required. Thus, there are reasons for believing that the first and fourth of *A Shrew*'s interludes correspond to passages which were originally present in the text of *The Shrew*. The fourth implies the existence of both the third (since Sly must be seen to go to sleep) and the epilogue (since it sets up a dramatic situation which must be resolved), and Wentersdorf has created a most convincing case for his conclusion that the framework of induction, interludes and epilogue was complete in Shakespeare's original version of *The Shrew*. Whether anything equivalent to the third interlude was present or not it is impossible to say, but there would have been no necessity for the compiler of *A Shrew* to invent one at that point in the action, and so we may conclude that he was reporting, however inaccurately, something which stood in the original. Wentersdorf goes on to speculate about how and when the 'abridgement' was made, and he concludes that it may have been because Heminge and Condell believed the abridgement to have been made with Shakespeare's approval that they submitted the cut text as copy to the printers of F. We need not follow him that far, but on the strength of his earlier demonstrations we may reasonably conclude that when Shakespeare completed *The Shrew* it had an induction, a dramatic epilogue, and four or five inter-

1. The so-called law is summarized in Irwin Smith, 'Their Exits and Re-entrances', *SQ* (1967). Smith says on p. 7: 'Shakespeare avoided having a character enter the stage at the beginning of an act or scene after having been on stage at the end of the preceding act or scene.' This was because there were no intermissions in the public playhouses for which Shakespeare wrote his earlier plays, and when a character left the stage he presumably left in order to do something. His immediate re-entry necessarily denied that any time had elapsed, and thus denied that he had accomplished his purpose. Smith states that out of approximately 750 scenes in the Shakespearean canon not more than sixteen show re-entrances that conceivably violate his usual practice. In nearly all sixteen Smith argues that the departure is more apparent than real; in the case of *The Shrew*, v.i he proposes that the characters either leave the stage 'momentarily' or not at all. Wentersdorf demonstrates that this is incorrect.

ludes, and that he intended these to form part of the whole play. The interludes and Epilogue in *A Shrew*, however garbled, are witnesses to their presence in Shakespeare's holograph.

Unless new, external evidence comes to light, the relationship between *The Shrew* and *A Shrew* can never be decided beyond a peradventure. It will always be a balance of probabilities, shifting as new arguments and opinions are added to the scales. Nevertheless, in the present century the movement has unquestionably been towards acceptance of the Bad Quarto theory, and this can now be accepted as at least the current orthodoxy. Two minor matters, which concern *A Shrew* alone, may be considered at this point, before we proceed to the dating of the plays and the reasons for *A Shrew*'s existence.

Although its title-page states, '*As it was sundry times acted by the Right honorable the Earle of Pembrook his servants*', the text of the 1594 Quarto of *A Shrew* can hardly, as it stands, have been the basis for performance. The stage-directions alone show that it cannot derive from a prompt-book. Exits and entrances are imperfectly marked, as, for example, at the opening of scene xiii where the Haberdasher, a speaking part, has neither entrance nor exit. Designations are often indefinite or permissive: 'Enter one' (i. 52); 'Enter two yoong Gentlemen, and a man and a boie' (iii, opening S.D.); 'Ex. Omnes' (iii. 29, where it is only Alfonso and his daughters who leave); 'Enter Sanders with two or three serving men' (ix, opening S.D.); 'Enter Kate thrusting Phylema and Emelia before her, and makes them come unto their husbands call' (xviii, opening S.D.). Other stage-directions seem an odd mixture of the definite and the imprecise: 'Enter two of the players with packs at their backs, and a boy' (i. 58) must be unacceptable to any prompter; 'Enter Ferando with a peece of meate uppon his daggers point and Polidor with him' (xi. 26) is surely a reminiscence of Tamburlaine's treatment of Bajazeth at *1 Tamburlaine*, iv. iv. 40; and the strange direction at iii. 21, 'Enter Simon, Alphonsus, and his three daughters', may well conceal the name of one of the actors.[1] The indications are that the copy for the 1594 Quarto was the compiler's foul papers with only rudimentary preparation for stage performance. Claims made on title-pages have less than the authority of holy writ, and, given the perpetual possibility of confusion between the titles of *The Shrew* and *A Shrew* in contemporary references, it is doubtful

1. There is no character called Simon. The Lord's name is Simon (ii. 27) but he cannot be on stage at iii. 21, nor can one actor double the Lord and Alfonso (see xvi. 111ff.). See Mary Edmond's proposed identification, pp. 51–2

whether the text of *A Shrew* as we have it in the Quarto of 1594 was thrown together for performance or publication.

While *A Shrew* was still regarded as a source-play the question of its authorship was itself the source of considerable critical speculation. Greene, Rowley, even Marlowe himself were proposed, and Bond, in 1904, summed up the current state of promiscuous attribution when he said:

> The model in this instance, *A Shrew*, has been assigned in turn to every near and important predecessor of Shakespeare save Lyly and Nash, and the idea of Shakespeare's own authorship . . . has even found a limited modern approval.[1]

If we accept the Bad Quarto theory all such contenders can be summarily dismissed. The text is a memorial reconstruction made by actors with or without the assistance of a writer. G. Blakemore Evans describes such a text as 'one based primarily on what an actor (or actors) could recall from having played one or more roles, usually of a comparatively minor sort, in an authorized production'.[2] They tend to be most reliable when the character is remembering his own part or recalling what was said by others when he was on stage. On this basis it has been proposed, for example, that the quarto of *The Merry Wives of Windsor* was reconstructed primarily by the actor who played the Host, and that Q1 *Hamlet* derives from the actor who doubled Marcellus and Lucianus. An analysis along these lines of the passages in *A Shrew* which are 'well remembered' shows a pattern (see facing table). Several other facts need to be added to the information provided by this table. If the performance(s) reported by *A Shrew* included the full Sly framework, then Sly was on stage throughout. No single character's part is substantially remembered, or better remembered than any other. *A Shrew* is closest to *The Shrew* in the taunting of Kate–Haberdasher–Tailor–time of leaving sequence, corresponding to IV.iii in *The Shrew*—i.e. IV.iii is the best remembered part of the play. The other well-remembered parts include the Induction, the main plot, and the final climax (V.ii).

Apart from the Induction, there are thirteen 'well-remembered' episodes, some brief, some long. Petruchio is on stage for eleven of them, Katherina for ten, Hortensio for eight, Grumio for seven, Tranio for two, and the remainder for one. Who, then, is responsible for reconstructing the text? If either Petruchio or

1. Bond, pp. xxxvii–xxxviii.

2. *A New Companion to Shakespeare Studies*, ed. Muir and Schoenbaum (Cambridge, 1971), p. 230.

Characters on stage in *The Shrew*

A Shrew	*The Shrew*	Pet.	Kate	Bap.	Gre.	Tra.	Hort.	Gru.	Bia.	Luc.	Hab.	Tail.	Vin.
i.1–89	Induction i	Sly, Hostess, Lord, 2 Huntsmen, Servant, ?3 Players											
ii.1–59	Induction ii	Sly, Lord, 3 Servants, 'Lady', Messenger											
v.13–39	II.i.182–273	Pet.	Kate										
vi.25–40	II.i.142–59	Pet.		Bap.	Gre.	Tra.	Hort.						
ix.22–40	IV.i.106–74	Pet.	Kate					Gru.					
ix.41–52	IV.i.175–98	Pet.											
x.25–7	IV.ii.55–7					Tra.			Bia.	Luc.			
xi.1–26	IV.iii.1–35	Pet.	Kate					Gru.					
xi.27–45	IV.iii.36–72	Pet.	Kate				Hort.	Gru.			Hab.		
xiii.1–15	IV.iii.63–86	Pet.	Kate				Hort.	Gru.					
xiii.16–52	IV.iii.87–165	Pet.	Kate				Hort.	Gru.				Tail.	
xiii.53–69	IV.iii.166–93	Pet.	Kate				Hort.	Gru.					
xv.5–19	IV.v.1–22	Pet.	Kate				Hort.						
xv.26–48	IV.v.27–57	Pet.	Kate				Hort.						Vin.
xvii+xviii	v.ii	All principal characters are on stage											

Katherina were involved one would have expected them to have remembered their own lines more accurately, or at least to have recalled portions of their larger speeches. But Petruchio's soliloquy (iv.i) is verbally distant, and Katherina's final speech (v.ii) is patched out with allusions to Du Bartas. If Hortensio were attempting to reconstruct his role he would hardly have forgotten his part in the sub-plot and his disguise. Grumio, on the other hand, is on stage for seven of the well-remembered scenes, including the 'taunting' scene at the beginning of iv.iii which he shares with Katherina alone, and the 'Tailor' scene, in which he plays a prominent part, is verbally the best remembered sequence in the play. He usually accompanies Petruchio, and it is *possible* (though F does not give entries for him) that he was among the 'Servants' accompanying Petruchio in iv.v. If we examine the role of his counterpart in *A Shrew*, Sander, we find that it is expanded and extended far beyond anything present in *The Shrew*. Sander is the fool for whom Sly calls, and he has two complete comic scenes with Polidor's boy which have no counterpart whatever in *The Shrew*; they are pure invention. It seems to me that the actor who played Grumio is primarily responsible for the memorial reconstruction of *A Shrew*'s text. He recalls some of his own words, many of the comic scenes in which he was concerned, he has a general sense of what others were saying and doing when he was on stage, and no clear recollection of the sub-plot in which he had no concern. He may well have remembered that there were three married couples in the final climactic scene (v.ii) since he was on stage for the whole of it, and this (as Alexander suggested) may account for the three sisters and three suitors sub-plot which *A Shrew* invents. One of the Players in scene i is given the speech-prefix 'San', and it may be that Sander doubled this part with his role in the play proper. If so, this would help to account for the well-remembered quality of *A Shrew*'s first two scenes. But I cannot believe that the actor who played Grumio and Sander wrote the text of *A Shrew*. As we have seen (pp. 33–7) there are several different stylistic levels in that text: garbled Shakespeare, Marlovian pastiche, comic dialogue and broken-backed hack verse. It seems unlikely that one man moved easily from one to the other. I would prefer to believe that Grumio/Sander gave as much as he could remember of the complex plot of *The Shrew* to a writer (whose identity we shall probably never know), recalled his own part in the action fairly well and suggested ways in which his part might be built up with additional comic scenes, and left the writer to construct the best sub-plot he could out of the confusion of odds and ends the actor could summon up. The writer may himself have seen a performance of the play, or heard it in rehearsal, or he may have consulted other actors who performed in it. This would account for the odd form '*Don Christo Vary*' at *A Shrew*, xvi.48 (Bullough, p. 101), which seems more likely to be a mishearing than a mistranscription. Bits and tags of Shakespeare's text seem to have been floating about in his mind, and where they were not sufficient for his purpose he fell back on the words of another dramatist he knew well, Marlowe, and generally tried to imitate his style whenever the material seemed appropriate.

We do not know the name of the actor who played Grumio. Baldwin assigns the part to William Kemp,[1] who, he thinks, also played Bottom in *A Midsummer Night's Dream*. Kemp is known to have played Dogberry, and Peter in *Romeo and Juliet*, and this would answer to Sly's description of Sander as 'fool' in *A Shrew*. Jean Robertson (in some unpublished material which she has kindly allowed me to use) argues strongly for John Sincklo (or Sincler). He first appears as a member of the cast in the 'plot' of *The Second Part of the Seven Deadly Sins*, probably staged about 1591, then in the F text of *3 Henry VI*, iii.i, where he plays a forester, then in the Quarto of *2 Henry IV* (v.iv) as the Beadle, and finally in the Induction to Marston's *The Malcontent* (1604). From what is said about him by Doll Tearsheet and the Hostess in *2 Henry IV* it would appear that he was abnormally thin (Doll calls him 'you thin man in a Censor'). In the Induction to *The Malcontent* Sly invites Sinklo to 'sit between my legs here', but Sinklo refuses because 'the audience then will take me for a viol-da-gamba, and think that you play upon me', which suggests that he was of less than average height. His appearance was obviously remarkable in one or more ways, and he seems to have been cast in roles which exploited this fact.[2] Jean Robertson points out that since he appears as one of the Players in *The Shrew*, Induction i, he must have played one of the characters in the play as well, and that Grumio is the most likely, since there is specific and significant jesting about Grumio's diminutive size at the opening of iv.i ('a little pot and soon hot', 'a taller man than I', 'Am I but three inches?'). She suggests that the text for *A Shrew* was probably compiled by Sincklo and other members of the company, as best they could, and delivered over to the 'writer' who filled in

1. T. W. Baldwin, *Organization and Personnel*, Table ii.

2. See Allison Gaw, 'John Sincklo as one of Shakespeare's Actors', *Anglia* (1926).

the substantial gaps. This 'writer probably confused Sincler with Sander (palaeographically this would be an easy error, especially with *Sin.* and *San.* as speech-prefixes). Hibbard, on the other hand, noting that Shakespeare thought of the pantaloon as 'lean' (*AYL*, II.vii.158), prefers to believe that Sincklo took the part of Gremio.[1] Harold Brooks does not believe that he would have played any parts so extensive, arguing that the evidence we have points to his being an actor of bit parts, in which capital could be made out of his sensational appearance, for which he was worth his place. He believes that in *The Shrew* Sincklo played the Tailor, and was probably the woman's tailor, Feeble, in *2 Henry IV*, and Starveling, the tailor, in *A Midsummer Night's Dream*.

Dover Wilson, however, believed that the jest on Grumio's stature indicated that the part was played by a boy, and this may well be so. He notes that in *A Shrew* 'the actor's name "Sander" (or "San") appears first as the principal Player in the Induction and later both in dialogue and speech-headings as the actual name of the character who corresponds with Grumio in the original'.[2] He proposes that Sander 'almost certainly stands for Alexander Cooke, who . . . had grown up to be a sharer in the King's company by 1605'.[3] On such evidence no one can do better than conjecture, but the case for Cooke seems to me marginally stronger than the case for Sincklo. At all events, whoever played Grumio/Sander we may feel reasonably sure that he was the principal progenitor, though not the onelie begetter, of the text of *A Shrew*. When and why it was begot remains to be considered.

3 . THE DATE

Much of the earlier scholarly speculation about the date of *The Shrew* can be disregarded once it is accepted that *A Shrew* is a Bad Quarto and therefore later than its original. It is possible, therefore, to date *The Shrew* before the publication of *A Shrew* in 1594, but precisely how long before remains a matter for speculation. The later limit depends on how accurately we can date the composition of *A Shrew*, and this must be our first concern.

A Shrew was entered on the Stationers' Register to Peter Short,

1. Hibbard, p. 167.

2. NCS, p. 119.

3. Baldwin, however, gives him the part of Katherina in *The Shrew*, and says that he was tall rather than short, and Jean Robertson believes he played one of the women, since he was cast as the Queene in *2 Seven Deadly Sins*.

'under master warden Cawoodes hande', on 2 May 1594,[1] and this gives us a later limit of April 1594. The earlier limit is established by the presence in the text of several quotations from Marlowe's *Faustus*. Many critics now believe that this was written after the publication of P.F.'s translation of the German *Faust Book* in 1592 (see p. 34). Greg states[2] that this was probably in print 'about May 1592' and so, if Marlowe's play was written and performed immediately after P.F.'s publication, the compiler of *A Shrew* can hardly have quoted from it in his text before August of that year at the earliest. This means that *A Shrew* was written at some time between August 1592 and April 1594.

One tantalizing possibility inclines the scales towards the earlier rather than the later limit. At iii.21 *A Shrew* has the stage-direction '*Enter Simon, Alphonsus, and his three daughters*', but there is no character in the play called Simon. The Lord's name is Simon (ii.27), but he cannot be on stage at iii.21, nor can one actor double the Lord and Alfonso (see xvi.111ff.). The most likely conjecture is that Simon is the name of one of the actors. Mary Edmond[3] identifies him as Simon Jewell, an actor in Pembroke's company, whose will states that he was buried on 21 August 1592. The will makes it quite clear that Jewell was closely concerned with one or other of the acting companies, and Miss Edmond argues for Pembroke's Men chiefly on the grounds of a reference in the will to 'ladie Pembrooke' from whom a contribution to the expenses of the company is expected. Miss Edmond goes on to connect some of the other persons mentioned in the will with Pembroke's company, but, as Scott McMillin points out,[4] the reference to Lady Pembroke does not necessarily mean that the company concerned was the one which bore her husband's name. He argues that the actors whose names are mentioned in the will could as easily be associated 'with a more famous company which by 1592 had fallen on hard days—the Queen's Men', though he acknowledges the force of G. M. Pinciss's suggestion[5] that in the year 1592 Pembroke's Men and the Queen's Men might have been one and the same company. Jean Robertson points out to me that if they were one and the same this would explain *The Shrew* as a property of the Lord

1. Arber, vol. II, p. 648.
2. Greg, *Marlowe's Doctor Faustus 1604–1616* (Oxford, 1950), p. 5.
3. 'Pembroke's Men', *RES* (1974), pp. 129–36.
4. 'Simon Jewell and the Queen's Men', *RES* (1976), pp. 174–7.
5. 'Shakespeare, Her Majesty's Players, and Pembroke's Men', *Sh.S.* (1974), pp. 129–36.

Chamberlain's company without any question of either purchase
or theft. At all events, Jewell's will states that he died in London
and, if Miss Edmond's identification of the company is accepted,
makes it sound as if the whole of Pembroke's company was there
too. No other actor called Simon is known to have been associated
with Pembroke's company, and if it were Simon Jewell who
played the part of Alfonso in *A Shrew* this would suggest either
that the compiler was here indicating the name of the actor
proposed for the role or that the copy had received the attention
of the book-keeper in at least one place. Miss Edmond's case seems
to me the best available explanation of the admittedly insub-
stantial evidence, and it suggests that *A Shrew* was compiled
before 21 August 1592, since neither author nor book-keeper
would knowingly cast a corpse.

Both the date of *A Shrew* and the reasons for its existence are
bound up with the rise and fall of Pembroke's Men. Whether that
company ever performed *A Shrew* or not (see above, p. 45—the
only unequivocal evidence is the statement on the title-page of
the 1594 Quarto) it seems to have had some rights or interest in
the play. Unfortunately, the whole history of the Pembroke company is shadowy, uncertain and full of conjecture.[1] We know that
it was playing at Leicester in the last three months of 1592. It
appeared at Court on 26 December 1592 and 6 January 1593. In
the following summer it was on tour, visiting York in June, Rye
in July. In 1592–3 it is also recorded at Ludlow, Shrewsbury,
Coventry, Bath and Ipswich. On 28 September 1593 Henslowe
wrote to Alleyn:

> As for my lorde a Penbrockes wch you desier to knowe wheare
> they be they ar all at home and hausse ben this v or sixe
> weackes for they cane not saue ther carges wth trauell as I heare
> & weare fayne to pane ther parell for ther carge.[2]

This means that they were back in London about 24 August 1593,
ready to pawn their costumes to defray the costs of a financially
unsuccessful tour of the provinces. Their name appears on the
title-pages of four plays published soon after: Marlowe's *Edward
the Second* (1594, S.R. 6 July 1593), *The Taming of A Shrew* (1594,
S.R. 2 May 1594). *The True Tragedy of Richard Duke of York* (1595)
and *Titus Andronicus* (1594). Upon this slender basis of facts
scholars have raised a glittering tower of conjecture, in an attempt

1. The best account is in NCS, *Henry VI: Part II*, ed. Wilson (1952), pp.
viii–xiv.
2. Dulwich MS. 1.14, quoted in Chambers, *ES*, vol. ii, p. 128.

to account for some aspects of Shakespeare's theatrical activity in the years preceding 1594, when he joined the newly-formed Chamberlain's Men. Some of the conjectures are more plausible than others, and need to be taken into account in explaining the genesis of *A Shrew*. For example, it is reasonable to suppose that the company which acted *The True Tragedy* also acted its companion piece *The First part of the Contention betwixt the two famous Houses of Yorke and Lancaster*, which was published in 1594 without the name of any acting company attached to it. It is now generally agreed that these two plays are Bad Quartos of Shakespeare's *3 Henry VI* and *2 Henry VI* respectively. Thus we have a group of five texts, two of which (*Edward II* and *Titus*) were printed from their authors' manuscripts, while the other three are memorial reconstructions by actors, to a greater or lesser degree. If the conjecture about *1 Contention* is accepted, all five are attached to Pembroke's Men, and appeared in print in 1594–5.

Chambers suggested that the Pembroke company came into being in the summer or autumn of 1592 for touring purposes, because the plague which raged in London from 1592 to 1594 closed the theatres for all but sporadic performance, and actors had to seek a living elsewhere. Dover Wilson proposes an earlier date. He points to the merger which had taken place towards the end of 1590 or earlier between Strange's and the Admiral's Men, and which brought together Edward Alleyn, the actor, and James Burbage, builder and owner of the Theatre. In May 1591 there was a violent quarrel between them, which resulted in Alleyn leaving the group, and entering into a close association with Philip Henslowe at his playhouse, the Rose on Bankside. It was the 1591 quarrel, not the 1592 plague, which, in Dover Wilson's view, brought about the formation of Pembroke's company. Richard Burbage, about twenty-four years old at the time, may have persuaded a number of the actors in the double company not to defect to the Rose but to stay with him. They would have needed a new patron, and Burbage may well have turned to the Earl of Pembroke, with whom we know him to have been closely associated in later years. This is guesswork, of course, but the theory permits us to accommodate some otherwise recalcitrant facts. It allows us to assume that Shakespeare's *2* and *3 Henry VI* were played at Burbage's Theatre in 1591–2 by a company called Pembroke's Men, led by Richard Burbage. This would explain the performances at Court during the Christmas festivities of 1592. *2* and *3 Henry VI* must have caused a stir when they were first produced; they would be strikingly unlike any previously-known play on English history, and Burbage was a notable actor. Such a company would attract attention. It would also suggest a reason for the presence of Marlowe's *Edward II* in the company's repertory. Dover Wilson's analysis of the parallels between *2* and *3 Henry VI* and *Edward II* show that Marlowe is 'unquestionably the borrower'[1] and it is generally agreed that Shakespeare's plays predate *Edward II*. It seems likely that Marlowe, attracted by the theatrical success of the two *Henry VI* plays, made his own contribution to the new mode utilizing the resources of the same, successful company.

The important plays, for our purposes, are the memorially reconstructed texts: *1 Contention*, *The True Tragedy* and *A Shrew*. Alexander believed[2] they were made after the failure of the 1593 tour, either in preparation for a further tour or for sale to a publisher. Madeleine Doran,[3] on the other hand, pointed out that the Bad Quartos of the Shakespeare histories were 'good acting versions' and proposed that the reconstructions were collaborative efforts by the company, who may have left their prompt-books in London while they were on tour. On the whole, scholars have followed Miss Doran's lead rather than Alexander's on this point. Scott McMillin's study[4] of the three texts is more closely concerned with the histories than with *A Shrew*, but by concentrating on the question of the casting McMillin wins a number of insights into the probable number of actors in the company. All three plays could be performed by eleven adult male actors, four boys, and approximately five supernumeraries —a total company of about twenty. He points out (p. 153, note 27) that *A Shrew* does not require more than fifteen performers at once, suggesting either 'a relaxed casting arrangement' or 'a company stripped of its supernumeraries'. The eleven principal actors and four boys could double all of the roles. In attempting to identify as many as possible of the actors McMillin finds a useful link between the actors' names believed to be present in some of the stage-directions and speech-prefixes of his three texts and the actors listed in the plot of *2 Seven Deadly Sins*.[5] He lists the correspondences:

1. NCS, *Henry VI: Part II*, p. xxv.

2. *Shakespeare's Henry VI and Richard III* (Cambridge, 1929).

3. *Henry VI, Parts II and III*, University of Iowa Humanistic Studies, IV.4 (Iowa, 1928).

4. *SQ* (1972), pp. 141–59.

5. Dulwich MS. xix. See Chambers, *ES*, vol. III, p. 496; *WS*, vol. I, p. 123. A 'plot' was a skeleton outline of the play's action, with actors' names attached to the characters they played.

Pembroke texts		*2 Seven Deadly Sins*
'Harry'	(*1 Contention*)	'Harry'
'Robin'	(*1 Contention*)	'Ro. Pallant'
'Tom'	(*1 Contention, A Shrew*)	'Tho. Goodale'
'Sander'	(*1 Contention, A Shrew*)	'Saunder'
'Nick'	(*1 Contention*)	'Nick'
'Will'	(*1 Contention, A Shrew*)	'Will'
'Slie'	(*A Shrew*)	'W. Sly'
'John Holland'	(*2 Henry VI*)	'J. Holland'
'Sinklo'	(*3 Henry VI*)	'John Sincler'
George (?) 'Bevis'	(*1 Contention, 2 Henry VI*)	
'Gabriel' Spencer	(*3 Henry VI*)	
'Humfrey' Jeffes	(*3 Henry VI*)	

The *Sins* plot also lists parts for 'Mr. Brian', 'Mr. Phillipps', 'Mr. Pope', 'R. Burbadg', 'R. Cowly', 'John Duke', 'Vincent', 'T. Belt', 'Ro. Go.', 'Ned', 'Kit', and two unnamed actors who played Henry VI and Lydgate. The nine actors whose names appear in the Pembroke texts and the *Sins* plot seem to have been the younger, less-experienced players in the *Sins* company about 1590.

2 Seven Deadly Sins is connected with Lord Strange's Men in the early 1590s.[1] McMillin shows that at least four actors named on the plot (Brian, Phillipps, Pope and Cowly) were with Strange's Men on a provincial tour which began some time after 6 May 1593, and no one of them corresponds with any of the twelve actors named in the Pembroke texts. He argues that the *Sins* plot represents a large company which existed about 1590, and which divided a year or so later into two groups: one, the established men, kept Lord Strange's name, the other, the younger element, sought and gained the patronage of the Earl of Pembroke. This is broadly in accord with the sequence of events proposed by Dover Wilson. Pembroke's Men would thus have included 'Saunder' and 'W. Sly', and, noting that men from Strange's company and Pembroke's company came together in 1594 to form the Chamberlain's Men (Shakespeare's company), McMillin identifies them as Alexander Cooke and William Sly, who are known on independent evidence to have been members of the Chamberlain's Men. It would fit neatly into the other evidence (see p. 48) if two of the men involved in the memorial reconstruction of *A Shrew* were William Sly, who played Sly, and Alexander Cooke, who played Sander.

1. Chambers, *ES*, vol. II, pp. 125–6.

Perhaps it is now possible to reconstruct the sequence of events which led to the compilation of *A Shrew*, and to account for some of its characteristics. In 1590 Strange's and the Admiral's Men amalgamated to produce a large company based on Burbage's Theatre. They included in their repertory *2* and *3 Henry VI*, *2 Seven Deadly Sins*, and other plays, including *The Taming of the Shrew*. In May 1591 the quarrel between Alleyn and the Burbages split the company, and part went off with Alleyn to the Rose, continuing to act and tour under the patronage of Lord Strange. I suggest that they took with them the existing copies of the texts of *2* and *3 Henry VI* and *The Taming of the Shrew* at least. The other group, now calling itself Pembroke's Men, either retained or acquired texts of *Edward II* and *Titus*. They were a normal theatrical company, acting successfully in the public play-houses to the extent that they were invited to play at Court in the Christmas season of 1592–3. On 23 June 1592 the London theatres were closed on account of some disorder, and they remained closed because of the plague, except for a brief season of about five weeks in the following January, for sixteen months. Pembroke's Men were obliged to tour the provinces, and we find them at Leicester in the last three months of 1592. It was for this tour that they reconstructed from memory *2* and *3 Henry VI*, in earlier productions of which some of them had acted, deliberately abridging them and reordering parts of the action to suit the resources of the company as it was then constituted. In this same period, from June to September 1592, they attempted to reconstruct *The Shrew* in the same way. William Sly and Alexander Cooke, perhaps with others of the company, re-created as much as they could of the Sly framework and the main plot but were unable to recall the details and complexities of the sub-plot and gave up the attempt after the first few scenes. Either themselves, or, more probably, with the aid of a writer,[1] they constructed a different but workable sub-plot, based on their recollection that there were three married couples on stage in the final scene, and working back from that. They remembered the title of the play almost accurately, but could not recall all the characters' names and so new ones were substituted throughout, except for Katherina, who became Kate, and Sly, who retained

---

1. Harold Brooks points out to me an implication of assuming a 'writer', i.e. that Shakespeare was not a member of Pembroke's Men when the reconstruction was made. If he had been, presumably they would have called on him as the writer; and if he had been, he would surely have remembered his own play better.

his name, while Alexander Cooke used his own name and greatly extended his role. The text thus produced was probably 'foul papers' which were rewritten to produce the company's prompt-book. With these texts, and possibly others, they went on tour in 1592 and 1593. As we know from Henslowe's letter, the tours were financially unsuccessful, and the company was back in London towards the end of August 1593. They were ready to pawn their costumes, and, it would seem, were already beginning to sell their texts to publishers, since *Edward II* was entered on the Stationers' Register on 6 July 1593. They continued to raise money in this way, selling their good text of *Titus* and their 'acting versions' of *2* and *3 Henry VI*, and the 'foul papers' of *A Shrew*. What they did, and whether they survived, the following winter and spring we do not know, but several of them joined the Chamberlain's Men when that company was formed in 1594. Henslowe records a performance of 'the Tamynge of A Shrowe' in June 1594, as part of a short season at Newington Butts given by 'my Lord Admeralle men & my Lorde Chamberlen men', and I believe that this must have been not *A Shrew* but *The Shrew* performed on the basis of the text of that play which had gone with Alleyn when the amalgamated company split up in 1591.[1]

The fact that Sly and Cooke and their fellows were unable to reconstruct fully the text of *The Shrew* suggests that it was some time since they had acted in it, whereas the company was reason-ably well able to recall the words of *2* and *3 Henry VI*. This does not mean that *The Shrew* must have been written before the *Henry* plays; it means simply that *The Shrew* had not been so recently performed. Nevertheless, the collocation of events lends credence to the idea that all these plays belong to the same period in Shakespeare's development, and points toward the year 1590, when the large, amalgamated company would have had the resources to stage *The Shrew* complete with framework, episodes and epilogue. At all events, with the probability established that *A Shrew* was constructed for the tour of September 1592, we can now feel fairly secure in seeking a date before August 1592 for *The Shrew*, if we accept the identification of Simon Jewell as the actor who played Alfonso in *A Shrew* (see pp. 51–2).

We may now turn to the problem of the dating of *The Shrew* itself, and at this point we run out of directly relevant facts. There is, for example, no internal evidence in the text of *The Shrew* to give any indication of its date of composition. The few contem-porary references to *The Shrew* and *A Shrew* are noted (see

1. Chambers, *WS*, vol. I, p. 327.

p. 64) for completeness's sake, but since the earliest of them is in 1593 they offer no help. Facts are few for the dating of all Shakespeare's early plays, and opinions vary widely about both the dates and the order of composition of the plays from *1 Henry VI* to at least *The Merchant of Venice*. No one is sure when Shakespeare 'commenced playwright' or which play was his first, so that much of the speculation about dating involves comparisons between one play and another in the attempt to establish precedence. In such circumstances we need a base line, if only to establish degrees of divergence; Chambers's chronology serves this purpose, though it must be stressed that most editors would now dissent from both its dates and its order. Chambers believed that Shakespeare's career began not earlier than 1590, and I give his list of the first ten plays, inserting in brackets the two poems, and adding in the right-hand column Marco Mincoff's refinement of Chambers's dates:

1590–1	*2 Henry VI*	autumn	1590
	3 Henry VI	spring	1591
1591–2	*1 Henry VI*	March	1592
1592–3	*Richard III*	autumn	1592
	The Comedy of Errors	spring	1593
	(*Venus and Adonis*)	April	1593
1593–4	*Titus Andronicus*	Jan.	1594
	The Taming of the Shrew	spring	1594
	(*The Rape of Lucrece*)	May	1594
1594–5	*The Two Gentlemen of Verona*	autumn	1594
	Love's Labour's Lost	winter	1594
	Romeo and Juliet	spring	1595[1]

Mincoff's revision of this chronology indicates the extent of the difference between scholars on the dating of these early plays. His proposal is as follows:

spring	1589	*Henry VI, 1*
autumn	1589	*The Taming of the Shrew*
spring	1590	*Henry VI, 2*
autumn	1590	*Henry VI, 3*
spring	1591	*Richard III*
autumn	1591	*The Comedy of Errors*
spring	1592	*Titus Andronicus*
autumn	1592	*The Two Gentlemen of Verona*

---

1. Chambers, *WS*, vol. 1, p. 270; Mincoff, *Zeitschrift für Anglistik und Amerikanistik* (1964), p. 173.

spring	1593	*Venus and Adonis*
autumn	1593	*Love's Labour's Lost*
spring	1594	*The Rape of Lucrece*[1]

If we add to this that J. C. Maxwell (Arden edn, 1953) prefers a date of 1589–90 for *Titus Andronicus*, and that Honigmann (Arden edn, 1954) argues strongly for a date of 'winter/spring of 1590/91' for *King John*, we find that the years before 1592 are becoming uncomfortably full. Either Shakespeare wrote with great speed and industry or his career as a playwright began earlier than Chambers believed. Chambers's date of 1590–1 for the start of Shakespeare's career is based on the earliest known reference to Shakespeare as a dramatist in Greene's *Groats-worth of Wit* (1592) where the reference to his 'Tygers hart wrapt in a Players hyde' parodies a line from *3 Henry VI*. It is on this evidence that Chambers assigns the three parts of *Henry VI* to the immediately preceding years.[2] But Shakespeare may quite possibly have left Stratford for London as early as 1585,[3] and we simply do not know where he was or what he was doing in the period 1585–90. He might, as Aubrey reports, have been 'a Schoolmaster in the Country'; he might have been writing *The Taming of the Shrew*.

Fortunately, it is no part of my task to attempt a revision of the chronology of Shakespeare's early plays. But there are certain agreements of scholarly opinion which may be adduced in attempting to find an acceptable date for *The Shrew*. I have argued that it must be earlier than August 1592. There is general agreement that by the end of that year Shakespeare had written the three parts of *Henry VI*, and probably *Richard III* as well.[4] Honigmann would add *John* and Maxwell *Titus* to that group. But the only comedy thought to predate 1592 is *The Comedy of Errors*, though some critics place that as late as 1594.[5] There are few

1. Mincoff, op. cit., p. 181.
2. Chambers, *WS*, vol. I, p. 59.
3. See Alexander, *Shakespeare* (1964), p. 51.
4. Dover Wilson (NCS, *1H6*, pp. xiv–xv) concludes, 'The Second and Third Parts, as all agree, must have been in existence and well known by the summer of 1592 . . . *1 Henry VI* was first produced on 3 March 1592'; Cairncross (Arden edn *3H6*, 1964, p. xlv) sets 'the trilogy within the period 1590 to mid-1591'. See also Greg, *SFF*, p. 189; Alexander, *Shakespeare* (1964), pp. 77, 81; Herschel Baker (Riverside Shakespeare, p. 588). The most recent editor of *Richard III* (Hammond, Arden edn, 1981) dates the play as 1591.
5. Sidney Thomas, *SQ* (1956), pp. 377–84. R. A. Foakes (Arden edn, 1962) notes that reasons can be found for dating *Errors* in 1589, 1591–3, and 1594, but says (p. xxiii), 'I prefer to think of it as written between 1590 and 1593'. Harold F. Brooks ('Marlowe and Early Shakespeare', in *Christopher Marlowe*,

points of possible comparison between *The Shrew* and the first tetralogy of history plays, but *The Shrew* and *Errors* have many features in common, and these have been analysed by Mincoff[1] in an attempt to establish which play was written first.

Both plays use Gascoigne's *Supposes* as a source. In *Errors*, the story of Aegeon is a translation into fact of the supposed situation of the pedant in *Supposes* and in *The Shrew*. Mincoff argues:

> Here an old man travelling to a foreign city is told that he has incurred the death penalty by entering enemy territory; the cause of the sudden hostilities in all three cases is quarrels over customs duties. In the earlier versions of the story this is quite a subsidiary incident, so subsidiary that it would need considerable familiarity with *The Supposes* for anyone to think of developing it. . . . It is surely more probable that Shakespeare decided to work up the passage after he had himself treated it in *The Shrew*, than that he should have first borrowed the idea from *The Supposes* and then taken that play for the subplot of his next comedy.

He finds *Errors* in every way more complex and sophisticated than *The Shrew*. The 'stagy monologues' by which Lucentio and Petruchio introduce themselves are not found in *Errors*, where 'Shakespeare was already paying considerable attention to methods of conveying his information less obtrusively'. The problem of marriage and the shrewish wife is common to both plays, but although it is less prominent in *Errors* it is expressed there with a deeper sense of its complexities. Adriana is both more subtle and less vivid than Katherina, and her assessment of a wife's rights and a wife's duties is intellectually more advanced than Katherina's, whose submission, in her final sermon (v.ii), is based on obedience to the will of God and the order of things. *Errors* 'begins where *The Shrew* ends, and on her first appearance Adriana counters Luciana's version of Katherina's sermon with the obvious retort that such a doctrine is easier to preach than to practise.' I find this a powerful argument, and an extended comparison of *The Shrew*, v.ii with *Errors*, ii.i would have enforced Mincoff's point. He prefers, however, to place more weight on matters of technique and style. He points to the passages of direct

Mermaid Critical Commentaries (1968), ed. Morris) accepts 'late in 1592' in the light of Shakespeare's indebtedness to Marlowe's *Edward II* in the matter of the vengeance on Pinch (p. 79).

1. Marco Mincoff, 'The Dating of *The Taming of the Shrew*', *ES* (1973), pp. 554–65.

Marlovian imitation in *The Shrew* (the description of the pictures
in Induction ii, and Gremio's account of his wealth in II.i),
which have no counterparts in *Errors*. He counts eleven 'decorative
classical similes' in *The Shrew*[1] where *Errors* has only one—'I think
you have all drunk of Circe's cup' (v.i.270), and notes that 'a
preponderant part of the imagery of *The Shrew* consists of similes'
which he (like Clemen)[2] finds characteristic of Shakespeare's
earliest style. In *Errors*, on the other hand, classical imagery and
poetical similes have almost disappeared, and metaphors abound.
The Shrew 'has nothing so imaginatively bold as:

> His heart's meteors tilting in his face. IV.ii.6.'

He finds connections between *Errors* and the *Sonnets*, especially in
the use of paradoxical word-play, and no such connections can
be made with *The Shrew*. And he examines the use of the compound epithet, often taken as an index of Shakespeare's maturity,
finding only five fairly ordinary forms (like proud-minded, mad-
brain) in *The Shrew*, while the much shorter *Errors* has three
times that number.

'All this', Mincoff admits, 'does not amount to actual proof',
but it does establish a strong probability, made all the stronger
if one tries to argue the opposite case. If *Errors* precedes *The Shrew*
we have to accept not only a reversion to an earlier style of
writing, but also a drastic simplification of Shakespeare's thinking
on the question of a woman's role in marriage. It is difficult to
give credence to such a prospect.

I find Mincoff's argument convincing, and its consequence
entirely acceptable: *The Taming of the Shrew* is Shakespeare's
earliest comedy.[3] As we shall see later, its roots are in native
English sources and an English translation of Ariosto's *I Suppositi*.
Shakespeare is aware of Roman drama and the *commedia dell' arte*
tradition, as is clear from the very names and descriptions of his
characters, but his deeper exploration of them is part of his
development as a comic dramatist, and we find it not here but
in the more 'classical' comedy, *Errors*.

It still remains to conjecture how early this first comedy should
be placed. Conjecture is all that can be offered, since there is no

1. For example, 'Softer and sweeter than the lustful bed / On purpose trimm'd
up for Semiramis' (Ind. ii.39–40).

2. W. Clemen, *The Development of Shakespeare's Imagery* (1951), p. 22.

3. Clifford Leech, *Two Gentlemen of Verona* (Arden edn, 1969) suggests that
Two Gentlemen preceded *Errors* (p. xxxiv). Of the date he says, 'We may guess
(and it is only a guess) at 1592 for the first phase (*not* version) and late 1593
for the putting of the play into its present shape' (p. xxxv).

external evidence on this point, and the internal evidence is indecisive. The actors afford no help. Supposing I am correct in assuming (pp. 55–6) that William Sly and Alexander Cooke acted in the original performances of *The Shrew*, we know only that Sly died in 1608 and Cooke in 1614,[1] which would allow a date for *The Shrew* at any time after Shakespeare is thought to have left Stratford. The only clear and unambiguous allusion within the play itself is Sly's quotation from *The Spanish Tragedy* in Induction i (his 'Go by, Saint Jeronimy' obviously echoes 'Hieronimo, beware: go by, go by', III.xii.31; see Commentary for this and other parallels). *The Shrew*, then, is later than *The Spanish Tragedy*. But the date of *The Spanish Tragedy* is uncertain, and the earlier and later limits are distressingly wide. It must have been written before 23 February 1592, because on that date there is a record of a performance for Henslowe by Strange's Men. It is probably later than 1582, since it adapts material from Watson's *Hekatompathia*, which was entered on the Stationers' Register in that year, though Kyd knew Watson and might have read his work in manuscript.[2] Within that decade, the majority of scholarly opinion inclines towards the latter end: Philip Edwards, Dover Wilson and Greg all favour a date of 1590–1,[3] but Freeman, in the most detailed and recent survey of the problem,[4] prefers to date the play before 1588 principally on the evidence of the 'pre-Armada tone' of the Spanish allusions. If we accept that *The Spanish Tragedy* was written at some time between 1587 and 1590 this would still permit a very early date for *The Shrew*. It might, indeed, be not simply Shakespeare's first comedy: it might be his first play.

One obvious, but often overlooked, fact supports an early date. Christopher Sly is a Warwickshire man, and the evocation of Warwickshire in the two Induction scenes is deliberate, powerful and detailed. Dramatically, it is not essential: a London setting would have been equally appropriate as a frame and contrast for the imaginary Padua, but Shakespeare's tinker goes out of his way to establish his origins at Burton Heath and Wincot, with Marian and Cicely Hacket, Peter Turph, and old John Naps of Greece. It is true that there were Slys enough in London, but the

1. Chambers, *ES*, vol. II, pp. 340, 312.
2. See *The Spanish Tragedy*, ed. Mulryne (New Mermaid edn, 1970), p. xvi.
3. Edwards (Revels edn, 1959—the standard edition), pp. xxi–xxvii; Wilson (NCS *King John*), pp. liii, 115–16; Greg, *MLQ* (1901), pp. 186–90.
4. Arthur Freeman, *Thomas Kyd: Facts and Problems* (Oxford, 1967), pp. 70–9.

name was well known in Warwickshire,[1] and the whole atmosphere—with its lord, its country house, its hunting, its pedlars, cardmakers and bear-herds—is redolent of the countryside around Stratford, which Shakespeare left for London at some time in the 1580s. No other play in the canon refers so specifically and extensively to the county of his birth. It may well be that when he began writing *The Shrew* Shakespeare was making dramatic capital out of personal nostalgia, recalling a countryside he had quite recently left.

Earlier scholars have tended towards the view that *The Shrew* was written in the second half of the 1590s, and, as a rough generalization, one might say 'the earlier the scholar, the later the date'. Bond quotes Fleay's date of Christmas 1599–1600,[2] depending on the recognition in Grumio's talk (IV.i) of an allusion to the great frost of that year, and the mention of patient Grissel (II.i.288), referring to the play of that title brought out in January 1600. But Grumio's words are not obviously specific, and, in any case, there may have been many frosts which seemed great before 1600. Similarly, I suspect that Grissel's patience was proverbial in Shakespeare's time.[3] Furnivall linked *The Shrew* with plays as late as *Henry IV*, and Boas noted likenesses to *A Midsummer Night's Dream*, but Bond probably represents the opinion of early-twentieth-century scholars when he says 'on the whole, I see no reason to attempt a more precise date than Professor Dowden's ?1597'.[4] Several critics placed weight on the fact that *The Shrew* is not mentioned in Meres's *Palladis Tamia* (1598), though some identified it with the mysterious 'Love labours wonne' in Meres's list.[5] Even if the two plays *are* the same, Meres's reference proves only that *The Shrew* existed by 1598, and since there is good reason to believe that *A Shrew* is a Bad Quarto we can confidently date *The Shrew* at least four years earlier—before the publication of *A Shrew* in 1594.[6] The omission of *The Shrew* from Meres's list is not particularly surprising, since he was not aiming for completeness. He says, 'For Comedy, witnes his *Gentlemen of Verona* . . .', and the word 'witnes' is significant. Meres leaves out the *Contention*, and was perhaps unaware that Shakespeare was the author of the *Henry VI* plays and *The Shrew*. He

1. C. J. Sisson, *New Readings*, vol. 1, p. 159.   2, Bond, p. xliv.
3. See II.i.288n.   4. Bond, pp. xlv–xlvi.
5. Chambers, *WS*, vol. 1, p. 273.
6. See also T. W. Baldwin, *Shakspere's Love's Labor's Won* (Carbondale, 1957), which shows that both *A Shrew* and *Love labours wonne* existed in a bookseller's manuscript catalogue in 1603.

seems simply to have chosen six comedies to balance six tragedies, as 'witnes' to his view that Shakespeare was 'the most excellent in both kinds for the stage'.[1] Chambers, in 1930, prefers an earlier date for *The Shrew*. From a combination of metrical tests, external reference and other evidence he arrived at a chronology which assigns *The Shrew* to 1593–4, and he adhered to the belief that *A Shrew* was used as a source-play. As we have seen, in the half-century since Chambers wrote scholars have moved steadily towards the opinion that *A Shrew* is a Bad Quarto, and so any date after the publication of *A Shrew* in 1594 will carry little conviction.

The idea of an early date for *The Shrew* is not vitiated by the lateness of the few contemporary references to the play. They are so few and casual as to suggest that its original performances did not take London by storm. This is not surprising. Contemporary references to the other early comedies are not abundant, and Shakespeare's reputation certainly seems to have been founded on the history plays rather than on anything else. The earliest reference is the most recently discovered. William H. Moore[2] found the line 'He calls his *Kate*, and she must come and kisse him' in Antony Chute's poem *Beawtie Dishonoured written under the title of Shores Wife* (1593). This must refer to *The Shrew* rather than *A Shrew*, since there is no evidence that Kate ever kisses Ferando whereas Petruchio twice demands a kiss from Katherina (v.i and v.ii). Harington, on the other hand, is clearly referring to the printed text of *A Shrew* when he says in his *Metamorphosis of Ajax* (1596), 'For the shrewd wife, read the book of Taming a Shrew, which hath made a number of us so perfect, that now every one can rule a shrew in our country, save he that hath her'. The only other allusion before the publication of the Folio in 1623 is by Samuel Rowlands in his *Whole Crew of Kind Gossips* (1609), where he says:

> The chiefest Art I have I will bestow
> About a worke cald taming of the Shrow.

Chambers links this with what he calls the 'counterblast' to *The Shrew*, Fletcher's *The Woman's Prize or the Tamer Tamed* (the date of which is uncertain) as possibly indicating a Jacobean revival of the play.[3]

---

1. Chambers, *ES*, vol. IV, p. 246.   2. *SQ* (1964), pp. 55–60.
3. Chambers, *WS*, vol. I, p. 328. Later allusions to *The Shrew* are to be found in Chambers, *WS*, and collected in *The Shakespeare Allusion Book*, ed. Ingleby, Smith and Furnivall; revised Munro, 2 vols (1909). See also Gordon Crosse

The lack of extensive contemporary enthusiasm for the play, as indicated by these few and unimpressive allusions, may even be taken to support an early dating. If, as I would like to think, *The Shrew* is the first play Shakespeare wrote after arriving in London from Stratford, he would have no reputation to command an audience's interest. This came when he exploited a very popular vein of public interest with the history plays, and I would conjecture a gap of two or three years before he returned to the kind of comedy he began with, and wrote *Errors*, in which he took up the trials and joys of marriage from where he had left them at the end of *The Shrew*. *The Shrew* must be dated before August 1592, and after *The Spanish Tragedy*. But I attach no small importance to the Warwickshire references in the Induction. I would propose 1589.

4. AUTHORSHIP AND SOURCES

In 1904 the original Arden edition of *The Shrew* devoted a substantial number of pages to discussion of the play's authorship, on the tacit assumption that Shakespeare could not have written it all.[1] Indeed, the editor stressed the importance of the question: 'The most intricate, as the most interesting, question with which an editor of *The Taming of the Shrew* has to deal is that of Shakespeare's precise share in it.'[2] The solution he adopts is marvellously diplomatic. He mentions a number of scholars who have 'the sense of other work than Shakespeare's . . . surviving in the existing text', but balances them with other scholars who 'assign him sole credit for the adaptation', saying that he himself is 'in accord with these latter so far as they hold the presence of Shakespeare's hand and mind in almost every part of the play'. Nevertheless, he shared the impression of unlikeness that certain parts of the play had left on many minds, and thought them best explained by the hypothesis of 'intermediate work, Shakespeare's *rifacimento* of which was not so thorough but that he accepted much structure and a good deal of actual verse from its author,

---

(*TLS*, 11 July 1936) quoting Henry Peacham, *The Worth of a Penny* (1641, misdated 1647): 'having many times no more shoes than feet: and sometimes more feet than shoes, as the *Beggar* said in the Comedy'. Cf. Induction ii. 10–11.

1. Yet (as Jean Robertson points out to me) the S.R. entry to Ling, Burby consenting, of 22 January 1607, consisted of *The Taming of a Shrew*, *Love's Labour's Lost* and *Romeo and Juliet*, which is at least a pointer to Shakespeare's authorship of *A Shrew*, and possibly *The Shrew*.

2. Bond, pp. xxix–xxxvii.

the precise amount of his own changes being indeterminable'. His general conclusion was that 'while admitting the presence of other work, I do not feel that we have ground enough for denying Shakespeare's revision, however hasty, of the whole'. Bond's view on this matter is, of course, controlled by his opinion of the relationship between *The Shrew* and *A Shrew*, and it was uncertainty on this matter which caused Kenneth Muir, in 1957, to yield up the whole problem of the play's origins: 'The state of our knowledge is such that it would be unprofitable to discuss the question of sources.'[1] Twenty years later he had revised that opinion,[2] and given a most authoritative account of *The Shrew*'s antecedents, but until quite recent years the position of *A Shrew* as either a source-play or a co-representative of a lost '*Ur-Shrew*' made it difficult to separate discussion of *The Shrew*'s authorship and sources from that of its relation to *A Shrew* (see above, pp. 12–50). Once it can be accepted that *The Shrew* predates *A Shrew*, and that the latter is a Bad Quarto of the former, the other problems are eased. In particular, there seems no reason to question Shakespeare's authorship of the whole of the F text of *The Shrew*. The disintegrators had already been fairly routed in 1925 by E. P. Kuhl (even though he believed that *A Shrew* was a source-play).[3] The general line of his exhaustive argument was that the so-called 'Shakespearean' parts of the play could not be distinguished from the 'non-Shakespearean' by any analysis of vocabulary, metrical peculiarity, syntactical characteristics, classical allusion, foreign language usage, or the like. He offered a detailed defence of the unified nature of plot and character as evidence against any form of double authorship, and shrewdly challenged the scholarly world to produce any dramatist who could so perfectly integrate his work with that of Shakespeare to produce such a seamless robe.

Quiller-Couch[4] and Peter Alexander[5] took the same view, but so distinguished a scholar as Chambers, so late as 1930, believed that in *The Shrew* 'Shakespeare had, exceptionally for him, the assistance of a collaborator', and he assigned to him almost two-fifths of the play though he was careful not to assign him a name.[6] It was left to Karl Wentersdorf to put the issue beyond reasonable doubt. In 1954 he offered an account of the play's imagery as

1. Kenneth Muir, *Shakespeare's Sources* (1957), p. 259.
2. In *The Sources of Shakespeare's Plays* (1977), pp. 19–22.
3. E. P. Kuhl, 'The Authorship of *The Taming of the Shrew*', *PMLA* (1925), pp. 551–618.
4. NCS (1928), pp. viiff.
5. *Shakespeare's Life and Art* (1939), pp. 69–70.
6. Chambers, *WS*, vol. I, p. 324.

evidence that it is the work of one man.[1] The strength of the method is obvious. As Wentersdorf says: 'In a play suspected of double authorship, we would not expect to find any affinity between the imagery of the portions assigned to the two writers' (p. 14). It is well attested that such collaborations as did take place were rough-and-ready affairs based on dividing responsibility for plot and sub-plot, or Act by Act, or scene by scene. Collaboration was never line by line, or image by image. Wentersdorf demonstrates that there are typically Shakespearean images in the sub-plot as well as in the Katherina–Petruchio scenes, that there are many parallels of imagery between those parts of the play Chambers assigns to Shakespeare and those he believes were written by the collaborator, and that the play contains some symbolic iterative imagery which runs through and unites plot and sub-plot. One example must suffice to illustrate the method. Shakespeare's mind was obviously deeply impressed by the unfathomed depth of the sea, and this often gives rise to an image which involves sounding the depth with a fathom-line.[2] Such an image occurs in the 'Shakespearean' part of *The Shrew*—

> Thy virtues spoke of, and thy beauty *sounded*,
> Yet not *so deeply* as to thee belongs. . . .
>
> (II. i. 192–3)

—and in the 'non-Shakespearean':

> But I will in, to be revenged for this villainy.
> And I, to *sound* the *depth* of this knavery.
> (v. i. 123–5)[3]

The accumulation of dozens of examples of this kind cannot but be convincing. Wentersdorf was quite justified in concluding, in 1954, that 'the imagery indicates that the play was the work of but one playwright and that this playwright was Shakespeare'. No one has since contested that claim, though Moody E. Prior challenged the validity of imagery tests as a criterion of authenticity.[4] Wentersdorf (obviously after lengthy thought) defended his method in an article published in 1972,[5] which made extensive

1. 'The Authenticity of *The Taming of the Shrew*', *SQ* (1954), pp. 11–32.

2. Examples are quoted from *Ven.*, *Wint.*, *Troil.*, *2H4*, *AYL*, *1H4*, *Tp.*, *2H6*, *Gent.*, and *H8*.

3. I quote from Wentersdorf, op. cit., p. 26, with his italics, and my line-numberings.

4. 'Imagery as a Test of Authorship', *SQ* (1955), pp. 381–6.

5. 'Imagery as a Criterion of Authenticity: A Reconsideration of the Problem', *SQ* (1972), pp. 231–59.

use of the techniques of 'cluster' criticism of imagery.[1] One of the most characteristically Shakespearean of these clusters is the death–kite–food–bed group, which is found from the earliest plays to the latest and is usually triggered by the underlying idea of death, especially violent death. Wentersdorf was able to show that all the component elements of this cluster are present within eighteen lines of Petruchio's soliloquy (IV. i. 177–94) where the pattern builds up to the metaphoric idea of death—'This is a way to kill a wife with kindness'.[2] *The Shrew*, despite its disparities of style (which a number of scholars now accept as evidence of the young poet's work), is typically Shakespearean in its use of images, and it is all of a piece throughout.

Wentersdorf's conclusion is supported by an analysis undertaken from an entirely different point of view. Waldo and Herbert[3] examine the musical references in *The Shrew*, and find that they point to one author, and that author Shakespeare. They present impressive statistics to show that Shakespeare's use of musical terms is more widespread as well as more complex than that of any possible collaborator. They compare the musical allusions in *The Shrew* with those in other early comedies, and argue that in all these plays 'the musical allusions . . . taken as a whole form a pattern' (from discord to harmony), and there is no differentiation to suggest collaborative work anywhere in *The Shrew*.

So far as I am aware, there has not been, since Chambers's in 1930, a single attempt to present a case for collaborative authorship in *The Shrew*. This is in accord with the general trend of criticism of the Shakespeare canon, and it seems likely that this trend will be supplemented and reinforced when computer-assisted analyses of the vocabularies and stylistic characteristics of these early plays become available. We may therefore accept that *The Shrew* was written by Shakespeare alone, and proceed to consider his sources.

It is no more than scholarly convention which decrees that the

1. See E. A. Armstrong, *Shakespeare's Imagination* (1946; rev. edn, Lincoln, Nebr., 1963).

2. The point about cluster imagery is that the presence of one element of the cluster will frequently suggest all the others to the poet's subconscious mind. This is especially telling when the connections are not obvious. Cf. Petruchio's soliloquy with *R3*, I. i. 132ff., where Hastings deplores 'that the *eagle* should be mewed / While *kites* and *buzzards prey* at liberty', and Richard comments on the news of the King's illness, 'Oh, he hath kept an evil *diet* long, / And overmuch *consumed* his royal person . . . / What, is he in his *bed*?'

3. Waldo and Herbert, 'Musical Terms in *The Shrew*: Evidence of Single Authorship', *SQ* (1959), pp. 185–99.

sources of a play shall be sought in the playwright's reading. Only when there is an identifiable objective fact—a story, a poem, a novella, a chronicle—can Shakespeare's process of dramatic transmutation of his material be studied and evaluated. If we were to ask what materials, and in what proportions, contributed to the creative act which issued in this play, we should never get an answer, but we would have displayed the fact that more than the reading of books is concerned in the writing of a play. In the case of *The Shrew* the most powerful tributaries are probably the most unchartable. Christopher Sly must be part of Shakespeare's personal experience, and his Warwickshire background—so richly evoked—must be Shakespeare's own recollection of his native county. There is no literary source for this, nor for Sly's drunken confusions of utterance, which derive from the poet's observation if not from his own experience. Similarly, the arrival of Lucentio and Tranio at 'fair Padua, nursery of arts' in 1.i may owe something to Gascoigne's *Supposes*, but it owes more to Shakespeare's personal sense of what it feels like to be a young stranger in a great town. Most importantly, we distort our understanding of the play if we labour long to establish which of the countless tales and stories that tell of the 'taming' of a headstrong woman comes closest to the particular circumstances of *The Shrew*. Shakespeare selected this topic as the basis for his comedy precisely because it was popular, and it was popular because it has a perennial appeal to the aggressive and competitive instincts and prejudices of men and women. It holds a mirror up to domestic life; it is the kind of thing which could disturb an audience's composure, if acted well. The real sources of *The Shrew* rise in Shakespeare's experience of Warwickshire, of the town houses of mercantile London, of the taverns and streets, and of all sorts and conditions of women, their expectations, frustrations, conquests and surrenders.

If *The Shrew* is dated about 1589, Shakespeare would have been about twenty-five when he wrote it, and his mind would not have been so well stocked with multifarious reading as it was later to become. It has never been supposed that the direct literary sources of *The Shrew* were many, and so long as it was assumed that *A Shrew* was the principal source there was little inducement to look beyond that play and Gascoigne's *Supposes*. Bond considered that Shakespeare 'had probably read an old prose tract . . . entitled The ancient, true and admirable history of Patient Grisel',[1] but in his account of 'Other Sources' he

1. Bond, pp. xxviii–xxix.

lists only a dozen or so texts which present situations analogous to some in *The Shrew*, and does not argue that Shakespeare knew and used any one of them.[1]

The same attitude underlies Bullough's account of the sources of this play in his standard work on Shakespeare's sources.[2] Bullough subscribed to what was by then very much the minority view, that *A Shrew* was a direct source. So he prints the text of the 1594 edition and discusses it at length. He also prints Simon Goulart's version of 'The Sleeper Awakened', in the translation by Edward Grimeston, as an analogue which best represents the theme of the beggar transported into luxury, and Gascoigne's *Supposes* (1566) as the direct source of the Bianca–Lucentio plot (which it undoubtedly is). We cannot rest content with this, as Hosley points out:

> Bullough prints only one generally acknowledged source (the *Supposes*), one representative version (Grimeston) of an acknowledged source or analogue (Heuterus), and one 'source' (*A Shrew*) which practically all modern scholars would consider to be neither a source nor an analogue; and he fails to print or discuss a number of other possible sources or analogues.[3]

Despite the title of his article, Hosley is not concerned to distinguish sharply between a source and an analogue, nor does he offer to evaluate the importance of analogues in discussing a play's origins. His principal concern is to assert the parallels with the anonymous verse tale called *Here Begynneth a Merry Jest of a Shrewde and Curste Wyfe, Lapped in Morrelles Skin, for Her Good Behavyour*, printed by Hugh Jackson about 1550. He calls this a 'source', and finds parallels with *The Shrew* in 'the basic situation, the characterization, the development of the action, and the language'. The tale tells the story of a man married to a shrewish wife, who has two daughters, the elder shrewish like her mother, the younger meek and gentle and her father's favourite. The younger daughter has many suitors, she marries one of them, and they fade out of the story. The elder has one suitor, the father tries to dissuade him, but, after seeking the mother's permission and hearing from her in some detail, he marries her. The wedding is normal and uneventful, and is followed by a fine wedding feast.

1. Ibid., pp. xlvi–lii. See also my Appendix III.
2. Bullough, pp. 57–158.
3. Richard Hosley, 'Sources and Analogues of *The Taming of the Shrew*', *HLQ* (1963–4), pp. 289–308, and reprinted in the Signet Shakespeare edn (1966).

The couple depart, and the marriage night is described at length. After some time, the wife starts to misuse the servants, and she abuses her husband when he admonishes her. She strikes him in her anger, and he rides off to give her time to cool down. When he returns she berates him and refuses him food. He orders his old horse, Morrel, to be killed and flayed, and the hide salted. He forces his railing wife into a cellar, beats her mercilessly with birch rods until she bleeds and faints, then fastens her naked body into the salted hide. The pain revives her, and he threatens to keep her tied up in the horse's hide for the rest of her life. With that, 'her moode began to sinke', and when he releases her she becomes meek and obedient. The husband gives a feast to demonstrate his wife's 'pacyence' before her father and mother. The wife serves them all, humbly and quickly, much to the surprise of her mother, who remonstrates with her in the kitchen, but is told that if she had been wrapped in Morrel's skin as her daughter had been she would be equally submissive and obedient. The colophon to the tale reads:

> He that can charme a shrewde wyfe
> Better then thus,
> Let him come to me, and fetch ten pound,
> And a golden purse.

This is very like Petruchio's challenge at the end of iv.i:

> He that knows better how to tame a shrew,
> Now let him speak: 'tis charity to show.

In Kenneth Muir's opinion this 'makes it fairly certain that Shakespeare did know the ballad',[1] but it must be said that the other verbal parallels which Hosley finds are very weak and general. A Shrewde and Curste Wyfe is over 1100 lines long, and it would be surprising if words like 'mad', 'fiend', 'devil', 'rout', 'wasp' and 'angry' did not occur both in it and in The Shrew. The parallels of action which Hosley adduces are equally unconvincing—the father's attempt to dissuade the suitor, the shrew striking her man, and the like. Far more important (and Hosley touches on this point but lightly) is the fact that A Shrewde and Curste Wyfe tells the story of two sisters, not three. In the vast majority of other shrew stories the shrew is the youngest of three sisters,[2] and the

---

1. The Sources of Shakespeare's Plays, p. 20.

2. The version most commonly quoted, and thought by some to be a source, is the Jutland tale of the Three Shrewish Sisters. See Reinhold Köhler, 'Zu Shakespeare's The Taming of the Shrew', SJ (1868), pp. 397–401.

rarity of the two-sister version is a stronger link between *A Shrewde and Curste Wyfe* and Shakespeare's play than the verbal echoes could ever be. Hosley might also have made more of the fact that in *A Shrewde and Curste Wyfe* the younger daughter disappears from the story very early, and if anything is certain about the sources of *The Shrew* it is that Shakespeare went to Gascoigne's *Supposes* for the development of the Bianca–Lucentio sub-plot. Perhaps he went there precisely because of this lacuna in *A Shrewde and Curste Wyfe*. Though I cannot be convinced by Hosley's arguments that Shakespeare had read a copy of *A Shrewde and Curste Wyfe*, I am quite ready to believe that he knew the story, or something very like it. I stress 'something very like it' because I think it indicates the area of error into which previous source-hunters have strayed. We should not be looking for a written document which tells a story as like as possible to Shakespeare's narrative of the taming of Katherina, which also exhibits as many verbal parallels as may be found by ingenuity. Stories about struggles for mastery between husband and wife are legion in every culture, and it is far more likely that Shakespeare knew many and various versions of such tales, deriving from both oral and written sources. The most fruitful approach to this multiplicity of material is likely to be through the discipline of folklore studies, in which all the known versions of a type of folk-tale, oral and written, are assembled and analysed in terms of the motifs exhibited and combined in any one version.

Fortunately, this has been done for *The Shrew* in the unpublished doctoral dissertation of Jan Harold Brunvand.[1] He bases his work on Aarne–Thompson Type 901,[2] the folk-tale in which the youngest of three sisters is a shrew, whose husband kills an animal to frighten his bride and bring her to submission, which submission is publicly shown by a wager amongst his friends on who has the most obedient wife. Aarne–Thompson identifies four motifs in this complex: the victorious youngest daughter, the taming of the shrew, the bride test for obedience, and the wager on the most obedient wife. Versions of this story are widespread in Europe, and have been recorded from France, Italy, Finland, Estonia, Lithuania, Sweden, Denmark, Iceland, Scotland,

1. '*The Taming of the Shrew*: A Comparative Study of Oral and Literary Versions', unpublished Ph.D dissertation, Indiana University (1961). Brunvand's article, based on his dissertation, 'The Folktale Origin of *The Taming of the Shrew*', is in *SQ* (1966), pp. 345–59.
2. *The Types of the Folktale: A Classification and Bibliography*, by Antti Aarne, translated and enlarged by Stith Thompson, second revision (Helsinki, 1964).

Ireland, Spain, Holland, Germany, Austria and the Balkans. It is known in the United States, India and Spanish America. Dr Brunvand assembled and examined 418 versions from thirty national groups, and his basic task was to ascertain the sub-types of the tales, their origins, developments, and paths of dissemination.

The tale was well known throughout western Europe,[1] and one of the versions may illustrate the type as well as suggesting a method of 'taming' much closer to Shakespeare's than that described in *A Shrewde and Curste Wyfe*. The Scottish tale of 'The Handsome Lazy Lass' has not survived in a complete form, but it is certainly recognizable as containing some elements of the 'Shrew' story:[2]

There was once a gentleman who had a farm, and kept serving-men and serving-women. There was a farmer living near him who had three daughters, and the gentleman made up his mind that he would seek one of the farmer's children in marriage.

He arrived at the farmer's house.

Two of the farmer's daughters were good and industrious. But the other one was handsome and lazy. And the gentleman chose this lazy and handsome one.

The farmer said to him, 'I do not wish thee to suffer loss. She will not do a hand's turn, she is so lazy.'

'Even if she will not, let that be my affair,' said the gentle-man, and he married her, and took her home with him.

'Now,' said the gentleman [to his servants], 'you are to give me the food that the serving-men eat, and give the serving-men the food that I have. You are to do this for a week.'

This was done, and the master had the food of the serving-men, and the serving-men were supplied with the master's food.

'Oh King! is it not an extraordinary thing,' said she, 'that the serving-men should have such good food, while we have such food as this.'

'It is the serving-men who have need of good food; they earn

1. See D. P. Rotunda, *Motif-Index of the Italian Novella in Prose* (Bloomington, Indiana, 1942); J. Bolte and G. Polívka, *Anmerkungen zu den Kinder- und Hausmärchen der Brüder Grimm* (Leipzig, 1913–31), vol. I, p. 443; Joseph Bédier, *Les Fabliaux* (2nd edn, Paris, 1895), p. 464; Victor Chauvin, *Bibliographie des ouvrages arabes* (Liège, 1892–1922), vol. II, p. 155.

2. J. G. McKay, *More West Highland Tales* (Edinburgh and London, 1940), vol. I, pp. 149–51. The difference is that the 'lass' is not a shrew; the similarity is in the method of taming.

it, but seeing that we do not work, food that is not so good will suffice for us.'

'What need is there to give such good food to the serving-men? what is the hardest and most exhausting work that they have to do?'

'Ploughing, threshing, and carting.'

'And which of those is the hardest?'

'Threshing.'

'Then certainly I myself will go and thresh to-day, if I get good food.'

'Thou certainly shalt not; it is not for that purpose that I took thee.'

'Now,' said he to the serving-woman, 'thou art to send me my own food again, and theirs to the serving-men. . . .'

Certain small, unimportant details occur here, in *The Shrew*, and in many versions of the tale, like the gentleman's 'Even if she will not, let that be my affair', which may be compared with Petruchio's comment in I.ii:

> I know she is an irksome brawling scold.
> If that be all, masters, I hear no harm.

But 'The Handsome Lazy Lass' differs from the majority of versions of the tale in that the wife is tamed by cunning rather than by violence. Brunvand's analysis of his 418 examples is convincing in that it shows that Shakespeare could not have derived his plot solely from the plot of *A Shrew* (the analysis, incidentally, helps to get rid of the idea of *A Shrew* as a source-play), and that he must have known the tale as it was developed in the oral tradition. Brunvand shows that *The Shrew* belongs to the 'Northern-European Elaborated Subtype' of Aarne–Thompson Type 901, and that in its basic outline as well as in a number of specific points the plot goes back to old and widespread elements of the story. Only a few traits of the main plot are not found in any folk-tales, and Brunvand comes to the conclusion that, allowing for such changes in the story as are necessary to dramatize it, the traditional pattern of the oral tales is well preserved in the play.

This is not to say that the shrew story is not well represented in surviving literary documents. M. C. Bradbrook has drawn attention to European antecedents like Jean de Meung's portrait of La Vieille, and Eustace Deschamps's *Miroir de Mariage*, *Les Quinze Joyes de Mariage* and the *sottie*, which have their English equivalents in Chaucer, the Miracle Plays and the interludes.[1] She also discusses the two early Tudor plays on the shrew theme, *Johan Johan* (1533–4) and *Tom Tyler and his Wife* (c. 1561), in both of which the husband is at the centre of the picture, and in both of which physical violence and fisticuffs are essential ingredients.

The 'shrew' tradition, in story, drama, and poem, is long, wide and richly varied, and Muir is perhaps too decisive when he says:

> The main plot, of the taming, seems to have no identifiable source. The taming of a shrew is a popular theme and there may well have been something closer to Shakespeare's plot than *A Shrewde and Curste Wyfe*.[2]

There were many things closer to Shakespeare's plot than that anonymous ballad, which in tone, morality, narrative and wit could hardly be more distant. Bradbrook mentions the ballad 'The Wife Wrapt in a Wether's Skin',[3] where, since his wife is too high-born to spin, wash or work, the husband wraps her in a wether's skin, and because he is afraid to beat her for fear of her family, he beats the wether's skin until he has tamed his wife. This is obviously related in some way to *A Shrewde and Curste Wyfe*, but it has a little more wit and ingenuity, and in that respect it stands closer to *The Shrew*. For the most important point to emerge from a study of the shrew tradition, both oral and written, is that no one has discovered a version in which the tamer goes to work in the way in which Shakespeare's Petruchio does. Some beat their wives, and some trick them. Petruchio deliberately

1. M. C. Bradbrook, 'Dramatic Role as Social Image: A Study of *The Taming of the Shrew*', *SJ* (1958), pp. 132–50. Chaucer's Wife of Bath is the grand exemplar of the 'shrew triumphant', a tradition at least as long as the 'shrew subdued'. Noah's wife has a long history in the Miracle cycles, though even in a late example like *The Townley Play of Noah* the relationship between husband and wife is less than subtle (see *Fourteenth Century Verse and Prose*, ed. Sisam (Oxford, 1921, reprinted 1950), pp. 185–203). A far wider range of tone, from the courtly to the scabrous, is exemplified in the slightly later poem of William Dunbar, 'The Tretis of the Tua Mariit Wemen and the Wedo', where the widow describes her shrewishness and her dissimulation (*The Poems of William Dunbar*, ed. Mackenzie (1932), p. 91):

> I schaw yow, sisteris in schrift, I wes a schrew evir,
> Bot I wes schene in my schrowd, and schew me innocent;
> And thought I dour wes, and dane, dispitous, and bald,
> I wes dissymblit suttelly in a sanctis liknes.

2. Muir, p. 20.
3. See Appendix III. For the fullest account of this ballad see B. H. Bronson, *The Traditional Tunes of the Child Ballads*, 4 vols (Princeton, 1959–72), vol. IV, pp. 143–73.

treats Katherina as if she were an untamed bird of prey, 'mans' her, tames her, and makes her obedient by 'killing her in her own humour'. This would appear to be Shakespeare's original contribution to the shrew tradition. It is the treatment, and that alone, which has 'no identifiable source'. The rest of the main plot is a *mélange* of incidents, motifs and commonplaces which would have been common knowledge to the playwright and his audience.

The same is true of the 'framework' plot. The real source lies in Shakespeare's personal experience of tinkers like Christopher Sly in the Warwickshire countryside, the country house, the tavern, and the hunting habits of lords, their servants and their hounds.[1] So strongly is this evoked that one might think the play had been written for performance in a Warwickshire manor house. There is no evidence for this, but it is not a ridiculous conjecture; it would give special point to the list of names (possibly of well-known local people) in Induction ii, which Sly quotes as his friends, and whom he is solemnly assured do not exist. The character of Sly is grafted on to a story which is itself age-old. In folklore studies it is known as 'le dormeur éveillé', or, in the Aarne–Thompson categorization, 'The Man thinks he has been in Heaven'.[2] It is widespread throughout Europe, appearing from Estonia to Turkey, and one of the earliest recorded versions appears in the *Arabian Nights*, where Haroun Al Raschid transports to a life of luxury a man found sleeping. The same story is told of Philip the Good of Burgundy, in Heuterus' *De Rebus Burgundicis* (1584). Muir suggests (p. 19) that Shakespeare 'could have read' Heuterus, but I find it difficult to believe that the young playwright would have been interested in Burgundian history for its own sake, or that he would have been likely to consult such a work when preparing a comedy about taming a wilful woman.[3] Warton, in his *History of English Poetry* (1774–81), says that the story was printed in a jest-book 'sett forth by maister Richard

1. See the extensive notes on 'literary hunting-scenes' in *A Midsummer Night's Dream*, ed. Brooks (Arden edn, 1979), pp. 92–4.

2. Aarne–Thompson, *The Types of the Folktale*, p. 438, Type 1531: 'The rich lord puts fine clothes on a drunken peasant and gives him good food and drink'. Cf. also Types 1313A* and 1526. See V. Chauvin, *Bibliographie des ouvrages arabes*, edn cit., vol. v, pp. 272–4, no. 155.

3. Bullough notes that Heuterus was translated into French by S. Goulart, in his *Thrésor d'histoires admirables et mémorables* (1606?), and that Goulart was translated into English in 1607 by Edward Grimeston; these versions were too late for Shakespeare. Burton summarizes Heuterus in *Anatomy of Melancholy* (1621), Pt II, Sect. ii, Mem. 4.

Edwardes, mayster of her maiesties revels', in 1570.[1] No trace of such a work has survived, but if Warton is correct this is a far more probable source than any of the extant versions. It is precisely the kind of book a young playwright planning a comedy might consult, or (in his youthful thirst for stories) know already.

Ballads like *The Waking Man's Dreame* and *The Frolicksome Duke, or the Tinker's Good Fortune* testify to the popularity of the story in Shakespeare's time, even though the extant versions are probably after *The Shrew*. The latter is found in Child's *English and Scottish Ballads* and in Percy's *Reliques of Ancient English Poetry*,[2] reprinted from a black-letter copy in the Pepys Collection. It begins:

> Now as fame does report a young duke keeps a court,
> One that pleases his fancy with frolicksome sport:
> But amongst all the rest, here is one I protest,
> Which will make you to smile when you hear the true jest:
> A poor tinker he found, lying drunk on the ground,
> As secure in a sleep as if laid in a swound.
>
> The duke said to his men, William, Richard, and Ben,
> Take him home to my palace, we'll sport with him then. . . .

This is very like the Christopher Sly story, but it is not obviously derivative from it, and many of the later details differ. It may well be quite independent of Shakespeare, whatever its date. Similarly, Baskervill notes that the drunken tinker theme was also a popular subject for jigs. He mentions a 1591 ballad called 'Alas the poor tinker', a jig published in 1595 with the title 'A pleasant jigge between a tinker and a clown', and a late example in which a drunken tinker is hauled out of a tavern by its hostess and left asleep on the cold ground.[3] This one may well be an echo of Shakespeare's play, but, in the case of ballads and jigs, the late date of an extant version does not preclude an earlier history, and it is probably safe to say that the story of the drunken tinker and his dream was well known in England when Shakespeare wrote *The Shrew*. So we need not strain credulity to decide which ballad, jig or story, of those which have survived, comes closest to the

1. Warton, Sect. LII, quoted in Bullough, p. 59. Chambers thought 'revels' a mistake for 'children' or 'chapel'; for full details of Richard Edwardes see *ES*, vol. III, pp. 309–11.

2. 1857 edition, vol. I, pp. 255–9.

3. Charles Baskervill, *The Elizabethan Jig* (Chicago, 1929), p. 315, referring to Jan van Arp's 'Singhende Klucht, Van Droncke Goosen', published in Amsterdam, 1639. Baskervill claims that there are 'distinct indications that "Droncke Goosen" is English in origin'.

events described in Induction i and ii of *The Shrew*. It would be a task more difficult than important, unless, as Bradbrook puts it, 'Shakespeare is held to be constitutionally incapable of inventing a plot' (p. 138).

The story of the wooing of Bianca by Lucentio forms the third strand in what Hosley describes as 'the brilliant threefold structure of induction, main plot, and subplot, unified as these elements are by the "Supposes" theme'.[1] Here it is quite clear that Shakespeare made use of Gascoigne's *Supposes*, and his reasons for doing so are attributed by Bradbrook to the nature of his theatre and audience: 'He was addressing a crowd socially heterogeneous, mostly masculine, who required a delicate adjustment of native popular traditional art with the socially more esteemed classical and foreign models' (p. 134). Ariosto was certainly a fashionable foreign model. Harington translated his *Orlando Furioso*, and Gosson, Sidney, Lodge and Puttenham were all interested in him, to say nothing of his influence on Spenser's *Faerie Queene*.[2] Gascoigne was one of the earliest to appreciate him,[3] as indeed he appreciated all things Italian. In the Prologue to the *Glasse of Government* (1575) he referred to 'Italian toyes' that 'are full of pleasaunt sporte', and his translation of Ariosto's comedy in 1566 was an entirely appropriate contribution to the new interest in Italian drama, which had even brought Italian actors to play in England as early as 1546/7.[4] Gascoigne was a member of Gray's Inn, and according to the title-page of the 1573 edition the play was 'there presented'. Chambers notes that there was probably a revival at Trinity, Oxford, on 8 January 1582, when Richard Madox recorded 'We supt at ye presidents lodging and after had ye supposes handeled in ye haul indifferently'.[5]

Gascoigne translated *I Suppositi* in the same year (1566) as he and another Gray's Inn lawyer, Francis Kinwelmershe, translated Lodovico Dolce's *Giocasta* (1549),[6] and both plays seem to have been originally intended for performance at the Inn, before an audience of fashionable young lawyers who made the various Inns of Court centres of elegance as much as seats of learning. As Prouty says, 'Importations from Italy, such as forks and fantastic

1. Hosley, 'Sources and Analogues', p. 294.
2. See A. Lytton Sells, *The Italian Influence in English Poetry* (1955), p. 171.
3. For details of Gascoigne's life and work see Chambers, *ES*, vol. III, pp. 320–2; C. T. Prouty, *George Gascoigne: Elizabethan Courtier, Soldier, and Poet* (New York, 1942); R. C. Johnson, *George Gascoigne* (New York, 1972).
4. See K. M. Lea, *Italian Popular Comedy* (1934), pp. 352–8.
5. *ES*, vol. III, p. 321.
6. Dolce's play was itself a paraphrase of the *Phoenissae* of Euripides.

styles in clothes, were received with enthusiasm, and exceptional hospitality was extended to Italy's poetry'.[1] The links with Roman comedy, though at second hand, were strong, since at the first performance of *I Suppositi* Ariosto himself is believed to have spoken the Prologue, which declared his sources unambiguously:

E vi confessa l'autore avere in questo e Plauto e Terenzio seguitato, de li quali l'un fece Cherea per Doro, e l'altro Filocrate per Tindaro, e Tindaro per Filocrate, l'uno ne lo *Eunuco*, l'altro ne li *Captivi*, supponersi: perché non solo ne li costumi, ma ne li argumenti ancora de le fabule vuole essere de li antichi e celebrati poeti, a tutta sua possanza, imitatore; e come essi Menandro e Apollodoro e li altri Greci ne le lor latine comedie seguitoro, egli cosí ne le sue vulgari i modi e processi de' latini scrittori schifar non vuole.[2]

The care which Gascoigne took in translating Ariosto's comedy is evidenced by J. W. Cunliffe's discovery[3] that he used not only the original prose version of the play but a later verse rendition, made between 1528 and 1531, and used them simultaneously.[4] Bond comments approvingly on the style of translation:

He translates with vigour and freedom, almost always speech by speech, but always rendering sense rather than words, keeping closely to it, condensing at whiles but making no important omission, inserting stage-directions and a line or two here and there in the actual text, besides his considerable development of Damon's mournful soliloquy on parents and children (III.iii), often introducing racy English phrases and proverbs unrepresented in the original, and substituting English equivalents for names or allusions that he felt would be unintelligible,

1. *George Gascoigne*, pp. 143–4.
2. Ariosto, *Le Commedie*, ed. M. Catalano (Bologna, 1933), vol. I, p. 86, quoted in Prouty, op. cit., p. 160. The passage may be translated thus: 'And the author confesses to you that in this matter he has followed both Plautus and Terence, of whom the one had Cherea substituted for Doro and the other Filocrate for Tindaro and Tindaro for Filocrate, in, respectively, the *Eunuch* of Plautus and the *Captives* of Terence; because the author wishes, as far as he can, to imitate not only the customs but even the arguments of the plots from ancient and celebrated poets. Just as the latter followed Menander, Apollodorus and the other Greeks in the Latin comedies, in the same way the author in his vernacular comedies does not wish to scorn the methods and processes of Latin writers.'
3. *Supposes and Jocasta*, ed. Cunliffe (Boston, 1906), pp. 109–11.
4. Details of all Gascoigne's departures from Ariosto's text are in R. W. Bond, *Early Plays from the Italian* (Oxford, 1911), pp. lviff.

but without making any change in the action or the characters beyond converting the Ferrarese stranger to whom Philogano appeals on his arrival into an Innkeeper.[1]

Prouty gives a number of illustrative examples, comparing the Italian closely with the English, to show that Gascoigne's translation is as vigorous as it is faithful.

A 'Suppose', as Gascoigne's Prologue tells us, 'is nothing else but a mystaking or imagination of one thing for an other', and in the 1575 edition each false supposition or mistake of identity is indicated by a marginal note. There are some twenty-four of these, suggesting that this 'errors' play is not deficient in complexity. As the play opens we learn that two years ago a young Sicilian, Erostrato, came to Ferrara to study, and fell in love with Polynesta, daughter of the merchant Damon. In order to gain access to her he changed name and position with his servant Dulipo, entered Damon's household, and with the help of her Nurse won Polynesta's love, slept with her, and declared his identity to her. The position has become critical because Damon has decided to marry Polynesta to the aged lawyer, Cleander, and to match Cleander's dowry the feigned Erostrato has had to declare himself a suitor and match the amount. He says this will be ratified by his father, Phylogano, who will come to Ferrara within a fortnight. He then induces a travelling Sienese to impersonate Phylogano, and installs him in a house in Ferrara. At this point the real Phylogano appears, intending to take his son home. At the feigned Erostrato's house he is confronted by the Sienese, who maintains himself to be Phylogano, and by the servant, Dulipo, who likewise denies him. Fearing foul play, the real Phylogano seeks legal remedy and consults Cleander. In discussion between them it emerges that Dulipo is really Cleander's son, lost eighteen years before when the Turks captured Otranto. Meanwhile, Damon, by overhearing a quarrel between the Nurse and another servant, has learned of the intrigue between the feigned Dulipo and Polynesta, and has imprisoned the feigned Dulipo in the house. News of this is brought to the feigned Erostrato by the parasite Pasiphilo, and the knowledge of his young master's peril causes the feigned Erostrato to confess all. His confession confirms Cleander's discovery, relieves Phylogano's anxiety, and reconciles Damon to marriage between Polynesta and Erostrato, since Erostrato is established as a man of rank, and Cleander, having recovered his son, relinquishes his suit.

1. Bond, *Early Plays*, p. lv.

Shakespeare takes over small things and large from *Supposes*.
Petrucio is the name of one of the servants of the Sienese, and
Lytio is a servant to Phylogano.[1] These would seem to have been
picked up at random and put to use. On the other hand, the
exchange of places by master and servant—'The first suppose &
grownd of all the suposes'[2]—is equally essential to the plot of
The Shrew. Shakespeare, since he is not bound to observe the
unities as *Supposes* does, can expand the retrospective narrative.
Polynesta says:

> The man whome to this day you have supposed to be *Dulipo*,
> is (as I say) *Erostrato*, a gentleman that came from *Sicilia* to
> studie in this Citie, & even at his first arivall met me in the
> street, fel enamored of me, & of suche vehement force were the
> passions he suffred, that immediatly he cast aside both long
> gowne and bookes, & determined on me only to apply his
> study. And to the end he might the more commodiously bothe
> see me and talke with me, he exchanged both name, habite,
> clothes and credite with his servant *Dulipo*.[3]

This is expanded to form a large part of I.i of *The Shrew*. Some
points touched on quite lightly in *Supposes* seem to have attracted
Shakespeare's imagination. In II.i Erostrato tells how he met the
Sienese:

> . . . as I passed the foorde beyonde *S. Anthonies* gate, I met at
> the foote of the hill a gentleman riding with two or three men:
> and as me thought by his habite and his lookes, he should be
> none of the wisest. He saluted me, and I him: I asked him from
> whence he came, and whither he would? he answered that he
> had come from *Venice*, then from *Padua*, nowe was going to
> *Ferrara*, and so to his countrey, whiche is *Scienna*. (Bullough,
> p. 122)

This becomes Biondello's account of the 'ancient angel' coming
down the hill in IV.ii. The names are changed (Rome, Tripoli,
Mantua), but the encounter and the incidents are closely similar.
In the same way, the servant Paquetto's remark in *Supposes*, II.ii—

> O you meane the foule waye that we had since wee came from
> this *Padua*, I promise you, I was afraide twice or thrice, that
> your mule would have lien fast in the mire. . . .

1. The only clear verbal link between the two texts is Lucentio's line at
v.i.107, 'While counterfeit supposes blear'd thine eyne'. But it is clear enough.
2. *Supposes*, I.ii; Bullough, p. 114.   3. Ibid.

—seems to have been the starting point for Grumio's extended account of the misfortunes which befell Katherina, and her falling in the mire on the journey to Petruchio's house (IV.i).

The two texts are quite sensitively in touch at moments like these, but in terms of the larger strategy of *The Shrew* Shakespeare took only what he needed. The window scene between the Sienese and Phylogano (IV.iv–vii) obviously attracted Shakespeare by its theatrical possibilities, and he makes it a point of inner climax in *The Shrew* (V.i). Most important of all, he greatly increases the narrative complexities by introducing the new character of Hortensio and making him a rival for the love of Bianca (Polynesta). The theme of rivalry is best served if the lady is an unattached virgin, and Shakespeare departs from his source in this respect; Bianca (like Katherina) has no previous wooers. Shakespeare enforces the essentially romantic quality of the sub-plot by adding the 'stolen marriage' (IV.iv–V.i) to the story in his source. There is no necessity for Lucentio and Bianca to marry surreptitiously 'at St Luke's', but the incident contributes something to the atmosphere in which love is sudden and irresistible, brooking no obstacle and no delay. The disguises of Litio and Cambio are greatly developed from the source—where Erostrato simply changes places with his servant in order to gain access to Polynesta—to further the same romantic end. And to sharpen the contrast the old lawyer, Cleander, becomes the rich old merchant, Gremio, and the light references in *Supposes* to the amount of Polynesta's dowry give rise to the 'auction' scene (II.i) in which Gremio and Tranio bid against one another to secure the lot.[1]

Several of the characters are quite radically changed. Lucentio is very different from Erostrato, or, indeed, from the typical young man of classical comedy. He is not seeking a wife with a fortune, he has not seduced Bianca, and he is seen to fall instantly, rapturously, romantically in love with her at first sight. Bianca is unlike Polynesta, in that she is a virgin, an obedient, submissive, and not unsubtle foil to her shrewish sister. Clearly, she has no need for any go-between, and the character of the Nurse, Balia, is dropped completely. The parasite, Pasiphilo, is also dropped; he would be an unnecessary encumbrance to the romance. Even the character of Damon, Polynesta's father, is subdued to the new emphasis. In *Supposes* he airs his opinions at length on the ingratitude of offspring to parents in a long speech (III.iii) which is one of Gascoigne's additions to Ariosto, and goes so far as to

1. Auction scenes are almost always good theatre. Cf. Bluntschli and Sergius bidding for Raina in Shaw's *Arms and the Man*.

imprison the feigned Erostrato, threatening him with dire penalties for seducing his daughter. There is nothing of this in Shakespeare's Baptista. He is a father and a merchant, and we learn little more about him than that. Along with Gremio and Vincentio he represents the mercantile world, the world of the old as against the young, the world which is the foil to the restless activity of the young lovers. This distinction is Shakespeare's far more strongly than it is Gascoigne's. Yet the 'romance' atmosphere does not extend to the finding of long-lost children (which becomes important later in Shakespeare's dramatic career). The episode in *Supposes* (v.v) where Cleander discovers that Dulipo is his son Carino, lost eighteen years earlier when the Turks took Otranto, finds no place in Shakespeare's play. The focus is on romantic, sexual love, leading to marriage, between young people; family love, the bond of affection between father and child, is but lightly handled in discourse.

Shakespeare uses *Supposes* primarily because it offers opportunities for complicating the action. Part of the theatrical appeal of *The Shrew* lies in the succession of disguises, deceptions and misprisions which accompany the contest for Bianca's hand, and which stand in such sharp contrast to the direct, forthright wooing of Katherina by Petruchio. *Supposes* provides a suitable 'Italian' background of intrigue and suspense, and it stands at a distinct remove from the hard, dry, unsentimental comedy of Plautus and Terence, from which, ultimately, it springs. All Shakespeare's changes are in line with what he does to the Plautine characters in *The Comedy of Errors*. It is this potential for romance, for love leading to marriage, which Shakespeare detected and exploited in Gascoigne's work. H. B. Charlton says of the play:

> *The Supposes* does not, indeed, break very considerably from the Latin comic tradition. But there are features in it which point to the future. It is, for instance, a play of love rather than of sex: the lovers mean honest matrimony and would welcome the ceremony which circumstance forbids. It is, however, not a play of wooing. . . . The germ of romanticism is beginning to leaven the classical tradition.[1]

Shakespeare would have known the classical dramatists from his schooldays. We cannot tell how or when he first made acquaintance with Gascoigne's work, but it may be relevant to the question

1. H. B. Charlton, *Shakespearian Comedy* (1938), p. 79. Ch. IV (pp. 73–99) is still one of the best accounts of the influence of the Italian comedies on Shakespeare.

84 THE TAMING OF THE SHREW

to note that *Supposes* (written in 1566, and first published in 1573) was reprinted in *The Whole woorkes of George Gascoigne Esquyre*, in 1587, only a year or so before (I believe) Shakespeare came to write *The Shrew*.

Sources have been proposed for a number of the incidents in *The Shrew*, with varying degrees of conviction and credibility. Hosley[1] recognizes an analogue to Lucentio's wooing of Bianca under the pretence of construing a Latin text (III.i) in R.W.'s play *The Three Lords and Three Ladies of London* (written c. 1589, published 1590).[2] Here Simplicity gives directions for the punishment of Fraud:

> O Singulariter *Nominativo*, wise Lord *pleasure*: *Genetivo* bind him to that poste, *Dativo.* give me my torch, *Accusat.* For I say he's a cosoner. *Vocat.* O give me roome to run at him. *Ablat.* take and blind me. *Pluraliter, per omnes casus.* Laugh all you to see mee in my choller adust to burne and to broile that false *Fraud* to dust.[3]

Hosley does not claim that this is a *source* for *The Shrew*, and Muir points out[4] that in view of the dates the debt may well be the other way round—a view which the early date I propose for *The Shrew* would support.[5]

The scolding of the Tailor (IV.iii) for cutting Katherina's gown in fantastic fashion has either a source or an analogue in Gerard Legh's *Accedens of Armory* (1562). Legh tells the story of Sir Philip Caulthrop of Norwich, who lived in the time of Henry VII. He commissioned his tailor to make a gown of some fine French tawny. A shoemaker happened to see the material at the tailor's and asked him to make him a gown of the same material and in the same style. The knight, when he came for a fitting, noticed the second gown and enquired about it. When told, he ordered that his own gown should be 'made as full of cuts as thy sheres can make it'. And so both gowns were treated the same. The shoemaker was furious when he saw what had happened to his, but 'I have done nothing quoth the Tailor, but that you bade mee, for as sir Philip Caltrops is, even so have I made yours'.[6]

1. Hosley, 'Sources and Analogues', p. 306.
2. See Chambers, *ES*, vol. III, p. 515.
3. Sig. 13ᵛ, quoted in Hosley, op. cit.   4. Muir, p. 20.
5. Bond quotes (ed. *The Shrew*, p. 72) two probable echoes of Shakespeare's scene: Middleton's *The Witch*, II.ii, '*Nocte tribus nodis*—Nick of the tribe of noddles; *Ternos colores*—that makes turned colours', and Nashe's *Four Letters Confuted* (1592); see *Works*, ed. McKerrow, rev. Wilson (1958), vol. I, p. 314.
6. F. 112, quoted in Hosley, op. cit., p. 302.

Legh may be giving a local habitation and some names to a widely-known story, but it is significant that no one has proposed a different source for this episode in *The Shrew*. Stories about tailors are recorded in the folklore of many countries,[1] but they usually concern the ways in which a tailor cheats his customer. There seems to be no extant story closer to the details in *The Shrew* than Legh's, and it may be that this is Shakespeare's source, though it is interesting to speculate why he should have been reading a treatise on the science of armorial bearings before 1590, and why he should have put this particular illustration to such use.

The incident in IV.v, where Katherina agrees with Petruchio that the sun is the moon, has an analogue in the collection of stories called *El Conde Lucanor* made by Don Juan Manuel, Infante of Castile, in 1335–47. Here, Vascuñana agrees with her husband Don Alvar that a herd of cows is a herd of mares, that a herd of mares is a herd of cows, and that a river is flowing backwards to its source, to demonstrate to Don Alvar's nephew how a dutiful wife will support her husband. It is highly improbable that Shakespeare had any direct knowledge of this story,[2] which must be regarded as an analogue and no more.

The wager between the three husbands on their wives' obedience is compared by Hosley to an episode in *The Book of the Knight of La Tour-Landry*, a collection of stories made by Geoffroy de la Tour-Landry in 1372–3, and translated into English by Caxton, who published his translation in 1484. Here the bet is on whose wife will be most obedient when ordered to jump into a basin set before her. There are three wives and three merchant husbands. The first two wives refuse. The third wife, at the dinner table, misunderstands something her husband says—'Sel sur table' (put the salt on the table) which she hears as 'Sayle sur table' (jump on the table). At once she jumps on the table, upsetting all the food and wine. The other two merchants concede the wager, and do not require the test of the basin. There are some significant points of contact between this story and *The Shrew*: three men wager, the wager is won by the third wife, and it is won during a dinner party. On the other hand, the wager on a wife's obedience is part of the complex of folk motifs which make up the Aarne–Thompson Type 901, and if Shakespeare had heard stories of the taming of a shrewish wife it is likely that the

---

1. Aarne–Thompson, *Types of the Folktale*, 1096, 1574–1574C, 1631, 1640.
2. See Hosley, op. cit., p. 302; M. Alcalá, 'Don Juan Manuel y Shakespeare: Una Influencia Imposibile', *Filosofía y Letras* (1945), pp. 55–67; Brunvand, *SQ* (1966), pp. 349–50.

wager on obedience would have formed part of at least some of them. As G. K. Hunter has said: 'The game of literary parallels is one that can be played with dashing but irrelevant freedom ... the point in the tradition that the modern critic selects as a "source" is often arbitrary and tendentious.'[1]

One of the most important things in Hosley's analysis of the play's sources and analogues is the way he directs attention to contemporary discussions of marriage, especially the humanist tradition of inducing a shrewish wife to mend her ways without resort to physical violence. He quotes from Juan Vives' *The Office and Duetie of an Husband*[2] and *A Very Fruteful and Pleasant Boke Callyd the Instruction of a Christen Woman*,[3] though stressing that these are neither sources nor analogues, to show evidence of a climate of opinion opposed to the rough reformatory methods favoured by the people described in folk-tales. Unfortunately, Hosley's anxiety to forge some link between this tradition and *The Shrew* forces him into one extravagant claim. Although he suggests only that it is 'either a source or an analogue' he clearly favours a close connection between *The Shrew* and the colloquy of Erasmus translated anonymously into English as *A Mery Dialogue, Declaringe the Propertyes of Shrowde Shrewes, and Honest Wyves* (1557).[4] There are a number of obvious similarities (given the subject), and Hosley allows that 'these resemblances of situation are admittedly general', but he believes their relevance is strengthened by 'two specific verbal links with Shakespeare's play'. In the colloquy Xantippa says: 'I gat me a thre foted stole in hand, and he had but ones layd his littell finger on me, he shulde not have found me lame.' Hosley compares Katherina's words to Hortensio: 'But if it were, doubt not her care should be/ To comb your noddle with a three-legg'd stoole.' But the phrase is proverbial. Tilley (H270) quotes an example from 1566–7:

Mer. Tales Skelton 5 in *Shak. Jest-Bks*, II 9: Hys wife woulde diuers tymes in the weeke kimbe his head with a iii footed stoole.

Smith and Wilson, *Oxford Dictionary of English Proverbs*, quotes this,

1. G. K. Hunter, 'Shakespeare's Reading', in *A New Companion to Shakespeare Studies*, ed. Muir and Schoenbaum (Cambridge, 1971), p. 55.

2. Trs. Thomas Paynell, *c.* 1553 (STC 24855).

3. Trs. Richard Hyrde, *c.* 1529 (STC 24856).

4. STC 10455. The analogue was first noted by R. A. Houk, *SAB* (1943), pp. 181–2. See also E. J. Devereux, *A Checklist of English Translations of Erasmus to 1700* (Oxford, 1968), pp. 7–8.

and the Erasmus colloquy, and other examples before Shakespeare. The same is true of Hosley's other link. He quotes from the colloquy the phrase 'she put the finger in the eye', which parallels Katherina's 'A pretty peat! it is best put finger in the eye, and she knew why'. This is Tilley F229, quoting several pre-Shakespearean examples. Hosley does not prove a link in this case, but this should not obscure the similarity between Erasmus's attitude to the rights and duties of wives and Shakespeare's. J. C. Maxwell informed Muir[1] of what looks like an echo from one of the other colloquies, *Senatulus* (which had not been translated), in Katherina's speech to the disobedient wives (v. ii).[2] Erasmus writes:

> our Condition is much preferable to theirs: For they, endeavouring to get a Maintenance for their Families, scamper thro all the Parts of the Earth by Land and Sea. In Times of War they are call'd up by the Sound of the Trumpet, stand in Armour in the Front of the Battle; while we sit at home in Safety.

Katherina says that the husband is

> one that cares for thee,
> And for thy maintenance; commits his body
> To painful labour both by sea and land,
> To watch the night in storms, the day in cold,
> Whilst thou liest warm at home, secure and safe.

It would be unsafe to claim that the *Senatulus* is a direct source for *The Shrew*, since similar claims might be made for the passages from Vives which Hosley quotes, and, indeed, any comment or commentary on St Paul's Epistle to the Ephesians might yield a comparable crop of parallel passages. There was a firm and articulate unanimity about wives submitting themselves unto their own husbands, and spokesmen tended to speak with one voice.

The deepest sources of *The Shrew* lie in the folk-tales and ballads Shakespeare would have known from boyhood. Woven into the strong simplicity of these stories of shrewish wives and drunken tinkers is the fashionable complexity of Italian comedy, which has its roots in the Latin *commedia erudita*.[3] In each case Shakespeare

1. Muir, p. 21. The translation is by N. Bailey (1725).

2. On Shakespeare's probable knowledge of Erasmus's colloquies see the notes to *A Midsummer Night's Dream*, ed. Brooks (Arden edn, 1979), i.i.76–7.

3. Muir (p. 22) notes crisply: 'The names of Tranio and Grumio, but nothing else, were taken from the *Mostellaria* of Plautus.' See also Leo Salingar, *Shakespeare and the Traditions of Comedy* (Cambridge, 1974), pp. 172ff.

modifies his material in the direction of romance, softening the element of physical and sexual confrontation to allow the more tender mysteries of love to be seen through the ritual parades of aggression and courtship. It is to be hoped that other sources and analogues will be discovered, especially in the field of humanist writings about marriage and the right relationships between the sexes, since it is in this area that Shakespeare's contribution to the 'taming' tradition seems at present so startlingly original. No doubt they will; source-hunting is still, as J. P. Brockbank has said, 'an acceptable mode of conspicuous leisure'.[1]

5. THE PLAY

ITS AFTERLIFE

It has become a commonplace of criticism to say that *The Taming of the Shrew* may not be Shakespeare's greatest comedy to 'any modern civilised man, reading . . . in his library'[2] but it is always a success in the theatre. This is both true and untrue. There have been many notable productions of *The Shrew*, and it is perhaps more popular in the present century than it has ever been. But for nearly two hundred years it was supplanted on the stage by adaptations, altered and partial versions, and its stage history cannot be said to have been an uninterrupted triumphal progress.

Like no other of Shakespeare's plays it provoked a direct answer in his lifetime. Fletcher's *The Woman's Prize; or, The Tamer Tamed*, written between 1604 and 1617 (probably *circa* 1611), is a comedy sequel to *The Shrew* in which Petruchio, now a widower, marries again and is effectively put down by his wife Maria, with the assistance of her cousin Bianca and her sister Livia.[3] This is evidence of the contemporary popularity of Shakespeare's play, though there are few records of any productions. Henslowe's *Diary* records that 'the tamynge of A Shrowe' was one of the plays performed at Newington Butts in June 1594, and since this is when the Admiral's and the Chamberlain's companies were there it is as likely as not that he meant *The Shrew* rather than *A Shrew*. The next reference is not until nearly forty years later, when Sir Henry Herbert, Master of the Revels, records: 'On Tusday night at Saint James, the 26 of Novemb. 1633, was acted before the

1. 'History and Histrionics in *Cymbeline*', *Sh.S.* (1958), p. 42.

2. Sir Arthur Quiller-Couch, in NCS, p. xvi. NCS, pp. 181–6, is still the best stage history of *The Shrew*. My account here is restricted to the history of the text, though it necessarily discusses that text in the theatre.

3. Chambers, *ES*, vol. III, p. 222.

Kinge and Queene, The Taminge of the Shrewe. Likt.'[1] Two
days later Herbert mentions that there was 'acted before the King
and Queene, The Tamer Tamd, made by Fletcher', and that this
was 'Very well likt'. In 1631 a Quarto edition of *The Shrew* had
appeared, including the following information on its title-page:
'A Wittie and Pleasant Comedie Called The Taming of the
Shrew. As it was acted by his Maiesties Seruants at the Blacke
Friers and the Globe.' There is no other evidence for such performances, the text of the Quarto is demonstrably printed from
F and not from any independent source, but not all Shakespeare's plays were reprinted in Quarto form after the procession
of the Folios began, and the appearance of this text in 1631
suggests that, for a publisher at least, the play retained some
popular interest nearly half a century after it was written.

The play's fortunes after the Restoration are a different matter.
Herbert, in his rough accounts for 1663–4, mentions a 'Revived
Play Taminge the Shrew',[2] and this may have been Shakespeare's
play. If so, it is the last recorded performance until the middle of
the nineteenth century, for with the Restoration came the adaptations which displaced it on the stage. Pepys comments on a
production he saw on 9 April 1667:

> To the King's house, and there saw 'The Tameing of a Shrew',
> which hath some very good pieces in it, but generally is but a
> mean play; and the best part, 'Sawny', done by Lacy; and
> hath not half its life, by reason of the words, I suppose, not
> being understood, at least by me.[3]

He saw the play again on 1 November, and described it as 'a silly
play and an old one'. Pepys was not without some discrimination
as a theatre critic. On the following night (2 November) he
records that he saw *Henry IV* at the same playhouse, and that he
'contrary to expectation, was pleased in nothing more than in
Cartwright's speaking of Falstaffe's speech about "What is
Honour?"'. Clearly, he had his favourite plays and parts of plays,
but, in the case of *The Shrew*, he seems not to have considered it
worth comment that the play he witnessed was very far removed
from Shakespeare's original. The fashion for adapting and varying
Shakespeare had already taken strong hold. John Lacey's *Sauny
the Scott: Or, The Taming of the Shrew: A Comedy* had been acted
some thirty years before it was printed in 1698, and it represents

1. Chambers, *WS*, vol. II, p. 352.
2. J. Q. Adams, *Dramatic Records of Sir Henry Herbert* (1917), pp. 53 and 138.
3. Pepys, *Diary*, Everyman edition (1906), vol. II, p. 215.

a complete rewriting of Shakespeare's text. The Induction and all the Sly material are omitted, the play is set in Restoration London, many of the characters are renamed (Hortensio becomes Geraldo, Baptista is Lord Beaufoy, Katherina is Margaret), though others, for no obvious reason, retain the Shakespearean names: Petruchio, Tranio, Curtis, Philip and Biancha. The basic movements of the taming plot and the lovers' plot are followed, though Lacey varies and adds incidents: after the scene at Petruchio's house in which Margaret (Katherina) is denied food he introduces a bedroom scene when Sauny (Grumio) is bidden to undress Margaret since there are no women in the house, and when this impropriety is avoided Petruchio keeps her up all night, making her drink beer and threatening to force a pipe of tobacco on her. The scene with the Tailor is retained, but the Haberdasher disappears, and the 'sun and moon' scene ends with Geraldo's line (taken straight from *The Shrew*) '*Petruchio*, go thy wayes, the Field is Won'. Yet in Act v Lacey adds a scene between Margaret and Biancha, in which Margaret is clearly vengeful, and this develops into the open, public defiance of Petruchio culminating in a physical attack on him. Margaret then vows not to speak 'one word more to thee these Two Months', and (as the stage-direction says) 'Sits Sullenly'. Petruchio attributes her silence to toothache, and sends Sauny for a Barber to perform an extraction. As soon as he offers to operate Margaret strikes him and forces him away. So Petruchio assumes that her silence means that she is dead, and summons bearers to bury her. She is tied, alive, on a bier, and is just about to be taken off for interment when she surrenders and promises amendment of life. The play ends with an abbreviated form of the wager scene, in which Margaret comes when she is called, but is not obliged to show the other women their duty, and has no climactic speech corresponding to Katherina's in v.ii. Lacey rewrites the whole of Shakespeare's dialogue in prose, though retaining many of *The Shrew*'s best-known lines. We still have 'Woe her, Wed her, and Bed her, and rid the House of her', 'Her Silence Flouts me, and I'll be Reveng'd', and longer pieces of verse reproduced as prose, as, for example:

What will you not suffer me; nay, now I see she is your Treasure; She must have a Husband; and I Dance Bare-foot on her Wedding-Day: And for your Love to her, lead Apes in Hell.[1]

1. All quotations are from *Sauny the Scott: Or, The Taming of the Shrew*, Written by J. Lacey (1698; facsimile reprint, Cornmarket Press, 1969).

Yet these are set in the midst of such typical Restoration prose as that of Snatchpenny (Pedant) to Tranio:

I warrant ye Sir, I know it to a hair, my Lord *Beaufoy* and I were School fellows together at *Worster*; my Estate lyes in the Vale of *Evesham*, Three thousand Pound a year, and Fifteen hundred a year I settle upon you upon the Marriage, let me alone *I* am Sir *Lyonell* himself.

But Lacey's most interesting alteration of Shakespeare lies in the character of Sauny himself. In *The Shrew* Petruchio's servant is Grumio, and the part, though significant, is not large. In *A Shrew*, however, Ferando's servant is Sander, and the part is much bigger than Grumio's, with some comic business which has no source in *The Shrew*. It may have been that the Elizabethan actor Alexander Cooke played both Grumio and Sander (see p. 55), and Harold Child has suggested[1] that it may have been the name which gave Lacey the hint for turning him into a Scot and writing his part in a language which Pepys failed to understand. His incomprehension is not surprising. When Petruchio, in Act v, makes Margaret 'Mistris both of my self and all I have', Sauny comments: 'S'breed bo ye'l nea gi *Saundy* tull her Sir?' and he is scarcely more comprehensible when sent to fetch Margaret at the climax of the wager scene: 'I'se gar her gea wuth me Sir, or I'se put my Durke to the hilt in her Weam.' We must assume that Restoration audiences found this funnier than Pepys did, but it is strange that Lacey's adaptation should ignore the humorous possibilities of Christopher Sly in favour of this Scottish transformation of a character from *A Shrew*, and it is noteworthy that Lacey rejected the skill and delicacy of Shakespeare's 'taming' techniques in favour of something much closer to the brutalism of *A Shrewde and Curste Wyfe*.[2]

Directly deriving from *Sauny the Scott* was James Worsdale's *A Cure for a Scold*, a ballad farce in two Acts, published in or about 1735.[3] It claimed on its title-page to be 'Founded upon Shakespear's taming of a Shrew', and the Prologue invites the audience to 'see Shakespear's Shrew revive, / A Lesson, to instruct us how to wive'. Worsdale retained the tooth-drawing threat from *Sauny the Scott*, but not the bedroom scene, or the threat to bury Margaret alive. The characters are again renamed (Baptista becomes Sir William Worthy, Petruchio is Mr Manly) and the

1. NCS, p. 182.
2. See pp. 70–2.
3. Facsimile reprint, Cornmarket Press (1969).

dialogue is freely interspersed with songs, in the manner of *The Beggar's Opera*. Nevertheless, the climax is, if anything, more brutally direct than Lacey's. Margaret has directly challenged her husband, and then vowed to speak no more. The tooth-drawing episode is then followed by the summoning of a Physician, who recommends drastic action:

> I find we must proceed in the most violent Way since the animal Spirits are so far exhausted; I wou'd by all Means have her Head shav'd immediately, and a large Blister apply'd, and lest Delays shou'd be dangerous, I will have four large Blisters on other Parts of her Body. . . . I've a Specifick which I will also force down her Throat, that never fails curing all Distempers.

Such threats effectively subdue Margaret, who becomes a loyal and loving wife, and she points the moral in the last lines of the play:

> By Manly taught, let Husbands bear the Sway,
> 'Tis Man's to rule, 'tis Woman's to obey.

Worsdale retains the Sander–Grumio–Sauny character, but anglicizes him and gives him comparatively little to do; the emphasis of the play is on hearty action and sentimental songs. All the subtleties and insights of Shakespeare's play have been left far behind.

Two other plays of the early eighteenth century derive directly from *The Shrew*, and show to what uses Shakespeare's play was put in the theatre of a very different age. Charles Johnson's *The Cobler of Preston* was produced at Drury Lane on 3 February 1716 and published in the same year.[1] It takes only the events of the Induction, and makes Sly the hero of the piece. He is discovered drunk and asleep at the roadside by Sir Charles Briton and his servants, returning from hunting, and they convey him to the manor house, dress him as a Spanish lord and disguise themselves as Spaniards to wait on him. Meanwhile, Sir Charles's butler, also drunk and asleep, is dressed in Sly's clothes and deposited at the roadside. Complications and reversals are numerous, so that Sly is forced to ask: 'The Question then, between me and my self, is, Whether I am a dreaming Lord and a waking Cobler, or a dreaming Cobler and a waking Lord?' The play is overtly political, with constant references to the 1715 Rebellion, and Sly at one point concludes, in his amazement: 'I am devilishly afraid

1. Facsimile reprint, Cornmarket Press (1969).

I am but a Pretender.' Johnson's play makes occasional verbal reference to Shakespeare's. In the first scene the Cobbler says: '. . . don't disparage my Family.—The *Sly's* came in with *Richard the Conqueror.*' Most of the verbal contacts take place in the early scenes, and as the play develops it leaves Shakespeare further and further behind.

There was rivalry, of course, between the theatres at Drury Lane and Lincoln's Inn Fields, and Christopher Bullock's farce, *The Cobler of Preston*, was written in direct competition to Johnson's. Bullock's Preface is frank:

> 'Tis true, I did hear, there was a Farce in Rehearsal at Drury-Lane Theatre, call'd, The Cobler of Preston, and that it was taken from the foremention'd Play of Shakespear's: I thought it might be of as good Service to our Stage as the other; so I set to work on Friday Morning the 20th of January, finish'd it on the Saturday following, and it was acted the Tuesday after.[1]

He probably knew a little more about Johnson's play than that, since both plays make use only of Shakespeare's Induction, modernizing and expanding the allusions and incidents, though Bullock makes more use of Shakespeare's language than his rival does. Indeed, Bullock makes it a matter of pride:

> . . . part of his Language I have made use of, with a little Alteration (which, for the satisfaction of my Readers, I have distinguish'd by this Mark " before each Line) and I hope I may be allow'd (without offence) to take Shakespear's Tinker of Burton-Heath, and make him the Cobler of Preston, as well as another: for no single Person has yet pretended to have a Patent for plundering Old Plays, how often soever he may have put it in practice.

Plunder is certainly Bullock's practice, and readers must be ill satisfied by his respectful marking of Shakespeare's lines. In the very first scene the lines

> "This Morning has produc'd us glorious Sport, sure fleeter Dogs ne'er ran: Sirrah take care they are well fed to-day, to-morrow I intend to hunt again

are marked as Shakespeare's while 'One either drunk or dead', a few lines later, is not. Like Johnson, Bullock appropriates lines

1. Christopher Bullock, *The Cobler of Preston* (fourth edn, 1723; reprinted Cornmarket Press, 1969), pp. ix–x.

and phrases from *The Shrew* for the early part of his play, but soars on his own wings as the plot develops.[1] Guzzle (Sly) is given a wife, Dorcas, who quarrels with Dame Hacket the ale-wife in a scene after Sir Jasper (the Lord) has removed the drunken, sleeping Guzzle to transform him into a magistrate. In this capacity he hears Dorcas's complaint against Dame Hacket, orders them both to be ducked, and arbitrates between Grist the Miller and Snuffle the Puritan, who have been involuntarily swapping wives. When he falls asleep again and is returned to the field Dorcas and Dame Hacket find him and assault him, but are beaten themselves until they cry for peace, when Guzzle invites them to 'laugh at all that has happen'd, and drown Animosities in a Dozen of Ale'. It is a vigorous and colourful little play, none the worse for having been written for an occasion, but it shows how *The Shrew* was seen in the early eighteenth century as a quarry for material, a treasury for plunder, rather than as any kind of inviolable theatrical masterpiece. In this respect it is no different from many other of Shakespeare's plays, but the degree to which authors felt they could make free with their original is perhaps greater than that which obtained for *Love's Labour's Lost* or *A Midsummer Night's Dream*. The apotheosis of Johnson's *Cobler* came when it was turned into a two-act musical farce, with no politics and an additional love story, and played at Drury Lane in September 1817.

Both versions of *The Cobler of Preston* were short-lived ephemera, but *Sauny the Scott* continued to be acted, at Drury Lane, Lincoln's Inn Fields, Goodman's Fields and the Queen's theatre, until it was displaced by Garrick's *Catharine and Petruchio*. This play was probably first performed on Monday, 18 March 1754 at Drury Lane,[2] and in subsequent years it became steadily more and more popular, until it was the only version on the stage. It was usually accompanied, in the early performances, by Garrick's version of *The Winter's Tale*, and the first printed edition (1756) included a Prologue written to precede the performance of the two plays on the same night. The Advertisement apologizes that 'Some of the Lines of the Prologue are only relative to the *Winter's Tale*', and,

---

1. He produces one riposte of which Shakespeare might not have been ashamed: when Dame Hacket threatens 'I'll fetch the Headborough to you' Guzzle responds, 'You may fetch the *Wheelbarrow* if you please, but I had much rather you'd fetch some more Ale'. Clearly, Bullock knew more of the play than the Induction, since Dame Hacket says, 'and if he comes to my House again, I'll comb his Head with a three-footed Stool' (cf. I. i. 64).

2. *The London Stage 1660–1800*, Part IV (1747–76), ed. G. W. Stone, Jr (1962), p. 415.

indeed, there is no mention of any character or incident in *The Shrew* in the Prologue at all. This may suggest that Garrick considered *Catharine and Petruchio* the lighter of the two pieces, but in performance at least they seem to have complemented each other well.

Garrick reduces the five Acts to three. The Induction and the Sly episodes are omitted, and Act I begins with Petruchio's arrangement with Baptista to woo Catharine. The wooing scene follows and the Act ends with Petruchio's 'To-morrow, *Kate*, shall be our Wedding-day' and a conversation between Baptista and Catharine. Shakespeare's entire sub-plot is despatched at a stroke by the expedient of announcing that Bianca is already married to Hortensio, though Garrick retains the lute scene and the head-breaking, making the victim of Catharine's assault a Music Master who appears for this scene only. The second Act jumps to III.ii, where the family await Petruchio's arrival on the wedding day, and then follows the main action of *The Shrew* more or less faithfully to Petruchio's 'taming' soliloquy at the end of IV.i. Act III opens with Grumio's taunting of Catharine (IV.iii) and contains the Tailor and Haberdasher scene, which ends with the conversation between Petruchio and Catharine about the sun and moon (IV.v), and a reduced version of the banquet and wager scene, in which Hortensio and Bianca are the only other couple concerned. The subtlest adjustment comes at the end. In *The Shrew* Katherina's speech on the rights and duties of women is given uninterrupted (V.ii.137–80). In *Catharine and Petruchio* it is verbally almost identical from the first line (137) to 'Too little Payment for so great a Debt' (155), though there are brief interjections from Petruchio and Bianca. But the lines which follow, from 'Such Duty as the Subject owes the Prince' to 'Where bound to love, to honour and obey', form the last lines of the play, and they are spoken not by Katherina but by Petruchio, who, according to the stage-direction, 'Goes forward with Catharine in his Hand' to say them.[1] This marks a distinct shift of Shakespeare's emphasis, towards a conventional, genial, eighteenth-century comedy resolution of the problems of marriage, and a simpler, more expository function for Petruchio in ending the play. There is nothing here of the mystery, the multiplicity of possibilities, of a line like 'Why, there's a wench! Come on, and kiss me, Kate.'

---

1. All quotations are from the Cornmarket Press reprint (1969) of the first edition of *Catharine and Petruchio* (1756). It is noteworthy that Garrick's alteration of 'serve, love, and obey' to 'to love, to honour and obey' neatly varies the 'obey … serve … love, honour, and keep' of the Book of Common Prayer (1662).

The actor who plays Shakespeare's Petruchio must make up his mind what that line means, and how it should be said, and what any chosen expression implies. Garrick's Petruchio need be in no doubt what his lines require of him.

Other small alterations indicate the care Garrick took in grooming the play for his audience. Explicit sexual references are often omitted, like the jesting about the wasp, his sting, and 'my tongue in your tail' in ii.i. In the same scene, when Shakespeare's Katherina invites Petruchio to 'keep you warm', he replies: 'Marry, so I mean, sweet Katherine, in thy bed.' Garrick's Petruchio is more circumspect: 'Or rather warm me in thy Arms, my *Kate*!' In iv.i the badinage about cuckoldry between Curtis and Grumio, with its references to 'you three-inch fool' and 'thy horn is a foot', is reduced to: 'Away, you thick-pated Fool, I am no Beast.' The most striking fact about Garrick's version, however, is its general fidelity to Shakespeare's text. In those parts of *The Shrew* which it selects it stays very close, verbally, to its original, even to the point of retaining readings like the improbable 'Soud, soud, soud, soud' at iv.i.129, and the 'censer in a barber's shop' at iv.iii.91. Yet this fidelity does not preclude pastiche invention where occasion calls for it. The very opening lines of the play have nothing to do with Shakespeare's text:

> *Baptista.* Thus have I, 'gainst my own Self-Interest,
> Repeated all the worst you are t'expect
> From my shrewd Daughter, *Cath'rine*; if you'll
> venture,
> Maugre my plain and honest Declaration,
> You have my free Consent, win her, and wed her.

Occasionally, Garrick feels the need to gloss even a famous Shakespearean phrase, as in the scene corresponding to iv.i, where the servant Peter says: 'He kills her in her own Humour. I did not think so good and kind a Master cou'd have put on so resolute a Bearing.'[1] And there are a few additions which seem to have been called for by the need to prepare some piece of stage business or costume, as when Grumio in iv.i is relating how Katherina fell from her horse into the mire, and Garrick's text adds to the details given in Shakespeare, '. . . how my Mistress

---

1. This unsolicited testimonial seems intended to inform the audience that Petruchio is by nature good and kind. Petruchio reminds them in his penultimate speech, when he has secured Catharine's obedience:

> *Petruchio* here shall doff the lordly Husband;
> An honest Mask, which I throw off with Pleasure.

lost her Slippers, tore and bemir'd her Garments, limp'd to the Farm-house, put on *Rebecca*'s old Shoes and Petticoat'. Shakespeare's play knows nothing of Rebecca, her shoes or her petticoat. Another of the additions draws attention to a crucial characteristic of Garrick's text: its treatment of the poetry of *The Shrew*. In Shakespeare's play the threatened fight between Grumio and the Tailor (iv.iii. 143–51) is controlled by Petruchio's decision, 'Well sir, in brief, the gown is not for me'. Garrick amplifies this incident, allowing Grumio and the Tailor to fight, adding a stage-direction 'Beats 'em off' for Petruchio, and giving him the following lines: 'What, Chickens sparr in Presence of the Kite! I'll swoop upon you both; Out, out, ye Vermin—.' This is the only significant *image* that Garrick adds to his text, though his radical selection and cutting of *The Shrew* mutilates the development of Shakespeare's image patterns. Garrick's selection of scenes is based entirely on the stage-worthiness of the incidents, and all other considerations (the relationships between plot and sub-plot, the development of character, the poetic structure, the deep analysis of themes) are subordinated to this criterion. Garrick's play is precisely what it appears to be: a comparatively brief, undemanding, uncluttered redaction of the main scenes from the taming plot of Shakespeare's play, skilfully excerpted and neatly joined together. It was deservedly popular, it held the London stage until the middle of the nineteenth century, and it was even revived, as a curiosity, at Her Majesty's Theatre in November 1897 by Beerbohm Tree. Major actors like Kemble and Macready performed Garrick's version of the play, and it was even turned into an opera by Frederic Reynolds, with an overture by Rossini and music composed or adapted by Braham and Cooke.[1] The operatic version was first performed in May 1828 at Drury Lane. It did not prove a lasting success.

Kemble's adaptation of Garrick's version illustrates the way the leading actors of the nineteenth century tailored texts to fit their own capacities and preferences.[2] One of the particular characteristics of the text Kemble performed is the cuts that are made in many of the longer speeches. At the opening of Act ii, the wedding scene (iii.ii in *The Shrew*), Catharine's outburst is gutted of some of its best lines:

1. See NCS, p. 184. A list of the principal operatic versions of *The Shrew*, incidental music for it and its adaptations, and concert-hall music related to it, is given in *Shakespeare in Music*, ed. Phyllis Hartnoll (1964), pp. 271–2.

2. Kemble's text is available in *Cumberland's British Theatre*, vol. XVIII (1828).

> I told you, I, he was a frantic fool,
> Hiding his bitter jests in blunt behaviour.
> And to be noted for a merry man
> He'll woo a thousand, 'point the day of marriage,
> Make feasts, invite friends, and proclaim the banns,
> Yet never means to wed where he hath woo'd.

What is left of the speech when this passage is omitted makes
Catharine sound more plaintive than passionate. Yet it is not a
case of reducing Catharine to build up Petruchio. The 'taming'
soliloquy which ends Act II (IV.i.175–98 in *The Shrew*), and
which Garrick takes with very little variation from Shakespeare,
is cut in Kemble's version by the omission of these lines:

> My falcon now is sharp and passing empty,
> And till she stoop she must not be full-gorg'd,
> For then she never looks upon her lure.
> Another way I have to man my haggard,
> To make her come and know her keeper's call.
> That is, to watch her, as we watch these kites
> That bate and beat and will not be obedient.
> She ate no meat today, nor none shall eat;
> Last night she slept not, nor tonight she shall not.

These lines are the essential explanation of Petruchio's method in
The Shrew, and to omit them changes the poetic structure of the
play. Kemble also altered Garrick's final scene, and he redistributed the maimed parts of Katherina's final speech to give
the last word to her and not Petruchio, though the play still
ends with the lines from the middle of that speech (*The Shrew*,
v.ii.162–5):

> How shameful 'tis, when women are so simple,
> To offer war where they should kneel for peace;
> Or seek for rule, supremacy and sway,
> Where bound to love, to honour, and obey!

Kemble is verbally more tender of his audience than is Garrick:
the word 'whoreson', which occurs three times in IV.i, and which
survived from F to Garrick, becomes consecutively 'stupid',
'careless' and 'blundering' in this chastened version. On the other
hand, Kemble's Petruchio must have been more physically threatening than many of his predecessors. Garrick adds some lines
for a servant, Pedro, in Act II, in which it is said that Petruchio
'shook his Whip in Token of his Love'. Kemble retains the
passage, and betters it with stage-directions in several parts of the

play, of the kind 'Exit Petruchio, R., cracking his whip', and these may have provided the inspiration for Cruickshank's drawing (said on the title-page of the *Cumberland's British Theatre* edition to have been 'taken in the Theatre') showing Petruchio laying about him with a whip, in illustration of his line to the servants 'There! take it to you—trenchers, cups, and all' (*The Shrew*, IV.i.152). The whip-cracking tradition lasted until well into the twentieth century, and the overall impression given by Kemble's text is of a short, fast-moving, vigorous version of the play, in which everything is sacrificed to stage action, and poetry has no place.

As Harold Child has pointed out,[1] 'Shakespeare's *The Taming of the Shrew* had to wait longer than any other of his plays for restoration to the stage.' This seems to have been because of the popularity of *Catharine and Petruchio* which continued to be acted long after the original version of the play had been reintroduced. In March 1844 Benjamin Webster, the manager of the Haymarket Theatre, commissioned J. R. Planché to prepare a production of the play as Shakespeare wrote it, to celebrate the return to the stage of Mrs Nisbett (Lady Boothby).[2] The choice of this play was probably Planché's suggestion in the first place, since not only did he think Mrs Nisbett would make an excellent Katherina, but the Haymarket company included at that time Mr Strickland, and Planché thought him especially suited to play Christopher Sly.[3] Given Planché's known antiquarian interests it is not surprising that he wished to present Shakespeare's text as opposed to what he called the 'miserable, mutilated form' of *Catharine and Petruchio*.[4] He probably used the Folio text, and certainly believed that the 'epilogue' was not lost, as Schlegel had suggested, but had never been written. In this production Sly was simply carried off-stage by servants at the end of the Katherina–Petruchio story. The reviews were, on the whole, enthusiastic, especially of the performances, but the *Morning Post* critic objected (among other things) to the restoration of the original text:

[The managers] overlook the fact that the original text was

1. NCS, p. 184.
2. NCS, pp. 184–5; Stanley Wells, 'Shakespeare in Planché's Extravaganzas', *Sh.S.* 16 (1963), pp. 103–17; Jan McDonald, '*The Taming of the Shrew* at the Haymarket Theatre 1844 and 1847', in *Nineteenth-Century British Theatre*, ed. Richards and Thomson (1971), pp. 157–70.
3. McDonald, op. cit., p. 157.
4. J. R. Planché, *Recollections and Reflections* (1872), vol. II, p. 83; McDonald, op. cit., p. 157.

not altered until it had been tried and found wanting in dramatic interest. We must plead guilty to the impeachment of preferring the pleasant abridgement of it in *Catherine and Petruchio* to the long, wearisome and yet unfinished comedy of five acts, with its preliminary induction without a conclusion.[1]

Other critics objected, more or less, to the attempt to stage the play in the Elizabethan manner, but in general their reception was favourable, and Webster revived the production for fourteen performances in October–November 1847. The *Illustrated London News* review tells us that Webster, playing Petruchio, continued the now traditional cracking of the whip as a feature of the role.[2]

Although public reaction to this performance of the full Shakespearean text of *The Shrew* was favourable, Webster's experiment did not encourage him to attempt any other play on an Elizabethan stage or in its entirety, nor did it banish *Catharine and Petruchio*. But a breakthrough had been made. Samuel Phelps used the full Folio text for a production at Sadler's Wells in 1856, and there was a strange, hybrid production in Edinburgh in February 1849, when the Garrick text preceded by the Induction was performed 'in the Baron's Hall, fitted up for a temporary theatre as in days of yore'.[3] Planché was perhaps more interested in re-creating the theatrical conditions of Shakespeare's plays than in restoring the full purity of their texts to the nineteenth-century stage, but it is to him that the credit belongs for allowing the public to witness (as they had not for nearly two centuries) the full play, with its three interweaving plots, as Shakespeare intended, and so bringing the theatre back into line with the textual and literary criticism of Shakespeare, which had always been based on the Folio text of *The Shrew*. Planché himself seems to have realized the significance of his experiment, for he wrote in his *Recollections and Reflections*: 'My restoration of this "gem" is one of the events in my theatrical career on which I look back with the greatest pride and gratification.'[4] By the middle of the nineteenth century, then, Shakespeare's play was once more available in the theatre, but it is strange to think that a whole range of critics, from Dr Johnson to Hazlitt, had been denied it.

In the United States, Garrick's *Catharine and Petruchio* seems to have held the stage unchallenged until 1887. William Winter

1. *The Morning Post* (18 March 1844); McDonald, op. cit., p. 165.

2. *Illustrated London News* (13 October 1847).

3. J. C. Dibdin, *Annals of the Edinburgh Stage* (Edinburgh, 1888), p. 407; McDonald, op. cit., p. 169.

4. Quoted in McDonald, op. cit., p. 169.

records, confidently: '. . . from the beginning of American stage history until the time of Mr. Daly's present revival of it, the comedy of "The Taming of the Shrew" has never been presented here as Shakespeare wrote it.'[1] The 'present revival' was first performed at Daly's Theatre, New York, on 18 January 1887, and reached its one hundredth performance on 13 April of that year. It was printed, privately, in New York (1887) in a text which the title-page claims was 'here Printed from the Prompter's Copy', with an Introduction by Winter and 'An Additional Word' by Augustin Daly himself. Winter is quite clear about why the play succeeded on the English stage: 'Aside from its rattling fun the subject itself seems to possess a particular interest for the average Briton—one of whose chief articles of faith is the subordination of woman to man.' He develops this point at some length, and concludes:

> . . . the predominance of John Bull, in any question between himself and Mrs. Bull, is a cardinal doctrine of the English social constitution, and . . . plays illustrative of the application of discipline to rebellious women have continually found favor with the English audience.

Daly felt that the popularity of his production with the New York audiences was due to the modernity of Shakespeare's play:

> In its varied and contrastive plots and characters, and its short, crisp dialogue, and in the absence of long philosophical monologues or soliloquies, it might have been constructed by a Shakspere of this century who had studied the methods and requirements of the modern comedy stage.[2]

The important point is that he was prepared to produce the whole play, Induction, taming plot and lovers' plot, for an audience which had hitherto seen only variations on *Catharine and Petruchio*. But the text Daly prepared was far from the pure milk of F, as he was well aware:

> I need not point out nor excuse the few excisions and transpositions of text which I have considered necessary, in order to bring Shakspere's work within the playing requirements of our day. I believe they have been found justified in every instance, by the result.[4]

1. *Taming of the Shrew*, as arranged by Augustin Daly, Centenary Edition, Privately Printed for Mr Daly (New York, 1887), p. 6.
2. Ibid., p. 9.
3. Ibid., p. 11.

There are changes in plenty, and they seem to have been made
for a variety of reasons. The very first line of the play is cut,
presumably because 'feeze' would not be understood, and so is
'Soud, soud, soud, soud' in iv. i. For reasons of propriety Sly does
not call upon his Maker at the opening of Induction ii, but says,
merely: 'For Love's sake, a pot of small ale.' For the same reasons
Gremio omits 'and bed her' in i. i, and there are many such
instances of moral grooming of the text. Daly also cuts the
snatches of Latin and Italian from the opening scenes, and he
does not scruple to reduce roles quite drastically, as when he cuts
the entry of Tranio/Lucentio in i. ii, or omits Katherina completely from the pre-wedding scene, iii. ii, so that her important
speech beginning 'No shame but mine' (iii. ii. 8 ff.) is absent from
the play. The effect is to direct far more sympathy towards
Katherina than Shakespeare's text does; through the central
scenes of the play she appears more sinned against than sinning.
Perhaps the most drastic variation in Daly's text is his transposition of iv. i and iv. ii, but it is noticeable that he makes
considerable use of Garrick's *Catharine and Petruchio*, retaining
many of Garrick's additional lines, like Baptista's reaction to
Katherina's assault on her music master:

> This is the third I've had within this month:
> She is an enemy to harmony.

Daly also follows Garrick in his treatment of some of the breezier
obscenities, like the 'wasp–sting–tail' joke in ii. i. Indeed, he tries
to get the best of all worlds, by reinstating Shakespeare's text
while keeping some of the better moments from the versions of
Garrick, Kemble and Booth. And he adds music to Shakespeare's
words. At Induction ii. 36–7 the Lord says:

> Wilt thou have music? Hark, Apollo plays,
> And twenty caged nightingales do sing.

Daly takes this as a cue for song, adding the stage-direction 'The
music of lutes is heard outside and several voices sing', together
with the following words:

> Say that he frown,
>   We will his care beguile:
>   Say he be mute—
> We'll answer with our lute! etc.

The 'etc.' suggests that the words were well known, and could be continued as necessary by the singers. Similar words are given, for 'Solo and Chorus', at the opening of the banquet scene, v. ii:

> Should he upbraid, I'll own that he prevail,
> And sing as sweetly as the nightingale;
> Say that he frown, I'll say his looks I view
> As morning roses newly washed with dew;
> Say he be mute, I'll answer with a smile,
> I'll dance and play and will his care beguile.

They are, of course, an adaptation of Petruchio's lines at II. i. 170–175, but they are not the work of Daly. They appear first in 1823 as the lyric of a song by Sir Henry Bishop (1786–1855), described by Charles Cudworth as 'the most fearsome despoiler of Shakespeare'.[1] Bishop composed many 'operatized' versions of Shakespeare, and made very free with his texts. The words of 'Should he upbraid' originally appeared in Bishop's version of *The Two Gentlemen of Verona*. It is not known who wrote the lyrics for many of Bishop's songs, and he may himself have been responsible for 'Should he upbraid', which, in many nineteenth- and twentieth-century song books, is attributed to Shakespeare. Clearly, Daly felt able to feature it in his 'revival', and expresses neither doubt nor opinion about its authenticity. The one point in the play where Daly presumably feels he cannot trust his author is the end. Katherina's 'submission' speech is cut and redistributed, Petruchio is obliged, in Garrick's words, to 'doff the lordly husband; / An honest mask, which I throw off with pleasure', but Daly outdoes his mentor in generosity by adding, at this point, the stage-direction, 'He kneels and kisses her hand', having him remain in this position for four lines, until Katherina 'Makes him rise'. The last lines of the play, as in Garrick's version, are given to Katherina, and Mr Daly's revival ends more unsubtly than Shakespeare's original.

By the end of the nineteenth century the full text of *The Shrew* was once again in regular production. The various adaptations of the long interim which began with Lacey's *Sauny the Scott* show that at different times different aspects of the play commanded theatrical attention. At first (and strangely) the potential for comedy between Petruchio and his servant was explored; later it was the colourful characterization of Christopher Sly which inspired emulation and development. But the long-continued popularity on the stage of Garrick's *Catharine and Petruchio* suggests

1. Charles Cudworth, 'Song and Part-Song Settings of Shakespeare's Lyrics, 1660–1960', in *Shakespeare and Music*, ed. Phyllis Hartnoll (1964), p. 75.

that it is the central taming plot, the complex, dynamic, developing relationship between Katherina and Petruchio, which lies at
the heart of the play's appeal to its audience. It is a special
example of the theme of 'the battle of the sexes' which has been
good dramatic material from Aristophanes' *Lysistrata* to Strind-
berg, and every live performance of *The Shrew* sets up a tension
between one half of the audience and the other, a tension which
can be resolved in many subtly different ways, depending on the
actors, the theatre, the aims of the production, and, above all,
the text. If the adaptations from 1667 to 1887 teach us anything
it is that Shakespeare's play, as preserved in F, is a marvellous
exhibition of adroit dramatic balance, offering solutions while
preserving uncertainties and mysteries. The twentieth century
has seen countless productions of *The Shrew*, for the most part
honouring the full text, since the fashion is now that Shakespeare
may be trusted in the theatre. But the spirit of irreverent adventure lives on, and adaptations have continued, from *Kiss Me Kate*
to Charles Marowitz's unorthodox version. The difference is that
these experiments can be seen as a set of variations on Shakespeare's text, which still continues in mainstream production as a
perpetual point of reference. Whereas Garrick's *Catharine and
Petruchio* displaced Shakespeare's play on the stage, the modern
adaptations complement it and maintain the vigour of its
continuing life.

STRUCTURES

The history of the text through its various adaptations is important because it focuses critical attention on what successive
generations of actors and dramatists considered essentially
dramatic in it. Garrick's *Catharine and Petruchio* dominated this
transmission, suggesting that in the *theatrical* structure the taming
plot makes the play's most powerful dramatic statement. It is,
after all, *The Taming of the Shrew*, not *Lucentio and Bianca*, or *Sly's
Dream*.

As we have seen, Garrick stitched together the large set pieces
of the taming plot: the bargain between Petruchio and Baptista,
the lute-breaking, the wooing, the wedding, the reception at
Petruchio's house, the Tailor and Haberdasher scene, the sun and
moon scene, and the last part of the final scene in which Petruchio
displays his wife's obedience and makes his peace with her. A
radical selection, made for purely theatrical purposes, it nevertheless lays bare one of the basic structures and rhythmic patterns
of Shakespeare's play, and the *enchaînement* of the scenes isolates

the process of domestication and reduction to conformity which lies at the heart of it.[1] After the Induction, Shakespeare's Act I is composed of relatively short episodes with little stage action (except for Petruchio's boisterous assault on Grumio), and mostly concerned with exposition or the creation of the various intrigues. Then follows what is by far the longest scene in the play (II.i), stretching to over four hundred lines, and presenting a four times repeated pattern of contest and recuperation, rising to a climax in the parodic 'wooing' and descending through the 'auction of Bianca' to the mundanities of plotting and intrigue. Balancing this overarching structure is a subsidiary pattern which contrasts physical violence with the eloquence of persuasions and the rituals of debate. The first contest opens the scene violently. Bianca, her hands tied, is haled about and struck by Katherina in a piece of stage action which reiterates and emphasizes the previous, lesser, conflicts between the Hostess and Sly, and Petruchio and Grumio. It is an angry episode, and when Baptista parts them Katherina leaves the stage in an outburst of frustration. Tension is released by the formal presentation to Baptista of the disguised lovers, Lucentio, Hortensio and Tranio, with civilized introductions and the giving of gifts until the 'tutors' are sent to meet their pupils off-stage. This leaves Petruchio and Baptista to begin the second contest, a brisk bargaining about Katherina's dowry (they are like merchants chaffering over a parcel of goods), which lacks the direct violence of the episode between the sisters. When the bargain is made, Hortensio enters 'with his head broke' and relates Katherina's off-stage attack on him. For the audience this is not a contest, since they are watching Hortensio's recuperation, but it repeats Katherina's propensity to violence, and creates anticipation for the third contest, the wooing, which is cunningly prepared and delayed by Petruchio's soliloquy—a moment of physical rest when he daringly reveals the first stage of his taming strategy. The wooing begins with a wit-bout, or, rather, a fast exchange of fairly crude insults, until Katherina takes an advantage by striking Petruchio. This provokes his reply: 'I swear I'll cuff you, if you strike again.' Katherina senses the danger and resumes wit-play: 'So may you lose your arms. . . .' It is a point of climax, marking a boundary in the dispute; this will not, we appreciate, be a matter of simple strength and brutality. The verbal jesting continues, Petruchio puts his plan into action, and

1. In considering the 'scenic structure' of *The Shrew* I have been much indebted to Emrys Jones's *Scenic Form in Shakespeare* (Oxford, 1971), especially chs 1–4.

so bewilders Katherina that she can offer only token resistance to his outrageous claims, made when Baptista, Gremio and Tranio enter. Recuperation follows, since Petruchio's announcement of the result of his wooing and his arrangements for the wedding go virtually unopposed. When Petruchio and Katherina leave the stage we witness the last contest, between Gremio and Tranio for the hand of Bianca. Baptista conducts this as a long, deliberate auction, and sells to the highest bidder. Tranio, having topped Gremio's bid, bandies a few words with the loser, plans how to make good his boast, and the scene ends.

Structurally, it is a theme and variations, the basic motif of a contest being repeated and modulated into different keys: a physical fight, the bargaining for a marriage contract, a contentious wooing, and an auction. And, each time, the form is related more and more obliquely to the content. The fight is natural, the marriage contract less so (since Petruchio talks of money and Baptista insists on love). The wooing is most abnormal, comprising insults, anger and the clash of wills, and the auction of Bianca's hand would have seemed as inappropriate to an Elizabethan audience (however well accustomed it was to hard bargaining over marriage contracts) as a broadly similar episode did to the first readers of Hardy's *The Mayor of Casterbridge*. The scene moves from the normal to the fantastic through repeated contests, separated by ever briefer episodes of rest, so that its pace increases steadily. As Jones says (of a scene in *Titus Andronicus*):

> If we look back for a moment to the scene just discussed, we can hardly fail to be struck by the bold simplicity of its shape. ... Shakespeare's big scenes are usually founded on such powerfully simple devices as this.[1]

Even in so early a play as *The Shrew* Shakespeare's constructive art is displayed in his elegant manipulation of such simplicities.[2]

The second big scene in the taming plot (a scene given full value in Garrick's adaptation) is the wedding scene (III.ii), which might be described as a 'displacement' scene, since the important action takes place off-stage, and is reported by witnesses. Petruchio's progress to Padua and the wedding itself are not allowed

1. Jones, op. cit., p. 13.
2. Other contrasting or distinguishing patterns might, of course, be observed: the double frustration of Katherina, silenced by her father in her rage, then stunned into acquiescence by Petruchio's behaviour; the contrasted marriage contracts, the one almost a parody of the other; or the central, cameo episode of the lute-breaking, an almost emblematic presentation of the union of comedy and violence which informs the taming plot.

on the stage, and the two are linked only by the comparatively brief appearance of Petruchio, fantastically dressed, to claim his bride. The scene begins with Baptista's complaints about Petruchio's lateness, and Katherina's outburst of shame and anger. Biondello's entry, with his long description of Petruchio's grotesque clothing and knackered horse, builds up his eventual appearance on stage, but also allows the audience to realize that the bridegroom is approaching his marriage disgracefully unprepared. Petruchio's point is that so is the bride. He displaces her emotional unpreparedness on to his own garments and means of transport, just as the dramaturgy of the scene displaces the simple sight of him so arrayed on to the more explicit and telling verbal description. The same is true of the wedding. Gremio reports Petruchio's antics at the ceremony, cuffing the priest, stamping and swearing 'As if the vicar meant to cozen him', when the action itself (or something like it) would have made a most effective stage spectacle. The displacement of the action by the description reflects Petruchio's displacement of the solemn 'union of this man with this woman' with a violent, disrespectful travesty of it—which is what he believes marriage to an unreformed shrew to be. It is both an image of his belief and a part of his treatment, and the displacement technique opens up a receding perspective of great dramatic depth.

The pattern of 'taming' scenes in Act IV (which Garrick's version excerpts into an unbroken sequence) forms the very heart of the play in the theatre. This process of taming, teaching and testing, by various and unexpected dislocations of normality, is strongly visual and comparatively direct.[1] In stage terms it is the busiest part of the play, with servants bustling about, food brought, meat thrown round the stage, the Haberdasher disdained and the Tailor abused, and all the preparations for the return to Padua as well as the journey itself. The climax comes at IV.v, in the form of what Jones recognizes as a 'transformation' or 'conversion' scene.[2] Either from weariness or because she at last recognizes the game her husband is playing, Katherina turns

1. There are some displacements, as when Petruchio's anger at Katherina's intransigence is directed at his offenceless and obedient servants. This may come from the folk-tale sources, where the husband kills his innocent dog or horse instead of beating his recalcitrant wife. Such obliquities seem to have attracted Shakespeare's imagination.

2. 'Another powerful device used by Shakespeare is a pattern of human transformation from one polar extreme to the other' (Jones, op. cit., p. 14). Cf. the Forum scene (*Caes.*, III.ii); the Lady Anne scene (*R3*, I.ii); the temptation scene (*Oth.*, III.iii).

from a contradicting shrew into an utterly compliant wife, agreeing with him that the sun is the moon, or the moon the sun:

> What you will have it nam'd, even that it is,
> And so it shall be so for Katherine.

This is the turning-point of the plot and the play, suitably and
tellingly marked by the metaphor in Hortensio's line: 'Petruchio,
go thy ways, the field is won.'[1] But, as before and after in the play,
there is one more test than seems strictly necessary, and Katherina
has to agree that Vincentio is either a budding virgin or an old
man, whichever Petruchio decrees. Like many other of Shakespeare's transformation scenes, this climactic scene has a compelling effect in the theatre. We recognize triumph, we sympathize
with surrender; we experience satisfaction in the completion of a
long pattern, and we regret that an interesting fight seems
finished.

Garrick's *Catharine and Petruchio* makes short work of Shakespeare's final ensemble scene, v. ii. By replacing Vincentio (in
IV. v) with Baptista, Garrick telescopes the closing scenes. He
omits both the feast and the wager, and severely cuts Katherina's
long 'obedience' speech, redistributing parts of it to Petruchio.
The result is brisk and bright, and it entirely falsifies Shakespeare's
sense of an ending. Shakespeare, in v. ii, is at pains to have as
many characters as possible on stage and involved in a series of
rituals. The scene opens with a banquet[2] at Lucentio's house
(almost the first time in the play anyone has had anything to eat).
Hospitality and generosity are the keynotes, but witty conversation soon gives rise to a verbal contest between Katherina and the
Widow. This, in turn, slowly moves on to the idea of a larger
contest and a formal wager on the obedience of the three wives.
This produces the thrice-repeated ritual of the summoned wife
and her response, culminating in the dutiful appearance of
Katherina and her obedient departure to bring in the other
wives. Petruchio has won his wager, but again there is the superfluous, and theatrically suspenseful, test. She must take off her
cap and trample on it, and she must 'tell these headstrong women /
What duty they do owe their lords and husbands'. She obeys.

1. The metaphor is immediately modified by Petruchio's following lines:
'Thus the bowl should run, / And not unluckily against the bias.'

2. A banquet, in this context, is a dessert course served after the principal
meal (which must have been served at Baptista's house). See *OED*, Banquet,
sb.[1] 3. The play has several examples of the 'broken feast' motif. Cf. *Err.*, III. i;
Mac., III. iv; *Tp.*, III. iii.

This part of the scene is complex and vitally important to any interpretation of the play, and it is fully discussed below (see pp. 143 ff.). For the moment, considering only its place in the theatrical structure of the taming plot, it is sufficient to say that the play ends with a long, full, formal, developed, public statement by Katherina, and Petruchio's recognition of the significance of that statement. This final ensemble scene, then, recapitulates the contests and the testings of the earlier Acts, in a strongly ritualized action, and guarantees the truth of the transformation brought about in IV.v, which was the climax of Petruchio's taming technique based on the dislocations of normal expectance and displacements which the wedding scene (III.ii) exemplifies and enacts. Shakespeare develops these various 'scenic patterns' in various ways throughout his dramatic career, but as they are deployed here they create a strong theatrical structure, forming the central statement of the play.

The strength of this structure is in no way vitiated by its refusal to employ the maximum of narrative suspense. We are told what is to happen, and we watch to see if it will. The theatrical pattern of 'the fulfilled declaration' creates a particular kind of audience participation. Petruchio's two soliloquies (II.i.168–81 and IV.i.175–98) make us privy to his intent as no one else in the play is permitted to be, and we watch the working out of his proposition, in two stages, like the demonstration of a mathematical proof. This places Petruchio squarely at the centre of the plot, and he is the focus of audience attention (it is surprising how small Katherina's part is, in terms of lines spoken). In the taming plot our principal concern is with the falconer, not with the bird.

Of all the post-Shakespearean adaptations of *The Shrew* only Lacey's *Sauny the Scott* has any use for the sub-plot, with its disguises and intrigues. The verdict of the theatre seems to have been that it is inferior, detachable and dispensable. As we have seen (p. 99), it was not until the Victorian period that it was restored to performance. Yet, almost alone among the early critics, Dr Johnson recognized that it is essential to Shakespeare's purposes. He says:

> Of this play the two plots are so well united, that they can hardly be called two without injury to the art with which they are interwoven. The attention is entertained with all the variety of a double plot, yet is not distracted by unconnected incidents.[1]

1. *Johnson on Shakespeare*, ed. Raleigh (1908), p. 96. It is curious to note that Charles and Mary Lamb's *Tales from Shakespeare* (1807) tells the story of *The*

Modern critics concur, virtually with one voice, and Hibbard is typical when he says, 'the first audience to witness a performance of the play . . . were seeing the most elaborately and skilfully designed comedy that had yet appeared on the English stage'.[1] Agreement about Shakespeare's constructional skills, however, should not blunt our recognition that the sub-plot is in quite a different key—less direct, less robust, more conventional in its characterizations, and by turns flatter and more ornate in its language. It does not work through such large set-piece scenes as the taming plot does. The lute-breaking episode in II.i and the scene (III.i) where Lucentio and Hortensio instruct Bianca in music and Latin are theatrically important and memorable, but for the most part the plot is conducted in comparatively brief episodes of scheming and deception. Shakespeare's skill in exposition may be illustrated from his delaying and integrating technique at the opening of the play. The title creates an expectation of conflict between a man and his wife, but the Induction[2] offers us immediately a dispute between the Hostess and a Beggar, followed by a long episode in which a Lord and his train plan to deceive the sleeping Beggar that he is a Lord. This is interrupted by the arrival of the actors, after which the Lord's plot is seen in operation, with Sly deceived for over a hundred lines until the actors come to play their comedy. The play-within-the-play then *begins* with the sub-plot, Lucentio and Tranio arriving in Padua to pursue a course of study and meeting Baptista, his daughters and suitors at I.i.47. Until this point (350 lines into a play only 2750 lines long) there is no hint of a shrew, yet all that has taken place proves, in the end, to be thematically and structurally relevant. At I.i.48, Baptista firmly links the two plots by his initial announcement:

> Gentlemen, importune me no farther,
> For how I firmly am resolv'd you know;
> That is, not to bestow my youngest daughter
> Before I have a husband for the elder.

It is from this decision that all the scheming of the sub-plot flows, with Hortensio, Lucentio and Gremio pursuing their various

---

Shrew, omitting the Sly scenes entirely and making only minimum mention of the sub-plot.

1. Hibbard, pp. 11–12.

2. It was Pope who labelled the first two scenes 'Induction'. The word does not occur in the Folio text, which begins 'Actus primus. Scoena Prima.'

ways to win Bianca. As Alexander Leggatt has suggested,[1] the taming plot, by coming later, may be seen as, in part, 'a reflection of it at a deeper level', but the contest *for* Bianca is also a parallel to the contest *between* Petruchio and Katherina. In both cases courtship is seen as a struggle, a conflict, and Shakespeare signals this by the way in which, after 1.i, the plots interweave.

Shakespeare derived several advantages from his choice of Gascoigne's *Supposes* as his sub-plot's source (see pp. 78–84). Italian literature was fashionable, Roman comedy was academically respectable, but not many vernacular plays had been built on these bases. As Charlton remarked, 'Not many English comedies of the sixteenth century are built directly on Italian models',[2] so that Shakespeare's work had the advantage of novelty. By a discreet 'italianizing' of the taming plot—giving the characters Italian names, setting the play in Padua, and so on—and by integrating it with Gascoigne's efficient translation from the popular Ariosto, Shakespeare, as M. C. Bradbrook says, adjusted 'native popular traditional art' to the 'socially more esteemed classical and foreign models'.[3] The title of the play, *The Taming of the Shrew*, would have sounded very like a contribution to the growing debate on the status of wives and the rights and duties of marriage, and the added Italian flavour provided a dash of sophistication.

The use of *Supposes* also adds a dimension of intrigue and indirection to *The Shrew*, counterpointing Petruchio's direct methods of courtship. Baptista's ban (1.i.48) on direct competition for Bianca makes subterfuge necessary, and brings about the disguises of Hortensio and Lucentio. These create both confusion and deception, prospering the action of the play, but they also imply a significant enlargement of Bianca's part. Polynesta (her original in *Supposes*) has been seduced two years ago, and is pregnant by Erostrato, but she rarely appears in the play. By making her a virgin, Katherina's younger sister, and by adding a third (Hortensio)[4] to the list of her suitors, Shakespeare

1. *Shakespeare's Comedy of Love* (1974), p. 49.

2. H. B. Charlton, *Shakespearian Comedy* (1938), p. 88. See also R. W. Bond, *Early Plays from the Italian* (Oxford, 1911); Leo Salingar, *Shakespeare and the Traditions of Comedy* (Cambridge, 1974). As Charlton says (p. 76): 'The sub-plot of *The Shrew* is one of the few English plots immediately traceable to a sixteenth-century Italian comedy.'

3. 'Dramatic Role as Social Image', *SJ* (1958), p. 134.

4. By also making Hortensio Petruchio's friend Shakespeare creates a strong narrative link between the two plots. For the alleged 'inconsistencies' in the presentation of Hortensio see pp. 37–9.

can increase the element of romance in the play (as with Lucentio's rapturous 'love at first sight' in i.i), and permit the younger sister to have a personality of her own, to complement the Shrew's. The development of Bianca is subtle. In i.i she appears the dutiful, submissive daughter, all 'mild behaviour and sobriety', though her first words, to Katherina, are beautifully barbed: 'Sister, content you in my discontent.' She obeys her father, suffers physical violence from her sister (ii.i), and publicly accepts the appointment of her 'tutors'. When she is alone with them, however, she is in complete, cool command:

> Why, gentlemen, you do me double wrong
> To strive for that which resteth in my choice.
> I am no breeching scholar in the schools,
> I'll not be tied to hours nor 'pointed times,
> But learn my lessons as I please myself.
> (iii.i.16–20)

It comes as small surprise, when she is married to Lucentio, that she assumes many of the characteristics of her shrewish sister when she is sent for in the final scene. The treatment of Bianca is typical of the 'room for development' which Shakespeare gives himself when he integrates the two plots.

The intrigues and the romantic quality of the sub-plot also allow Shakespeare to make comparisons and contrasts which clarify and deepen the thematic development. Leggatt points out that the two plots 'present a contrast in conventions, both social and dramatic'.[1] And the contrasts are not simple. Leggatt adds: 'The courting of Bianca follows literary convention: and this is played off against the social conventions followed by her father, the romanticism of the one contrasting with the realism of the other.'

Lucentio's rapturous passion in i.i is contrasted not only with Petruchio's realistic declaration 'I come to wive it wealthily in Padua' (i.ii.74) and with his brisk financial bargaining over Katherina's dowry (ii.i.119–27), but also with Baptista's thoroughly commercial auction of his daughter later in the scene. Contrasts of social and dramatic convention of this kind are the staple of the play's development, and they comment ironically one on the other, refusing to allow any single attitude to love and marriage to go unchallenged.[2] But the sub-plot is patient of other kinds of contrast, some superficial, some deep. From its Roman and

1. Leggatt, op. cit., pp. 46–7.
2. Cf. the central scenes of *AYL* (iii.i–iv.iii).

Italian sources comes the opposition of youth and age: Baptista, Vincentio, the Pedant and Gremio are the targets of the scheming young men, Lucentio, Tranio and Hortensio, made explicit in Grumio's comment: 'Here's no knavery. See, to beguile the old folks, how the young folks lay their heads together' (1.ii.137–8). Then there is the direct comparison between Petruchio and Lucentio as the principal wooers in their respective actions. Petruchio is superficially direct, simple, overbearing and business-like (though, on inspection, his methods are seen to be more subtle and based on a shrewd psychological appreciation); Lucentio, on the other hand, is lovesick, devious (employing Tranio in disguise to do all his real work for him),[1] and proceeds by expediency rather than plan. There is also the larger contrast between the stock, stereotyped characters, inherited from the sub-plot's sources, and the more highly-individualized personalities of the taming plot (though in this group we may include Bianca, created by Shakespeare from mere hints in his source). Lucentio, in this respect, is little more than the romantic young man of Italian comedy, and Tranio displays his origin as the resourceful slave of Roman drama. Baptista is a type of the anxious father (we know nothing more of him except that he is a rich merchant), the Pedant is not even allowed the dignity of a name, and Gremio is specified in the stage-direction at 1.i.47 as 'a pantaloon', the stock 'old man' character of the *commedia*. Such characters are circumscribed, they act in predictable ways and within defined limits. Against them are ranged the individualized, unpredictable, developing figures of Katherina and Petruchio. The creative tension set up between the conventions and the different modes of characterization in the two plots is epitomized in the climax of the sub-plot (v.i), when the true and false Vincentios at last come face to face, and the intrigues are resolved. Shakespeare is careful to place Katherina and Petruchio (who have resolved their differences and come together in the previous scene) as eavesdropping witnesses to this action: Petruchio says, 'Prithee, Kate, let's stand aside and see the end of this controversy', and from a position of dramatic superiority they watch the events of the dénouement.

The two plots comment on each other at a deeper level as well. The most obvious example is in the matter of disguise. Lucentio

---

1. Tranio (disguised as Lucentio) is a major character in the play. He creates almost all the intrigue in the sub-plot; it is he who 'propels the action and who of all the characters best corresponds with Petruchio in the Katherina plot'. See E. M. W. Tillyard, *Shakespeare's Early Comedies* (1965), pp. 92ff.

and Hortensio are disguised as private tutors simply to gain access to their mistress; Tranio is disguised as Lucentio to further his master's designs by his own ingenuity. These are simple changes of identity. But Petruchio disguises his true nature by his assumption of the 'tamer's role', for it is a role, a performance, for a particular purpose, and this is made perfectly clear at the end of the play (though there have been hints before) when he is asked what his reform of Katherina implies. He answers:

> Marry, peace it bodes, and love, and quiet life,
> An awful rule, and right supremacy,
> And, to be short, what not that's sweet and happy.
>
> (v.ii. 109–11)

Mutatis mutandis, a similar case might be made for the emergence of Katherina from her disguise as a shrew, a role forced on her by a neglectful father, a sly sister and an unsympathetic society.

It has also been argued that the plots are united by the pervasive presence of 'supposes', or mistakings, but since this concerns the Sly material as well it is discussed below (see p. 19). In his chapter on 'Double plots in Shakespeare' Salingar sums up the structural importance of the sub-plot and its integration with the story of Petruchio and Katherina:

Above all, he applies the lesson of the balanced and interconnected double plot, which he is more likely to have learned from *Supposes* than anywhere else. In his first act, the marriage of Kate is introduced only as a means to another end, the release of Bianca, and the rivalry over Bianca occupies most of the dialogue, although Shakespeare ensures the momentum of his double plot by interesting the audience more in Kate. He maintains the latent contrast between the two halves of his plot by devising scenes dealing with the pretended tutoring of Bianca before he comes to Petruchio's 'schooling' of Kate in Act IV. He then links the two plots causally together, first by making Hortensio and his real or pretended rivals join in offering Petruchio inducements to 'break the ice' for them [I.ii. 265] by wedding the elder sister, and then by making Tranio point out to Lucentio 'our vantage in this business' in the midst of Kate's marriage-scene [III.ii. 142], before he brings the two marriages together (with Hortensio's added) for comparison in the final scene. This is not mere imitation of New Comedy or Italian plots, but the application of Italian methods to new purposes.[1]

1. Salingar, op. cit., p. 225.

One might only add that the union of the two plots is not, in Johnson's phrase, 'distracted by unconnected incidents' to appreciate the subtlety and complexity of Shakespeare's constructional art.

What Hosley has described as 'the brilliant threefold structure of induction, main plot, and subplot . . . perhaps all the more remarkable for being without parallel in Elizabethan drama'[1] is completed by the two Induction scenes and the episode which ends I.i.[2] This 'Sly framework' is at once the most realistic and the most fantastic and bewildering structure in the play, closely related as it is to the play it encloses, in matters of theme, tone and proleptic irony.

Sly himself is a memorable creation[3]—earthy, addicted to ale, fond of ease, firmly rooted in the Warwickshire countryside, and garrulously eloquent either as beggar or supposed lord. Yet he is only one part of what is the widest social spectrum in the play, comprising a beggar, an innkeeper, huntsmen, actors, a page, servants and a lord (to say nothing of Stephen Sly, and old John Naps of Greece). This social group is strongly contrasted with the narrower, bourgeois-mercantile society of Padua where money is master and marriage is commerce, just as the rural English setting of the Induction guarantees a certain artificiality and sophistication to the main play's locations in Italy. We move easily from realism to romance, just as Sly assumes the role of 'a mighty lord' with alacrity, remembering that 'the Slys are no rogues. Look in the Chronicles, we came in with Richard Conqueror.' To explore the relationships between the Induction and the play is to skin an onion, or open a set of Chinese boxes, so interwoven are the anticipations of the one in the other. This is a vital part of *The Shrew*'s larger strategy.

The most obvious link is between Sly's assumption of a new personality and Katherina's translation into a loving wife. In each case, the victim is 'practised upon', deluded, and the result is bewilderment. 'What, would you make me mad?' asks Sly (Ind. ii. 17), enumerating his friends by name to prove his sanity, but a little later it is 'Am I a lord, and have I such a lady? / Or do I

1. Hosley, *HLQ* (1964), p. 294. See also Donald A. Stauffer, *Shakespeare's World of Images* (New York, 1949), p. 46; Maynard Mack, 'Engagement and Detachment in Shakespeare's Plays', in *Essays . . . in Honor of Hardin Craig*, ed. Hosley (Columbia, 1962), pp. 279–80.

2. I believe there were other episodes, and an epilogue. See pp. 39–45.

3. It is noteworthy that he attracted considerable attention from the early adaptors of the play, especially Johnson and Bullock. See pp. 92 ff.

dream? Or have I dream'd till now?' and then 'Upon my life, I am a lord indeed'. We may compare Katherina's stunned incomprehension at Petruchio's behaviour in the wooing scene (II.i), her ineffectual resistance after the wedding, and her few and feeble words before the Haberdasher and the Tailor. Once Sly is convinced that he is a lord he adopts what he feels to be an appropriate utterance ('Well, bring our lady hither to our sight'), and Katherina, after Petruchio's 'field is won', learns gradually to speak the dialect of the obedient wife. Katherina's new role is anticipated by the Page's description of a wife's duties (the more ironic as the Page is not what he seems): 'My husband and my lord, my lord and husband'. In different ways, both Sly and the Page parody what Katherina is to become.

The Induction's use of music similarly foreshadows the play's concern with it as a part of the action and a metaphor for harmony. The Lord commands his huntsmen to 'Procure me music when he wakes, / To make a dulcet and a heavenly sound', and in the following scene music is called for in a stage-direction, when the Lord suggests:

> Wilt thou have music? Hark, Apollo plays,
> And twenty caged nightingales shall sing.

Here music is a means to deception, just as in the play Hortensio is disguised as a musician to gain access to Bianca, who is described as 'the patroness of heavenly harmony', and there follows all the business of the lute-breaking and the music lesson, the wedding music (III.ii) and Petruchio's scraps of old songs (IV.i).

The sense of gracious living created in the Induction (with its music, its soft beds, its fine pictures, its perfumed rooms) includes hunting with hawk and hound. The Lord first enters 'from hunting', and the talk of Silver, Belman and Echo opens the play with an extended evocation of field sports. Sly is told that his 'hounds shall make the welkin answer them', and if he prefers hawking, 'Thou hast hawks will soar / Above the morning lark'. All this gives a local habitation and a name to the hunting imagery of the main play, both in Petruchio's taming methods and all that is summed up from the sub-plot in Tranio's comment in V.ii:

> O sir, Lucentio slipp'd me like his greyhound,
> Which runs himself, and catches for his master.

Once again, the comparison produces a bewildering mixture of fantasy and reality, since the Lord's hounds and huntsmen are credible and real, while Sly's are imaginary, and Petruchio's and

Lucentio's hunting is in the field of courtship only. Petruchio calls for his 'spaniel Troilus' (IV.i), but it never comes.

The Induction makes great play with actors and acting. The Players are courteously and expansively received, the Lord clearly knows something of their art, and Sly himself, although we are told he has never seen a play, garbles a phrase from *The Spanish Tragedy* in his opening lines. As Anne Righter points out,[1] 'The theatrical nature of the deception practised upon the sleeping beggar is constantly stressed': the huntsman promises 'we will play our part', the Page will 'well usurp the grace' of a gentlewoman, and the Players promise to contain themselves, 'Were he the veriest antic in the world'. This foreshadows the main play's concern with plays and the acting of parts, from Tranio's belief in I.i that Baptista and his party represent 'some show to welcome us to town', through the various disguises and performances of Tranio, Lucentio, Hortensio and the Pedant.

These analogies, anticipations and ironic prolepses between the Induction and the main play subserve a larger purpose—the relentless questioning of the boundaries between appearance and reality. As we shall see (pp. 133 ff.), *The Shrew* is deeply concerned with processes of change, metamorphosis and transformation, and the movement through the Induction into the play itself deliberately dislocates our sense of what is true and what is fiction. As Stauffer puts it:[2]

> Most of the conflicts here between appearance and reality, between shadow and substance, are generated from the outside. How can Christopher Sly be sure he is a drunken tinker when all those around him assure him that he is a lord? And is not the old father Vincentio almost justified in doubting his identity when everyone on the stage is crying away to prison with the dotard and impostor?

Tillyard sees the conflict between appearance and reality as the play's overriding theme, and says:[3]

> There is exquisite comedy in Sly, newly awakened in his gorgeous surroundings, demanding a pot of the smallest ale; and there is the hint, through his bewilderment and his final acquiescence in the reality of the moment, that the limits of the

1. *Shakespeare and the Idea of the Play* (1962), p. 105. See her perceptive remarks on 'the play within the play' in *The Shrew*, pp. 104ff.

2. *Shakespeare's World of Images*, p. 46.

3. *Shakespeare's Early Comedies*, p. 106.

apparent and the real are not easily charted. Such thoughts would well occur in an age of allegory, with Spenser the chief poet, to any thoughtful man.

Marjorie B. Garber argues that the formal device of the induction affects the play as a whole especially because the Induction purports to tell a dream, and the dream metaphor, like the stage metaphor, 'presents the audience with the problem of comparative realities and juxtaposes a simple or "low" illusion with the more courtly illusions of the taming plot itself'.[1] She adds:

> The 'dream' to which the lord and his servants refer is Sly's conviction that he is a tinker named Christopher Sly. Thus, what they call his dream is actually the literal truth, while the 'truth' they persuade him of is fictive.[2]

Shakespeare's Induction sets up the problem of appearance and reality as a puzzle, a corridor of mirrors, and this conditions our experience of the whole play. Leggatt sums it up:[3]

> it would certainly be too simple to say that each new perspective takes us one step closer to reality, or one step further away from it. . . . The audience remains detached from Sly's experience when he becomes a lord, but begins to share it when he watches the play. . . . The barriers that separated different experiences of life in the earlier plays are now less tight, and there is more traffic across them.

This has ramifications for our understanding of the play as a whole, which, in one sense, may be no more than 'Sly's Dream', and it is the direct result of Shakespeare's decision to preface the story of the taming of the shrew with the story of 'the waking man's dream' as well as undergirding it with the sub-plot of intrigue, competition in courtship, and romance. These structures are brilliantly reticulated, or interwoven, both at narrative and thematic levels, to create a seemingly seamless web of story (*The Shrew* is dazzling, but not difficult to follow, in the theatre). Its structural unity may well be compared to that of plays like *The Merchant of Venice* or *Twelfth Night*.

Examination of structures and sources has also revealed what is widely felt to be the feature which unifies the three plots and informs Shakespeare's whole dramatic intention. C. C. Seronsy

1. *Dream in Shakespeare* (New Haven and London, 1974), p. 27.

2. Ibid., p. 29. Cf. Brooks's note on Lyly's interest 'in the idea that his plays were "unreal"', in his Arden edn of *MND* (1979), p. cxlii.

3. Leggatt, op. cit., pp. 43–4.

has proposed the idea that 'the sub-plot, with its theme of "supposes" which enters substantially into both the shrew action and the induction . . . will account in large measure for Shakespeare's superior handling of all three elements of the plot'.[1] As Gascoigne's Prologue states, a 'suppose' is 'nothing else but a mystaking or imagination of one thing for an other' (see p. 80), and he indicates twenty-four of them in his play, marking them carefully in the margins of his text. Seronsy argues that the term need not be so confined as to mean only one character disguised as another, and if we accept a wider sense for the word—'supposition', 'expectation', 'to believe', 'to imagine', 'to guess', 'to assume'—we may see how it becomes 'a guiding principle of Petruchio's strategy in winning and taming the shrew'. He sees the Induction, too, as 'a steady play of suggestion, of make-believe, and of metamorphosis': Sly is to be persuaded that he has been lunatic, the Page is subtly transformed into his supposed new identity, the Players are to join in the Lord's game and imagine that they are not playing before a drunken tinker but before a lord. Sly's transformation comes when he wakes in the second scene, and though it is never complete, it forms the central action of that scene. Seronsy concludes that *The Shrew*'s artistic success 'lies chiefly in the union of the three strands, in their having a fundamental likeness, the game of supposes or make-believe'. This is a strong argument, and it provides insights into many areas of the play. It links and contrasts Sly's assumption of his false lordly role with Katherina's final conformity to the image Petruchio has made of her: thinking has made it so. And it connects each of these with the comedy of errors and misprisions in the sub-plot. Nevertheless, I feel it does not fully comprehend the organic unity of the play; it relates principally to the narrative and constructional conduct of the action, and pays less than full attention to the deeper and more primitive structures of the play. To these we must now turn.

The play grows from two primal images—the shrew and the hawk. These are far more than metaphors to illustrate the vagaries and varieties of human behaviour. They are the basic raw material from which story, character and poetic structure are formed. In places, the very scenic structure of the action arises from the natural characteristics of the animal and the bird. And it is not a simple matter of character-correspondences: Katherina is both shrew and haggard; Petruchio is both falconer and fool.

1. C. C. Seronsy, '"Supposes" as the Unifying Theme in *The Taming of the Shrew*', *SQ* (1963), pp. 15–30.

We need to see how both images are rooted in myth and nature and folklore to appreciate how organic the play's unity is.

The play's title sounds proverbial, but, surprisingly, neither Tilley nor Smith and Wilson records it. There are many proverbs about shrews (e.g. Tilley, A9, E229, I59, M684, S412–14), but they are concerned with the habits of the animal, and 'Every man can rule a shrew but he that has her' (M106), the closest to Shakespeare's phrase, is not recorded before 1546. In this context 'shrew' clearly means 'a woman given to railing or scolding' (*OED*, sb.² 3), but the word has many earlier meanings. Originally, of course, it referred to any animal belonging to the genus *Sorex* (*OED*, sb.¹ 1), and occurs in Old English as early as *c.* 725. But by the middle of the thirteenth century it had come to mean 'a wicked, evil-disposed, or malignant man' (sb.² 1), and by the end of the fourteenth century it was regularly applied to the Devil.[1] The earliest recorded example of its application to a *woman* 'given to railing or scolding' is in Chaucer's Epilogue to *The Merchant's Tale*: 'But of hir tonge a lobbyng shrewe is she.' By the end of the sixteenth century this had become the dominant meaning, but behind Shakespeare's use of the word lies a long sense of the shrew as evil, malign, even satanic, and this must inform our understanding of what Shakespeare meant by it.

In natural history, too, the shrew has had a uniformly bad and wholly undeserved report.[2] Topsell gives a fair idea of what Shakespeare's contemporaries would have believed:[3]

It is a rauening beast, feygning it selfe to be gentle and tame, but being touched it biteth deepe, and poisoneth deadly. It beareth a cruell minde, desiring to hurt any thing, neither is there any creature that it loueth, or it loueth him, because it is feared of al. The cats as we haue saide do hunt it and kil it,

---

1. *OED*, sb.² 1b. See Langland, *Piers Plowman*, A. x. 209; Chaucer, *Can. Yeo. Tale*, 364. For the transference from male to female in the medieval period cf. Witch (*OED*, sb.¹, sb.²). Derivatives like 'shrewd', 'shrewish', originally meant 'rascally or villainous'; the verb 'to shrew' meant 'to curse'. Cf. beshrew.

2. See Emma Phipson, *The Animal-Lore of Shakespeare's Time* (1883); H. W. Seager, *Natural History in Shakespeare's Time* (1896); C. Plinius Secundus, *The Natural Historie*, trans. Philemon Holland (1601; 1634, 43e, 50i, 55e, 56m, 71e, 167a, 168m, 277c, 322k, 360m, 361a); Gordon Corbet, *The Terrestrial Mammals of Western Europe* (1966); Peter Crowcroft, *The Life of the Shrew* (1957).

3. Edward Topsell, *The Historie of Foure-footed Beasts* (1607), pp. 536–40. See also Thomas Lupton, *A Thousand Notable Things* (1579, 1601, etc.); John Swann, *Speculum Mundi* (1635); Robert Plot, *The Natural History of Stafford-shire*, vi. 51 (1686), p. 222; Gilbert White, *Natural History of Selborne* (1776); *OED*, Shrew, sb.¹ 2, for shrew-ash, shrew-bitten, shrew-running, shrew-struck, etc.

but they eat not them, for if they do, they consume away in time. . . . They go very slowly, they are fraudulent, and take their prey by deceipt. Many times they gnaw the Oxes hooues in the stable. They loue the rotten flesh of Rauens. . . . The Shrew being cut and applyed in the manner of a plaister, doth effectually cure her owne bites. . . . The Shrew falling into the furrow of a Cart wheele doth presently dye: the dust thereof in the passage by which she went being taken, and sprinkled into the woundes which were made by her poysonsome teeth, is a very excellent and present remedy for the curing of the same . . . if horses, or any other labouring creature do feede in that pasture or grasse in which a Shrew shall put her venome or poyson in, they will presently die.

So absorbed were the natural historians with these (totally imaginary) venomous and maleficent qualities of the shrew that they failed to record what every countryman would have observed as its dominant peculiarities. Shakespeare was country-bred, and his play virtually ignores the old wives' tales, but shows striking affinities with what modern mammalogists have identified as the true characteristics and behaviour patterns of the shrew. Corbet's standard work summarizes what is now generally believed:[1]

Shrews are very active, solitary, surface-dwellers. . . . They are very voracious and suffer from lack of food within a few hours. . . . Shrews are preyed upon extensively by birds, but much less so by mammalian carnivores. . . . Dispersion is maintained by aggressive behaviour at all times except during the brief period of oestrus and copulation. The fighting is stereotyped and involves great use of the voice, resulting in 'squeaking matches'.[2]

1. Corbet, op. cit., pp. 106–10.
2. Cf. Crowcroft, op. cit.: 'It is typical of the animal's general behaviour that when it digs, it digs furiously and with a great show of energy' (p. 36); 'it is clear that newly caught shrews always eat about their own weight of food daily' (p. 25); 'What is astonishing is that the shrew should require so much food of such high energy content' (p. 26); 'The explanation seems to be that their physiology is adjusted for a rapid turnover of energy' (p. 28); [a shrew] 'having disembowelled a comrade, attacked with equal ferocity snakes, slow-worms and vipers, from an unequal conflict with which it was removed unhurt in body and unsubdued in spirit' (p. 20, quoting Barrett-Hamilton); 'most "fights" do not involve actual physical contact, the outcome being decided by screaming contests. If one shrew encounters another and the other does not give way, the first raises its muzzle and squeaks loudly. When a shrew is squeaked at . . . its reaction is to return the compliment—or insult—and a screaming contest takes

These primary characteristics, energy, irascibility and noise, have their analogies in Shakespeare's play.

The Shrew is much concerned with the search for food. In the Induction the Lord proposes 'a most delicious banquet', and Sly (to whom drink is food) calls for it repeatedly; conserves are offered, and Sly smells 'sweet savours'. Katherina is denied her bridal dinner (III.ii), starved at Petruchio's house (IV.i), mocked with the promise of food by Grumio (IV.iii), and not finally satisfied until Lucentio's banquet in v.ii, where there is nothing to do 'but sit and sit, and eat and eat'. From Act I she is presented as vigorously active, in contrast to Bianca's 'mild behaviour and sobriety': she is a 'fiend of hell', whose 'gifts are so good here's none will hold you'. She fights with Bianca in II.i, strikes her, 'flies after her', breaks a lute on Hortensio's head, strikes Petruchio, weeps on her wedding day, and opposes Petruchio on the matter of the bridal dinner because 'a woman may be made a fool / If she had not a spirit to resist'. Her raging energy is amply demonstrated throughout the play's first three Acts.

We are left in no doubt about her fiery temperament and irascibility. Gremio (I.i.55) says at once 'She's too rough for me', and five lines later Hortensio rejects her, 'Unless you were of gentler, milder mould'. She threatens 'To comb your noddle with a three-legg'd stool', as we have seen she attacks both Bianca and Petruchio physically, and her anger is even more emphasized in word than in action. The long verbal dispute with Petruchio in II.i has been inaccurately described as a 'wit-bout'; it is far more of a flyting match, in which the contestants vie in vilification. As it concludes, Petruchio sums up her temperament in ironic inversions:

> I find you passing gentle.
> 'Twas told me you were rough, and coy, and sullen. . . .
> Thou canst not frown, thou canst not look askance,
> Nor bite the lip, as angry wenches will,
> Nor hast thou pleasure to be cross in talk.   (II.i.236–43)

---

place, the two animals only a few inches apart, facing one another. Many fights are decided without anything more serious than the one contestant apparently becoming intimidated by the squeaks of the other' (p. 51); 'whereas [rodents] usually fight in grim silence, shrews continue to squeak loudly' (p. 52); 'The noisy nature of the fighting of shrews is its most prominent feature' (p. 61); 'It has a particularly scolding and complaining note, which immediately convinces the hearer that a fight is going on' (p. 48); 'the various species of *Sorex* utter sounds of at least two distinct types: (1) staccato squeaks and (2) soft twittering sounds' (p. 62).

These are, of course, precisely the qualities she has just displayed. We have already heard of her as 'an irksome brawling scold' (I.ii) and Petruchio describes her as 'a wasp' (II.i), and as late as III.ii, after the wedding, she has an outburst of anger which draws from her husband the mockingly suave request: 'O Kate, content thee, prithee be not angry.' She insists, even at this late stage, on her right to free expression of wrath: 'I will be angry; what hast thou to do?' In Acts IV and V things are different, but until then Katherina's shrewish nature is predominantly emphasized by her shrew-like irascibility. She is, as Hortensio says, 'Renown'd in Padua for her scolding tongue'.

Although not averse to using her fists, Katherina fights principally by noise. We are told that Petruchio's 'taming-school' (IV.ii) exists 'To tame a shrew and charm her chattering tongue'. Tranio's first comment on her (I.i) notes how she

> Began to scold and raise up such a storm
> That mortal ears might hardly endure the din.

She loses no opportunity for verbal contest, with Bianca, with Petruchio, or with her father, when Petruchio is late arriving on the wedding day (III.ii):

> No shame but mine. I must forsooth be forc'd
> To give my hand, oppos'd against my heart,
> Unto a mad-brain rudesby, full of spleen,
> Who woo'd in haste and means to wed at leisure. . . .

Her freedom of speech is almost the last liberty she surrenders, making a spirited stand for it as late as IV.iii:

> Why, sir, I trust I may have leave to speak,
> And speak I will. I am no child, no babe.
> Your betters have endur'd me say my mind,
> And if you cannot, best you stop your ears.
> My tongue will tell the anger of my heart,
> Or else my heart concealing it will break,
> And rather than it shall, I will be free
> Even to the uttermost, as I please, in words.

Her resistance is ignored, her angry words silenced, and her most 'shrewish' quality subdued to the tamer's hand.

Shakespeare's presentation of Katherina subsumes several of the available characteristics of the shrew. From the history of the word comes the sense of her as a devil: the word (and its derivatives) is applied to her no less than fifteen times. As Hortensio says

(I.i.66): 'From all such devils, good Lord deliver us!' From the observed characteristics of the animal itself come the distinguishing features of energy, irascibility and (above all) noise. By dramatizing Katherina in this way in the first movement of the play Shakespeare puts down deep roots into social, verbal and natural history.

Shrew imagery dominates the first half of the play. Petruchio's first soliloquy (II.i.168–81), outlining his plan for dealing with his shrew, says nothing about taming her. He will 'woo her with some spirit when she comes' and the only bird mentioned is a nightingale. His technique will be to oppose reality with a created fiction, and make the appearance more real than the fact:

> Say that she rail, why then I'll tell her plain
> She sings as sweetly as the nightingale.

The plan is to confuse, to baffle, to bewilder her by presenting her with a perpetual image of what he thinks her behaviour ought to be. And it is important that Katherina should fail to understand what he is doing. Throughout the play she is presented as not particularly intelligent, and she never stops to analyse his behaviour, to plan, to counter. She simply reacts, violently, to stimuli. In this respect, too, she is like the animal: her reactions are 'shrewish'.

The play's title, *The Taming of the Shrew*, is, in the literal sense, an absurdity. Men tame animals either for companionship or for use. In Shakespeare's day there is no evidence to suggest that men ever kept shrews as pets[1] and such a tiny beast could do no useful work. At one level, Petruchio is a fool for making the attempt, and his technique is certainly seen by others as eccentric and fantastic. Katherina, not surprisingly, enquires after his 'coxcomb' (II.i), and refers to him as 'one half lunatic', 'A madcap ruffian', 'a mad-brain rudesby' and 'a frantic fool', but Bianca points out, after the wedding (III.ii), 'That being mad herself, she's madly mated'. It is left to Tranio, commenting on Petruchio's fantastic clothing as he arrives for his wedding, to make the crucial point: 'He hath some meaning in his mad attire.' Petruchio is playing the Fool, just as Lear's Fool does, presenting unpalatable truths under the cloak of entertainment, displacing his master's folly on to himself. It is Katherina who is ill prepared for marriage, and Petruchio, in his foolishness, is telling her so. To 'tame the shrew', then, is, in one sense, to exorcize an evil and irascible spirit (in

1. The best-known of the few recorded modern attempts to tame a shrew is in Konrad Lorenz, *King Solomon's Ring*, trs. Wilson (1952), ch. 9.

this case by outdoing it—he 'kills her in her own humour'), and in another, to reduce a wild bird to obedience, so that she can hunt for you and with you. It is this taming image, the reclaiming of the haggard, which controls the second half of the play.

Falconry was so well known and so widely practised in Shakespeare's day that little needs to be said about it.[1] As Lascelles says: 'To the reader or playgoer of Shakespeare's time the technical terms describing the training of hawks for the sport of falconry were household words.' In *The Shrew*, however, Shakespeare focuses attention almost exclusively on one part of that training: the watching, or 'manning'[2] of the wild bird, by keeping it awake day and night, and by limiting its food, until from sheer fatigue it settles down into docility and tameness.[3] This is often a long, exhausting process, but, when successfully completed, it sets up a close and special relationship between the falconer and his bird which makes them an efficient hunting team. It is as if Shakespeare's imagination focused as narrowly and intensively on the 'hawk' image as it had ranged extensively when exploring the 'shrew'. His dramatic presentation of it alerts a particular kind of audience attention by its directness, explicitness, and an almost Euclidian insistence on stating a theorem and proceeding to prove it. It is also surprising that it is introduced so late in the play.

Allusions to falconry are not absent from the first three Acts of the play, but they are slight, passing, almost incidental. The Induction is strongly concerned with hunting, but mainly it is hare coursing, with only one direct bird-image:

> Dost thou love hawking? Thou hast hawks will soar
> Above the morning lark.[4]

Apart from the buzzard at II.i.206–8 (which comes in for its value in word-play) the allusions to falconry before Act IV are oblique, and apply to Bianca, not Katherina. Gremio asks Baptista 'will you mew her up . . . ?'[5] and Tranio explains to Lucentio that her father has 'closely mew'd her up', but the term carries little metaphoric force. The first overt reference to taming does not

---

1. See Hon. Gerald Lascelles, in *Shakespeare's England* (Oxford, 1916), vol. II, pp. 351–66, who lists and describes the principal Elizabethan authorities.
2. 'To man' is 'to accustom (a hawk, occas. other birds) to the presence of men': *OED*, Man, v. 10.
3. See Commentary on IV.i.175–98.
4. Probably flight 'at the high mountee' as opposed to 'at the river'. See Lascelles, op. cit., p. 359.
5. A hawk was 'mewed up' (confined in a 'mew' or cage) at moulting time: *OED*, v.[2] 1.

occur until II.i.269–71 (concerning Katherina), when Petruchio intends to 'bring you from a wild Kate to a Kate / Conformable as other household Kates', and the allusion is to cats, not birds. At III.i.87–90 Hortensio, suspecting Bianca of inconstancy, refers to her as 'ranging', and casting her 'wandering eyes on every stale', which probably refers to a straying hawk stooping to any lure,[1] and at IV.ii.39 he calls her a 'haggard', Shakespeare's usual word for wildness and inconstancy.[2]

All this amounts to very little compared with Petruchio's direct declaration of intent in the soliloquy at IV.i.175–98. This arises quite naturally from the 'displacement' activity in the earlier part of the scene, when he beats the servants, flings the meat about, and refuses to allow the weary, bemoiled Katherina anything to eat.[3] He announces that 'this night we'll fast for company', and Curtis reports that the 'manning' has begun with Petruchio 'Making a sermon of continency to her' so that she 'Knows not which way to stand, to look, to speak'. Petruchio's soliloquy begins with a reference to his hierarchical position vis-à-vis his wife ('Thus have I politicly begun my reign') which foreshadows Katherina's words in V.ii ('Thy husband is thy lord, thy life, thy keeper, / Thy head, thy sovereign'), and he then develops at length his metaphor of Katherina as an untrained falcon who must be 'manned'. What follows is an extended, almost conceited, image, addressed directly to the audience, and introducing the technical terms of the 'manning' technique: the bird must be 'sharp', and not 'full-gorg'd' until she has 'stooped', he will man his 'haggard' by watching, and so on. The force, the directness of this speech impart a new impetus to the play's action, and in the scenes which follow we witness a clear, relentless demonstration of the programme which has been announced. This is carried out in the terms of the metaphor, applied plainly—there is no dense 'hawking' imagery in Acts IV and V. In IV.iii we see Katherina, starving, tempted with the prospect of food by Grumio and Petruchio. Then her natural inclinations towards fashionable dress are systematically checked and frustrated in the scene with the Haberdasher and the Tailor. Even her speech is checked by Petruchio's resolute attention to her desires—his 'reverend care

---

1. See *OED*, v.[1] 8, quoting *Shr.*; cf. *Caes.*, II.i.118, 'So let high-sighted tyranny range on'.

2. Cf. *Oth.*, III.iii.264–7; *Ado*, III.i.35–6.

3. It was not normally considered advisable to starve hawks during manning (see Lascelles, op. cit., p. 357), but obviously a full-fed hawk would not respond so readily to the technique.

of her'. By the end of the scene she is not even allowed to say what time it is, since Petruchio interprets this as 'crossing' him. She relapses into silence, baffled, thwarted, and, above all, weary. This is the first stage of 'manning'.

Once tameness and docility are assured, the hawk must be taught and tested in obedience. Lascelles describes the process:

> ... in a few weeks our hawk will display no fear of men or dogs, even when bareheaded in the open air. ... When this stage has been reached, there is no more in the way of training to be done but to accustom the hawk to fly to the lure ... and not to leave it on the falconer's approach. At first she is for safety's sake confined by a creance or long light line, but ere long she is flown loose altogether and ... is ready to be entered to the quarry which she is destined to pursue.[1]

This process is reproduced in human terms in a series of scenes which show Katherina being tested, and permitted to operate at steadily increasing distances from her handler's control. It begins in IV.v, on the journey to Padua, when Petruchio comments provocatively on the brightness of the moon. A dispute arises:

> *Kath.* The moon? The sun! It is not moonlight now.
> *Pet.* I say it is the moon that shines so bright.
> *Kath.* I know it is the sun that shines so bright.
> *Pet.* Now by my mother's son, and that's myself,
> It shall be moon, or star, or what I list,
> Or e'er I journey to your father's house.

This is a simple test in obedience, taking up the 'what time is it?' test which ended IV.iii. Katherina has not learned her lesson, however, and Petruchio threatens to go back to square one and begin the process all over again. Hortensio provides her the clue: 'Say as he says, or we shall never go.' Katherina shrugs, obeys, and the journey is resumed. Petruchio naggingly insists that she repeats her lesson—'I say it is the moon'—and she does as she is told. The second test, the encounter with Vincentio, follows immediately. This is a more advanced examination since it involves a third person and exposes her to more than private ridicule. But Katherina has learned what is expected of her; as we have seen (pp. 107–8) the fulcrum is placed between these two episodes in IV.v. In the following scene (v.i) Petruchio and Katherina witness and eavesdrop on the climax of the sub-plot;

1. Op. cit., pp. 357–8.

having made their own peace they watch the resolution of the other intrigues. But the scene ends with yet another test of Katherina's education: she must kiss her husband in the public street. She demurs, he threatens, she obeys. But what is far more important, she offers a tiny gesture of affection: 'Nay, I will give thee a kiss. Now pray thee, love, stay.' This is not lost on Petruchio. There is great depth of implication in his question 'Is not this well?'; in the theatre it can be a most moving and expressive moment, a moment of reconcilement, replete with unspoken understanding. The final scene represents the greatest test, because it is not only the most extensive but the most public. Katherina must display her obedience before the entire household, and Petruchio insists on the most rigorous standards:[1]

> Katherine, that cap of yours becomes you not.
> Off with that bauble, throw it under foot. [*She obeys.*]

This comes perilously close to a public degradation, and, theatrically, it provides no small element of suspense, from which the 'obedience' speech issues almost as a release.

The twofold pattern of manning and testing, announced in Petruchio's soliloquy and systematically applied in a cumulative sequence of scenes, dominates the second part of the play and creates its dramatic form. So beneath the complex organization of the narrative—Hosley's 'brilliant threefold structure'—lies a deeper, contrasting, two-part organization arising from the controlling symbols of the shrew and the hawk. These anchor the play in the realities of man's commerce with nature, his dealings with birds and animals, following God's command to Adam that he should have dominion 'over every living thing that moveth upon the earth'. The first three Acts of the play explore the peculiar characteristics of the shrew, ranging extensively through the analogies between human and animal behaviour; the last two Acts focus intensively on the single action of manning a wild hawk, translating it relentlessly into human terms. What unites the two symbolic patterns, at this deeper level, is the concept of all life as contest—the noisy, fighting shrew opposed by another of her kind, the battle of wills between the bird and its tamer. The result, in this case, is a particular and peculiar kind of peace, a

---

1. Among all the hunting, sporting and gaming images of v.ii there is only one allusion to hawking, but its irony is important. Of the twenty crowns' wager Petruchio says:

> I'll venture so much of my hawk or hound,
> But twenty times so much upon my wife.

resolution of conflict, that happy issue out of all our afflictions which is the essence of comedy.

Education
All formal education is, in some sense, a reduction to conformity, a restraint upon freedom. The child is subjected to experiences not of its own choosing, introduced to preferred patterns of social behaviour, expected to comply. Before anything can be drawn out of the individual mind, much is put in, and the line between liberal education and socio-cultural indoctrination is difficult to draw and harder to hold. Elizabethan educationists were less concerned with liberating the pupil's consciousness by encouragement to free-ranging enquiry than with inculcating an approved body of knowledge in the context of a serenely accepted social order, to the end that the young might grow up literate, useful citizens of the commonwealth, and, if possible, good and wise as well. *The Shrew* both illustrates this and explores its limitations. But the accepted background must be borne in mind.[1]

The Induction offers the theme obliquely. In his 'practice' upon Sly the Lord conducts an experiment in human nature, so that Sly is offered a picture of himself as a cultured English gentleman —hunting, hawking, but also taking delight in music, pictures, and the performance of plays.[2] Sly, however, remains resolutely himself, rural, vulgar and illiterate, although vastly attracted by the pleasures of gentility, illustrating the truth that education cannot be imposed, it must be achieved. Sly belongs with Barnadine and Caliban in Shakespeare's gallery of the incorrigible and ineducable, upon whose natures nurture can never stick. The opening of the main play sets up a strong contrast. Lucentio comes to Padua to institute 'A course of learning and ingenious studies' and seeking the 'happiness / By virtue specially to be achiev'd'.[3] Padua was famous throughout Europe as a university city, the centre of Aristotelianism, and a debate ensues between Lucentio and Tranio about the curriculum to be followed. Tranio advocates a wide syllabus, philosophy, logic, rhetoric, music, poetry and mathematics, balancing the discipline of Aristotle against sweet witty Ovid on the doubtful principle that 'no profit

1. See Louis B. Wright, *Middle Class Culture in Elizabethan England* (Ithaca, 1958).
2. Cf. the image of himself which the Lord offers Sly with the image of herself which Petruchio offers Katherina in II.i and later.
3. The principal concern in Aristotle's *Ethics*.

grows where is no pleasure ta'en', and ends with the permissive prescription 'study what you most affect'. We feel that this intellectual voyage 'is but for two months victuall'd'.[1] The entry of Bianca with her family puts an end to this academic planning and we never hear of it again. But the brisk bargaining and match-making which follows in I.i creates a contrast between the world of romantic love, allied to cultural and intellectual pursuits, and the world of realistic marriage contracts, made in a society of merchants and adventurers.

Education has a high social value in Padua, as we see from the stately conduct of the episode (in II.i) in which the disguised suitors are presented to Baptista as tutors. Both are described as 'cunning' men, and he is careful to instruct that they should be 'used well'. Yet the formal lessons we hear of or witness are parodies of instruction. Hortensio's impatient pupil breaks his lute over his head, and when he and Lucentio wrangle over who shall instruct Bianca first (III.i), the pupil seizes the opportunity to assume the master's role. Lucentio makes his Latin lesson a cover for declaring his love, and Hortensio puts his music to the same use. The effect of all this is to depreciate the value of book-learning, or, at least, to show that artistic and intellectual pursuits have little attraction against the pull of 'love, first learned in a lady's eyes'.[2] This is precisely the demonstration Shakespeare makes in his most intellectual and erudite comedy, *Love's Labour's Lost*. It is epitomized in *The Shrew* at the opening of IV.ii, where Tranio and Hortensio overhear the brief love-conversation between Lucentio and Bianca:

> *Luc.* Now, mistress, profit you in what you read?
> *Bian.* What, master, read you? First resolve me that.
> *Luc.* I read that I profess, *The Art to Love*.
> *Bian.* And may you prove, sir, master of your art.

The point is that Ovid's *Ars Amatoria* is anything but a manual for romantic lovers.[3] It is a witty, cynical textbook for seducers, offering here an ironic comment on Lucentio's wooing methods and Bianca's mixture of naïveté, sentiment and calculation.

The play makes clear that the true paths to learning are not those of the school or university. Formal education is contrasted to its detriment against the practical academy of experience. Here,

1. Cf. the response evoked by Navarre's 'edict' in *LLL*, I.i.
2. *LLL*, IV.iii.323.
3. It was considered so licentious when it appeared that it was made the pretext for the poet's banishment.

as elsewhere, Petruchio stands at the centre of the stage. He is the
teacher, Katherina is his pupil. His task is to inculcate such
knowledge and instil such behaviour as will fit her to take a useful
place in the existing society. The play gives his qualifications, and
is significantly concerned to demonstrate his teaching methods in
an exemplary way. His first appearance, in I.ii, shows him ready
to use his fists to teach Grumio how to knock at a door when he
is told; this teacher is direct, practical, distinctly rough and very
ready, and intent on being master. When presented with the
prospect of educating Katherina into conformity he presents his
credentials:

> Have I not in my time heard lions roar?
> Have I not heard the sea, puff'd up with winds,
> Rage like an angry boar chafed with sweat?
> Have I not heard great ordnance in the field,
> And heaven's artillery thunder in the skies?
> Have I not in a pitched battle heard
> Loud 'larums, neighing steeds, and trumpets' clang?
> And do you tell me of a woman's tongue,
> That gives not half so great a blow to hear
> As will a chestnut in a farmer's fire?
> Tush, tush, fear boys with bugs!   (I.ii.199–209)

He has faced many things, and his experience gives him confidence that he is a strong candidate for this post.[1]

His teaching technique is a rich and strange mixture of the
academic and the practical. At the heart of it lies the most commendable pedagogic principle of presenting his pupil with an
image of what he wants her to become:

> Take this of me, Kate of my consolation,
> Hearing thy mildness prais'd in every town,
> Thy virtues spoke of, and thy beauty sounded,
> Yet not so deeply as to thee belongs,
> Myself am mov'd to woo thee for my wife.   (II.i.190–4)

Throughout the play this ideal picture is constantly kept before
Katherina, and she is gradually wooed and induced into conformity with it. Part of Petruchio's technique is coercive: he gives
as good as he gets in the flyting match of II.i, he subjects his pupil
to disgrace and humiliation in the wedding scene, and he
deliberately keeps her without food or sleep in the testing scenes

1. He adds enthusiasm to his credentials in his self-recommendation to
Baptista at II.i.130 ff.

of Act IV. But it is significant that he never physically assaults or chastises her, and this sharply distinguishes *The Shrew* from earlier plays on the taming theme like *Tom Tyler and his Wife*. The larger part of Petruchio's teaching method is puzzlement. Katherina is reluctantly fascinated by his energetic and outrageous behaviour (there is no precedent for it in the Padua of her upbringing), and she only gradually comes to recognize it as a travesty of her own wild behaviour. The audience, duly instructed by Petruchio's two explicit soliloquies, can watch the series of lessons from a position of informed superiority. Katherina has to work out, incident by incident, the significance of the instruction she is being given. All this is so unlike the normal processes of Elizabethan education, with its rote learning of grammar and syntax, its translation and retranslation, its imitation of approved literary and philosophical models, that it hardly looks like a teaching process at all. But the subject, the bringing to conformity of an aberrant member of a social group, was no part of any school curriculum, though it was the first premise and ultimate object of all schooling. Petruchio's teaching task, self-imposed, is to bring Katherina into conformity with the acceptable social image of a marriageable young woman in 'Paduan' society. No one has analysed this aspect of the play better than M. C. Bradbrook in the essay I have already cited.[1] She says:

> In real life, to see persons as merely fulfilling one or two rôles, as merely a lawyer, a priest, a mother, a Jew, even as merely a man or a woman is to see them as something less than images of God; for practical purposes this may be necessary. . . . Assigning and taking of rôles is in fact the basis of social as distinct from inward life.

She goes on to describe the unique way in which Petruchio instructs Katherina in the assumption of the role he, and her society, have decreed for her:

> The wooing of Katherine takes up rather less than half the play, and her part is quite surprisingly short; although she is on the stage a good deal, she spends most of the time listening to Petruchio. The play is his; this is its novelty. Traditionally, the shrew triumphed; hers was the oldest and indeed the only native comic rôle for women. If overcome, she submitted either to high theological argument or to a taste of the stick.

1. 'Dramatic Role as Social Image; a Study of *The Taming of the Shrew*', *SJ* (1958), pp. 132–50.

Here, by the wooing in Act II, the wedding in Act III, and the 'taming school' in Act IV, each of which has its own style, Petruchio overpowers his shrew with her own weapons—imperiousness, wildness, inconsistency and the withholding of the necessities of life—combined with strong demonstrations of his natural authority.

The unorthodoxy, and novelty, of this educational programme is the central point of interest in the play's exploration of teaching and learning, and all the other lessons are subservient and contributory to it.

Katherina, however, is not Petruchio's only pupil, and he varies his methods according to his students. Grumio, in I.ii, is taught by the most direct method, a box on the ear. Hortensio and Lucentio, the pupil-teachers, are given the example of the 'taming school', and exhorted to follow it. These are the traditional and time-honoured techniques; Petruchio's innovation in educational methodology lies in his treatment of Katherina. It is still capable of raising heated debate when the play is performed on the stage, and perhaps this is because it presents with alarming directness the dichotomy which underlies all educative processes. On the one hand, education is designed to liberate and bring to full fruition the innate capabilities of the pupil. On the other, it is a means of reducing the individual to social conformity through the imparting of approved knowledge and acceptable skills. To some extent it is always a taming procedure, at odds with the very human desire for liberty. But it also works on the deep human need to conform and to be socially approved within the tribe. The tension between these contrary impulses is always present. *The Taming of the Shrew* makes them uncomfortably evident.

Metamorphosis

Education is one way of transforming a person into someone else, but it is not the only form of change the play investigates. The theme of transformation, of metamorphosis, raises perhaps some of the subtlest questions in the play but it does so through the medium of very direct allusion and reference, and in some of the play's most obvious stage action. It is notable that most of the reference to classical mythology takes place in the early part of the play, where it serves a variety of purposes. Douglas Bush points out:[1]

1. Douglas Bush, 'Classical Myth in Shakespeare's Plays', in *Elizabethan and Jacobean Studies Presented to F. P. Wilson in Honour of his 70th Birthday* (1959), pp. 68–9.

Even in such a boisterous farce as the *Shrew* (which has much
less, and less detailed, allusion than *A Shrew*) the sophisticated
Lucentio can speak to his man-servant with stilted irrelevance
—'That art to me as secret and as dear / As Anna to the queen
of Carthage was' [1. i. 153–4]—or with the undramatic elabora-
tion of the allusion to Europa in [1. i. 168–70]. . . . Now and then
Ovidianism is less high-flown and more dramatic. The luscious
pictures offered to the drunken Sly in the Induction to the
Shrew have their point.

They have their point indeed, and they are very firmly placed to
make it. At the very opening we are presented with the spectacle
of a man transformed into a beast.[1] The Lord, approaching the
sleeping Sly, comments: 'O monstrous beast, how like a swine
he lies.' He at once resolves to 'practise on this drunken man' and
transform him into a lord, asking his huntsmen: 'Would not the
beggar then forget himself?' Such transformations, up and down
the social scale, with the participants either losing their old
identities or shrewdly retaining them, are to become essential
ingredients of the play's action. No sooner has the transformation
of Sly been agreed than the actors enter, themselves professional
shape-shifters, and they are enlisted to take part in the sport
'Wherein your cunning can assist me much'. The scene ends with
instructions sent to 'Barthol'mew my page' to transform himself
into a lady and play the drunkard's wife. In the second scene of
the Induction Sly stubbornly resists the possibility that he has
been metamorphosed into a lord, until he is seduced by the
images of Cytherea, Io and Daphne, all taken directly from
Ovid's *Metamorphoses*, into exclaiming: 'Upon my life, I am a lord
indeed.' The comic significance of what he then says and does in
performance of his new role lies, of course, in his inability to play
the part. His metamorphosis must be imperfect because he is
ignorant of how to behave. But the whole game of shape-changing
in the Induction is proleptic of the metamorphoses in the main
play. One character after another assumes a disguise, practises to
deceive, and takes on a new identity. As we have seen (p. 116),
the disguised Page of the Induction prefigures the obedient and
compliant wife which Katherina becomes in v. ii. The bewildered
Sly, incapable through ignorance of changing himself, contrasts
with the Katherina who slowly and painstakingly learns her part.
   As the main play opens, Lucentio hopes, by the study of

1. A possibility which Shakespeare takes up later, and in greater detail, in
MND.

Aristotelian virtue, to transform himself into a scholar, but Tranio reminds him that this might be a barren role if 'Ovid be an outcast quite abjured', which links the poet of the *Metamorphoses* with that of the *Amores*, which is to be the lovers' textbook. The first sight of Bianca transforms Lucentio instantly into a lover, and he likens her beauty to that of 'the daughter of Agenor'. According to Ovid (*Metamorphoses*, ii. 846–75) Agenor's daughter, Europa, was the beloved of Jupiter, who appeared before her transformed into a snow-white bull. And so the transformation game goes on, through allusion and action. The love-plot brings about the exchange of clothing and identity between Lucentio and Tranio (the first of the 'disguisings' in the play), and Tranio *becomes* his master for most of the rest of the action. In ii.i Lucentio becomes Cambio, and Hortensio becomes Litio, so that, through the central Acts of the play, nearly half the cast are not what they seem. These metamorphoses are relatively simple, parts of the machinery of the plot, and true identities can be resumed by so simple a device as the changing of clothes. Like the Pedant, and Vincentio, later, they are all, as Biondello says, 'busied about a counterfeit assurance', and no one of them is ever in doubt about his true identity.

Sly, however, is unsure of himself. If, as I believe, the play originally contained Induction, episodes and Epilogue (see p. 44), it seems clear that he was intended to remain bewildered. Reluctantly, and because it seemed the best thing to do, he assumes the identity of the Lord, and at the end of the play he equally reluctantly becomes a beggar again. He is perpetually bewildered, and in this he is the prefiguration of Katherina, who, once Petruchio accosts her, is never allowed to be sure of her own nature until she surrenders to the character he has created for her. She is secure, if discontented, as the typical 'shrew' in ii.i, and this is the identity she offers to Petruchio in the flyting match. But, in spite of the evidence, he refuses to believe her, assuming that she is 'pleasant, gamesome, passing courteous, . . . sweet as spring-time flowers'. This is the dislocating picture, held up to her as a mirror to nature for the rest of the play. And the mutation of her personality which takes place is achieved not with the ease of a change of clothes, but with difficulty, with reluctance, with recalcitrance. Yet the metamorphosis is permanent. Just as the changes in Ovid's *Metamorphoses* are mutations which preserve the life of the subject, or apotheosize his or her state, so the change in Katherina is shown as a development into a better, and enduring, condition. And, in keeping with the bewildering changes in which the play abounds, Petruchio brings her change about by himself assuming a variety of roles. The bluff, rough wooer of Act II is succeeded in III.ii by the fantastic bridegroom, coming to his wedding 'in a pair of old breeches thrice turned'. The purpose of this disguise is to enforce upon Katherina her own unpreparedness for marriage, just as the roistering bully Petruchio becomes in IV.i and IV.iii is a means of displaying to his wife her own inability to manage a household and command her servants. As Peter says (IV.i), 'He kills her in her own humour'.

Although the majority of references to Ovid occur in the earlier scenes of the play, the poet maintains a presence as late as Act IV. In III.i Lucentio invites Bianca to construe a passage from the *Heroides*, and in IV.ii he instructs her in the *Ars Amatoria*. It is as if the mythological Ovid of the *Metamorphoses* gives place, as the play progresses, to the sweet, witty poet of love. The play's development is in tune with this, for the dazzling changes of identity in the manifold disguisings take place, for the most part, in the first two Acts, while the later part of the play is concerned with the longer rhythms of the change of personality which overcomes Katherina. It is upon her transformation that we focus, though we may note the foil which Shakespeare provides for her in her sister. Bianca is the only major character who assumes no disguise, and achieves no development. She begins, in I.i, with her own form of covert and clever shrewishness to her sister, securing herself the sympathy of her father and all his household, and she ends the play bidding fair to take up where her sister left off. The morality of *The Shrew* is a morality of change.

Love and marriage

Unlike *Love's Labour's Lost* and the later comedies, *Much Ado, As You Like It* and *Twelfth Night*, *The Shrew* is concerned with both love and marriage. It takes the romantic action on beyond the wedding, contemplating not only the coming together of lovers but the relationship between man and wife. It belongs with *The Comedy of Errors*, *A Midsummer Night's Dream* and *The Merchant of Venice*. Once again, this theme is explored in a rich mixture of modes: romance, a kind of knockabout farce, realism and parody.

The Induction offers extensive and subtle parody of all the play's attitudes to love. As we have noted already (p. 110), the opening lines offer what appears to be the Shrew of the play's title roundly berating an unfortunate man. It looks like a version of the traditional quarrelling between Noah and his wife in the

Moralities, and echoes of this persist in the attacks made by Katherina on Bianca and on Hortensio, and in the flyting match between Petruchio and Katherina in II.i. Sly is the befuddled victim of the Hostess's outburst, and he falls asleep as bemused and bewildered as Katherina is, at several points in the main play, when faced with expressions of Petruchio's outrageous energy. The Lord and his huntsmen, with their elaborate talk of the chase, suggest the play's concern with the royal hunt of love, culminating in Tranio's greyhound image at v.ii.52–3. Petruchio sums up the two kinds of hunting when he says of the wager:

> I'll venture so much of my hawk or hound,
> But twenty times so much upon my wife.

The actors, in the Induction, are welcome, and remembered, because one of them had previously played a romantic lead— ''Twas where you woo'd the gentlewoman so well'—and the main play's element of romance is thus delicately introduced in the Lord's memory of a player's play. It is carried through in Induction ii, by the proffers to Sly made by the Lord and his servants: 'Apollo plays', 'twenty caged nightingales do sing', 'the lustful bed / On purpose trimm'd up for Semiramis', and the evocative pictures of Adonis, Cytherea, Io and Daphne.[1] But the most prolonged and direct anticipatory parody occurs in the Lord's instructions for the behaviour of 'Barthol'mew my page', who is to enact Sly's wife:

> Tell him from me, as he will win my love,
> He bear himself with honourable action,
> Such as he hath observ'd in noble ladies
> Unto their lords, by them accomplished.

1. Cf. Marlowe, *2 Tamburlaine*, I.ii.31ff. (*Plays*, ed. Gill, pp. 126–7):
> Choose which thou wilt; all are at thy command. . . .
> The Grecian virgins shall attend on thee,
> Skillful in music and in amorous lays,
> As fair as was Pygmalion's ivory girl
> Or lovely Iö metamorphosèd. . . .
> And as thou rid'st in triumph through the streets,
> The pavements underneath thy chariot wheels
> With Turkey carpets shall be coverèd,
> And cloth of Arras hung about the walls,
> Fit objects for thy princely eye to pierce. . . .
> And, when thou go'st, a golden canopy
> Enchas'd with precious stones, which shine as bright
> As that fair veil that covers all the world,
> When Phoebus, leaping from his hemisphere,
> Descendeth downward to th' Antipodes.

Such duty to the drunkard let him do,
With soft low tongue and lowly courtesy,
And say 'What is't your honour will command,
Wherein your lady and your humble wife
May show her duty and make known her love?'

This precisely predicts the compliant and obedient Katherina of
v.ii, who enters with the line: 'What is your will, sir, that you
send for me?' In the same way the Page, in Induction ii, says:

My husband and my lord, my lord and husband;
I am your wife in all obedience.

And this pre-echoes Katherina's phraseology:

Thy husband is thy lord, thy life, thy keeper,
Thy head, thy sovereign. . . .

The analogies are too close and too numerous for coincidence or
accident. Shakespeare clearly intended the comic incidents of the
Induction to throw a forward light on the main play's concern
with the development of love in marriage.

But the technique of parody is not confined to the Induction.
Petruchio's arrival at his wedding, fantastically dressed, is a
deliberate parody of the bridegroom's approach. The uneaten
feast, in iv.i, is a parody of the wedding breakfast, and the night
spent in fasting and watching, with Petruchio 'Making a sermon
of continency to her', is a travesty of the wedding night. The
purpose of parody in the play is to illuminate by distortion the
true lineaments of love, by imbalance to suggest balance, by
impersonation to propose the truth of nature, by comic exaggera-
tion to seek out the lovers' real estimate of one another.

Realism[1] adds a second dimension to the presentation of love.
In *The Shrew* there are neither seductions nor adulteries, love is
indissolubly linked with marriage, and marriage with money.
John Russell Brown,[2] after examining *Errors*, turns to *The Shrew*
and says:

In this play love and commerce are brought closer together.
Petruchio, as he determines to woo Baptista's elder daughter
Katharina, blatantly identifies the two:

1. In using this vexed critical term I intend no more than 'a powerful illusion
of actuality, a sense of conformity to real life'.
2. John Russell Brown, *Shakespeare and his Comedies* (1957), pp. 57–8; see also
pp. 94–9.

> *I come to wive it* wealthily *in Padua*;
> *If* wealthily, *then happily in Padua.*

Grumio immediately and brutally underscores Petruchio's statement: 'Why, give him gold enough and marry him to a puppet or an aglet-baby, or an old trot with ne'er a tooth in her head.' Hortensio maintains the commercial imagery in describing his love for Bianca:

> For in Baptista's keep my treasure is.
> He hath the jewel of my life in hold.

In the following scene the exchange between Baptista and Tranio sets the scene for the 'auction' of Bianca in appropriately mercantile terms:

> *Bap.* Faith, gentlemen, now I play a merchant's part,
>   And venture madly on a desperate mart.
> *Tra.* 'Twas a commodity lay fretting by you,
>   'Twill bring you gain, or perish on the seas.

The 'auction' itself, with its catalogues of plate and gold, Tyrian tapestry, ivory coffers, cypress chests, apparel, tents, canopies, and the like, may appear fantastic to modern sensibilities, and it is certainly comic, since the audience knows that Tranio has no title whatever to the wealth he bids, but it would not have seemed very odd to the Elizabethans. Marriages depended upon satisfactory contracts being agreed between the participating families. A manuscript in the Shakespeare Centre, Stratford-upon-Avon (Shakespeare's Birthplace Record Office, Willoughby de Brooke Collection, DR 98/1027A) records 'Articles of agreament Indented hadd and made betweene Elianor Peyto widowe . . . And William Jeffes of Walton', dated '20 May, 10 James I', in which William agrees to marry Elinor 'before the feast of St John Baptist next ensuinge'. In consideration of this marriage the said William Jeffes to the intent 'that he may haue possesse & enioye . . . all the goodes chattels cattles household stuffe money & plate wch shee the said Elianor hath or claimeth to haue as administratrix to the said William Peyto hir late husband', and that he may 'quietly & peaceably likewise haue hold possesse & enioy all such landes tenementes pastures meadowes groundes comons & comodities whatsoeuer' which William Peyto in his lifetime conveyed to Elinor, seals and delivers 'Six seuerall obligacions . . . in the seuerall sommes in such obligacions appearinge'. These obligations amount to some £3000 in all, and so Elinor agrees to make an absolute deed of gift of all her goods and chattels to

Jeffes before they marry. Such a marriage contract is typical of thousands in Shakespeare's day, and the original audience of *The Shrew* would have seen nothing strange in hard bargaining over money and domestic possessions before a marriage. In *The Shrew*, as nowhere else, Shakespeare roots his presentation of romantic love in the rich soil of finance.

If the fiscal background to courtship is strongly presented in the first part of the play, the domestic realities of the married state are made crystal clear in Acts IV and V. The first three Acts offer only a sketchy outline of Baptista's household. It is true, as Bradbrook says,[1] 'Katherine is the first shrew to be given a father, the first to be shewn as maid and bride; she is not seen merely in relation to a husband.' But, like almost all the heroines of Shakespearean comedy, she is not shown to have a mother. Baptista is a rich merchant who has two daughters. Beyond this, we know nothing of him. The domestic dimension does not appear until IV.i, with Grumio's arrival at Petruchio's house, but this scene marks a turning-point in the play, with its insistence on the daily duties and drudgeries of domestic life, a life into which Katherina is pitched as precipitately as she had been pitched from her horse on her journey (IV.i.65–6). It is a world with servants concerned with practical household tasks: there are fires to be lit, the cook to be enquired after, and Grumio asks:

> Is supper ready, the house trimmed, rushes strewed, cobwebs swept, the serving men in their new fustian, their white stockings, and every officer his wedding-garment on? Be the Jacks fair within, the Jills fair without, the carpets laid, and everything in order?

This realistic presentation of the details of everyday living is maintained in Petruchio's concern for his boots, his spaniel, his slippers and his supper, and (in IV.iii) with the cut, colour, fashion and material of Katherina's dress. Realism depends upon the convincing evocation of relevant detail, and the last two Acts are full of such things. In a different key it even enters into the plotting between Lucentio and Biondello in IV.iv, where Biondello, with superb irrelevance, says: 'I cannot tarry. I knew a wench married in an afternoon as she went to the garden for parsley to stuff a rabbit.' It is this constant presence, throughout the play, of concrete, unromantic detail about love and marriage —whether it be dowries or marriage contracts, pots, pans or parsley—which creates the strong sense of actuality. As Hibbard

1. Bradbrook, op. cit., p. 139.

has said:[1] '*The Taming of the Shrew*, unlike most of Shakespeare's other comedies—the nearest to it in this respect is *All's Well that Ends Well*—deals with marriage as it really was in the England that he knew.'

The idea that *The Shrew* is in any sense a farce derives less from the text than from the history of that text in the theatre. As we have seen (pp. 91–9), Worsdale's *A Cure for a Scold* and Bullock's *The Cobler of Preston* are farces derived from parts of Shakespeare's play, and Kemble's adaptation of Garrick's version of the play is responsible for popularizing the 'whip-cracking' Petruchio and sacrificing everything to vigorous, knockabout stage action. But the essence of farce is the dramatist's intention to provoke laughter in his audience, and laughter is by no means our dominant response when watching or reading *The Shrew*. Anne Barton's estimate is judicious:[2]

> There are undeniable elements of farce in the Katherina/ Petruchio plot, as well as a robust glee in that age-old motif of the battle between the sexes which Shakespeare does, at moments in the play, exploit for its own, eminently theatrical, sake.

The elements of farce are 'eminently theatrical', no doubt, but they occur only 'at moments in the play'. Apart from the opening exchanges between Sly and the Hostess the two scenes of the Induction are not farcical. Neither is the opening scene of the main play. Knockabout begins in 1.ii, with Petruchio wringing Grumio by the ears, and by then the other tones of the play have been firmly set. It is continued with Katherina's assault on her sister in the following scene, but, far from developing, it is thereafter subtly controlled and diminished. In the same scene, Katherina's attack on Hortensio with her lute takes place offstage, and the battle between Katherina and Petruchio is conducted verbally until the crucial moment when 'She strikes him', and he replies: 'I swear I'll cuff you, if you strike again.' Katherina backs down, faced (and outfaced) by the utterly serious prospect of superior physical strength. This is a point of inner and lesser climax in the play. From this moment on it becomes clear that the traditional methods of shrew-taming are not going to be used, and the traditional methods, the 'Punch and Judy' methods, are matter of farce.

Farce is not exploited, but transcended. Nevertheless, the basic

1. Hibbard, p. 30.
2. Anne Barton, Introduction to *The Taming of the Shrew* (Riverside edn, Boston, 1974), p. 107.

situations and techniques of farce remain. Petruchio's entry to his wedding, fantastically attired, would be farcical if it were not obvious that he is playing the fantastic in order to teach Katherina how inappropriate is her approach to marriage. Similarly, when he abuses and beats his servants in IV.i, and throws the food around the room, he is employing farcical methods to teach his new wife the true order of domesticity. Even this is subdued in the Tailor and Haberdasher scene (IV.iii), where the lesson continues, though no one is beaten and the only abuse is verbal. The relationship between Petruchio and Katherina is too serious, too delicate, for farce, and the play's strongest strain of farce is reserved for the association of master and servant between Petruchio and Grumio. This obviously has its source in the beatings regularly inflicted on the clumsy or impertinent *zanni* in Italian comedy, and the knockabout, verbal abuse and jest, and the general low comedy which opens IV.i clearly derive from this tradition. It is not surprising that Lacey's farcical adaptation *Sauny the Scott* (see pp. 89–91) is centrally concerned with developing the comic possibilities in the character of Grumio. Love and marriage, in *The Shrew*, are too important to be presented as farce.

Romantic love is a presence in the play from beginning to end, and it functions as a kind of prolonged and delicious illusion, sustained in the face of a plethora of contrary facts. Not the least of the achievements of Shakespeare's dramaturgy is the way in which he interweaves the passion of Lucentio for Bianca with the Katherina–Petruchio plot. Nothing could be more patently Petrarchan than Lucentio's confession of love at first sight in I.i:

> Tranio, I burn, I pine, I perish, Tranio,
> If I achieve not this young modest girl. . . .
> Tranio, I saw her coral lips to move,
> And with her breath she did perfume the air.
> Sacred and sweet was all I saw in her. . . .
> And let me be a slave, t'achieve that maid
> Whose sudden sight hath thrall'd my wounded eye.

Through all the disguises and deceptions of the lovers' plot he maintains this tone, and at the dénouement in V.i he is still singing in the same key:

> Love wrought these miracles. Bianca's love
> Made me exchange my state with Tranio,
> While he did bear my countenance in the town,
> And happily I have arriv'd at the last
> Unto the wished haven of my bliss.

It is not until he loses the wager in v.ii that Lucentio is unde-
ceived, and even then he is let down easily, with little more than
a grumble:

> The wisdom of your duty, fair Bianca,
> Hath cost me a hundred crowns since supper-time.

Romantic love is allowed full weight in the play. It is not mocked.
It is seen as the source of endless ingenuity, invention and
youthful exuberance. It invites adventure and collusion: 'Here's
no knavery. See, to beguile the old folks, how the young folks lay
their heads together.' But the illusions and delusions of romantic
love are seen as essentially a young man's passion. One thinks of
Petruchio as somehow *older* than the other characters. When he
became a man he put away the adolescent fantasies of romance,
and learned to see his mistress not through a glass, darkly, but
face to face. And, by contrast with Lucentio's romanticism, this
makes his few, hard-won moments of tenderness all the more
moving and convincing. At the end of v.i he demands a kiss from
Katherina in the middle of the public street (see p. 128). After
some demur, she kisses him, and he says:

> Is not this well? Come, my sweet Kate.
> Better once than never, for never too late.

'Is not this well?' establishes, in one brief question, a mutuality,
a gentle and loving concern for union which shows that the
teaching is over, the pupil has graduated, and all that is left is love.

The last scene of the play marks the climax of its exploration
of the theme of love and marriage, and this scene has given rise
to more differences of interpretation than anything else in the
play. The earliest adaptations were uneasy with it. Lacey's *Sauny
the Scott*, though vastly more brutal than Shakespeare's play,
omits Katherina's 'obedience' speech entirely, and the same is
true of Worsdale's *A Cure for a Scold*. As we have seen (p. 95),
Garrick's *Catharine and Petruchio* distributes the 'obedience' speech
between Petruchio and his wife, presumably on the grounds that
what Shakespeare wrote represented an unacceptable presentation of marriage at the end of a comedy, and Garrick's judgement
held the stage until Shakespeare's text was reinstated in the nineteenth century. But the restoration of the text meant the restoration of the problem. What was taken to be the abject and un-
conditional surrender, in public, of the 'tamed', broken-spirited
wife was uncomfortable to the male self-esteem of the Victorian
or Edwardian gentleman. Though he might, privately, most

powerfully and potently believe it, yet he held it not honesty to have it thus set down. Shaw was offended:[1] 'the last scene is altogether disgusting to modern sensibility'. Sir Arthur Quiller-Couch was embarrassed:[2]

> the whole Petruchio business . . . may seem, with its noise of whip-cracking, scoldings, its throwing about of cooked food, and its general playing of 'the Devil amongst the Tailors', tiresome—and to any modern woman, not an antiquary, offensive as well.

Later in the twentieth century the robustly feminist view of the final scene as essentially an ironic performance by Katherina was first and most strongly argued by Margaret Webster,[3] but perhaps most persuasively expressed by Harold C. Goddard:[4]

> the play ends with the prospect that Kate is going to be more nearly the tamer than the tamed, Petruchio more nearly the tamed than the tamer, though his wife naturally will keep the true situation under cover. So taken, the play is an early version of *What Every Woman Knows*—what every woman knows being, of course, that the woman can lord it over the man so long as she allows him to think he is lording it over her. This interpretation has the advantage of bringing the play into line with all the other Comedies in which Shakespeare gives a distinct edge to his heroine. Otherwise it is an unaccountable exception and regresses to the wholly un-Shakespearean doctrine of male superiority, a view which there is not the slightest evidence elsewhere Shakespeare ever held.

More recent critics have seen it as part of Petruchio's wooing dance,[5] an example of 'the Games People Play',[6] or even as Petruchio's reward,[7] and it is not surprising, in the light of the recent importance of feminist studies, that this final scene should be the subject of critical dispute.

There can be no question but that the 'obedience' speech is

1. *Shaw on Shakespeare*, ed. Edwin Wilson (1961; reprinted Penguin, 1969), p. 198.

2. NCS, p. xvi.

3. Margaret Webster, *Shakespeare Without Tears* (New York, 1942), p. 142.

4. *The Meaning of Shakespeare* (Chicago, 1951), vol. 1, pp. 68ff.

5. Michael West, 'The Folk Background of Petruchio's Wooing Dance: Male Supremacy in *The Taming of the Shrew*', *Shakespeare Studies* (1974).

6. Ralph Berry, *Shakespeare's Comedies* (Princeton, 1972), p. 7.

7. Germaine Greer, *The Female Eunuch* (New York, 1971), pp. 220–1.

meant to be a final statement on the subject of love and marriage.[1]
It is forty-four lines long, and only ten lines after it the play is
finished. It is a great set piece and no one challenges it. So it is
important to be quite clear what Katherina says, and what
implications her words would have had for the play's original
audience.

She begins by rebuking the Widow for darting scornful glances
designed 'To wound thy lord, thy king, thy governor'. Straight
away this establishes her argument on the basis of degree, status
in 'the chain of being', and this is one theory which Shakespeare
endorses totally from the first scene of *1 Henry VI* to *The Tempest*,
where it is the principle which disqualifies Caliban's claim that
'This island's mine'.[2] When Ulysses, in *Troilus and Cressida*, I.iii,
enunciates the theory at length he is simply establishing the norm
from which the Greek army has declined with such disastrous
results. What has been called 'the Elizabethan world picture'
asserted a hierarchy, a series of correspondences, which descended
from God to inanimate nature, and on this ladder a wife stands
one rung lower than a husband. Katherina's speech accepts this,
and reiterates it:

> Thy husband is thy lord, thy life, thy keeper,
> Thy head, thy sovereign.

As the lord is to the servant, as the head is to the body, as the
sovereign is to the subject, so is the husband to the wife. Katherina
goes on to emphasize the benefits which accrue to accepting your
place in the hierarchy of degree. When you accept your status
you enter into the enjoyment of its rights and privileges; a dutiful
wife may lie 'warm at home, secure and safe' for no other tribute
than 'love, fair looks, and true obedience'. It cannot be too
strongly stressed that this does not make a husband into some
kind of 'lord of creation'. Katherina states the relationship with
perfect clarity:

> Such duty as the subject owes the prince
> Even such a woman oweth to her husband.

The wife is vassal to the husband, the husband is vassal to the
prince, the prince is vassal to God, the only Lord of Creation. If
a wife denies her duty to her husband, if she is not 'obedient to his
honest will', Katherina has very strong words for her:

1. See Ruth Nevo, *Comic Transformations in Shakespeare* (1980), esp. p. 50.
2. See *The Tempest*, ed. Kermode (Arden edn, 1954), pp. xxxivff.

> What is she but a foul contending rebel,
> And graceless traitor to her loving lord.

Shakespeare's audience would have seen the heads of rebels exposed in public places; they would have heard in their parish churches the Homily Against Wilful Rebellion. 'Graceless' meant not only 'unpleasing' but 'lacking the grace of God'. In emphasizing a wife's duty 'to serve, love, and obey' Katherina clearly alludes to the well-known phraseology of the Book of Common Prayer, where, in the Marriage Service, the priest says to the woman: 'Wilt thou obey him, and serue him, loue, honor, and kepe him in sickenes and in health?'[1] Even Katherina's reference to woman's comparative physical weakness finds an echo in so impeccably orthodox and familiar a source as the Homily 'Of the State of Matrimonie', first published in the *Second Book of Homilies* (1563):

> For the woman is a weake creature, not indued with like strength and constancy of minde, therefore they bee the sooner disquieted, and they bee the more prone to all weake affections and dispositions of minde, more then men bee, and lighter they bee, and more vaine in their fantisies and opinions.[2]

The 'obedience' speech, taken as a whole, is completely in accord with normal Elizabethan opinion on the rights and status of wives. This opinion assumed, as we do not, that a wife was inferior in degree to her husband, and owed him submission and obedience which he repaid with protection and maintenance. For this opinion there was the authority of Holy Writ: 'Wives, submit yourselves unto your own husbands, as unto the Lord. For the husband is the head of the wife, even as Christ is the head of the church.'[3] The speech is rooted and grounded in well-known, sacred and serious expressions of the duty of wives. Shakespeare cannot possibly have intended it to be spoken ironically.

So the great final speech of *The Shrew* is a solemn affirmation of the great commonplace. The play's exploration of the theme of love and marriage comes to rest in that. But there is more to

1. In 'The Forme of Solemnizacion of Matrimonie', *The First & Second Prayer-Books of Edward VI* (Everyman's Library, 1910), p. 253.
2. Quoted in Helen Gardner, *The Business of Criticism* (Oxford, 1959), p. 71, in the context of a discussion of Donne's 'Air and Angels'. This poem, and the recent extensive critical debate about it (see *The Elegies and The Songs and Sonnets of John Donne*, ed. Gardner (Oxford, 1965), pp. 75 and 205) are very relevant to any full understanding of Katherina's final speech.
3. Ephesians, v. 22–3.

this final scene than one speech, and Shakespeare's dramaturgy personalizes what Katherina expresses generally. The real irony lies in the context. We, the audience, know from the last lines of v.i that Katherina and Petruchio have made their peace, and that she is in love with him as he is with her. Act v, scene ii opens with a wit-bout in which Petruchio attacks the Widow and Katherina surreptitiously comes to his aid. The alliance between them is, to the audience, another example of their developing trust, though to the other characters on stage it shows no more than the 'shrewish' Katherina acting aggressively to another woman, just as she had to her sister in II.i. Petruchio supports his wife, 'A hundred marks, my Kate does put her down', honouring the new alliance, but betraying nothing of it to the other characters. When the women withdraw the men agree upon the wager. It is important to note the terms in which Petruchio proposes it:

> ... he whose wife is most obedient,
> To come at first when he doth send for her,
> Shall win. ...

It is to be a simple test of obedience, nothing more. There is a continuing flicker of irony in Petruchio's comment on the amount of the wager:

> I'll venture so much of my hawk or hound,
> But twenty times so much upon my wife.

It hints that the falconer's training, the manning and the coming to the lure, forms the basis for his confidence. Nevertheless, he is taking a risk, he is giving his wife the freedom to humiliate him if she chooses to do so. The three women are together off-stage, 'conferring by the parlour fire', and so Katherina has ample opportunity to see what the game is, as Biondello summons first Bianca and then the Widow. When Grumio comes for her she obeys her husband's command, but it is no cowed, broken-spirited compliance, but a duty which she does and a gift which she offers freely. It is a gift which Petruchio values highly because, as Germaine Greer has pointed out:[1] 'The submission of a woman like Kate is genuine and exciting because she has something to lay down, her virgin pride and individuality.' With the stage-direction 'Enter Katherina' the test is over, the suspense is lifted, the wager is won, and the love relationship triumphs. As Anne Barton puts it:[2]

1. Greer, op. cit., p. 221.
2. Anne Barton (Riverside edn, Boston, 1974), p. 106.

What Petruchio wants, and ends up with, is a Katherina of unbroken spirit and gaiety who has suffered only minor physical discomfort and who has learned the value of self-control and of caring about someone other than herself.

What follows may *appear* to be a stern continuation of the testing and humiliation, but it is in fact a willing 'display' by Katherina in response to a series of coded messages from her husband, which have a secret meaning for the two of them alone. Petruchio enquires after the Widow and Bianca, and instructs Katherina to 'fetch them hither'. But he adds: 'If they deny to come, / Swinge me them soundly forth unto their husbands.' In other words, he offers her the chance to use physical violence on the Widow who has insulted her, and the sly and shrewish sister she has been itching to beat since Act II. And it would all be legitimate, praiseworthy and 'obedient'. Katherina sees and appreciates the clever, generous point he makes. When she returns with the 'froward wives' Petruchio makes what looks like an impossibly humiliating demand:

> Katherine, that cap of yours becomes you not.
> Off with that bauble, throw it under foot.

The audience, and Katherina, recall the episode with the Haberdasher in IV.iii, when, in her unregenerate state, she stubbornly insisted on keeping the cap, and Petruchio refused to allow her to do so because she was wild:

> *Kath.* I'll have no bigger. This doth fit the time,
>   And gentlewomen wear such caps as these.
> *Pet.* When you are gentle, you shall have one too,
>   And not till then.

Now she has learned the pointlessness of such selfish stubbornness, and the gesture of throwing down her cap when told to do so has a deeper, private meaning for the two participants, the shared secret bringing them closer together. Petruchio's third order to his wife is the most subtly and brilliantly phrased of all:

> Katherine, I charge thee, tell these headstrong women
> What duty they do owe their lords and husbands.

He does not say 'Tell the assembled company what duty *you* owe your husband', nor does he say 'Rehearse the duties of wives to husbands'. He deliberately abstains from humiliating her in any way. He offers her the opportunity publicly to instruct her cunning little sister and the Widow who has been insulting her in their marital duties. He offers her a position of superiority from which to lecture. And the tiny exchange before she begins permits Petruchio covertly to direct his wife's performance even more carefully:

> *Wid.* Come, come, you're mocking. We will have no telling.
> *Pet.* Come on, I say, and first begin with her.
> *Wid.* She shall not.
> *Pet.* I say she shall. And first begin with her.

The angry Widow is pointed out as the target for the regenerate shrew, and Katherina can begin with a just rebuke: 'Fie, fie!' The particular form of Petruchio's command, 'tell these headstrong women', allows Katherina to avoid any reference to her own changed state. She does not have to say anything about her relationship with her own husband. She is permitted and encouraged to take refuge in the most bland and incontrovertible generalities—'What duty they do owe'.

She is grateful for the delicate way in which he has handled the situation. And she expresses her gratitude in the full and expansive exposition she gives not only of the duty of the Widow to Hortensio, but the duty of all wives to their husbands. She gives more than Petruchio asked. She gives full measure, pressed down, shaken together, and running over. And she ends by doing something that was never required of her. She refers openly to her own situation, 'My mind hath been as big as one of yours', and to her own change of heart: 'But now I see our lances are but straws.' Finally, and quite gratuitously, she offers a public gesture of subservience freely and unasked:

> place your hands below your husband's foot.
> In token of which duty, if he please,
> My hand is ready, may it do him ease.

Petruchio responds to this unsolicited act of love and generosity with one of the most moving and perfect lines in the play, almost as if he is lost for words, taking refuge in action: 'Why, there's a wench! Come on, and kiss me, Kate.' I believe that any actor striving to represent Petruchio's feelings at this moment in the play should show him as perilously close to tears, tears of pride, and gratitude, and love.

THE TAMING OF THE SHREW

DRAMATIS PERSONÆ

INDUCTION

CHRISTOPHER SLY, a Tinker.
Hostess.
A Lord.
Page, Huntsmen, and Servants attending on the Lord.
A company of Players.

THE TAMING OF THE SHREW

BAPTISTA MINOLA, *a rich citizen of Padua.*
KATHERINA, *the Shrew, elder daughter of Baptista.*
PETRUCHIO, *a gentleman of Verona, suitor to Katherina.*
GRUMIO, *Petruchio's personal servant.*
CURTIS, *Petruchio's chief servant at his country house.*
A Tailor.
A Haberdasher.
Five other servants of Petruchio.

BIANCA, *younger daughter of Baptista.*
GREMIO, *rich old citizen of Padua, suitor to Bianca.*
HORTENSIO, *a gentleman of Padua, suitor to Bianca.*
LUCENTIO, *a gentleman of Pisa, suitor to Bianca.*
TRANIO, *personal servant to Lucentio.*
BIONDELLO, *servant to Lucentio.*
VINCENTIO, *rich citizen of Pisa, father of Lucentio.*
A Pedant of Mantua.
A Widow.
Servants attending on Baptista.

Note. The list of characters is first given in Rowe, though this does not include Curtis, who is added in Capell. The name Petruchio must be pronounced with the 'ch' as in English 'much'; never as 'Petrukkio'.

THE TAMING OF THE SHREW

INDUCTION

SCENE I

Enter CHRISTOPHER SLY *and the* HOSTESS.

Sly. I'll feeze you, in faith.
Host. A pair of stocks, you rogue.
Sly. Y'are a baggage, the Slys are no rogues. Look in the
Chronicles, we came in with Richard Conqueror.
Therefore *paucas pallabris*, let the world slide. Sessa!   5

INDUCTION SCENE 1] *Pope; Actus primus. Scoena Prima. F.*   S.D. *Enter . . .*
Hostess.] *This edn; Enter Begger and Hostes, Christophero Sly. F.*   1. *Sly.*] *Rowe;*
Begger. F (Beg. throughout Induction).

Induction] This is the only play in
which Shakespeare uses an induction,
though the device was common in
plays written around 1590. The most
famous examples are in Kyd's *The
Spanish Tragedy* (to which Sly refers)
and Peele's *The Old Wives' Tale*. The
Induction is in two distinct scenes,
though they are not distinguished in
F, the first set outside an alehouse, the
second in a large country house.

S.D.] Both here and in all speech-
prefixes F describes Sly as 'Begger'.
He is in fact a tinker, but the distinction was not sharp. F's 'Christophero
Sly' is obviously an addition, derived
from Ind. ii. 5, and possibly made by
the prompter. The 'Hostess' is referred
to as 'boy' in l. 12, and the S.D. in
A Shrew (Bullough, *Narrative and
Dramatic Sources*, I. 69) reads 'Enter a
Tapster, beating out of his doores Slie
Droonken', which suggests that, at some
point, the part may have been played
by a man.

1. *feeze*] 'do for', beat, flog (*OED*,
feeze, *v.* 3. a and b, quoting *Shr.*).

The word, spelt 'pheeze' in F and
commonly by editors, originally meant
'to drive off, put to flight, frighten
away', but it developed a more abus-
ive sense in proverbial usage. Tilley,
Dictionary of the Proverbs in England,
V22, 'I will vease thee'; cf. *Troil.*,
II. iii. 200. 'Feeze' provides the first
of the comparatively few points of
direct verbal contact between *Shr.* and
A Shrew, which reads 'Ile fese you
anon'.

4. *Richard Conqueror*] Sly confuses
Richard Coeur-de-Lion with William
the Conqueror. 'He came in with the
Conqueror' was a proverbial phrase
(Tilley, C594; F. P. Wilson, *Shakespearian and other Studies*, p. 160). Sly's
drunken tongue is rich in proverbs
and garbled erudition.

5. *paucas pallabris*] a corruption
of the Spanish *pocas palabras*, few
words. Cf. *Spanish Tragedy*, III. xiv. 118,
'Pocas Palabras, mild as the Lamb';
Ado, III. v. 16.

let the world slide] let the world go by.
Cf. Tilley, W879, which quotes Sly's

Host. You will not pay for the glasses you have burst?

Sly. No, not a denier. Go by, Saint Jeronimy, go to thy
     cold bed and warm thee.

Host. I know my remedy, I must go fetch the third-
     borough.   [*Exit.*]   10

Sly. Third, or fourth, or fifth borough, I'll answer him
     by law. I'll not budge an inch, boy. Let him come,
     and kindly.   *Falls asleep.*

Wind horns. Enter a LORD *from hunting, with his* Train.

Lord. Huntsman, I charge thee, tender well my hounds.
     Breathe Merriman, the poor cur is emboss'd,   15

7. Go by,] *Theobald;* go by *F.*   Saint] *F* (S.), *Dyce.*   9–10. thirdborough]
Theobald; Head-/borough *F.*   10. S.D.] *Rowe; not in F.*   15. Breathe]
Sisson; Brach *F;* Leech *Hanmer;* Trash *Dyce;* Broach *NCS.*

very similar phrase at Ind. ii. 142;
Cotgrave, *A Dictionary of the French and
English Tongues* (1611), s.v. Chargé,
'To take no thought, passe the time
merrily, let the world slide'.

   Sessa] From this and other contexts
it would seem to mean something like
'Off you go'. *OED* says 'An exclamation of uncertain meaning', quoting this line in *Shr.* and Edgar's two
uses of the word in *Lr* (III. iv. 98 and
III. vi. 72), where the sense requires
an incitement to speed. Other editors
have conjectured variously: Bond
compares German *sasa*, Theobald
understands it as 'Cessa' (Spanish),
'be quiet', and Halliwell suggests
French 'cessez', 'cease'. 'C'est ça' has
also been suggested (*N&Q* (1952),
p. 393, and answer on p. 437).

   6. *burst*] broken (*OED*, Burst, *v.* 7,
'To break, snap, shatter', quoting
Marlowe, *2 Tamburlaine*, v. i. 71,
'Whose chariot-wheels have burst the
Assyrians' bones').

   7. *denier*] a French coin, one-
twelfth of a sou. Cf. *R3*, I. ii. 251.

   Go by, Saint Jeronimy] Sly, confusing
Hieronimo with St Jerome (Latin
Hieronymus), misquotes *Spanish
Tragedy*, III. xii. 31, '*Hieronimo*, beware;
go by, go by'. The phrase was widely

quoted in Elizabethan drama to sug-
gest impatient dismissal of something
disagreeable. Cf. Beaumont and
Fletcher, *The Captain*, III. v. 38, and
Jonson, *Every Man in his Humour*,
I. iv. 49.

   7–8. go . . . *thee*] Exactly these
words are used by Edgar in *Lr* (Q1),
III. iv. 46–7, the F text omitting the
word 'cold'. Edgar is on the heath,
disguised as Poor Tom, and the settings are similar, so the phrase may
have been traditionally associated
with vagrancy.

   9–10. *thirdborough*] the petty con-
stable of a township or manor (*OED*).
F's 'Headborough' means the same
thing, but the emendation is called
for by Sly's response. Bond quotes
Dalton's *Countrey Justice* (1620): 'There
be officers of much like authority to
our constables, as the borsholders in
Kent, the thirdborow in Warwickshire, and the tythingman and bur-
rowhead or headborow, or chief-
pledge in other places.'

   12. *I'll . . . inch*] proverbial
(Tilley, I52).

   15. *Breathe*] Sisson's emendation
(*New Readings in Shakespeare*, I. 159)
is preferred because, although sense
can be made of F's reading, the

And couple Clowder with the deep-mouth'd brach.
Saw'st thou not, boy, how Silver made it good
At the hedge corner, in the coldest fault?
I would not lose the dog for twenty pound.

First Hun. Why, Belman is as good as he, my lord.   20
He cried upon it at the merest loss,
And twice today pick'd out the dullest scent.
Trust me, I take him for the better dog.

Lord. Thou art a fool. If Echo were as fleet,
I would esteem him worth a dozen such.   25
But sup them well, and look unto them all.
Tomorrow I intend to hunt again.

First Hun. I will, my lord.

Lord. What's here? One dead, or drunk? See, doth he
breathe?

Sec. Hun. He breathes, my lord. Were he not warm'd with ale,
This were a bed but cold to sleep so soundly.   31

Lord. O monstrous beast, how like a swine he lies!
Grim death, how foul and loathsome is thine image!

20, 28. *First Hun.*] *Capell; Hunts. F.*   30–1.] *as verse, Rowe; as prose, F.*

---

sentence seems to require a verb not a noun here, Merriman is an odd name for a brach (i.e. a *bitch*-hound), and in ll. 15–16 the Lord is instructing his huntsman *how* to tender his hounds. F's 'Brach' could easily be a misreading of 'Breath' in the MS. Sisson adds: 'I suggest further that the two lines now go together very closely, if poor Merriman had been coupled or leashed with "the deep-mouthed brach", a thruster and a stayer (as deep-mouthed hounds were), and was now to be 'breathed' while Clowder took his place in leash with the brach.'

emboss'd] exhausted, foaming at the mouth. The word originally referred to the quarry, who took shelter in a wood (bois) when exhausted. But it came to mean 'foaming, beaded with sweat', as if from 'emboss', to raise protuberances (*OED*). Cf. D. H. Madden, *The Diary of Master William

Silence (1897), pp. 37, 55.

18. *hedge corner*] 'This lord, as the "hedge-corner" seems to indicate, had been hunting the hare' (*Shakespeare's England*, II. 349).

the coldest fault] A 'fault' is a break in the scent, and, strictly, it is the scent not the fault which is 'cold'. But the phrase had become a common hunting expression, and NCS quotes *Ven.*, 691–4, where the hare runs among sheep or conies: 'For there his smell with others being mingled,/The hot scent-snuffing hounds are driven to doubt,/Ceasing their clamorous cry till they have singled/With much ado the cold fault cleanly out.'

21. *cried . . . loss*] gave tongue when the scent was utterly lost. This is Shakespeare's only use of 'merest', meaning 'completely'.

33. *image*] counterpart, copy, likeness (Onions, 3).

Sirs, I will practise on this drunken man.
What think you, if he were convey'd to bed,   35
Wrapp'd in sweet clothes, rings put upon his fingers,
A most delicious banquet by his bed,
And brave attendants near him when he wakes,
Would not the beggar then forget himself?
First Hun. Believe me, lord, I think he cannot choose.   40
Sec. Hun. It would seem strange unto him when he wak'd.
Lord. Even as a flatt'ring dream or worthless fancy.
Then take him up, and manage well the jest.
Carry him gently to my fairest chamber,
And hang it round with all my wanton pictures.   45
Balm his foul head in warm distilled waters,
And burn sweet wood to make the lodging sweet.
Procure me music ready when he wakes,
To make a dulcet and a heavenly sound.
And if he chance to speak, be ready straight   50
And with a low submissive reverence
Say 'What is it your honour will command?'
Let one attend him with a silver basin
Full of rose-water and bestrew'd with flowers,
Another bear the ewer, the third a diaper,   55
And say 'Will't please your lordship cool your hands?'
Some one be ready with a costly suit,
And ask him what apparel he will wear.
Another tell him of his hounds and horse,
And that his lady mourns at his disease.   60
Persuade him that he hath been lunatic,

---

37. *banquet*] not necessarily 'a feast, a sumptuous entertainment of food and drink' (*OED*, *sb.*¹ 1). Shakespeare, in view of the 'sack' and 'conserves' mentioned at the opening of Ind. ii, may have intended 'a course of sweetmeats, fruit and wine, served either as a separate entertainment, or as a continuation of the principal meal' (*OED*, *sb.*¹ 3). *Shr.* is much concerned with food and meals or the lack of them. Cf. S.D.

opening v. ii.

38. *brave*] finely arrayed. Cf. *Pilgr.*, xii. 4, 'Youth like summer brave, age like winter bare'. The sense survives in Scots 'braw'.

47. *burn sweet wood*] Juniper was commonly used. Cf. *Ado*, i. iii. 50, 'Being entertain'd for a perfumer, as I was smoking a musty room'.

48. *me*] for me (Abbott, *Shakespearian Grammar*, 220).

And when he says he is, say that he dreams,
For he is nothing but a mighty lord.
This do, and do it kindly, gentle sirs.
It will be pastime passing excellent,   65
If it be husbanded with modesty.

First Hun. My lord, I warrant you we will play our part
As he shall think by our true diligence
He is no less than what we say he is.

Lord. Take him up gently, and to bed with him,   70
And each one to his office when he wakes.
                    [*Sly is carried off.*] *Sound trumpets.*
Sirrah, go see what trumpet 'tis that sounds—
                                    [*Exit Servingman.*]
Belike some noble gentleman that means,
Travelling some journey, to repose him here.

                    Enter SERVINGMAN.

How now? Who is it?
Serv.   An't please your honour, players
That offer service to your lordship.   76
Lord. Bid them come near.

                    Enter PLAYERS.

                    Now, fellows, you are welcome.

62. is,] *F; is* Sly *Johnson.*   71. S.D. *Sly . . . off.*] *Theobald* (*subst.*); *not in F.*
72. S.D.] *Theobald; not in F.*   77. S.D.] *F* (*after l. 76*).

62. *And . . . is*] F's reading, retained here, contrasts 'hath been' in l. 61 with 'is' in l. 62, and makes acceptable sense. It also scans correctly, and the lines in the Lord's speech are very regular. But many editors feel the need to emend, and the most popular and persuasive suggestion has been Johnson's to supply 'Sly' after 'is', on the argument that F's compositor might easily have read 'Sly, say' in his copy as a repetition. The emendation receives support from the fact that in Ind. ii Sly does indeed make this play with his name. Against it must be noted that at this point in Scene i the Lord does not know Sly's

name. Sisson discounts this objection (*New Readings*, 1. 160), and NCS (1968 edn) accepts the emendation in its text, but argues against it in the Notes (p. 130).
64. *kindly*] convincingly, spontaneously (Onions, kindly, adv. 2).
66. *modesty*] moderation, i.e. so long as it is not overdone. Cf. *Caes.*, III. i. 214.
71. S.D. *Sound trumpets*] Greg notes (*SFF*, p. 213) that this is one of the stage-directions which may have been added by the book-keeper. In the text, the following line mentions only one trumpet.
77. *Now, fellows*] The Lord's attitude to the Players anticipates in

Players. We thank your honour.
Lord. Do you intend to stay with me tonight?
First Player. So please your lordship to accept our duty.   80
Lord. With all my heart. This fellow I remember
　　Since once he play'd a farmer's eldest son.
　　'Twas where you woo'd the gentlewoman so well.
　　I have forgot your name; but, sure, that part
　　Was aptly fitted and naturally perform'd.   85
Second Player. I think 'twas Soto that your honour means.

80. *First Player.*] *This edn; 2. Player. F.*　　86. *Second Player.*] *This edn; Sincklo. F;*
1. Play. Capell.

several respects Hamlet's welcome to
the actors at Elsinore. See *Ham.*, II. ii.

80. *So please*] F assigns this speech
to '2. *Player*', though no First Player
has yet been mentioned. It may be
that Shakespeare had the compliment
to Sincklo (see below) uppermost in
his mind.

81–5.] Editors have generally assumed that everything in this speech
after 'This fellow' is addressed to the
Second Player. Jean Robertson, in a
private letter incorporating her as yet
unpublished research, points out that,
since there is a group of players on the
stage, it is far more likely that the
Lord speaks successively to more than
one of them. If ll. 81–2 are addressed
to the Second Player, l. 83 to the
First Player, and ll. 84–5 to the
Second Player, the difficulty over the
text of *Women Pleased* (see below)
disappears.

86. *Soto*] F assigns this speech to
'*Sincklo*'. John Sincklo, or Sincler, was
a member of the King's company,
though he is not mentioned among
the 'Principall Actors' at the beginning of F. For Sincklo's appearance
see A. Gaw, *Anglia* (1926), 289.
The earliest reference is to him
as an actor in *The Second Part of the
Seven Deadly Sins*, acted about 1591
(see Chambers, *ES*, III. 496–7).
In the F text of *3H6* (III. i. 1) he
plays a keeper, in the Q (1600) of
2H4 he appears as a Beadle, and there

are several jokes about his thinness,
and he appears in his own person with
other actors in Webster's Induction to
Marston's *Malcontent* (1604). NCS
reports the opinion that he probably
played Lucentio in *Shr.*, Hibbard (ed.,
Taming of the Shrew, Penguin, 1968)
suggests that he may have played
Gremio, but Jean Robertson (see n. to
ll. 81–5) argues for Grumio, and suggests that Sincklo was a very small
man rather than a tall thin one (he is
compared to a viol da gamba in *The
Malcontent*, and Grumio makes several
jokes about his small stature in the
first 25 lines of *Shr.*, IV. i). Harold
Brooks does not believe he would have
played parts so extensive, arguing that
the evidence points to his being an
actor of 'bit parts' in which capital
could be made out of his sensational
appearance, and suggesting that in
Shr. he played this actor and the
Tailor—and possibly the woman's
tailor, Feeble, in *2H4*, the legitimate
Falconbridge in *John*, the Apothecary
in *Rom.*, and Starveling in *MND*.

Soto, 'a farmer's eldest son', appears in Fletcher's *Women Pleased*
(*c.* 1620), but does not woo a gentlewoman. This led NCS to propose that
the Lord must be referring to an
earlier scene which 'Fletcher dis-
pensed with on revision', But if l. 83
is addressed to the First Player, who
played Silvio, who wooed the gentlewoman Belvedere, in *Women Pleased*

Lord. 'Tis very true, thou didst it excellent.
　　　Well, you are come to me in happy time,
　　　The rather for I have some sport in hand
　　　Wherein your cunning can assist me much.　　　　　　90
　　　There is a lord will hear you play tonight;
　　　But I am doubtful of your modesties,
　　　Lest over-eyeing of his odd behaviour—
　　　For yet his honour never heard a play—
　　　You break into some merry passion　　　　　　95
　　　And so offend him; for I tell you, sirs,
　　　If you should smile, he grows impatient.
First Player. Fear not, my lord, we can contain ourselves,
　　　Were he the veriest antic in the world.
Lord. Go, sirrah, take them to the buttery,　　　　　　100
　　　And give them friendly welcome every one.
　　　Let them want nothing that my house affords.

　　　　　　　　　　　　　Exit one with the Players.

　　　Sirrah, go you to Barthol'mew my page,
　　　And see him dress'd in all suits like a lady.

98. *First Player.*] *Capell* (*subst.*); *Plai.* F.

there is no discrepancy between the Lord's account of the plot and Fletcher's play as we now have it (I owe this suggestion to Jean Robertson). Commenting on the date, G. E. Bentley says: '*Women Pleased* is a curiously ill-constructed play, with various elements which seem too old-fashioned for the latter part of Fletcher's career. . . . It seems to me that an original version by some other dramatist in the nineties is much more likely' (*Jacobean and Caroline Stage*, III. 432). This would be congruent with Sincklo's other recorded performances, and the compliment to him in *Shr.* would be pointless unless the audience could be assumed to have seen him fairly recently in the part of Soto.

88. *in happy time*] opportunely. Cf. *All's W.*, v. i. 6; *Caes.*, II. ii. 60; *Ham.*, v. ii. 198.

89. *The rather*] the more so.

90. *cunning*] art, skill (Onions, 2).

Cf. *H5*, v. ii. 148.

92. *modesties*] self-restraint.

93. *over-eyeing*] This is usually glossed as 'observing', 'casting an eye over' (Onions, p. 155), but the editors of the Bantam text (New York, 1967) suggest that Shakespeare uses the verb 'eye' much as we do in modern English, and 'over' to indicate excess in such forms as 'overbold', 'overdone' and 'overpay'. The Lord is warning the Players not against 'observing' but against eyeing excessively. Shakespeare's only other use of the word (*LLL*, IV. iii. 76) is clearly in the sense of 'observe, oversee', but the context in *Shr.* is certainly patient of the Bantam editors' gloss.

95. *merry passion*] fit of merriment. Cf. *MND*, v. i. 70; *John*, III. iii. 45–7.

99. *veriest antic*] most complete buffoon. Cf. *Ado*, III. i. 63.

104. *suits*] respects (with a pun on 'garments').

That done, conduct him to the drunkard's chamber,   105
And call him 'madam', do him obeisance.
Tell him from me, as he will win my love,
He bear himself with honourable action,
Such as he hath observ'd in noble ladies
Unto their lords, by them accomplished.   110
Such duty to the drunkard let him do,
With soft low tongue and lowly courtesy,
And say 'What is't your honour will command,
Wherein your lady and your humble wife
May show her duty and make known her love?'   115
And then with kind embracements, tempting kisses,
And with declining head into his bosom,
Bid him shed tears, as being overjoy'd
To see her noble lord restor'd to health,
Who for this seven years hath esteemed him   120
No better than a poor and loathsome beggar.
And if the boy have not a woman's gift
To rain a shower of commanded tears,
An onion will do well for such a shift,
Which in a napkin being close convey'd,   125

120. this] *F*; twice *Theobald*.

108. *bear . . . action*] comport himself like one of the nobility. Onions glosses 'action' as 'gesture, gesticulation', quoting this line in *Shr.*, and comparing *Caes.*, III. ii. 221: 'For I have neither wit, nor words, nor worth,/Action, nor utterance, nor the power of speech . . .'; this obviously uses 'action' in the sense of 'gesture', but the context in *Shr.* clearly requires the more extended sense of 'deportment'.

110. *accomplished*] performed.

112. *low*] gentle, not loud, the opposite of shrill. Cf. *Ant.*, III. iii. 12, 'Is she shrill-tongu'd or low?' Lear commends this quality of voice in Cordelia (*Lr*, v. iii. 272–3): 'Her voice was ever soft,/Gentle, and low—an excellent thing in woman.'

courtesy] curtsy (*OED*, *sb*. 8).

113–15. *What . . . love*] In its formal

syntax this is like Olivia's question to the Duke in *Tw.N.*, v. i. 95–6: 'What would my lord, but that he may not have,/Wherein Olivia may seem serviceable?'

117. *with . . . bosom*] This could mean either 'leaning upon his (Sly's) breast', or 'hanging his head'. The pronoun is ambiguous but the latter reading is preferable.

120. *seven years*] 'a long period' (Onions; cf. *1H4*, II. iv. 302). Proverbial (Tilley, Y25; other examples in Smith and Wilson, *Oxford Dictionary of English Proverbs*).

esteemed him] considered himself.

124. *An onion*] 'the tears live in an onion that should water this sorrow' (*Ant.*, I. ii. 166; cf. Tilley, O67).

shift] stratagem, contrivance (Onions, 2). Cf. *Err.*, III. ii. 180.

125. *close convey'd*] secretly carried.

Shall in despite enforce a watery eye.
See this dispatch'd with all the haste thou canst,
Anon I'll give thee more instructions.   *Exit a Servingman.*
I know the boy will well usurp the grace,
Voice, gait, and action of a gentlewoman.   130
I long to hear him call the drunkard husband,
And how my men will stay themselves from laughter
When they do homage to this simple peasant.
I'll in to counsel them. Haply my presence
May well abate the over-merry spleen   135
Which otherwise would grow into extremes.   [*Exeunt.*]

133. peasant.] *Johnson;* peasant, *F.*   136. S.D.] *Capell; not in F.*

126. *in despite*] notwithstanding anything (Onions, 3).

129. *usurp*] assume, take on (*OED, v.* 1. b, quoting this line). Cf. *Meas.,* III. ii. 87.

133. *simple*] 'of poor or humble condition' (Onions, *adj.* 1).

134. *Haply*] perhaps.

135. *spleen*] The organ itself was viewed as the seat of all emotions and passions. Cf. *Tw.N.,* III. ii. 64; *Troil.,* I. iii. 178. Onions quotes Holland's *Pliny,* 'Untemperate laughers have alwaies great Splenes'.

[SCENE II]

Enter aloft SLY, *with* Attendants; *some with apparel,*
basin and ewer, and other appurtenances; and LORD.

Sly. For God's sake, a pot of small ale.
First Serv. Will't please your lordship drink a cup of sack?
Sec. Serv. Will't please your honour taste of these conserves?
Third Serv. What raiment will your honour wear today?
Sly. I am Christophero Sly, call not me 'honour' nor   5
     'lordship'. I ne'er drank sack in my life. And if you
     give me any conserves, give me conserves of beef.
     Ne'er ask me what raiment I'll wear, for I have no

Scene II

SCENE II] *Capell; not in* F.   S.D. *Sly*] *Hibbard; the drunkard* F.   2. lord-
ship] Q; Lord F.

The setting of this scene presents a
problem. The S.D. in F '*Enter aloft* . . .'
(reinforced by the S.D. near the end
of I. i '*The Presenters above speakes*')
makes it clear that the action takes
place on some sort of upper stage or
gallery. It may not always have been
played so. The S.D. for the corresponding scene in *A Shrew* (Bullough,
p. 71) reads '*Enter two with a table and*
a banquet on it, and two other, with Slie
asleepe in a chaire, richlie apparelled, &
the musick plaieng', and nowhere in that
text is an upper level indicated. But
F's text requires one. The scene is
long, at least six, and possibly nine,
characters are on stage, and it is
difficult to see how it could be played
on the narrow, balustraded gallery, or
'Lords' Room', usually thought to
form the upper level of the Elizabethan public playhouse. For discussion of the problem see Richard
Hosley, 'The Gallery over the Stage
in the Public Playhouse of Shakespeare's Time', *SQ* (1957), and
'Shakespeare's Use of a Gallery
over the Stage', *Sh.S.* (1957). The
best solution is probably that of
C. Walter Hodges (*The Globe Restored*,
1953, pp. 56 ff.), who proposes a

temporary structure jutting out from
the façade of the tiring-house, and
raised about seven feet above the main
stage: 'I will allow myself to imagine
the porch-like booth hung with its
arras, standing between the two
tiring-house doors. It backs up to the
gallery floor, where, behind closed
curtains, Sly lies snoring. A light
stairway leads up on one side,
and up this from below come the
servants with apparel, basin and
ewer. They are now standing on top
of the porch-booth in front of the
curtain which represents the bed.
They draw the curtain. Sly emerges.'
(pp. 64–5)

1. *small ale*] the weakest and cheap-
est beer. Bond suggests that the ale is
actually brought, and most modern
editors agree, though there is no
direction to do so in F. See note to
l. 25 S.D.

2. *sack*] a general name for a class
of white wines formerly imported from
Spain and the Canaries. Cf. *Tw.N.*
II. iii. 180.

3. *conserves*] candied fruits. The
noun occurs only here in Shakespeare.

7. *conserves of beef*] salt beef hung.

    more doublets than backs, no more stockings than
    legs, nor no more shoes than feet—nay, sometime   10
    more feet than shoes, or such shoes as my toes look
    through the overleather.
Lord. Heaven cease this idle humour in your honour!
    O, that a mighty man of such descent,
    Of such possessions, and so high esteem,   15
    Should be infused with so foul a spirit!
Sly. What, would you make me mad? Am not I
    Christopher Sly, old Sly's son of Burton-heath, by
    birth a pedlar, by education a cardmaker, by
    transmutation a bear-herd, and now by present   20
    profession a tinker? Ask Marian Hacket, the fat
    ale-wife of Wincot, if she know me not. If she say I
    am not fourteen pence on the score for sheer ale,

18. Sly's] *Q* (Slies)*; Sies *F*.

13. *idle humour*] foolish fancy.

16. *infused*] imbued (Onions, 2). Cf. *Ven.*, 928.

17–21. *Am . . . tinker*] Sly tests his own sanity by rehearsing certain facts about himself. This was a common test for sanity. See C. J. Sisson, 'Tudor Intelligence Tests', in *Essays . . . in Honour of Hardin Craig*, ed. Hosley (1963), pp. 183–200; *Tw.N.*, IV. iii. 1–21.

18. *Burton-heath*]   Barton-on-the-Heath, a village about sixteen miles south of Stratford, on the southern border of Warwickshire, where Shakespeare's aunt Joan Lambert lived, is now the generally accepted identification. Barton, on the south side of the Avon, just opposite Bidford and about eight miles from Stratford, has been proposed but is less likely.

19. *cardmaker*] one who makes cards for combing wool. A card was an instrument with iron teeth for parting, combing out, and setting in order the fibres of wool, hemp, etc. (*OED*, *sb.*[1] 2. a). Cf. *H8*, I. ii. 33, 'The spinsters, carders, fullers, weavers'.

20. *bear-herd*] one who keeps and

exhibits a bear. Cf. *Ado*, II. i. 37 (Berrord).

21–2. *Marian . . . Wincot*] probably a real person. Hibbard notes that 'Sara, the daughter of Robert Hacket, was baptized in Quinton church on 21 November, 1591. The hamlet of Wincot, four miles south of Stratford, lay partly in the parish of Quinton and partly in that of Clifford Chambers.' The only other plausible but not really likely suggestion has been Wilmcote, the home of Shakespeare's mother, a few miles north of Stratford.

23. *on the score*] in debt. The 'score' was originally kept by cutting notches in a stick, later by making marks on a wall or door.

sheer ale] probably 'nothing but ale' (*OED*, Sheer, *a.* and *adv.* 7. b, 'taken alone, without solid food'). Bond notes that 'harvest ale' has been suggested ('shear' being used for 'reap' in Warwickshire), that it has been taken to allude to the doles on 'Sheer-Thursday' (i.e. Maundy Thursday), and that 'sheer' could be used in the sense of 'undiluted', as in *R2*, V. iii. 61, 'Thou sheer, immaculate, and silver

score me up for the lying'st knave in Christendom.
[*A Servant brings him a pot of ale.*] What! I am not   25
bestraught. Here's— [*He drinks.*]
Third Serv. O, this it is that makes your lady mourn.
Sec. Serv. O, this is it that makes your servants droop.
Lord. Hence comes it that your kindred shuns your house,
    As beaten hence by your strange lunacy.   30
    O noble lord, bethink thee of thy birth,
    Call home thy ancient thoughts from banishment,
    And banish hence these abject lowly dreams.
    Look how thy servants do attend on thee,
    Each in his office ready at thy beck.   35
    Wilt thou have music? Hark, Apollo plays,   *Music.*
    And twenty caged nightingales do sing.
    Or wilt thou sleep? We'll have thee to a couch
    Softer and sweeter than the lustful bed
    On purpose trimm'd up for Semiramis.   40

25. S.D.] *Hibbard (subst.); not in F.*   26. S.D.] *Hibbard; not in F.*   27. *Third
Serv.*] *Capell (subst.);* 3 *Man. F (throughout scene).*   28. *Sec. Serv.*] *Capell (subst.);*
2 *Man. F (throughout scene).*

fountain'. But cf. *1H4*, II. iv. 519–21, 'O monstrous! but one halfpenny-worth of bread to this intolerable deal of sack!', showing that Shakespeare elsewhere found humour in heavy drinking with light eating.

24. *score*] mark.

lying'st . . . Christendom] Cf. *2H6*, II. i. 125–6, where Gloucester uses exactly these words to Simpcox.

25. S.D.] not in F, but something more than the Third Servant seems needed to break into Sly's speech, and I follow Hibbard's suggestion that this is when the pot of ale demanded in l. 1 actually arrives.

26. *bestraught*] distracted, mad. A form of 'distraught' (*OED*, Bestraught, 2).

30. *As*] as if. See Onions, as 4, and cf. *Tp.*, II. i. 115.

31. *bethink thee*] consider. Shakespeare usually, but not invariably, uses the verb reflexively (bethink me, bethink you), to mean 'reflect, remember'.

32. *ancient thoughts*] former (sane) state of mind.

35. *beck*] nod.

36. *Apollo*] here, the god of music and song. In classical mythology he is also god of medicine, archery, prophecy, light, and youth. Apart from the references to Apollo's oracle in *Wint.*, and a few to the story of Apollo and Daphne (see below, l. 58 and *MND*, II. i. 231), the great majority of Shakespeare's references to Apollo are to his musical skill. Cf. *LLL*, IV. iii. 339, V. ii. 917 ff.; *Troil.*, III. iii. 298 ff.

39. *lustful*] provocative of lust. This predates *OED*'s earliest example (Lustful, *a.* 5, '1610 Fletcher *Faithf. Shepherdess* II. ii. (1629) C4b lustfull Turpentine').

40. *trimm'd up*] arrayed, dressed up (*OED*, *v.* 7, quoting T. Wright, *Passions*, v. i. 151, 'Salomon . . . exhorteth us . . . not to looke upon a woman trimmed and decked up').

Semiramis] legendary Assyrian

Say thou wilt walk; we will bestrew the ground.
Or wilt thou ride? Thy horses shall be trapp'd,
Their harness studded all with gold and pearl.
Dost thou love hawking? Thou hast hawks will soar
Above the morning lark. Or wilt thou hunt?   45
Thy hounds shall make the welkin answer them
And fetch shrill echoes from the hollow earth.

First Serv. Say thou wilt course, thy greyhounds are as swift
As breathed stags, ay, fleeter than the roe.   49

Sec. Serv. Dost thou love pictures? We will fetch thee straight
Adonis painted by a running brook,
And Cytherea all in sedges hid,
Which seem to move and wanton with her breath
Even as the waving sedges play with wind.

Lord. We'll show thee Io as she was a maid,   55
And how she was beguiled and surpris'd,

---

48. *First Serv.*] *Capell (subst.)*; 1 *Man.* F *(throughout scene).*   54. with] *F;* wi'th'
Hibbard.

---

queen, famous for her licentiousness.
Shakespeare mentions her only here
and twice in *Tit.* He probably knew
of her from Ovid. See *Met.*, iv. 58,
where she is associated with Pyramus
and Thisbe (*Shakespeare's Ovid*, trs.
Golding, ed. Rouse, 1961, p. 83), and
Amores, I. v. 11, which Marlowe translates as 'Resembling fair Semiramis
going to bed'.

41. *bestrew*] cover. Probably rushes
would be used. Cf. *Tp.*, IV. i. 20.

42. *trapp'd*] protected or adorned
with trappings (*OED, ppl. a.*²). Cf.
Tim., I. ii. 179–80.

46–7. *Thy . . . earth*] Cf. the more
extended description of the hounds'
music in *MND*, IV. i. 106–24, and
Brooks's notes in the Arden edition.

46. *welkin*] sky. Cf. *Tw.N.*, III. i. 58
(and note in Lothian and Craik's
Arden edn); *LLL*, III. i. 62.

48. *course*] generally, to pursue or
hunt game with hounds; especially, to
hunt hares by view (not scent) with
greyhounds.

49. *breathed*] strong-winded, in good
wind. Cf. *LLL*, v. ii. 645.

50–61. *Dost . . . drawn*] Cf. Ind.
i. 45. Shakespeare probably does not
have actual pictures in mind. See A.
Lytton Sells, *The Italian Influence in
English Poetry* (1955), pp. 188 ff. The
descriptions of Adonis, Io, and
Daphne derive from Ovid. Shakespeare would know them from school
and from Golding's translation of the
Metamorphoses (1567).

51. *Adonis*] See Ovid, *Met.*, x. 520–
739 (Golding, pp. 211 ff.), for Adonis
and Cytherea (Venus). Both here and
in *Ven.* Shakespeare depicts a reluc-
tant Adonis and an amorous Venus,
possibly influenced by the story of
Salmacis and Hermaphroditus in
Met., iv. See Shakespeare, *Poems*, ed.
F. T. Prince, Appendix I (b); Spenser,
FQ, III. i. 34–8, and Douglas Bush,
*Mythology and the Renaissance Tradition
in English Poetry* (1932), pp. 140 ff.

55. *Io*] Ovid, *Met.*, i. 588–600
(Golding, pp. 35 ff.).

As lively painted as the deed was done.

Third Serv. Or Daphne roaming through a thorny wood,
  Scratching her legs that one shall swear she bleeds,
  And at that sight shall sad Apollo weep,   60
  So workmanly the blood and tears are drawn.

Lord. Thou art a lord, and nothing but a lord.
  Thou hast a lady far more beautiful
  Than any woman in this waning age.

First Serv. And till the tears that she hath shed for thee 65
  Like envious floods o'er-run her lovely face,
  She was the fairest creature in the world;
  And yet she is inferior to none.

Sly. Am I a lord, and have I such a lady?
  Or do I dream? Or have I dream'd till now?   70
  I do not sleep. I see, I hear, I speak.
  I smell sweet savours and I feel soft things.
  Upon my life, I am a lord indeed,
  And not a tinker nor Christophero Sly.
  Well, bring our lady hither to our sight,   75
  And once again a pot o' th' smallest ale.

Sec. Serv. Will't please your mightiness to wash your hands?
  O, how we joy to see your wit restor'd!
  O, that once more you knew but what you are!
  These fifteen years you have been in a dream, 80
  Or when you wak'd, so wak'd as if you slept.

Sly. These fifteen years! By my fay, a goodly nap.

---

74. Christophero] *F2;* Christopher *F.*

---

57. *As ... done*] Shakespeare invariably praises works of art for their verisimilitude. See (above) ll. 53–4 and 58–61, and cf. *Lucr.*, 1371 ff., *Tim.*, I. i. 33–41, *Cym.*, II. iv. 68–85, and *Wint.*, v. ii. 91–100 and v. iii. 65–8. See also Lee, in *The Art Bulletin*, XXII. 4 (1940), 197–203.

58. *Daphne*] Ovid, *Met.*, i. 452–567 (Golding, pp. 31 ff.). Note also Bush, op. cit., p. 141.

64. *this waning age*] The idea that the history of man was a steady decline from the perfection of Eden or the golden age (soft primitivism) was widely believed. See Spenser, *FQ*, v. Proem. 1–9, and Panofsky, *Studies in Iconology* (1939), pp. 33–67.

66. *o'er-run*] overflowed (past tense).

68. *yet*] still.

70–2. *Or ... things*] Cf. Sebastian's soliloquy in *Tw.N.*, IV. iii. 1–21.

76. *And . . . ale*] This might be taken as indicating an exit for one of the servants.

78. *wit*] mental powers or faculties (Onions, wit, sb. 1).

82. *fay*] faith.

But did I never speak of all that time?
First Serv. O yes, my lord, but very idle words,
   For though you lay here in this goodly chamber,   85
   Yet would you say ye were beaten out of door,
   And rail upon the hostess of the house,
   And say you would present her at the leet,
   Because she brought stone jugs and no seal'd quarts.
   Sometimes you would call out for Cicely Hacket.   90
Sly. Ay, the woman's maid of the house.
Third Serv. Why, sir, you know no house, nor no such maid,
   Nor no such men as you have reckon'd up,
   As Stephen Sly, and old John Naps of Greece,
   And Peter Turph, and Henry Pimpernell,   95
   And twenty more such names and men as these,
   Which never were nor no man ever saw.
Sly. Now Lord be thanked for my good amends.
All. Amen.

---

94. Greece] *F; Greete conj. Halliwell.*

83. *of*] during (Onions, of, 8). Cf. *H8*, II. i. 147; *LLL*, I. i. 43.

88. *present . . . leet*] bring her to trial before the manorial court. Bond quotes Kitchen, on *Courts*, ed. 1663, p. 21, enumerating among charges brought at the Court-leet, 'Also if tiplers sell by cups and dishes, or measures sealed, or not sealed, is inquirable'. Underhill (*Shakespeare's England*, I. 388) notes that 'probably even in Shakespeare's time the Leet was but little used'.

89. *seal'd quarts*] quart measures officially marked with a stamp as a guarantee of accurate size. Malone quotes *Characterismi, or Lenton's Leasures* (1631): 'He [an informer] transforms himself into several shapes, to avoid suspicion of inne-holders, and inwardly joyes at the sight of a blacke pot or jugge, knowing that their sale by sealed quarts, spoyles his market.'

90. *Cicely Hacket*] See note to Ind. ii. 21–2.

91. *woman's . . . house*] landlady's maid.

93. *reckon'd up*] enumerated.

94. *Stephen Sly*] There was a Stephen Sly living in Stratford in January 1615 (E. K. Chambers, *William Shakespeare* (1930), II. 144), and Sisson (*New Readings*) notes: 'To the known Warwickshire Slys I might add Edward Slye of Wooton (Wawen), husbandman, aged 40 in 1607. . . . There were Slys enough in London, apart from the actor William Slye, and a John Slye appears in 1517 as leader of a company of London actors in the Drapers' records' (I. 159).

94–5. *John . . . Pimpernell*] These also may be the names of real people. Halliwell suggests that 'Greece' is an error for 'Greete', a village not far from Stratford, but on the Greeks in England, and the possible derivation of the name 'John Naps' from Greek, see T. J. B. Spencer, in *MLR* (1954).

Enter [PAGE *as a*] *lady, with* Attendants.
[*One gives Sly a pot of ale.*]

Sly. I thank thee, thou shalt not lose by it.   100
Page. How fares my noble lord?
Sly. Marry, I fare well, for here is cheer enough.
  Where is my wife?
Page. Here, noble lord, what is thy will with her?
Sly. Are you my wife, and will not call me husband?   105
  My men should call me 'lord', I am your goodman.
Page. My husband and my lord, my lord and husband;
  I am your wife in all obedience.
Sly. I know it well. What must I call her?
Lord. Madam.   110
Sly. Alice madam, or Joan madam?
Lord. Madam and nothing else, so lords call ladies.
Sly. Madam wife, they say that I have dream'd
  And slept above some fifteen year or more.
Page. Ay, and the time seems thirty unto me,   115
  Being all this time abandon'd from your bed.
Sly. 'Tis much. Servants, leave me and her alone.

                                        [*Exeunt Attendants.*]
  Madam, undress you and come now to bed.
Page. Thrice noble lord, let me entreat of you
  To pardon me yet for a night or two;   120
  Or, if not so, until the sun be set.

---

99. S.D. *Page as a*] *Capell (subst.); not in* F.   *One gives Sly a pot of ale.*]
Hibbard; not in F.   101. *Page.*] *Capell; Lady.* F (*or La.*) (*throughout scene*).
111. Alice] *Capell* (Al'ce); *Alce* F.   117. S.D.] *NCS (subst.); not in* F; *Exeunt
Lord and Servingmen*/*Hibbard.*

99. S.D.] F reads '*Enter Lady with
Attendants*'. The Lady must be played
by the Page (see Ind. i. 103–4), and
the pot of ale Sly has called for at
l. 76 should arrive at this point since
his next line clearly refers to it.

102. *fare*] a pun on 'fares' in the
previous line. Here it means 'take
(liquid) nourishment'.

106. *goodman*] husband.

107–8. *My . . . obedience*] Cf.
Katherina's words at v. ii. 137–80.

116. *abandon'd*] banished. Shakespeare nowhere else uses the word in
this sense.

117. S.D.] There is no S.D. in F,
but NCS points out the necessity for
one in obedience to Sly's command
and in order to clear the stage of all
but the 'Presenters' before the play
proper can start.

119–21. *let . . . set*] Cf. *A Shrew*
(Bullough, p. 71), i. 76–7: 'And if he
desire to goe to bed with thee,/Then
faine some scuse and say thou wilt
anon.'

For your physicians have expressly charg'd,
In peril to incur your former malady,
That I should yet absent me from your bed.
I hope this reason stands for my excuse.   125

Sly. Ay, it stands so that I may hardly tarry so long. But
   I would be loath to fall into my dreams again. I will
   therefore tarry in despite of the flesh and the blood.

Enter a MESSENGER.

Mess. Your honour's players, hearing your amendment,
   Are come to play a pleasant comedy;   130
   For so your doctors hold it very meet,
   Seeing too much sadness hath congeal'd your blood,
   And melancholy is the nurse of frenzy.
   Therefore they thought it good you hear a play
   And frame your mind to mirth and merriment,   135
   Which bars a thousand harms and lengthens life.

Sly. Marry, I will. Let them play it. Is not a comonty

---

128. S.D.] *F; Enter the Lord as a Messenger/Hibbard.*   137. will . . . Is] *Capell;*
will let them play, it is *F.*   comonty] *F;* commodity *NCS.*

---

123. *In . . . incur*] on pain of bringing on yourself.

125. *stands for*] is acceptable as.

126. *stands*] is erect (referring to the
penis). A pun on the previous line.

128. S.D.] F reads 'Enter a Messenger.' NCS assigns this role to the First
Servant, on the grounds that he is
still on stage at the end of I. i.
Hibbard suggests *Enter the Lord as a
Messenger,* arguing that since the Lord
has suggested the play he must be
where he can best observe Sly's reaction to it, and also that in *A Shrew* it is
the Lord who announces the play to
Sly in words which are very close to
ll. 129–30 here: 'May it please you,
your honors plaiers be come/To
offer your honour a plaie.' But it may
be that F's direction simply represents
a lack of precise instruction on Shakespeare's part. In practice, either the
Lord or the First Servant could play

the Messenger without causing any
difficulty.

130. *pleasant*] merry. Cf. *LLL,* v. i.
4, 'pleasant without scurrility'.

131. *For . . . meet*] because your
doctors believe it very suitable.

132–3. *Seeing . . . frenzy*] NCS compares *MND,* III. ii. 96–7, and Bond
cites *John,* III. iii. 42–4: 'Or if that
surly spirit, melancholy,/Had bak'd
thy blood and made it heavy-thick,/
Which else runs tickling up and down
the veins.'

137. *Marry . . . comonty*] F reads
'Marrie I will let them play, it is not
a Comontie . . .', which (see Sisson,
I. 161) makes sense of a kind. But all
editors emend. NCS suggests 'commodity' for 'Comontie', on the grounds
that Sly's perversion should have some
logic and connection with 'stuff' and
'household stuff' following, and that
'comoditie' appears as a perversion of

A Christmas gambol or a tumbling-trick?
Page. No, my good lord, it is more pleasing stuff.
Sly. What, household stuff?
Page.   It is a kind of history.   140
Sly. Well, we'll see't. Come, madam wife, sit by my side
   And let the world slip, we shall ne'er be younger.

140.] *as verse, Capell; as prose, F.*

'comedy' in *A Shrew*. Sisson finds both arguments unconvincing. It seems necessary only to repunctuate F's reading, and accept 'comonty' as Sly's error for 'comedy'.

138. *gambol*] frolic, entertainment; F's 'gambold' is a variant spelling of 'gambol'; it may indicate Sly's pronunciation.

140. *household stuff*] furnishings (with pun on 'stuff' in the sense of 'matter' in the previous line).

history] story. Onions distinguishes two senses in Shakespeare: (i) 'tale, narrative' and (ii) 'story represented dramatically', quoting this occurrence, and *H5*, Prol. 32, 'Admit me Chorus to this history'.

142. *And . . . younger*] Sly combines two proverbs: see Tilley, W879, 'Let the world wag (slide, pass)', and Y36, 'You shall never be younger'.

[ACT I]

[SCENE I]

Flourish. Enter LUCENTIO *and his man* TRANIO.

Luc. Tranio, since for the great desire I had
    To see fair Padua, nursery of arts,
    I am arriv'd for fruitful Lombardy,
    The pleasant garden of great Italy,
    And by my father's love and leave am arm'd   5
    With his good will and thy good company,
    My trusty servant well approv'd in all,
    Here let us breathe and haply institute
    A course of learning and ingenious studies.

ACT I
Scene 1

ACT I SCENE 1] *Pope; not in* F.   S.D. *Tranio*] F2; *Triano* F.   3. for] *F;*
from *Theobald; in Capell.*

S.D.] F reads *Triano*, and NCS
points out (p. 101) that although the
name 'Tranio' is always correctly
spelt in the dialogue, it sometimes
appears as 'Trayno' or 'Triano' in the
stage-directions, suggesting that a different hand was responsible for the
stage-directions in the copy. See
pp. 11–12.

   1–24.] a conventional piece of
dramatic exposition. Cf. the opening
of *Err.*, and especially the intermin-
able speeches of Aegeon.

   1. *Tranio*] In Plautus' comedy
Mostellaria the plot rests on the
effrontery and resourceful lying of the
slave, Tranio.

   since for] because of.

   2. *Padua*] Padua was famous for its
university, founded in 1228, and a
centre of Aristotelianism. See Sells,
The Italian Influence in English Poetry
(1955), pp. 82–4, who notes that

'English students had been flocking in
increasing numbers both to Bologna
and Padua, and by 1535 or 1540 they
were sufficiently numerous in the
latter university to require the super-
vision of a senior among their com-
patriots'.

   3. *am arriv'd for*] have arrived in.
See Abbott, 295, Verbs Passive.

   Lombardy] Padua is not and never
was in Lombardy, though Shakespeare seems to have thought it was.
Elizabethan cartography was not
always precise: Ortelius' map of
Europe has 'Lombardy' written right
across northern Italy from the French
Alps to Trieste. See Ethel Seaton,
'Marlowe's Map', *E & S* (1924).

   8. *breathe*] pause, take rest (*OED*,
Breathe, *v.* I. 5). Cf. *John*, IV. ii. 137–9.

   haply] perhaps, maybe.

   9. *ingenious*] appropriate (*OED*, Ingenious, *a.* I. 6, 'Of employment,

Pisa renowned for grave citizens   10
Gave me my being and my father first,
A merchant of great traffic through the world,
Vincentio, come of the Bentivolii.
Vincentio's son, brought up in Florence,
It shall become to serve all hopes conceiv'd   15
To deck his fortune with his virtuous deeds.
And therefore, Tranio, for the time I study
Virtue, and that part of philosophy
Will I apply that treats of happiness
By virtue specially to be achiev'd.   20
Tell me thy mind, for I have Pisa left
And am to Padua come as he that leaves
A shallow plash to plunge him in the deep,
And with satiety seeks to quench his thirst.

Tra. *Mi perdonato*, gentle master mine.   25
I am in all affected as yourself,
Glad that you thus continue your resolve
To suck the sweets of sweet philosophy.
Only, good master, while we do admire
This virtue and this moral discipline,   30
Let's be no stoics nor no stocks, I pray,

13. Vincentio] *Hanmer; Vincentio's F.*   14. brought] *F2;* brough *F.*   25. *Mi
perdonato*] *Capell* (perdonate)*; Me perdonato F.*   26. am] *F;* am, *Riverside.*

education etc.: Befitting a well-bred
person; "liberal" ', quoting this line).
    10. *Pisa . . . citizens*] This line is
repeated at IV. ii. 95.
    12. *traffic*] business. Cf. *Err.*, I. i. 15.
    13. *Bentivolii*]   Historically,   the
Bentivogli were not Pisans; they were
the leading family of Bologna, and a
powerful political force. See Machi-
avelli, *History of Florence*, esp. Book VI.
    14–16. *Vincentio's . . . deeds*] It is
appropriate   that   Vincentio's   son,
brought up in Florence, should fulfil the high hopes people have of him
by embellishing his good fortune with
deeds of virtue.
    17. *for the time*] at present.
    19. *apply*] apply myself to.
    19–20. *happiness . . . achiev'd*] The
idea that only virtuous living brings

happiness is central to Aristotle's
Ethics. See esp. Books I and II.
    23. *plash*] pool, puddle (*OED, sb.*[1]).
Cf. Spenser, *FQ*, II. viii. 36.
    24. *And . . . thirst*] an early example
of an idea to which Shakespeare often
returns. Cf. *Gent.*, III. i. 219–20; *MND*,
II. ii. 137–42; *Tw.N.*, I. i. 1–3; *Troil.*,
III. ii. 17–28; *Ant.*, II. ii. 239–44; *Cym.*,
I. vi. 46–9.
    25. *Mi perdonato*] excuse me. With
one exception ('mercatante', at IV. ii.
63), the Italian phrases in this play
are confined to Act I.
    26. *affected*] inclined. Cf. *Gent.*, I. iii.
60; *Lr*, II. i. 98.
    31. *stoics . . . stocks*] Onions glosses
'stoic' as 'severe or rigorous person'
(Shakespeare uses the word nowhere
else), and 'stock' as 'blockhead'. For

Or so devote to Aristotle's checks
As Ovid be an outcast quite abjur'd.
Balk logic with acquaintance that you have,
And practise rhetoric in your common talk,   35
Music and poesy use to quicken you,
The mathematics and the metaphysics
Fall to them as you find your stomach serves you.
No profit grows where is no pleasure ta'en.
In brief, sir, study what you most affect.   40
Luc. Gramercies, Tranio, well dost thou advise.
   If, Biondello, thou wert come ashore,

---

32. checks] *F; ethicks conj. Blackstone.*   33. Ovid] *F3; Ouid; F.*   34. Balk]
F; Talk Rowe; Chop conj. Capell.

---

the play on words in stoics and stocks
see Kökeritz (*Shakespeare's Pronunciation*), pp. 83 and 223, and cf. Lyly,
Euphues (*Works*, ed. Bond, I. 190),
'Who so seuere as the *Stoyckes*, which
lyke stockes were moued with no
melody?'
   32. *devote*] devoted (Abbott, 342).
   checks] restraints, counsels of moderation. Blackstone conjectured 'ethics',
which is attractive in view of ll. 18–20,
and the two words could easily be
confused in manuscript.
   33. *Ovid*] clearly the Ovid of the
Ars Amatoria. Lucentio quotes from
Ovid's *Heroides* at III. i. 28–9, and the
Ars Amatoria is mentioned specifically
at IV. ii. 8. F's punctuation here is
obviously erroneous, making Ovid a
student of Aristotle. The historical
Ovid was literally an 'outcast' when
he was exiled to Tomi; cf. *AYL*, III.
iii. 5–6.
   34. *Balk . . . have*] chop logic with
your friends (*OED*, Balk, *v*.[1] 6). Cf.
Spenser, *FQ*, III. ii. 12, 'Her list in
strifull termes with him to balke'.
   36. *quicken*] enliven, refresh. Cf.
Mer.V., II. viii. 52.
   38. *stomach serves*] inclination moves.
The line suggests that Lucentio should
'fall to' his studies as he would 'fall to'
his dinner.
   39. *No . . . ta'en*] Horace, *Ars*

Poetica, 343–4, 'omne tulit punctum
qui miscuit utile dulci,/lectorem
delectando pariterque monendo' (He
has won every vote who has blended
profit and pleasure, at once delight-
ing and instructing the reader). The
phrase is one of the great commonplaces of Renaissance criticism.
   40. *affect*] like. Cf. II. i. 14; *Lr*,
I. i. 1.
   42. *Biondello*] Bond notes that
Tranio and Biondello are both Lucentio's (or Vincentio's) servants, as in
the *Supposes* the real Dulipo and Lytio
are both dependants of Philogano.
   come ashore] This has been taken as
evidence that Shakespeare thought
Padua was a port. But at this time the
whole of Northern Italy was a network
of canals and waterways, much used
by travellers, and this fact would be
well known. Bond quotes Elze (*Essays*,
trans. 1874, 'The Supposed Travels of
Shakespeare', pp. 295, 296): 'Upper
Italy as early as the sixteenth century
was intersected by canals. . . . There
appears indeed to have been a regular
system of communication by these
watercourses; the barks which were
employed were called "corriere" by
the Venetians.' Sells (*The Paradise of
Travellers*, 1964, pp. 114–15) comments on the practice of 17th-century
students: 'If you were merely visiting

We could at once put us in readiness,
And take a lodging fit to entertain
Such friends as time in Padua shall beget.   45
But stay awhile, what company is this?

Tra. Master, some show to welcome us to town.

Lucentio [and] Tranio stand by.

Enter BAPTISTA *with his two daughters* KATHERINA
and BIANCA, GREMIO, *a pantaloon*, HORTENSIO,
suitor to Bianca.

Bap. Gentlemen, importune me no farther,
For how I firmly am resolv'd you know;
That is, not to bestow my youngest daughter   50
Before I have a husband for the elder.
If either of you both love Katherina,
Because I know you well and love you well,
Leave shall you have to court her at your pleasure.

Gre. To cart her rather. She's too rough for me.   55
There, there, Hortensio, will you any wife?

Kath. I pray you, sir, is it your will
To make a stale of me amongst these mates?

47. S.D. *Katherina*] *F2*; *Katerina F* (*occasionally throughout*). *suitor*] *F2* (shuiter);
sister F.   57. *Kath.*] *Rowe*; *Kate. F* (*throughout*).

Padua and then proceeding to Venice,
you would hire a boat which left from
the canal behind the University and
took about seven hours.'

44. *lodging fit*] 'It seems to have
been usual, on arriving in Padua, to
put up at the principal inn, which was
the "Stella d'Oro" in the Piazza della
Paglia. . . . It was within three or four
minutes of the University' (Sells, op.
cit., p. 114).

47. S.D.] The name Katherina
appears variously as Katerina, Katherina, and Kate in F. F's 'sister' for
'suitor' is an obvious error, and is
taken by NCS as 'almost proof that
the direction was written in Italian
script, since the mistake would be very
difficult to account for in the English
hand'. The description of Gremio as
'a pantaloon' identifies him as the

stock figure of a foolish old man in the
Italian *commedia dell' arte*. See Allardyce Nicoll, *The World of Harlequin*
(1963), pp. 44–55. Cf. also III. i. 36;
AYL, II. vii. 157–63.

50. *youngest*] The superlative was
often used when only two objects were
being compared (Abbott, 10). Cf.
1H6, II. iv. 11–16.

53. *I . . . well*] Cf. *R3*, III. iv. 31.

55. *cart*] A whipping at the cart's
tail was a punishment for bawds and
whores. For the pun on 'court/cart'
see Kökeritz, p. 72, and cf. Lyly,
Euphues (*Works*, ed. Bond, I. 190),
'*Aristippus* a Philosopher, yet who more
courtely? *Diogenes* a Philosopher, yet
who more carterly?'

58. *To . . . mates*] complex word-
play. Among other things, the word
'stale' could mean (i) decoy, (ii) pros-

Hor. Mates, maid, how mean you that? No mates for you

  Unless you were of gentler, milder mould.   60

Kath. I' faith, sir, you shall never need to fear.

  Iwis it is not half way to her heart.

  But if it were, doubt not her care should be

  To comb your noddle with a three-legg'd stool,

  And paint your face, and use you like a fool.   65

Hor. From all such devils, good Lord deliver us!

Gre. And me too, good Lord!

Tra. Husht, master, here's some good pastime toward.

  That wench is stark mad or wonderful froward.

Luc. But in the other's silence do I see   70

  Maid's mild behaviour and sobriety.

  Peace, Tranio.

Tra. Well said, master. Mum! and gaze your fill.

Bap. Gentlemen, that I may soon make good

  What I have said—Bianca, get you in.   75

  And let it not displease thee, good Bianca,

  For I will love thee ne'er the less, my girl.

Kath. A pretty peat! it is best put finger in the eye, and

  she knew why.

71. Maid's] *Rowe;* Maids F.   78–9.] *as prose,* F; *as verse, Capell.*

titute, (iii) someone whose love is ridiculed for the amusement of a rival, (iv) stalemate in chess (*OED*, Stale, *sb*.³, *sb*.⁶). A 'mate' could be (i) the final position in a game of chess, (ii) a habitual companion, (iii) one of a pair, especially husband or wife (*OED*, Mate, *sb*.², *sb*.³). The dominant sense of Katherina's question is 'Do you want to make me a laughing-stock among these fellows?', but the several other meanings play beneath the surface.

  59. *Mates . . . mates*] fellows . . .husbands.

  62. *Iwis . . . heart*] Assuredly it (i.e. marriage) is something in which she has no interest.

  64. *To . . . stool*] to beat you over the head. See Tilley, H270, quoting Skelton's *Merry Tales,* 'Hys wife woulde diuers tymes in the weeke kimbe

his head with a iii. footed stoole'.

  65. *paint*] i.e. with your own blood, brought by scratching. Cf. *Troil.,* I. i. 90.

  66. *From . . . us*] an allusion to 'The Litany' in the *Boke of Common Prayer,* (1552) where the Priest prays 'from all the disceites of the world, the fleshe, and the deuill' and the people respond 'Good Lord, deliuer us'.

  68. *Husht*] hush, be quiet (a 16th–17th century form which survives only in dialect).

  toward] about to take place.

  69. *froward*] wilful, perverse.

  78. *peat*] pet, darling. Onions says of this form 'Common from about 1570 to 1640'; Bond quotes Corydon in Lodge's *Rosalynd,* 'Heigh-ho the pretty peat'.

  78–9. *it . . . why*] She ought to weep, if only she could find some excuse. 'To

Bian. Sister, content you in my discontent.   80
      Sir, to your pleasure humbly I subscribe.
      My books and instruments shall be my company,
      On them to look and practise by myself.
Luc. Hark, Tranio, thou may'st hear Minerva speak.
Hor. Signor Baptista, will you be so strange?   85
      Sorry am I that our good will effects
      Bianca's grief.
Gre.   Why, will you mew her up,
      Signor Baptista, for this fiend of hell,
      And make her bear the penance of her tongue?
Bap. Gentlemen, content ye. I am resolv'd.   90
      Go in, Bianca.   [*Exit Bianca.*]
      And for I know she taketh most delight
      In music, instruments, and poetry,
      Schoolmasters will I keep within my house
      Fit to instruct her youth. If you, Hortensio,   95
      Or Signor Gremio, you, know any such,
      Prefer them hither; for to cunning men
      I will be very kind, and liberal
      To mine own children in good bringing-up.
      And so farewell. Katherina, you may stay,   100
      For I have more to commune with Bianca.   *Exit.*
Kath. Why, and I trust I may go too, may I not? What,
      shall I be appointed hours, as though, belike, I knew
      not what to take and what to leave? Ha?   *Exit.*
Gre. You may go to the devil's dam. Your gifts are so   105

90. resolv'd] *Q;* resould *F.*   91. S.D.] *Theobald; not in F.*   98. kind, and liberal] *Theobald;* kinde and liberall, *F.*

put finger in the eye' was proverbial (Tilley, F229). Cf. *Err.,* II. ii. 202–3.

85. *strange*] distant, unfriendly (Onions, 5). Cf. *Tw.N.,* II. v. 155.

86. *effects*] brings about.

87. *mew her up*] confine her, shut her up. A hawk was put in a 'mew' or cage at moulting time. Cf. *R3,* I. i. 38 and 132–3.

92. *for*] because.

97. *Prefer*] introduce, recommend. *cunning*] knowledgeable, learned

(*OED,* Cunning, *a.,* 1). Cf. Tindale's translation of Matthew, xiii. 52, 'Every scrybe which is coninge vnto the kyngdom of heven' (AV 'instructed').

101. *commune with*] communicate to. Accented on the first syllable.

105. *the devil's dam*] The devil's mother was thought worse than he (Tilley, D225). Cf. *1H6,* I. v. 5; *Err.,* IV. iii. 46–7.

105–6. *Your . . . you*] Your personal

good here's none will hold you. Their love is not so
great, Hortensio, but we may blow our nails together, and fast it fairly out. Our cake's dough on
both sides. Farewell. Yet, for the love I bear my
sweet Bianca, if I can by any means light on a fit   110
man to teach her that wherein she delights, I will
wish him to her father.

Hor. So will I, Signor Gremio. But a word, I pray.
Though the nature of our quarrel yet never brooked
parle, know now, upon advice, it toucheth us both—   115
that we may yet again have access to our fair
mistress and be happy rivals in Bianca's love—to
labour and effect one thing specially.

Gre. What's that, I pray?

Hor. Marry, sir, to get a husband for her sister.   120

Gre. A husband? A devil.

Hor. I say a husband.

Gre. I say a devil. Thinkest thou, Hortensio, though her
father be very rich, any man is so very a fool to be
married to hell?   125

Hor. Tush, Gremio. Though it pass your patience and
mine to endure her loud alarums, why, man, there
be good fellows in the world, and a man could light

108. cake's] *F3;* cakes *F.*

qualities are such that no one wants
to keep you. NCS says 'There is some
quibble here, which we cannot explain'. The phrase sounds proverbial,
but no such proverb is recorded.

106. *Their love*] so F, meaning
'women's love'. Q's 'There love' is
accepted by some editors, including
Hibbard (in the form 'There! Love'),
who points out that Gremio is fond of
'There' as an exclamation (cf. I. i. 56).

107. *blow our nails*] wait patiently,
'twiddle our thumbs'. Cf. *LLL*, v. ii.
900, 'And Dick the shepherd blows
his nail'. Bond quotes Nashe's *Wonderful Prognostication for this Year* (1591),
'watermen that want fares shall sit and
blowe their fingers till their fellowes
row betwixte the Old Swanne and
Westminster'.

108. *Our cake's dough*] We have both
failed (Tilley, C12). Cf. v. i. 128, and
Jonson, *Case Is Altered* (H. & S., III.
187), v. xii. 102; 'Steward your cake
is dow, as well as mine'.

112. *wish*] commend. See I. ii. 59,
'And wish thee to a shrewd ill-favour'd
wife'.

114–15. *brooked parle*] allowed nego-
tiations. 'Parle' is a shortened form of
'Parley' (*OED*, Parle, *sb.* 2).

115. *advice*] consideration.

118. *labour and effect*] strive to bring
about.

124. *very a fool*] complete a fool. Cf.
Tw.N., I. iii. 22, 'he's a very fool and
a prodigal'.

127. *alarums*] disturbances, out-
cries. See Onions, alarm, alarum.

128. *and*] if.

on them, would take her with all faults, and money
    enough.   130

Gre. I cannot tell. But I had as lief take her dowry with
    this condition, to be whipped at the high cross every
    morning.

Hor. Faith, as you say, there's small choice in rotten
    apples. But come, since this bar in law makes us   135
    friends, it shall be so far forth friendly maintained
    till by helping Baptista's eldest daughter to a
    husband we set his youngest free for a husband,
    and then have to't afresh. Sweet Bianca! Happy
    man be his dole. He that runs fastest gets the ring.   140
    How say you, Signor Gremio?

Gre. I am agreed, and would I had given him the best
    horse in Padua to begin his wooing that would
    thoroughly woo her, wed her, and bed her, and rid
    the house of her. Come on.   *Exeunt Gremio and Hortensio.*

Tra. I pray, sir, tell me, is it possible   146
    That love should of a sudden take such hold?

Luc. O Tranio, till I found it to be true,

145. S.D.] *This edn; Exeunt ambo. Manet Tranio and Lucentio. F.*

131. *as lief*] as soon.

132. *high cross*] a cross set on a
pedestal in a market-place in the
centre of a town or village (*OED*,
High, 21).

134–5. *small . . . apples*] proverbial
(Tilley, C358). Tilley records no
example earlier than Shakespeare's
here, and Smith and Wilson gives only
this one, plus a distant paraphrase by
De Luna (1622), and one in Lacey's
Sauny the Scott, which clearly derives
from *Shr.* The phrase may be Shakespeare's invention.

135. *bar in law*] presumably
Baptista's refusal to let them woo
Bianca, though this does not, strictly
speaking, form any legal impediment.

136. *it . . . maintained*] we shall
continue friends.

139–40. *Happy . . . dole*] May his
lot be that of a happy man. The
phrase was proverbial, and equivalent

to 'Good luck' or 'May the best man
win' (Tilley, M158). Cf. *1H4*, II. ii.
73–4; *Wiv.*, III. iv. 64; *Wint.*, I. ii. 163.

140. *He . . . ring*] again, equivalent
to 'May the best man win' or 'Winner
take all'. The proverbial phrase is
usually found in the form 'He that
hops best gets the ring', but Shakespeare here seems to be referring to
jousting, where 'running (or riding)
at the ring' was part of the game
(Tilley, R130).

144. *woo . . . bed her*] a common
proverb for the progress of a courtship
(Tilley, W731, quoting, among many
examples, 1594 *Knack to Know a Knave*,
sig. C4, 'So may I see the Maid, woo,
wed, I and bed her to'). Shakespeare
does not use precisely this locution
elsewhere, but cf. IV. ii. 51; *LLL*,
IV. iii. 367–8.

144–5. *rid . . . her*] Gremio adds his
own phrase to the proverb.

I never thought it possible or likely.
But see, while idly I stood looking on,   150
I found the effect of love in idleness,
And now in plainness do confess to thee,
That art to me as secret and as dear
As Anna to the Queen of Carthage was,
Tranio, I burn, I pine, I perish, Tranio,   155
If I achieve not this young modest girl.
Counsel me, Tranio, for I know thou canst.
Assist me, Tranio, for I know thou wilt.
Tra. Master, it is no time to chide you now;
Affection is not rated from the heart.   160
If love have touch'd you, naught remains but so,
Redime te captum quam queas minimo.
Luc. Gramercies, lad. Go forward, this contents.
The rest will comfort, for thy counsel's sound.
Tra. Master, you look'd so longly on the maid,   165

---

162. *captum*] *F2*; *captam F.*   164. counsel's] *F2*; counsels *F.*

---

151. *I . . . idleness*] I fell in love.
Lucentio brings together the proverbial idea that idleness begets love (Tilley, I19), and the supposed effect of the flower called 'love-in-idleness' (the 'heartsease', or *Viola tricolor*). Cf. Ovid, *Rem. Amor.*, 139, 'Otia si tollas, periere Cupidinis arcus'; Lyly, *Loves Metamorphosis*, II. i. 109 (*Works*, ed. Bond, III. 309), where Ceres asks the causes of love and Cupid replies 'Wit and idlenesse'; *Euphues* (*Works*, ed. Bond, I. 250), 'idlenes is the onely nourse and nourisher of sensual appetite'; and *MND*, II. i. 165–8, with Brooks's notes and examples in the Arden edn.

152. *in plainness*] openly. Cf. *Oth.*, I. i. 98, 'In honest plainness thou hast heard me say'.

153. *as secret*] as much in my confidence. Cf. *Rom.*, I. i. 147, 'to himself so secret and so close'.

154. *Anna . . . was*] Virgil, *Aen.*, iv. 8–30. See also Marlowe's *Dido*,

Queen of Carthage (published in 1594), III. i. 57–79 (*Plays*, ed. Gill, pp. 22–3). On classical allusions in *Shr.* see Niall Rudd in *Hermathena* (1980).

160. *rated*] scolded. *OED*, Rate, *v.*[2] I quotes Tindale, Colossians, iii. 21, 'Fathers rate not youre children' (AV, 'provoke not your children to anger').

162. *Redime . . . minimo*] Ransom yourself from captivity as cheaply as you can. Shakespeare quotes from Lily's *Latin Grammar*, the standard school-book (ed. with Introduction by Vincent J. Flynn, New York, 1945). The line 'is literally copied from Lily's Latin syntax—of the ablative after the verb, whereas the original line in the current Elizabethan (and other) editions of Terence runs: "quid agas? nisi ut te redimas captum quam queas minimo" (*Eun.*, I. i. 30)' (*Shakespeare's England*, I. 232).

165. *longly*] persistently, for a long time.

Perhaps you mark'd not what's the pith of all.

Luc. O yes. I saw sweet beauty in her face,
   Such as the daughter of Agenor had,
   That made great Jove to humble him to her hand,
   When with his knees he kiss'd the Cretan strand.   170

Tra. Saw you no more? Mark'd you not how her sister
   Began to scold and raise up such a storm
   That mortal ears might hardly endure the din?

Luc. Tranio, I saw her coral lips to move,
   And with her breath she did perfume the air.   175
   Sacred and sweet was all I saw in her.

Tra. Nay, then 'tis time to stir him from his trance.
   I pray, awake, sir. If you love the maid,
   Bend thoughts and wits to achieve her. Thus it stands:
   Her elder sister is so curst and shrewd   180
   That till the father rid his hands of her,
   Master, your love must live a maid at home,
   And therefore has he closely mew'd her up,
   Because she will not be annoy'd with suitors.

Luc. Ah, Tranio, what a cruel father's he!   185
   But art thou not advis'd he took some care
   To get her cunning schoolmasters to instruct her?

Tra. Ay, marry, am I, sir—and now 'tis plotted.

Luc. I have it, Tranio.

Tra.   Master, for my hand,
   Both our inventions meet and jump in one.   190

Luc. Tell me thine first.

---

166. *pith of all*] central issue.

168. *daughter of Agenor*] Europa. See Ovid, *Met.*, ii. 837 ff. Jupiter wooed Europa in the form of a bull. Shakespeare seems not to have followed the story exactly. In Ovid the courtship is conducted on a beach at Tyre, and Europa is carried off *to* Crete (Golding, p. 62).

169. *humble him*] Final unaccented syllables are commonly elided before a vowel or 'h'. See Abbott, 465, and cf. 'hardly endure' in l. 173.

174. *coral lips*] Cf. *Ven.*, 542; *Lucr.*, 420; *Sonn.*, cxxx. 2. In the plays,

Shakespeare uses the word 'coral' only once, at *Tp.*, I. ii. 397.

180. *curst and shrewd*] cantankerous and sharp of tongue. Cf. *MND*, III. ii. 300–1.

183. *mew'd her up*] confined her.

184. *Because*] so that (Abbott, 117). Cf. *2H6*, III. ii. 99–100.

189. *for my hand*] probably 'by my hand' (so Hibbard), but Abbott does not record this sense. It may be an ellipsis for 'I'll wager my hand' (Abbott, 150). Cf. *R3*, IV. i. 3.

190. *jump*] coincide. Cf. *Tw.N.*, v. i. 244, 'cohere and jump'.

Tra.   You will be schoolmaster,
And undertake the teaching of the maid.
That's your device.
Luc.   It is. May it be done?
Tra. Not possible. For who shall bear your part
And be in Padua here Vincentio's son,   195
Keep house and ply his book, welcome his friends,
Visit his countrymen and banquet them?
Luc. Basta, content thee, for I have it full.
We have not yet been seen in any house,
Nor can we be distinguish'd by our faces   200
For man or master. Then it follows thus:
Thou shalt be master, Tranio, in my stead,
Keep house, and port, and servants, as I should;
I will some other be, some Florentine,
Some Neapolitan, or meaner man of Pisa.   205
'Tis hatch'd, and shall be so. Tranio, at once
Uncase thee, take my colour'd hat and cloak.
When Biondello comes, he waits on thee,
But I will charm him first to keep his tongue.
Tra. So had you need.   210
In brief, sir, sith it your pleasure is,
And I am tied to be obedient—
For so your father charg'd me at our parting,
'Be serviceable to my son' quoth he,
Although I think 'twas in another sense—   215

207. colour'd] *F2;* Conlord *F.*

193. *device*] plan, contrivance.
196. *ply his book*] study. Cf. Middleton, *A Chaste Maid in Cheapside* (ed. Parker), I. ii. 107–8, 'Go to school, ply your books, boys, ha?'
198. *Basta*] enough.
203. *port*] social station, style of living (Onions, port, 2).
205. *meaner*] poorer. NCS accepts Capell's emendation of F's 'meaner' to 'mean' as an improvement both in metre and sense, and compares the S.D. at II. i. 38.
207. *Uncase thee*] Take off your top clothes. Cf. *LLL*, v. ii. 689–90.

colour'd hat] An Elizabethan gentleman would wear variously coloured clothing, whereas a servant would wear a livery, usually of blue. Cf. IV. i. 81; *1H6*, I. iii. 47. See also *Shakespeare's England*, II. 112.
209. *charm*] influence, exercise power over. 'Charm' retains much of its original meaning of 'enchant'. For the phrase 'charm the tongue' meaning 'keep quiet' cf. IV. ii. 58; *2H6*, IV. i. 64; *3H6*, v. v. 31; *Oth.*, v. ii. 187.
210.] The broken line, followed by the irrelevant 'In brief', suggests that there has been a cut.

  I am content to be Lucentio,
  Because so well I love Lucentio.
Luc. Tranio, be so, because Lucentio loves;
  And let me be a slave, t'achieve that maid
  Whose sudden sight hath thrall'd my wounded eye. 220

    Enter BIONDELLO.

  Here comes the rogue. Sirrah, where have you been?
Bion. Where have I been? Nay, how now, where are you?
  Master, has my fellow Tranio stol'n your clothes,
  Or you stol'n his, or both? Pray, what's the news?
Luc. Sirrah, come hither. 'Tis no time to jest, 225
  And therefore frame your manners to the time.
  Your fellow Tranio here, to save my life,
  Puts my apparel and my countenance on,
  And I for my escape have put on his.
  For in a quarrel since I came ashore 230
  I kill'd a man, and fear I was descried
  Wait you on him, I charge you, as becomes,
  While I make way from hence to save my life.
  You understand me?
Bion.   I, sir? Ne'er a whit.
Luc. And not a jot of Tranio in your mouth. 235
  Tranio is chang'd into Lucentio.
Bion. The better for him. Would I were so too.
Tra. So could I, faith, boy, to have the next wish after, 238
  That Lucentio indeed had Baptista's youngest daughter.
  But, sirrah, not for my sake but your master's I advise

226. time.] *F2;* time *F.* 234. I] *F;* Ay *Rowe.* 238–43.] *as verse, Capell;*
as prose, F.

216–17. *I . . . Lucentio*] This balanced repetition of a word is
characteristic of Lyly's style. Cf. ll.
157–8 above, and see examples given
in Lyly's *Works*, ed. Bond, I. 124. It is
not uncommon in Shakespeare's early
comedies: Cf. *Gent.*, III. ii. 20–1.
 228. *countenance*] outward appearance. Cf. v. i. 35.
 232. *as becomes*] as is fitting. An
impersonal use; cf. *1H6*, v. iii. 170.

238–43.] F prints as prose. The
lines are, in fact, doggerel verse of the
kind found elsewhere in the comedies.
Cf. *Err.*, III. i. 11–83; *Gent.*, II. i. 124–9;
LLL, IV. ii. 26–33.
 238–9. *after . . . daughter*] probably
a good rhyme in Shakespeare's day.
Cf. the string of such rhymes in *Lr*,
I. iv. 318–22, and for discussion of the
pronunciation, Kökeritz, p. 183.

You use your manners discreetly in all kind of companies.
When I am alone, why then I am Tranio,
But in all places else your master Lucentio.
Luc. Tranio, let's go.
One thing more rests, that thyself execute,   245
To make one among these wooers. If thou ask me why,
Sufficeth my reasons are both good and weighty. *Exeunt.*

The Presenters above speak.

First Serv. My lord, you nod, you do not mind the play.
Sly. Yes, by Saint Anne, do I. A good matter, surely.
Comes there any more of it?   250
Page. My lord, 'tis but begun.
Sly. 'Tis a very excellent piece of work, madam lady.
Would 'twere done.   *They sit and mark.*

---

243. your] *F2;* you *F.*   247. S.D. *The . . . speak*] *This edn; The Presenters above*
speakes F.   248. *First Serv.*] *Capell (subst.); Lord|Hibbard; 1. Man. F.*

245. *that thyself execute*] which is for
you to carry out (Abbott, 368).
246–7.] doggerel verse, and so
printed in F.
247. *Sufficeth*] I need only say
(Abbott, 297). Cf. III. ii. 104.
S.D.] In Elizabethan drama the
'Presenter' or 'Presenters' were usually
placed 'above' the stage, and introduced the play or commented on
the action. See Chambers, *ES*, III.
91–3 and 128–9, where the Presenters
in Greene's *James IV, Soliman and
Perseda, The Spanish Tragedy* and
Every Man Out of his Humour are discussed. In *Shr.* the Lord is technically
the 'Presenter', but Sly and his 'wife'
also fulfil the function.
248.] F gives this line to '1. *Man.*',

but Hibbard argues that it should be
assigned to the Lord.
mind] pay attention to.
249. *Saint Anne*] mother of the
Virgin Mary, though not mentioned
in the Bible. The cult of Saint Anne
was specially attacked by Luther and
the Reformers. Cf. *Tw.N.,* II. iii. 111,
the only other occurrence of this oath
in Shakespeare, though said by the
Arden edition of *Tw.N.* to be 'still a
common oath in Shakespeare's time'.
253. S.D.] F's '*They sit and marke*'
implies that they are to remain on
stage. But they never speak again. For
Sly's part in the rest of the play, and
the relationship of *Shr.* to *A Shrew,*
see Intro., pp. 39–45.

[SCENE II]

Enter PETRUCHIO *and his man* GRUMIO.

Pet. Verona, for a while I take my leave,
To see my friends in Padua, but of all
My best beloved and approved friend,
Hortensio; and I trow this is his house.
Here, sirrah Grumio, knock, I say.   5
Gru. Knock, sir? Whom should I knock? Is there any
man has rebused your worship?
Pet. Villain, I say, knock me here soundly.
Gru. Knock you here, sir? Why, sir, what am I, sir, that
I should knock you here, sir?   10
Pet. Villain, I say, knock me at this gate,
And rap me well, or I'll knock your knave's pate.
Gru. My master is grown quarrelsome. I should knock you
first,
And then I know after who comes by the worst.

Scene II

SCENE II] *Capell; not in F.*

1–4. *Verona . . . house*] This exposition of necessary information is much
more economical than Lucentio's
in I. i.

2. *but of all*] especially. 'Of' is used
for 'out of', 'from' (Abbott, 166). Cf.
Cor., V. vi. 14–15, 'we'll deliver you/
Of your great danger'.

4. *I trow*] I am pretty sure, I
daresay (Onions, 4, idiomatic uses
(i), comparing *R2*, II. i. 218, 'and
'tis time, I trow', and distinguishing
this from the more common sense of
'believe', 'know').

his house] 'Having come on to the
stage by one of the main doors,
Petruchio and Grumio cross to the
other main door, which now becomes
the entrance to Hortensio's house'
(Hibbard).

7. *rebused*] Grumio's version of
'abused', a technique for verbal
comedy which Shakespeare exploits

with Dogberry and Verges in *Ado*.

8. *knock me here*] 'Me' is a survival
of the old dative, where we should use
'for me'. Grumio takes it as an accus-
ative (Abbott, 220). Cf. Ind. i. 48;
Mer. V., I. iii. 79, 'The skilful
shepherd pill'd me certain wands'.
By Shakespeare's time this 'ethic
dative' had become equivalent to
'I tell you', as in *1H4*, II. iv. 100–2,
'he that kills me some six or seven
dozen of Scots at a breakfast'.

13–14. *I . . . worst*] You want me to
hit you so that you will have an excuse
to beat me. For 'should' (half-way
between the meaning of 'ought' and
'was to') see Abbott, 324. Note the
exchange of doggerel rhyming couplets in ll. 13–14 and 16–17. NCS
proposes (unconvincingly) that rhyming couplets embedded in prose
suggest revision.

Pet. Will it not be?   15
     Faith, sirrah, and you'll not knock, I'll ring it.
     I'll try how you can solfa and sing it.
                              He wrings him by the ears.
Gru. Help, masters, help! My master is mad.
Pet. Now knock when I bid you, sirrah villain.

                    Enter HORTENSIO.

Hor. How now, what's the matter? My old friend   20
     Grumio, and my good friend Petruchio? How do
     you all at Verona?
Pet. Signor Hortensio, come you to part the fray?
     Con tutto il cuore ben trovato, may I say.
Hor. *Alla nostra casa ben venuto, molto honorato signor mio*   25
     Petrucio.
     Rise, Grumio, rise. We will compound this quarrel.
Gru. Nay, 'tis no matter, sir, what he 'leges in Latin. If
     this be not a lawful cause for me to leave his service,
     look you, sir. He bid me knock him and rap him   30
     soundly, sir. Well, was it fit for a servant to use his

---

18. masters] *Theobald;* mistris *F.*   24. *Con . . . trovato*] *Theobald (after Rowe);*
Contutti le core bene trobatto F.   25. *ben*] *F2; bene* F.   *molto*] *Theobald;*
multo F.   *honorato*] *F2; honorata* F.   28. 'leges] *Capell;* leges *F.*

---

16. *ring*] with a pun on 'wring'.

17. *solfa*] The sol-fa is the set of
syllables 'do (or ut) re mi fa sol la si'
sung to the respective notes of the
major scale. Rules for this method of
teaching music first appeared among
the Greeks, and were developed in the
early 11th century by Guido d'Arezzo.
In Shakespeare's time the system is
discussed in Thomas Morley's *Plaine
and Easie Introduction to Practicall Music*
(1597). There are references to it at
LLL, IV. ii. 96, and *Lr,* I. ii. 131, but
in *Shr.* it is demonstrated (briefly) in
the music lesson in III. i. Cf. Lyly,
Euphues (*Works,* ed. Bond, II. 3), 'the
Musition, who being entreated, will
scarse sing sol fa, but not desired,
straine aboue Ela'. See also Grove's

Dictionary of Music, s.v. Solmization.

18. *masters*] F's 'mistris' probably
arises from the presence in its copy of
the contracted form 'Mrs'. Cf. v. i. 5
and 47.

24. *Con . . . trovato*] With all my
heart well met. F's irregular Italian
is regularized here and elsewhere in
this edition.

25–6. *Alla . . . Petrucio*] Welcome to
our house, my much-honoured Signor
Petruchio. For the pronunciation of
Petrucio/Petruchio see note to Dra-
matis Personæ.

27. *compound*] settle.

28. *'leges*] alleges.

in Latin] Grumio (Italian only in
his name) cannot tell Italian from
Latin.

master so, being perhaps, for aught I see, two and
thirty, a pip out?
Whom would to God I had well knock'd at first,
Then had not Grumio come by the worst.   35

Pet. A senseless villain. Good Hortensio,
I bade the rascal knock upon your gate,
And could not get him for my heart to do it.

Gru. Knock at the gate? O heavens! Spake you not these
words plain, 'Sirrah, knock me here, rap me here,   40
knock me well, and knock me soundly'? And come
you now with 'knocking at the gate'?

Pet. Sirrah, be gone, or talk not, I advise you.

Hor. Petruchio, patience, I am Grumio's pledge.
Why, this a heavy chance 'twixt him and you,   45
Your ancient, trusty, pleasant servant Grumio.
And tell me now, sweet friend, what happy gale
Blows you to Padua here from old Verona?

Pet. Such wind as scatters young men through the world
To seek their fortunes farther than at home,   50
Where small experience grows. But in a few,

33. pip] *Rowe;* peepe *F.*   34–5.] *as verse, Rowe; as prose, F.*   49. young
men] *F3;* yongmen *F.*   51. grows . . . few,] *Hanmer (subst.);* growes but
in a few. *F.*

32–3. *two . . . out*] Several interpretations are possible. Grumio may be
referring to Petruchio's age, 32, i.e. he
is too old to be beaten by his servant.
He may be suggesting that Petruchio
is drunk, since Tilley (O64, He is
One-and-Thirty) quotes '1678 Ray,
p. 87: Proverbiall Periphrases of one
drunk'. But probably the allusion is
to the card game of Thirty-one, where
the object was to amass cards whose
'pips' (i.e. the spots on each card)
totalled exactly 31. Thus, to score 32
was to overshoot, to 'go bust', and
Grumio is implying that Petruchio has
overshot the bounds of reason, gone
off his head. See *OED*, Thirty-one,
quoting French *trente et un:* 'il consiste
à complèter 31 points; qui passe perd'
(Littré), and *OED*, Pip, *sb.*[2] 1. b.
Smith and Wilson gives additional
examples of 'Thirty-one' meaning a

card game. Cf. iv. ii. 57.
38. *for my heart*] for my life. Cf.
Cym., ii. i. 53, 'Cannot take two from
twenty, for his heart'.
44. *pledge*] bail, surety.
45. *this*] this is. The contracted
form is not uncommon in Shakespeare.
Cf. *Meas.*, v. i. 131, 'this 'a good Fryer
belike' (quoted from F text); *Lr*,
iv. vi. 184, 'This a good block'. See
also Abbott, 461.
heavy chance] sad happening.
47. *what happy gale*] Cf. *2H4*, v. iii.
84, 'What wind blew you hither,
Pistol?', and Marlowe, *The Jew of
Malta* (*Plays*, ed. Gill), iii. v. 2–4:
'*Ferneze.* What wind drives you thus
into Malta road?/*Basso.* The wind
that bloweth all the world besides,/
Desire of gold.'
51. *in a few*] briefly.

Signor Hortensio, thus it stands with me:
Antonio, my father, is deceas'd,
And I have thrust myself into this maze,
Haply to wive and thrive as best I may.   55
Crowns in my purse I have, and goods at home,
And so am come abroad to see the world.

Hor. Petruchio, shall I then come roundly to thee,
And wish thee to a shrewd ill-favour'd wife?
Thou'dst thank me but a little for my counsel,   60
And yet I'll promise thee she shall be rich,
And very rich. But th'art too much my friend,
And I'll not wish thee to her.

Pet. Signor Hortensio, 'twixt such friends as we
Few words suffice; and therefore, if thou know   65
One rich enough to be Petruchio's wife—
As wealth is burden of my wooing dance—
Be she as foul as was Florentius' love,
As old as Sibyl, and as curst and shrewd

---

69. Sibyl] *Theobald;* Sibell F.

---

54. *maze*] chance wandering.

55. *Haply*] with luck, perchance. F reads 'Happily'.

to wive and thrive] a combination of several proverbs. 'First thrive and then wive' (Tilley, T264, with additional examples in Smith and Wilson, p. 263), 'Who weds ere he be wise shall die ere he thrive' (W229), 'In wiving and thriving a man should take counsel of all the world' (W592), and 'It is hard to wive and thrive both in a year' (Y12). All have ironic relevance to Petruchio's condition.

58. *come roundly*] speak plainly. Cf. III. ii. 212; *1H4*, I. ii. 21–2, 'Well, how then? Come, roundly, roundly'.

59. *wish thee to*] commend you to.

ill-favour'd] Normally, in Shakespeare 'ill-favoured' means 'ugly'. See *Gent.*, II. vii. 53–4; *Wiv.*, I. i. 272, III. iv. 32–3; *AYL*, III. v. 53, v. iv. 57–8; *Tit.*, III. ii. 66. But Hortensio describes Katherina as 'beauteous' at l. 85. Either he is underprizing her

here, or 'ill-favour'd' must mean 'lacking good-nature'.

67. *burden*] musical accompaniment.

68. *Florentius' love*] Florent is a knight in Gower's *Confessio Amantis* (*Works*, ed. Macaulay (1901), I. 74) who keeps his promise to marry an old hag because she had given him the answer to the question on which his life depended, 'What is it that all women desire?', that answer being 'That alle wommen lievest wolde / Be soverein of mannes love'. On the wedding-night she turned into a beautiful girl. The story is told to illustrate the deadly sin of 'Inobedience' (*Conf. Aman.*, i. 1235–1875). It also appears, with the knight unnamed, in Chaucer's *The Wife of Bath's Tale*, and a similar story is in *The Weddynge of Sir Gawane and Dame Ragnell* (ed. Madden, 1839).

69. *Sibyl*] In Ovid (*Met.*, xiv. 104 ff.) the Cumaean Sibyl tells Aeneas of

As Socrates' Xanthippe, or a worse,   70
She moves me not, or not removes at least
Affection's edge in me, were she as rough
As are the swelling Adriatic seas.
I come to wive it wealthily in Padua;
If wealthily, then happily in Padua.   75

Gru. Nay, look you, sir, he tells you flatly what his mind
is. Why, give him gold enough and marry him to a
puppet or an aglet-baby, or an old trot with ne'er a
tooth in her head, though she have as many diseases
as two and fifty horses. Why, nothing comes amiss,   80
so money comes withal.

Hor. Petruchio, since we are stepp'd thus far in,
I will continue that I broach'd in jest.
I can, Petruchio, help thee to a wife
With wealth enough, and young and beauteous,   85
Brought up as best becomes a gentlewoman.
Her only fault, and that is faults enough,
Is that she is intolerable curst,
And shrewd, and froward, so beyond all measure
That, were my state far worser than it is,   90
I would not wed her for a mine of gold.

Pet. Hortensio, peace. Thou know'st not gold's effect.
Tell me her father's name and 'tis enough.

70. Xanthippe] *Theobald;* Zentippe *F.*   72. me, were she] *F2 (subst.);* me.
Were she is *F;* me. Whe'er she is *Riverside.*   73. seas.] *F;* seas, *Rowe.*

Apollo's gift to her of as many years of
life as there were grains in a handful
of sand she picked up (Golding,
p. 278). Cf. *Mer.V.*, i. ii. 95, 'If I live
to be as old as Sibylla'; *Oth.*, iii.
iv. 70-3.

70. *Xanthippe*] Socrates' wife, famed
for her bad temper. See Xenophon,
Memorabilia, ii. 2. *OED*, Xantippe,
quotes *Shr.* as its earliest example.

72-3. *rough . . . seas*] Horace, *Odes*,
iii. ix. 23, 'iracundior Hadria'.

78. *aglet-baby*] *OED* offers '? A doll
or (grown-up) 'baby' decked with
aglets (Explained by some as an aglet
shaped like a human figure)', quoting
only this example (Aglet, 6. Comb.).

An aglet was originally the metal tag
of a lace, but it came to mean any tag
or pendant attached to a fringe, or
any metallic stud, plate or spangle
worn on the dress. See Nashe, *Pierce
Penilesse* (*Works*, ed. McKerrow, rev.
Wilson (1958), i. 167), 'his Cappe . . .
all to be tasseld with Angle-hookes, in
stead of Aglets'. But no one is certain
exactly what an 'aglet-baby' was.

trot] hag (*OED, sb.*[2], quoting *Shr.*).
Cf. *Meas.*, iii. ii. 48 (applied to a
man).

80-1. *nothing . . . withal*] a common
proverb, in many forms (Tilley,
M1041a-84).

90. *state*] fortune, estate (Onions, 2).

For I will board her though she chide as loud
As thunder when the clouds in autumn crack.   95
Hor. Her father is Baptista Minola,
An affable and courteous gentleman.
Her name is Katherina Minola,
Renown'd in Padua for her scolding tongue.
Pet. I know her father, though I know not her,   100
And he knew my deceased father well.
I will not sleep, Hortensio, till I see her,
And therefore let me be thus bold with you
To give you over at this first encounter,
Unless you will accompany me thither.   105
Gru. I pray you, sir, let him go while the humour lasts.
O' my word, and she knew him as well as I do, she
would think scolding would do little good upon him.
She may perhaps call him half a score knaves or so.
Why, that's nothing; and he begin once, he'll rail in   110
his rope-tricks. I'll tell you what, sir, and she stand

---

94. *board*] address, woo. Cf. *Tw.N.*,
I. iii. 52–4, ' "Accost" is front her,
board her, woo her, assail her'.

104. *To . . . encounter*] to leave you
even though we have just met.

110–11. *he'll . . . rope-tricks*] Many
explanations have been offered of this
line; none is certain. *OED* records no
other instance of 'rope-tricks' (*sb.*[2] 8).
In the Epistle Dedicatory to *Have With
You to Saffron-Walden* Nashe writes of
Harvey's 'Paracelsian rope-rethorique'
and later in the same pamphlet refers
to him as 'Archibald Rupenrope'
(*Works*, ed. McKerrow, rev. Wilson,
III. 15 and 65). Rupenrope is possessed by 'the spirit of foolery'. *OED*
gives several examples of 'rope-ripe'
applied to language, among them
T. Wilson's *Art of Rhetoric* (1553), p. 59,
'if we firste expresse our mynde in
plaine wordes, and not seeke these
rope rype termes, whiche betraie
rather a foole, than commende a wyse
man'. McKerrow (IV. 335) notes
R. W.'s *Three Ladies of London* (1584),
B1, 'Thou art very pleasant & ful of

thy roperipe (I would say Retorick)',
and *Rom.*, II. iv. 154 (Alexander, 142;
Arden edn, 143), where Q has 'rope-
ripe', and Q2 and F1 'ropery' (though
the Nurse's comment on Mercutio's in-
decent badinage. All these examples
are concerned either with the art of
rhetoric or with jesting (often in-
decent jesting). Probably, then, the
nonce-word 'rope-tricks' is Grumio's
perversion of 'rhetorics', or 'rope-
rhetoric' (meaning 'rhetoric for which
the author deserved hanging'), or
'tropes of rhetoric', or (as Hibbard
suggests) 'trope-tricks' (though the
word is not known to exist). Or it may
be a confused recollection of all these.
The sense of 'rhetoric' is supported by
'figure' in l. 112. At the same time,
'stand' (l. 111) and 'throw a figure in
her face' (l. 112) suggest sexual innuendo. Cf. Anne C. Lancashire,
'Lyly and Shakespeare on the Ropes',
JEGP (1969); Richard Levin,
'Grumio's "Rope-tricks" and the
Nurse's "Ropery" ', *SQ* (1971).
Grumio is a known corrupter of words

him but a little, he will throw a figure in her face,
and so disfigure her with it that she shall have no
more eyes to see withal than a cat. You know him
not, sir.   115
Hor. Tarry, Petruchio, I must go with thee,
For in Baptista's keep my treasure is.
He hath the jewel of my life in hold,
His youngest daughter, beautiful Bianca,
And her withholds from me and other more,   120
Suitors to her and rivals in my love,
Supposing it a thing impossible,
For those defects I have before rehears'd,
That ever Katherina will be woo'd.
Therefore this order hath Baptista ta'en,   125
That none shall have access unto Bianca
Till Katherine the curst have got a husband.
Gru. Katherine the curst,
A title for a maid of all titles the worst.
Hor. Now shall my friend Petruchio do me grace,   130
And offer me disguis'd in sober robes
To old Baptista as a schoolmaster
Well seen in music, to instruct Bianca,
That so I may by this device at least
Have leave and leisure to make love to her,   135
And unsuspected court her by herself.
Gru. Here's no knavery. See, to beguile the old folks, how
the young folks lay their heads together.

Enter GREMIO, *and* LUCENTIO *disguised.*

Master, master, look about you. Who goes there, ha?

120. me and other] *Capell;* me. Other *F.*   138. S.D.] *F (after l. 136).*

(cf. 'rebused' at l. 7), and the trick is
comparable with Sly's 'comonty' (Ind.
ii. 137).
    112. *throw . . . face*] cast a figure of
speech at her (see also note to ll. 110–
111, above).
    113–14. *no . . . cat*] Cats' eyes are
proverbially sharp (Tilley, C180), but
the allusion may be to the saying
'Well might the cat wink when both

her eyes were out' (Tilley, C174).
    117. *keep*] custody.
    120. *other*] others. The use of the
singular for the plural is common
(Abbott, 12). Cf. *Troil.,* I. iii. 89–91.
    130. *do me grace*] do me a favour.
    133. *Well seen*] highly qualified. 'A
common expression, but not found
elsewhere in Shakespeare' (NCS).

Hor. Peace, Grumio. It is the rival of my love.   140
    Petruchio, stand by awhile.
Gru. A proper stripling and an amorous.
Gre. O, very well; I have perus'd the note.
    Hark you, sir, I'll have them very fairly bound—
    All books of love, see that at any hand—   145
    And see you read no other lectures to her.
    You understand me. Over and beside
    Signor Baptista's liberality,
    I'll mend it with a largess. Take your paper too,
    And let me have them very well perfum'd,   150
    For she is sweeter than perfume itself
    To whom they go to. What will you read to her?
Luc. Whate'er I read to her, I'll plead for you
    As for my patron, stand you so assur'd,
    As firmly as yourself were still in place,   155
    Yea, and perhaps with more successful words
    Than you, unless you were a scholar, sir.
Gre. O this learning, what a thing it is!
Gru. O this woodcock, what an ass it is!
Pet. Peace, sirrah.   160
Hor. Grumio, mum! God save you, Signor Gremio.
Gre. And you are well met, Signor Hortensio.
    Trow you whither I am going? To Baptista Minola.
    I promis'd to enquire carefully
    About a schoolmaster for the fair Bianca,   165

149. paper] *F;* papers *Pope.*

142. *proper stripling*] handsome youth (sarcastic comment on Gremio).
    143. *the note*] Lucentio's list of books.
    144. *fairly*] finely, handsomely (Onions, 1). Cf. *Troil.,* I. iii. 84.
    145. *at any hand*] in any case. Cf. Marlowe, *Doctor Faustus,* IV. iv. 19–20 (*Plays,* ed. Gill, p. 398), 'ride him not into the water at any hand'.
    146. *read . . . lectures*] give no other lessons. A lecture could be either a discourse delivered before an audience, or personal instruction. The second sense is required here. Cf. *1H4,*

III. i. 46, 'Which calls me pupil or hath read to me'.
    149. *mend . . . largess*] add to it with a gift. Cf. *Ant.,* I. v. 45, 'To mend the petty present'.
    paper] the 'note' referred to in l. 143.
    150. *them*] the books.
    155. *still in place*] present all the time.
    159. *woodcock*] the type of stupidity. Cf. *Ham.,* I. iii. 115, 'Ay, springes to catch woodcocks', and Gosson, *Sch. of Abuse,* Apol. (Arber), 72, 'Cupide sets vpp a Springe for Woodcockes, which

And by good fortune I have lighted well
On this young man, for learning and behaviour
Fit for her turn, well read in poetry
And other books, good ones, I warrant ye.

Hor. 'Tis well. And I have met a gentleman   170
Hath promis'd me to help me to another,
A fine musician to instruct our mistress.
So shall I no whit be behind in duty
To fair Bianca, so belov'd of me.

Gre. Belov'd of me, and that my deeds shall prove.   175

Gru. And that his bags shall prove.

Hor. Gremio, 'tis now no time to vent our love.
Listen to me, and if you speak me fair,
I'll tell you news indifferent good for either.
Here is a gentleman whom by chance I met,   180
Upon agreement from us to his liking,
Will undertake to woo curst Katherine,
Yea, and to marry her, if her dowry please.

Gre. So said, so done, is well.
Hortensio, have you told him all her faults?   185

Pet. I know she is an irksome brawling scold.
If that be all, masters, I hear no harm.

Gre. No, say'st me so, friend? What countryman?

Pet. Born in Verona, old Antonio's son.
My father dead, my fortune lives for me,   190
And I do hope good days and long to see.

Gre. O sir, such a life with such a wife were strange.

171. *me to*] *Rowe;* one to F.   189. *Antonio's*] *Rowe; Butonios* F.

are entangled ere they descrie the line'. See also Tilley, W748.

176. *bags*] money-bags. Cf. *John*, III. iii. 7–8, 'see thou shake the bags/ Of hoarding abbots'.

177. *vent*] express. Cf. Marston, *Antonio's Revenge* (ed. Gair), II. iv. 33, 'Come, I must vent my griefs, or heart will burst'.

179. *indifferent*] equally. See *OED*, Indifferently, *adv.* 1. Onions incorrectly glosses 'tolerably, fairly'.

181. *Upon . . . liking*] if we agree to his terms (see ll. 213–14).

184. *So . . . well*] Tilley cites this line under S117, 'No sooner said than done', but it seems at least equally applicable to S116, 'It is sooner said than done'. Cf. *3H6*, III. ii. 90, ''Tis better said than done'. Gremio's point is that 'words and performances are no kin together' (*Oth.*, IV. ii. 184–5; cf. Tilley, P602, 'Great promise small performance').

188. *say'st me so*] Is that what you tell me? (Abbott, 201).

192. *O . . . strange*] NCS suggests that the hypermetrical 'O' is probably

But if you have a stomach, to't a God's name,
You shall have me assisting you in all.
But will you woo this wildcat?
Pet.   Will I live?   195
Gru. Will he woo her? Ay, or I'll hang her.
Pet. Why came I hither but to that intent?
Think you a little din can daunt mine ears?
Have I not in my time heard lions roar?
Have I not heard the sea, puff'd up with winds,   200
Rage like an angry boar chafed with sweat?
Have I not heard great ordnance in the field,
And heaven's artillery thunder in the skies?
Have I not in a pitched battle heard
Loud 'larums, neighing steeds, and trumpets' clang? 205
And do you tell me of a woman's tongue,
That gives not half so great a blow to hear
As will a chestnut in a farmer's fire?
Tush, tush, fear boys with bugs!
Gru.   For he fears none.
Gre. Hortensio, hark.   210
This gentleman is happily arriv'd,
My mind presumes, for his own good and yours.

205. trumpets'] *Capell;* trumpets *F.*   207. to hear] *F;* to th'ear *Hanmer.*
208. chestnut] *Singer;* Chesse-nut *F.*   212. yours] *F;* ours *Theobald (conj.*
Thirlby).

derived from the last syllable of the speech-heading 'Gremi-o' and cites examples from *LLL.* But unmetrical lines are common enough in the early comedies.

193. *stomach*] inclination. Cf. *Ado,* I. iii. 15–16, 'eat when I have stomach'.

195. *Will I live?*] Yes, certainly. Cf. *2H4,* II. i. 154–5, 'You'll pay me all together?/*Fal.* Will I live?'

196. *Will ... hang her*] Tilley, H130. Cf. *Tw.N.,* I. v. 18–19, 'Many a good hanging prevents a bad marriage' (though Feste's remark probably includes an obscene sense which is not present in Grumio's).

201. *chafed*] irritated. The coincidence of 'lion', 'sea' and 'boar' with the word 'chafed' occurs again at

Tit., IV. ii. 138–9; 'The chafed boar, the mountain lioness,/The ocean swells not so as Aaron storms.'

205. *'larums*] alarums, or alarms, which were calls to arms on the drum and trumpet. Cf. *Cor.,* I. iv. 9, 'Then shall we hear their 'larum, and they ours'. The old form of the word is usually retained in modernized texts, in preference to 'alarm'.

207. *to hear*] Hanmer's emendation 'to th'ear' is mentioned with approval by Bond, NCS and Hibbard, but no one adopts it.

209. *fear ... bugs*] frighten children with bugbears (Tilley, B703). Cf. *3H6,* v. ii. 2.

212. *yours*] Many editions since Theobald (including Perry, Bond

Hor. I promis'd we would be contributors
  And bear his charge of wooing, whatsoe'er.
Gre. And so we will, provided that he win her.   215
Gru. I would I were as sure of a good dinner.

        Enter TRANIO *brave, and* BIONDELLO.

Tra. Gentlemen, God save you. If I may be bold,
  Tell me, I beseech you, which is the readiest way
  To the house of Signor Baptista Minola?
Bion. He that has the two fair daughters, is't he you   220
  mean?
Tra. Even he, Biondello.
Gre. Hark you, sir, you mean not her too?
Tra. Perhaps him and her, sir. What have you to do?
Pet. Not her that chides, sir, at any hand, I pray.   225
Tra. I love no chiders, sir. Biondello, let's away.
Luc. Well begun, Tranio.
Hor.   Sir, a word ere you go.
  Are you a suitor to the maid you talk of, yea or no?
Tra. And if I be, sir, is it any offence?
Gre. No, if without more words you will get you hence.   230
Tra. Why, sir, I pray, are not the streets as free
  For me as for you?
Gre.   But so is not she.
Tra. For what reason, I beseech you?
Gre.   For this reason, if you'll know,
  That she's the choice love of Signor Gremio.
Hor. That she's the chosen of Signor Hortensio.   235

223. *too?*] *conj. Tyrwhitt;* to— *F;* to woo? *conj. Malone.*

and NCS) have accepted his emendation 'ours'. But, as Hibbard points
out, to do so obscures the dramatic
point that Gremio is anxious to shift
any expense involved on to Hortensio.
  216. S.D. *brave*] finely dressed
(*OED*, Brave, *a.* A. 2). Cf. Ind. i. 38
and note.
  220-1. *He . . . mean?*] Biondello's
question is obviously part of a prearranged plan.
  223. *you . . . too?*] F reads 'you
meane not her to—'. If the dash

denotes a missing word that word
must be 'woo', but then Tranio's reply
makes odd sense. If F is correct, and
Tranio's reply is an interruption, the
sense is little better. Tyrwhitt's emendation gives meaning to the whole
passage. Since 'to' and 'too' are interchangeable spellings in Shakespearean
texts F's reading is explicable, though
it seems to have puzzled the compositor.
  225. *at any hand*] see note to l. 145,
above.

Tra. Softly, my masters. If you be gentlemen,
　　Do me this right; hear me with patience.
　　Baptista is a noble gentleman,
　　To whom my father is not all unknown,
　　And were his daughter fairer than she is,   240
　　She may more suitors have, and me for one.
　　Fair Leda's daughter had a thousand wooers,
　　Then well one more may fair Bianca have.
　　And so she shall. Lucentio shall make one,
　　Though Paris came, in hope to speed alone.   245
Gre. What, this gentleman will out-talk us all!
Luc. Sir, give him head, I know he'll prove a jade.
Pet. Hortensio, to what end are all these words?
Hor. Sir, let me be so bold as ask you,
　　Did you yet ever see Baptista's daughter?   250
Tra. No, sir, but hear I do that he hath two:
　　The one as famous for a scolding tongue
　　As is the other for beauteous modesty.
Pet. Sir, sir, the first's for me, let her go by.
Gre. Yea, leave that labour to great Hercules,   255
　　And let it be more than Alcides' twelve.
Pet. Sir, understand you this of me in sooth,
　　The youngest daughter whom you hearken for
　　Her father keeps from all access of suitors,
　　And will not promise her to any man   260
　　Until the elder sister first be wed.
　　The younger then is free, and not before.
Tra. If it be so, sir, that you are the man

242. *Fair . . . wooers*] Leda's daughter was Helen of Troy. NCS and Hibbard compare Marlowe, *Doctor Faustus* (*Plays*, ed. Gill, p. 383), v. i. 97, 'Was this the face that launch'd a thousand ships', as a possible source for the 'thousand wooers', but Shakespeare is probably quoting Ovid, *Heroides*, xvii. 103–4: 'Tunc ego te vellem celeri venisse carina,/cum mea virginitas mille petita procis.'

245. *came*] should come, were to come.

247. *jade*] a poor or worn-out

horse. If 'given his head' he would soon tire. Cf. II. i. 201.

254. *let . . . by*] leave her alone. Cf. *Meas.*, II. ii. 41, 'And let go by the actor'.

256. *Alcides' twelve*] Hercules was also called Alcides, after Alcaeus, a family ancestor. For his labours see Apollodorus, II. 5.

258. *hearken for*] ask for, enquire after (*OED, v.* 6). Bond and NCS gloss 'lie in wait', Onions gives 'wait for', but the sense may be similar to that in *LLL,* I. i. 212–13, 'Such is the

Must stead us all and me amongst the rest,
And if you break the ice and do this feat,   265
Achieve the elder, set the younger free
For our access, whose hap shall be to have her
Will not so graceless be to be ingrate.

Hor. Sir, you say well, and well you do conceive.
And since you do profess to be a suitor,   270
You must, as we do, gratify this gentleman,
To whom we all rest generally beholding.

Tra. Sir, I shall not be slack. In sign whereof,
Please ye we may contrive this afternoon,
And quaff carouses to our mistress' health,   275
And do as adversaries do in law,
Strive mightily, but eat and drink as friends.

Gru., Bion. O excellent motion! Fellows, let's be gone.

Hor. The motion's good indeed, and be it so.
Petruchio, I shall be your *ben venuto.*   *Exeunt.* 280

264. stead] *Capell;* steed *F.*   265. feat] *Rowe;* seeke *F.*   274. contrive] *F;*
convive *Theobald.*   280. ben] *F2;* Been *F.*

simplicity of man to hearken after the
flesh'.

264. *stead*] help, render service to
(*OED, v.* I. 1. c). Cf. *Oth.,* I. iii. 338–9.

265. *break the ice*] Tilley, I3.

267. *whose . . . be*] he whose good
luck it shall be.

268. *ingrate*] ungrateful (*OED, a.* 3).

271. *gratify*] reward, give a present
to (*OED, v.* 2). Cf. *Mer.V.,* IV. i. 401.

274. *contrive*] pass the time. A rare

use, not found elsewhere in Shakespeare. See Onions, contrive[2], and
OED, v.[2], quoting *Shr.* and Spenser,
FQ, II. ix. 48, 'Three ages, such as
mortall men contrive', though
Spenser's sense would seem to be more
like 'reckon' or 'divide the time into'.

278. *motion*] proposal.

280. *ben venuto*] literally, 'welcome'. Hortensio is offering Petruchio
his hospitality.

[ACT II]

[SCENE I]

Enter KATHERINA *and* BIANCA.

Bian. Good sister, wrong me not, nor wrong yourself,
To make a bondmaid and a slave of me.
That I disdain. But for these other gawds,
Unbind my hands, I'll pull them off myself,
Yea, all my raiment, to my petticoat,   5
Or what you will command me will I do,
So well I know my duty to my elders.

Kath. Of all thy suitors here I charge thee tell
Whom thou lov'st best. See thou dissemble not.

Bian. Believe me, sister, of all the men alive   10
I never yet beheld that special face
Which I could fancy more than any other.

Kath. Minion, thou liest. Is't not Hortensio?

Bian. If you affect him, sister, here I swear
I'll plead for you myself but you shall have him.   15

ACT II

Scene 1

ACT II SCENE I] *Pope; not in F.*   3. gawds] *Theobald; goods F.*   8. thee]
F2; not in F.

S.D.] F, which has neither act- nor
scene-heading here, simply gives the
entry of the sisters, though l. 4 makes
it clear that Bianca must enter with
her hands tied.

2. *bondmaid*] Shakespeare does not
use this word elsewhere, though he
would have known it from Scripture:
See Leviticus, xix. 20, xxv. 44, etc.
Bianca is literally 'bound'.

3. *gawds*] playthings, baubles.
Theobald's emendation of F's 'goods'
is generally adopted.

8. *thee*] F omits. NCS (p. 97) notes

a number of lines in which the omission of some small word or words ruins
the metre (and often the sense). It is
one of the most obvious characteristics of the text of *Shr.* in F.

14. *affect*] like (cf. I. i. 40; *Lr*,
I. i. 1), but possibly including the
sense of 'aim at, aspire to' (Onions, 1).
Cf. *2H6*, IV. vii. 92, 'Have I affected
wealth or honour?'

15. *but . . . him*] either 'if you shall
not have him otherwise', or 'but in
any case you shall have him' (Abbott,
126).

197

Kath. O then belike you fancy riches more.
  You will have Gremio to keep you fair.
Bian. Is it for him you do envy me so?
  Nay then you jest, and now I well perceive
  You have but jested with me all this while. 20
  I prithee, sister Kate, untie my hands.
Kath. If that be jest, then all the rest was so.   *Strikes her.*

Enter BAPTISTA.

Bap. Why, how now, dame, whence grows this insolence?
  Bianca, stand aside. Poor girl, she weeps.
  Go ply thy needle; meddle not with her. 25
  For shame, thou hilding of a devilish spirit,
  Why dost thou wrong her that did ne'er wrong thee?
  When did she cross thee with a bitter word?
Kath. Her silence flouts me, and I'll be reveng'd.
                    Flies after Bianca.
Bap. What, in my sight? Bianca, get thee in.   *Exit [Bianca].*
Kath. What, will you not suffer me? Nay, now I see 31
  She is your treasure, she must have a husband,
  I must dance barefoot on her wedding-day,
  And for your love to her lead apes in hell.
  Talk not to me, I will go sit and weep, 35
  Till I can find occasion of revenge.   [*Exit.*]

30. S.D. *Bianca*] *Rowe; not in F.*   36. S.D.] *Rowe; not in F.*

17. *fair*] finely dressed, (and so) beautiful.
18. *envy*] The verb was accented on the second syllable until well into the seventeenth century (Abbott, 490).
23. *dame*] madam (as a term of rebuke). Not a common use in Shakespeare, but cf. *2H6*, I. ii. 42, 'Presumptuous dame, ill-nurtur'd Eleanor!'
26. *hilding*] jade, baggage. 'A late word, of obscure etymology' (*OED*). The earliest example quoted (applied to a horse) is 1589. In Shakespeare it describes a contemptible or worthless person of either sex, but is specially applied to a woman here, and at *Rom.*, III. v. 168.

28. *cross*] annoy, contradict (*OED*, v. 14).
29. *flouts*] mocks, insults. Cf. *MND*, II. ii. 128.
33. *I . . . wedding-day*] An elder unmarried sister was supposed to dance barefoot on her sister's wedding-day. So the phrase became proverbial for remaining unmarried (Tilley, D22). Bond quotes a reference to show that the custom survived in Dorset until at least 1871.
34. *lead . . . hell*] Old maids were said to lead apes in (or into) hell, because they had no children to lead them into heaven (Tilley, M37). Cf. *Ado*, II. i. 34–41, and Lyly, *Euphues* (*Works*, ed. Bond, I. 230), 'For I had

Bap. Was ever gentleman thus griev'd as I?
      But who comes here?

Enter GREMIO, LUCENTIO [*disguised as Cambio*] *in the habit of a mean man;* PETRUCHIO, *with* [HORTENSIO *disguised as Litio; and*] TRANIO [*disguised as Lucentio*], *with his boy* [BIONDELLO], *bearing a lute and books.*

Gre. Good morrow, neighbour Baptista.
Bap. Good morrow, neighbour Gremio. God save you,   40
      gentlemen.
Pet. And you, good sir. Pray, have you not a daughter
      Call'd Katherina, fair and virtuous?
Bap. I have a daughter, sir, call'd Katherina.
Gre. You are too blunt, go to it orderly.   45
Pet. You wrong me, Signor Gremio, give me leave.
      I am a gentleman of Verona, sir,
      That hearing of her beauty and her wit,
      Her affability and bashful modesty,
      Her wondrous qualities and mild behaviour,   50
      Am bold to show myself a forward guest
      Within your house, to make mine eye the witness
      Of that report which I so oft have heard.
      And for an entrance to my entertainment
      I do present you with a man of mine, [*Presents Hortensio*]
      Cunning in music and the mathematics,   56
      To instruct her fully in those sciences,
      Whereof I know she is not ignorant.

38. S.D. *disguised as Cambio . . . Hortensio disguised as Litio; and . . . disguised as Lucentio . . . Biondello*] Hibbard (*after Rowe*); *not in* F.   42–3.] *as verse,* Capell; *as prose,* F.   55. S.D.] Rowe (*Presenting Hortensio*); *not in* F.

rather thou shouldest leade a lyfe to thine owne lykeinge in earthe, then to thy greate tormentes leade Apes in Hell'.

    38. S.D.] F makes no mention of Hortensio (perhaps the omission arose because he does not speak for nearly 150 lines), though he is certainly required on stage. The 'boy' must be Biondello. The description of Lucentio 'in the habit of a meane man' recalls I. i. 205. In reading 'Litio' I accept

Hosley's emendation in *HLQ* (1964), pp. 304–5. Most editions from Rowe onwards read 'Licio' but F has only 'Litio' or 'Lisio'.

    45. *orderly*] properly, in due order (*OED, adv.* 2). Cf. *Mer.V.*, II. ii. 155.
    54. *entrance*] entrance-fee. *OED* quotes no example before 1681.
    56. *Cunning*] See note to I. i. 97.
    57. *sciences*] branches of knowledge. Cf. *H5*, v. ii. 58.

Accept of him, or else you do me wrong.

His name is Litio, born in Mantua.   60

Bap. Y'are welcome, sir, and he for your good sake.

But for my daughter Katherine, this I know,

She is not for your turn, the more my grief.

Pet. I see you do not mean to part with her,

Or else you like not of my company.   65

Bap. Mistake me not, I speak but as I find.

Whence are you, sir? What may I call your name?

Pet. Petruchio is my name, Antonio's son,

A man well known throughout all Italy.

Bap. I know him well. You are welcome for his sake.   70

Gre. Saving your tale, Petruchio, I pray

Let us that are poor petitioners speak too.

Baccare! You are marvellous forward.

Pet. O pardon me, Signor Gremio, I would fain be doing.

Gre. I doubt it not, sir, but you will curse your wooing.   75

Neighbour, this is a gift very grateful, I am sure of it.

To express the like kindness, myself, that have been

more kindly beholding to you than any, freely give

unto you this young scholar [*Presents Lucentio*], that

---

60. Litio] *F;* Licio *F2* (*followed by Rowe and most subsequent edns*).   71–3.] *as verse,*
Steevens (*after Capell*); *as prose, F.*   74.] *as verse, Hanmer; as prose, F.*
75–6. wooing. Neighbour,] *Theobald;* wooing neighbors: *F.*   76–87. Neighbour . . . coming?] *as prose, Pope; as verse, F.*   76. it.] *Rowe;* it, *F.*   79. you]
Capell; not in F.   S.D.] *Rowe* (*presenting Lucentio*); *not in F.*

---

63. *She . . . turn*] She is not the girl
for you (*OED*, Turn, *sb.* 30 '. . .
purpose, use, convenience . . . 1602
Life T. Cromwell II. iii, We hardly
shall finde such a one as he, To fit
our turnes'). Cf. II. i. 265.

66. *I . . . find*] Tilley, S724.

71. *Saving*] with all respect to
(Onions, 2). Cf. *Err.*, IV. i. 27.

72. *poor petitioners*] Gremio adopts
the humble tone always used in formal
petitions. Bond quotes Sylvester's Du
Bartas, *Weekes,* II, 'Heare the Cries,
see the Teares of all distressed poor
Petitioners'. Cf. *2H6,* I. iii. 24, 'I am
but a poor petitioner of our whole

township'.

73. *Baccare!*] Stand back! *OED*
(Backare, baccare) quotes Nares's
view that 'the allusion is to an ignorant man who affected to speak Latin'.
In the form 'Backare, quoth Mortimer
to his sow' it was proverbial (Tilley,
M1183, where the earliest example is
1546). See Lyly, *Midas* (*Works,* ed.
Bond, III. 119), I. ii. 3, 'The Masculin
gender is more worthy then the fem-
inine, therefore *Licio,* backare'.

74. *I . . . doing*] I am eager to get
on with things (with a pun on 'doing'
in its sexual sense).

76. *grateful*] acceptable.

hath been long studying at Rheims; as cunning in   80
Greek, Latin, and other languages, as the other in
music and mathematics. His name is Cambio. Pray
accept his service.

Bap. A thousand thanks, Signor Gremio. Welcome,
good Cambio. [*To Tranio*] But, gentle sir, methinks   85
you walk like a stranger. May I be so bold to know
the cause of your coming?

Tra. Pardon me, sir, the boldness is mine own,
That, being a stranger in this city here,
Do make myself a suitor to your daughter,   90
Unto Bianca, fair and virtuous.
Nor is your firm resolve unknown to me
In the preferment of the eldest sister.
This liberty is all that I request,
That, upon knowledge of my parentage,   95
I may have welcome 'mongst the rest that woo,
And free access and favour as the rest.
And toward the education of your daughters
I here bestow a simple instrument,
And this small packet of Greek and Latin books.   100
If you accept them, then their worth is great.

Bap. Lucentio is your name? Of whence, I pray?

Tra. Of Pisa, sir, son to Vincentio.

Bap. A mighty man of Pisa. By report

---

85. S.D.] *Rowe; not in F.*   90. a suitor] *Q*; as utor *F.*   104. Pisa. By report]
Rowe (subst.); Pisa by report, F.

---

80. *Rheims*] The university was
founded in 1547, but the schools
founded by Abp. Adalberon had been
famous since the 10th century. In
Greene's *Friar Bacon and Friar Bungay*
(ed. Lavin, sc. ix) Vandermast includes it in his list of famous European
universities: 'I have given nonplus to
the Paduans,/To them of Sien,
Florence, and Bologna,/Rheims,
Louvain, and fair Rotterdam,/
Frankfort, Utrecht, and Orleans.'
Richard H. Perkinson argued (*N&Q*,
5 March 1938) that, in Shakespeare's
day, Rheims would have been 'recog-

nized as the most important source of
Catholic activity in England rather
than as a seat of general culture' since
the English college at Douai was
transferred there from 1578 to 1593.

93. *preferment*] preference, advantage (*OED*, II. 4, quoting 1526
Tindale, Romans, iii. 1, 'What preferment then hath the Jewe?'). AV
reads 'advantage'.

102. *Lucentio . . . name?*] Baptista
has not so far been told Lucentio's
name. Editors have suggested various
ways of giving him this information.
The simplest is that, after being given

I know him well. You are very welcome, sir.   105
[*To Hortensio*] Take you the lute, [*To Lucentio*] and you
   the set of books.
You shall go see your pupils presently.
Holla, within!

Enter a Servant.

                    Sirrah, lead these gentlemen
To my daughters, and tell them both
These are their tutors. Bid them use them well.   110
              [*Exeunt Servant, Hortensio, Lucentio, Biondello.*]
We will go walk a little in the orchard,
And then to dinner. You are passing welcome,
And so I pray you all to think yourselves.

Pet. Signor Baptista, my business asketh haste,
And every day I cannot come to woo.   115
You knew my father well, and in him me,
Left solely heir to all his lands and goods,
Which I have better'd rather than decreas'd.
Then tell me, if I get your daughter's love,
What dowry shall I have with her to wife?   120

---

106. *To Hortensio . . . To Lucentio*] *after NCS; not in* F.   110. S.D.] *Capell (Exit Servant with Lucentio and Hortensio, Biondello following) ; not in* F.

the books (l. 100), he opens one of
them and reads Lucentio's name on
the fly-leaf.

104–5. *A . . . well*] F's reading
cannot be correct. It would make
nonsense of the plot in v. i. 1–99.
Rowe's emendation has been universally accepted.

107. *presently*] immediately, at once.
See Onions: 'Very frequent in Shakespeare, and the usual Elizabethan
sense; the modern sense of "in a little
while, shortly" is not evidenced with
certainty before 1650, but there are
possible instances in Shakespeare, e.g.
Wiv., IV. ii. 102' (l. 85 in Alexander's
text).

109. *To . . . both*] The line is unmetrical, and something seems to have
been omitted (Capell added 'from me'
at the end of the line). But it is impossible to say what has been left out.

112. *dinner*] The main meal of the
day, served between 11 a.m. and
noon. See *Shakespeare's England*, II.
134 ff.

   passing] very (*OED*, Passing, B. *adv.*).

114. *asketh*] demands, requires. Cf.
2H6, I. ii. 90.

115. *And . . . woo*] 'the burden of
several old English ballads' (Bond).
See Durfey's *Pills to Purge Melancholy*
(ed. 1707), I. 135: 'Saie, Joan, quoth
John, what wilt thou doe? / I cannot
come every daie to woo.' The ballad
'Joan, quoth John, when wyll this be'
has a long history in the literature of
English ballads. See John M. Ward,
'Joan qd. John', in *Aspects of Mediæval
and Renaissance Music: A Birthday
Offering to Gustave Reese*, ed. Jan La
Rue (New York, 1966), pp. 832–55.
I am grateful to Dr F. W. Sternfeld
for help with this identification.

Bap. After my death the one half of my lands,
  And in possession twenty thousand crowns.
Pet. And for that dowry I'll assure her of
  Her widowhood, be it that she survive me,
  In all my lands and leases whatsoever.   125
  Let specialties be therefore drawn between us,
  That covenants may be kept on either hand.
Bap. Ay, when the special thing is well obtain'd,
  That is, her love; for that is all in all.
Pet. Why, that is nothing. For I tell you, father,   130
  I am as peremptory as she proud-minded;
  And where two raging fires meet together,
  They do consume the thing that feeds their fury.
  Though little fire grows great with little wind,
  Yet extreme gusts will blow out fire and all.   135
  So I to her, and so she yields to me,
  For I am rough and woo not like a babe.
Bap. Well mayst thou woo, and happy be thy speed.
  But be thou arm'd for some unhappy words.
Pet. Ay, to the proof, as mountains are for winds,   140
  That shakes not, though they blow perpetually.

---

131. proud-minded] *hyphened, Rowe; unhyphened, F.*   141. shakes] *F;* shake *F2.*

---

122. *in possession*] at the time of the marriage.

124. *widowhood*] the estate settled upon a widow at the time of the marriage contract (*OED*, 2, quoting only *Shr.*). Cf. *Meas.*, v. i. 420–3.

126. *specialties*] explicit contracts; a specialty was 'a special contract, obligation, or bond, expressed in an instrument under seal' (*OED*, II. 7). Cf. *LLL*, II. i. 164. Specialties between two or more parties were 'indented' as a precaution against forgery (*Shakespeare's England*, I. 407).

131. *peremptory*] always accented on the first syllable, in Shakespeare.

134–5. *Though . . . all*] The proverb was 'A little wind kindles, much puts out the fire' (Tilley, W424), or 'The wind puts out small lights but enrages

great fires' (Tilley, W448a). Cf. *John*, v. ii. 83–7; *Lucr.*, 647–8. Petruchio's point is that Katherina's fiery temper has met with only feeble opposition from her father, whereas his own 'extreme gusts' will subdue her.

138. *happy . . . speed*] good luck to you. 'Speed' here means 'fortune' (Onions, speed, 2). Cf. *Wint.*, III. ii. 141–2.

140. *proof*] 'proved or tested strength of armour or arms, impenetrability' (Onions, proof, 4). Cf. *Rom.*, I. i. 208.

141. *shakes*] The third person plural in -s is extremely common in F. See Abbott, 333, and cf. *Tp.*, III. iii. 2, where F reads 'My old bones akes' and Alexander 'corrects' to 'ache'.

Enter HORTENSIO *with his head broke.*

Bap. How now, my friend, why dost thou look so pale?
Hor. For fear, I promise you, if I look pale.
Bap. What, will my daughter prove a good musician?
Hor. I think she'll sooner prove a soldier.   145
        Iron may hold with her, but never lutes.
Bap. Why then, thou canst not break her to the lute?
Hor. Why no, for she hath broke the lute to me.
        I did but tell her she mistook her frets,
        And bow'd her hand to teach her fingering,   150
        When, with a most impatient devilish spirit,
        'Frets, call you these?' quoth she, 'I'll fume with them.'
        And with that word she struck me on the head,
        And through the instrument my pate made way,
        And there I stood amazed for a while,   155
        As on a pillory, looking through the lute,
        While she did call me rascal fiddler
        And twangling Jack, with twenty such vile terms,
        As had she studied to misuse me so.
Pet. Now, by the world, it is a lusty wench.   160
        I love her ten times more than e'er I did.

---

153. struck] *Capell* (strook); stroke *F.*   157. rascal fiddler] *Capell;* Rascall,
Fidler, *F.*

S.D.] The editors of the Bantam
text of *Shr.* (New York, 1967) point
out that it has become traditional in
the theatre for Hortensio to enter
with the broken lute over his head,
but that there is no justification for
this in F. It is better to follow F in
this respect, and let the words do
their work. Cf. Greene, *Orlando
Furioso* (*Plays and Poems*, ed. Collins,
I. 255), IV. ii, '*He strikes and beates him
with the fiddle . . . He breakes it about
his head*'.

144. *prove*] (i) become, (ii) test.
Baptista's pun is ironic.

146. *hold*] remain unbroken, not
break or give way (Onions, hold, B.
9). Cf. *Wint.*, IV. iii. 34.

147. *break*] train, discipline (*OED*,
v. 14), with special reference to horse-

breaking. This is the first of the play's
many images in which the taming of
Katherina is compared to the training of an animal or bird. Cf. the word-
play in ll. 147–8 with *Err.*, III. i. 73–7.

149. *frets*] bars or ridges placed on
the fingerboard of the lute to regulate
the fingering (*OED*, *sb.*[3]).

152. *Frets*] irritations, vexations
(*OED*, *sb.*[2] 3). *OED* notes the phrase
'fret and fume', but its earliest example
is 1885.

156. *pillory*] a kind of stocks for
head and arms. The offender stood
with his head, as it were, framed in
wood.

158. *Jack*] base or silly fellow. Cf.
l. 281, and *Ado*, v. i. 91, 'Boys, apes,
braggarts, Jacks, milksops!'

160. *lusty*] vigorous, merry (the

O, how I long to have some chat with her.

Bap. Well, go with me, and be not so discomfited.
Proceed in practice with my younger daughter;
She's apt to learn and thankful for good turns.   165
Signor Petruchio, will you go with us,
Or shall I send my daughter Kate to you?

Pet. I pray you do.   *Exeunt all except Petruchio.*
          I'll attend her here,
And woo her with some spirit when she comes.
Say that she rail, why then I'll tell her plain   170
She sings as sweetly as a nightingale.
Say that she frown, I'll say she looks as clear
As morning roses newly wash'd with dew.
Say she be mute and will not speak a word,
Then I'll commend her volubility,   175
And say she uttereth piercing eloquence.
If she do bid me pack, I'll give her thanks,
As though she bid me stay by her a week.
If she deny to wed, I'll crave the day
When I shall ask the banns, and when be married.   180
But here she comes, and now, Petruchio, speak.

Enter KATHERINA.

Good morrow, Kate, for that's your name, I hear.

Kath. Well have you heard, but something hard of hearing;

168. S.D.] *F (after l. 167).*

common Elizabethan sense was 'pleasing, pleasant', but see Onions, 1 and 2).

162. *chat*] conversation (*OED, sb.* 2). Under Chat, *sb.*⁶, *OED* notes the meaning 'Cate', and quotes '1584 B.R. tr. *Herodotus* 43 The greatest part of theyr provision consisting in choise chats and junkettinge dishes'. Cf. ll. 189 and 271.

163. *discomfited*] discouraged. Cf. *2H6,* v. i. 62–3.

164. *Proceed in practice*] continue your lessons.

173. *As . . . dew*] Cf. *A Shrew,* xv. 37 (Bullough, p. 99), where a form of

this line is transferred to Kate in her conversation with the Duke of Cestus.

177. *pack*] go away. Cf. *Wiv.,* i. iii. 79.

179. *deny*] refuse. Cf. v. ii. 104.

180. *ask the banns*] This detail, which would require a delay of three weeks in the practice of the Church of England, is omitted in the play, but see III. ii. 16, and *Shakespeare's England,* II. 144–8.

183. *heard . . . hard*] Both words would have been pronounced 'hard', producing a pun. See Kökeritz, 112 and 250.

They call me Katherine that do talk of me.

Pet. You lie, in faith, for you are call'd plain Kate,   185
And bonny Kate, and sometimes Kate the curst;
But Kate, the prettiest Kate in Christendom,
Kate of Kate Hall, my super-dainty Kate,
For dainties are all Kates, and therefore, Kate,
Take this of me, Kate of my consolation,   190
Hearing thy mildness prais'd in every town,
Thy virtues spoke of, and thy beauty sounded,
Yet not so deeply as to thee belongs,
Myself am mov'd to woo thee for my wife.   194

Kath. Mov'd, in good time! Let him that mov'd you hither
Remove you hence. I knew you at the first
You were a movable.

Pet.   Why, what's a movable?

186. bonny] *F4;* bony *F.*

185–217. *You . . . try*] This wit-
combat is comparable with those in
LLL (e.g. v. ii. 337–415) and *Ado,*
I. i. 99–124.

186. *bonny*] F 'bony', a common
variant spelling (Kökeritz, p. 96). The
word has several senses in Shakespeare
from 'comely' to 'big, stout' (Onions,
1–3), but here something like 'fine,
big, strapping' is required. Cf. *AYL,*
II. iii. 8.

188. *Kate . . . Hall*] The reference
seems specific but probably is not.
Bond notes 'The suggestion of an
allusion to St. Catherine's Hall at
Cambridge has nothing to recommend it', but NCS refers to Stopes,
Life of Southampton (p. 45): 'In Aug.
1591 the queen's harbinger was
allowed payment "for making ready a
dining-house at Katharine Hall", one
of the places in the South of England
at which Elizabeth stopped on a
summer progress which included visits
to Cowdray, the house of Southampton's grandfather, and Titchfield,
the house of Southampton himself'
(NCS, p. 149). With the known links
between Shakespeare and the Earl of
Southampton, the coincidence is
tantalizing, but the evidence adds

nothing to our understanding of this
line in *Shr.*

super-dainty] The word is not found
anywhere else in Shakespeare, and
OED (Super-, III. 9. a) quotes only
this instance.

189. *dainties . . . Kates*] punning on
the sense of 'cates' as 'delicacies'. Cf.
Err., III. i. 28; Greene, *A Looking
Glasse for London and England (Plays and
Poems,* ed. Collins, I. 198), v. i. 2,
'These curious cates are gratious in
mine eye'.

190. *consolation*] comfort.

192. *sounded*] proclaimed. Cf. *R2,*
III. iv. 74. It also means 'fathomed'.
See p. 67.

193. *deeply*] with deep sound, i.e.
loudly (*OED, adv,* 6). Cf. *Ven.,* 832.
It also means 'to such a depth', taking
up the nautical sense of 'sounded'
(plumbed) in the previous line.

195. *in good time*] indeed. The phrase
is 'an interjection with various shades
of meaning used to express acquiescence, astonishment, or indignation'
(NCS).

197. *movable*] a piece of furniture
(cf. *R2,* II. i. 161), and hence also,
here, a man easily moved, given to
change (*OED,* B. 3 and 5).

Kath. A joint-stool.
Pet.   Thou hast hit it. Come, sit on me.
Kath. Asses are made to bear, and so are you.
Pet. Women are made to bear, and so are you.   200
Kath. No such jade as you, if me you mean.
Pet. Alas, good Kate, I will not burden thee!
     For, knowing thee to be but young and light—
Kath. Too light for such a swain as you to catch,
     And yet as heavy as my weight should be.   205
Pet. Should be? Should—buzz!
Kath.   Well ta'en, and like a buzzard.
Pet. O slow-wing'd turtle, shall a buzzard take thee?
Kath. Ay, for a turtle, as he takes a buzzard.

206. be] *F;* bee *Theobald.*

198. *A joint-stool*] Bond retains F's 'ioyn'd stoole' as 'join'd-stool', on the analogy of 'ioyned bed' in Harrison's *Description of England*, II. 12, and also the forms 'joyned chair' and 'joyned press'. A joint-stool was a low stool with three or four legs fitted into it, made by a joiner, as opposed to a carpenter. Cf. *Lr*, III. vi. 51, 'Cry you mercy, I took you for a joint-stool', a proverbial phrase (Tilley, M897) which was a taunting apology for overlooking someone; Lyly, *Mother Bombie* (*Works*, ed. Bond, III. 209), IV. ii. 28.

199. *bear*] carry burdens.

200. *bear*] bear children (with a second sexual sense evidenced by Petruchio's 'burden' in l. 202).

201. *jade*] worn-out horse, which soon tires (used of either sex). Cf. I. ii. 247.

202. *burden*] (i) lie heavy on, (ii) accuse. For sense (ii) cf. *Err.*, v. i. 209.

203. *light*] (i) light in weight, (ii) frivolous, wanton.

204. *Too . . . catch*] 'Too quick for rustic wit like yours' (Bond).

205. *heavy . . . be*] carrying the weight of importance my position in society requires. NCS suspects a reference to catch-weights in horse-racing. Hibbard suggests the allusion is to coinage: counterfeit coins were 'too light', and Katherina claims she she is good, sound currency.

206. *Should . . . buzz!*] Petruchio puns on 'be' and 'bee', and on 'buzz' in the senses of (i) the buzz of a bee, and (ii) a busy rumour, or scandal (*OED, sb.*[1] 1 and 3. b). Cf. *Lr*, I. iv. 326, 'Each buzz, each fancy, each complaint, dislike'. *OED* adds, under a separate entry (Buzz, *int. Obs.*), 'Said in the Variorum Shakespeare (1803) to have been a common exclamation (of impatience or contempt) when any one was telling a well-known story'. Cf. *Ham.*, II. ii. 389, and Jonson, *Alchemist* (H. & S., v. 308), I. ii. 169–70.

buzzard] a bird of the falcon family, regarded as useless for falconry, and hence (*OED, sb.*[2] 2) 'a worthless, stupid, or ignorant person'. Hibbard suggests the sense of 'scandal-monger' or 'tale-bearer' as better fitting the context, and quotes *R3*, I. i. 133, 'Whiles kites and buzzards prey at liberty'.

207. *turtle*] turtle-dove, symbol of faithful love.

208. *Ay . . . buzzard*] NCS paraphrases 'the fool will take me for a faithful wife, as the turtle-dove swallows the cockchafer'. *OED* records

Pet. Come, come, you wasp; i' faith, you are too angry.

Kath. If I be waspish, best beware my sting.   210

Pet. My remedy is then to pluck it out.

Kath. Ay, if the fool could find it where it lies.

Pet. Who knows not where a wasp does wear his sting?
      In his tail.

Kath.   In his tongue.

Pet.   Whose tongue?

Kath. Yours, if you talk of tales, and so farewell.   215

Pet. What, with my tongue in your tail? Nay, come again,
      Good Kate. I am a gentleman—

Kath.   That I'll try.   *She strikes him.*

Pet. I swear I'll cuff you, if you strike again.

Kath. So may you lose your arms.

      If you strike me, you are no gentleman,   220
      And if no gentleman, why then no arms.

Pet. A herald, Kate? O, put me in thy books.

213–14.] *as verse, Rowe; as prose,* F.   215. tales] F; tails Q.

Buzzard, *sb.*², *dial.*: 'A name applied to various insects that fly by night, e.g. large moths and cockchafers.' This seems the best interpretation of a difficult line, and the dialect sense of 'buzzard' is taken up by 'wasp' in the following line.

209. *Come . . . angry*] Tilley, W76 and W705, 'Women are wasps if angered'. Cf. Peele, *Old Wives' Tale* (1595), sig. B4, 'As curst as a waspe'.

214. *In his tail*] Tilley, S858, 'The sting is in the tail'. Cf. *Troil.*, v. x. 41–4.

215. *tales*] idle stories, gossip, with a pun on 'tails' meaning fundaments or pudenda (*OED*, *sb.*¹ 5). Kökeritz (p. 149) describes this as 'one of Shakespeare's favorite bawdy puns' and cites *Oth.*, iii. i. 6–11, *AYL*, ii. vii. 28, *Rom.*, ii. iv. 91–6, *Gent.*, ii. iii. 41–5, etc.

216. *What . . . again*] Petruchio keeps up the obscene jest in 'tongue . . . tail', but the phrase also means 'What, are you running away, and leaving me the last word?' So 'come again' means both 'come back', and 'have at you!' Cf. *Ham.*, v. ii. 294, 'Nay,

come again'. Many editors follow this line with some such S.D. as '*he takes her in his arms*', on the grounds that it is required by Katherina's words in l. 219. But F has none, and the point may safely be left to a producer's discretion.

217. *try*] put to the test.

219. *So . . . arms*] F makes no spelling distinction between 'loose' and 'lose', and the pronunciation was probably identical. Kökeritz (p. 125) says 'The possibility of a pun on *loose* "to let fly" and *lose* should probably be admitted'. The two basic senses of the line are 'It makes you let me go', and 'Thus you would forfeit your claim to being a gentleman'. A coat-of-arms from the College of Heralds was proof of a gentleman's status, and the pun on 'arms' was common. Cf. *Ham.*, v. i. 31–8; Lyly, *Mother Bombie* (*Works*, ed. Bond, iii. 182), i. iii. 187–8, 'and wee must wearie our legges to purchase our children armes'.

222. *O . . . books*] 'To be in the herald's books was to be registered as a gentleman' (Hibbard), and to be

Kath. What is your crest, a coxcomb?

Pet. A combless cock, so Kate will be my hen.

Kath. No cock of mine, you crow too like a craven.   225

Pet. Nay, come, Kate, come; you must not look so sour.

Kath. It is my fashion when I see a crab.

Pet. Why, here's no crab, and therefore look not sour.

Kath. There is, there is.

Pet. Then show it me.

Kath.   Had I a glass, I would.   230

Pet. What, you mean my face?

Kath.   Well aim'd of such a young one.

Pet. Now, by Saint George, I am too young for you.

Kath. Yet you are wither'd.

Pet.   'Tis with cares.

Kath.   I care not.

Pet. Nay, hear you, Kate—in sooth, you scape not so.

Kath. I chafe you, if I tarry. Let me go.   235

Pet. No, not a whit. I find you passing gentle.

    'Twas told me you were rough, and coy, and sullen,

    And now I find report a very liar;

    For thou art pleasant, gamesome, passing courteous,

'in someone's books' was to be in their favour. Cf. Tilley, B534; *Ado*, I. i. 64, 'I see, lady, the gentleman is not in your books'.

223. *crest*] (i) a figure or device borne above the shield and helmet in a coat of arms, (ii) a 'comb' or tuft of feathers, or the like, on the head of a bird or animal (*OED, sb.*[1] 1 and 3).

coxcomb] the professional fool's cap, like a cock's comb in shape and colour. Cf. *Lr*, I. iv. 96–108.

224. *A combless cock*] an unaggressive cock, the cut comb being indicative of humiliation. Cf. Tilley, C526, quoting '1581 Pettie, *Civ. Conv.* II. i. 197: Princes should . . . cut the combes of these clownish cocks-combes'.

225. *craven*] a cock that 'is not game' (*OED*, B. *sb.* 1). Cf. Lyly, *Euphues* (*Works*, ed. Bond, I. 247), 'though he [Curio] be a Cocke of the

game, yet *Euphues* is content to bee crauen and crye creeke'.

227. *crab*] crab-apple: 'wild apple, esp. connoting its sour, harsh, tart, astringent quality' (*OED, sb.*[2] 1). Hence, also, 'a sour person' (*sb.*[2] 6).

232. *I . . . you*] I am too strong for you (*OED*, Young, *a.* 3, 'Having . . . the freshness or vigour of youth'). Cf. *Ado*, v. i. 118–19, 'Had we fought, I doubt we should have been too young for them'.

235. *chafe you*] (i) excite you, inflame your feelings, (ii) vex you, irritate you (*OED, v.* I. 2 and 5).

238. *report . . . liar*] Tilley, F44, 'Fame (Report) is a liar', and R84, 'Report has a blister on her tongue'.

239. *gamesome*] merry, playful. Cf. Lyly, *Euphues* (*Works*, ed. Bond, II. 54), 'I now taking heart at grasse, to see hir so gamesome, as merely [i.e. merrily] as I could, pledged hir in this manner'.

But slow in speech, yet sweet as spring-time flowers. 240
Thou canst not frown, thou canst not look askance,
Nor bite the lip, as angry wenches will,
Nor hast thou pleasure to be cross in talk.
But thou with mildness entertain'st thy wooers,
With gentle conference, soft and affable.   245
Why does the world report that Kate doth limp?
O slanderous world! Kate like the hazel-twig
Is straight and slender, and as brown in hue
As hazel-nuts and sweeter than the kernels.
O, let me see thee walk. Thou dost not halt.   250
Kath. Go, fool, and whom thou keep'st command.
Pet. Did ever Dian so become a grove
   As Kate this chamber with her princely gait?
   O be thou Dian, and let her be Kate,
   And then let Kate be chaste and Dian sportful.   255
Kath. Where did you study all this goodly speech?
Pet. It is extempore, from my mother-wit.
Kath. A witty mother, witless else her son.
Pet. Am I not wise?
Kath.   Yes, keep you warm.

---

241. askance] *Capell;* a sconce *F.*   257. mother-wit] *hyphened, Rowe; un-*
hyphened, F.   *hyphened, F.*

240. *slow in speech*] not sharp-
tongued. (*OED,* Slow, *a.* 5). Cf.
Gent., III. i. 293 ff. and esp. 324–7,
'. . . To be slow in words is a woman's
only virtue', and Exodus, iv. 10.

241. *askance*] scornfully (*OED, adv.*
2, quoting *Shr.*). Cf. Spenser, *Shep-*
heardes Calender, March, 21, 'That
scornefully lookes askaunce'.

243. *cross*] contradicting, perverse.
Cf. *R3,* III. i. 126.

244. *entertain'st*] treatest (Onions,
3).

245. *conference*] conversation (*OED,*
sb. 5).

247. *like the hazel-twig*] Cf. Lyly,
Euphues (*Works,* ed. Bond, I. 254), 'If
she be well sette, then call hir a Bosse,
if slender, a Hasill twigge, if Nut-
browne, as blacke as a coale . . . '

251. *whom . . . command*] order your

own servants about, not me. Cf.
Tilley, C245, 'Thou dost not bear my
charges that thou shouldst command
me'. Bond says 'derived from the
slave Stasimus' answer in Plautus'
Trinummus, IV. iii. 54, "Emere meliu'st
cui imperes" '.

255. *sportful*] playful, sportive
(*OED, a.* 2), probably also with the
sense of 'amorous'. Cf. *3H6,* v. i. 18,
'Is sportful Edward come?' (Edward
was notorious for his lust).

256. *study*] learn by heart, commit
to memory (*OED, v.* 9. b). It is very
much the actor's term. Cf. *Tw.N.,*
I. v. 182; *Ham.,* II. ii. 535; *MND,*
I. ii. 59–60.

257. *from my mother-wit*] Tilley, O87.

259. *Am . . . warm*] The allusion is
to the proverb 'He is wise enough that
can keep himself warm' (Tilley, K10).

Pet. Marry, so I mean, sweet Katherine, in thy bed.   260
　　And therefore, setting all this chat aside,
　　Thus in plain terms: your father hath consented
　　That you shall be my wife; your dowry 'greed on;
　　And will you, nill you, I will marry you.
　　Now, Kate, I am a husband for your turn,   265
　　For by this light, whereby I see thy beauty,
　　Thy beauty that doth make me like thee well,
　　Thou must be married to no man but me.
　　For I am he am born to tame you, Kate,
　　And bring you from a wild Kate to a Kate   270
　　Conformable as other household Kates.

　　　　　　　　Enter BAPTISTA, GREMIO, TRANIO.

　　Here comes your father. Never make denial;
　　I must and will have Katherine to my wife.
Bap. Now, Signor Petruchio, how speed you with my
　　　　daughter?
Pet. How but well, sir? How but well?   275
　　It were impossible I should speed amiss.
Bap. Why, how now, daughter Katherine? In your dumps?
Kath. Call you me daughter? Now I promise you
　　You have show'd a tender fatherly regard
　　To wish me wed to one half lunatic,   280
　　A madcap ruffian and a swearing Jack,
　　That thinks with oaths to face the matter out.

---

270. wild Kate] *F;* wild Kat *F2–4.*   271. S.D.] *F (after l. 268).*   Tranio] *Q;*
Trayno F.

Cf. *Ado*, I. i. 57–8, and Jonson, *Cynthia's Revels* (H. & S., IV. 67), II. ii. 47. Katherina implies that Petruchio has no more than minimum wisdom.

264. *will you, nill you*] one way or another, willy-nilly (*OED*, Will, *v.* VI. 50. b). See also Tilley, W401; *Ham.*, V. i. 18.

265. *for your turn*] See note to II. i. 63.

270. *wild Kate*] a pun on 'wild-cat'.

271. *Conformable*] tractable, submissive (*OED*, *a.* 3. b).

274. *how speed you . . . ?*] How are you getting on?

277. *In your dumps?*] Are you feeling depressed? A 'dump' was originally a mournful melody or song, though little is known about them (there is a *Triste Dumpe* in the Fitzwilliam Virginal Book, and it is not particularly doleful). See *Rom.*, IV. v. 103–25, and *OED*, Dump, *sb.*[1] 3.

281. *Jack*] See note to II. i. 158, and Onions, 2.

282. *face . . . out*] brazen it out, get his way. Cf. *Err.*, III. i. 6.

Pet. Father, 'tis thus: yourself and all the world
     That talk'd of her have talk'd amiss of her.
     If she be curst it is for policy,   285
     For she's not froward, but modest as the dove.
     She is not hot, but temperate as the morn.
     For patience she will prove a second Grissel,
     And Roman Lucrece for her chastity.
     And to conclude, we have 'greed so well together   290
     That upon Sunday is the wedding-day.
Kath. I'll see thee hang'd on Sunday first.
Gre. Hark, Petruchio, she says she'll see thee hang'd first.
Tra. Is this your speeding? Nay then, good night our part.
Pet. Be patient, gentlemen, I choose her for myself.   295
     If she and I be pleas'd, what's that to you?
     'Tis bargain'd 'twixt us twain, being alone,
     That she shall still be curst in company.
     I tell you 'tis incredible to believe
     How much she loves me. O, the kindest Kate!   300

294. good night] *F3;* godnight *F.*

285. *policy*] tactical advantage.

286. *modest . . . dove*] Tilley cites this line under D573, 'As loving (tame, patient) as a Dove', and compares *MND*, I. ii. 74–5, *Pilgr.*, vii. 2 and *Ham.*, v. i. 280–1. But the sense is very close to that of D572, 'As innocent (harmless) as a Dove', and behind both lies Matthew, x. 16.

287. *hot*] passionate, ardent. Cf. *Gent.*, II. v. 42, 'a hot lover'.

temperate] (i) of genial temperature: cf. *Sonn.*, xviii. 2, (ii) chaste: cf. *Tp.*, IV. i. 132, 'temperate nymphs'.

288. *a second Grissel*] Griselda, 'the flour of wyfly pacience', is first described in Boccaccio's *Decameron* (x. x), and later by Chaucer in the *Clerkes Tale.* Bond notes that the story 'had been the subject of ballads and tracts long before our play appeared', and lists a song and two ballads entered on the Stationers' Register in 1566, a play on the subject by Ralph Radcliff (*fl.* end of Henry VIII), of which the title only is preserved by John Bale, and two black-letter tracts, 'the first of which, dated 1590, but probably originally printed earlier, was used by Dekker, Chettle, and Haughton for their play *Patient Grissell*, acted 1600, and had, I believe, been read by Shakespeare'. There is also (unknown to Bond) the *Patient Grissell* play by John Phillip (*c.* 1560). The phrase 'As patient as Grissel' is quoted as proverbial by Tilley (G456), though apart from this line in *Shr.*, he quotes only one example, dated 1681. Smith and Wilson quotes nothing between Chaucer and Shakespeare. Despite all this, and the obvious attraction of the allusion in a play like *Shr.*, Griselda is not mentioned anywhere else in Shakespeare.

289. *Lucrece*] Shakespeare published *Lucrece* in 1594. He found the story in the first book of Livy's *History of Rome*, and the second book of Ovid's *Fasti.*

294. *good . . . part*] goodbye to our share in the business.

She hung about my neck, and kiss on kiss
She vied so fast, protesting oath on oath,
That in a twink she won me to her love.
O, you are novices. 'Tis a world to see
How tame, when men and women are alone,   305
A meacock wretch can make the curstest shrew.
Give me thy hand, Kate, I will unto Venice,
To buy apparel 'gainst the wedding-day.
Provide the feast, father, and bid the guests.
I will be sure my Katherine shall be fine.   310

Bap. I know not what to say, but give me your hands.
God send you joy, Petruchio, 'tis a match.

Gre., Tra. Amen, say we. We will be witnesses.

Pet. Father, and wife, and gentlemen, adieu,
I will to Venice; Sunday comes apace.   315
We will have rings, and things, and fine array,
And kiss me, Kate, we will be married o' Sunday.
                              Exeunt Petruchio and Katherina.

Gre. Was ever match clapp'd up so suddenly?

Bap. Faith, gentlemen, now I play a merchant's part,

---

302. *vied*] (i) increased in number by addition or repetition (*OED, v.* 6), (ii) in card-playing: hazarding a certain sum on the strength of one's hand (*OED, v.* 2). Rider's *Bibliotheca Scholastica* (1589) glosses 'vie' as 'Augere, Admittere, Accipere Sponsionem'.

304. *'Tis a world*] It is worth a world. Cf. Tilley, W878; *Ado,* III. v. 34–5; Lyly, *Euphues* (*Works,* ed. Bond, I. 202), 'It is a worlde to see the doating of theyr louers'.

306. *meacock*] tame, spiritless (*OED, obs.* I). Not found elsewhere in Shakespeare.

311–12. *give . . . match*] Hibbard argues that this brief ceremony constitutes a 'pre-contract', an essential part of an Elizabethan marriage, after which neither party could marry another person. But the pre-contract, or *sponsalia per verba de futuro,* was a sworn declaration of intention to marry in the future, and required the presence and verbal consent of both parties. Katherina is silent, so there is no consent, and the contract is not binding. See Henry Swinburne, *A Treatise of Spousals* (1686), pp. 219–20; E. Schanzer, 'The Marriage-Contracts in *Measure for Measure*', *Sh.S.,* 13 (1960), 81–9; and *Measure for Measure* (ed. J. W. Lever, 1965, pp. liv–lv). Cf. *Troil.,* III. ii.

317. *we . . . Sunday*] Bond notes that this is the burden of several ballads, one of which occurs in *Ralph Roister Doister* as 'I mun be married a Sunday'.

318. *clapp'd up*] hastily agreed. Cf. *John,* III. i. 235, 'To clap this royal bargain up of peace'; Ford, *'Tis Pity She's a Whore,* III. i. 14–15, 'There's no way but to clap up a marriage in hugger-mugger'.

And venture madly on a desperate mart. 320

Tra. 'Twas a commodity lay fretting by you,
'Twill bring you gain, or perish on the seas.

Bap. The gain I seek is quiet in the match.

Gre. No doubt but he hath got a quiet catch.
But now, Baptista, to your younger daughter; 325
Now is the day we long have looked for.
I am your neighbour, and was suitor first.

Tra. And I am one that love Bianca more
Than words can witness or your thoughts can guess.

Gre. Youngling, thou canst not love so dear as I. 330

Tra. Greybeard, thy love doth freeze.

Gre. But thine doth fry.
Skipper, stand back, 'tis age that nourisheth.

Tra. But youth in ladies' eyes that flourisheth.

Bap. Content you, gentlemen, I will compound this strife.
'Tis deeds must win the prize, and he of both 335
That can assure my daughter greatest dower
Shall have my Bianca's love.
Say, Signor Gremio, what can you assure her?

Gre. First, as you know, my house within the city

323. in] *Rowe;* me *F.*

320. *a desperate mart*] a chancy piece
of business, likely to fail. Cf. *OED,*
Mart, *sb.*⁴ 4, and Spenser, *Shepheardes Calender*, Sept., 37, 'And maken
a Mart of theyr good name'.

321. *commodity*] article of commerce,
object of trade (*OED*, 6). Cf. *Err.,*
IV. iii. 6.

fretting] (i) rotting, decaying, and
hence deteriorating in value (*OED,*
*v.*¹ 7), (ii) chafing, irritating (*OED,*
*v.*¹ 8). Tranio applies both senses to
Katherina.

323. *in*] F's reading, 'me', probably
arose from a misreading of 'inne' in
the copy. The same mistake occurs
at IV. ii. 71.

326. *Now . . . for*] Tilley, L423,
'Long looked for comes at last'. Two
examples in Smith and Wilson predate the earliest in Tilley (1605).

330. *Youngling*] novice, stripling

(*OED*, 2). Cf. *Tit.*, II. i. 73.

dear] deeply, and also (proleptic-
ally) 'expensively'.

332. *Skipper*] light-brained, skipping fellow. Cf. *1H4*, III. ii. 60, 'The
skipping King', and *OED*, *sb.* 1. b,
which quotes only this line from *Shr.*

334. *compound*] settle. Cf. Bacon,
Essays, 'Of Honour and Reputation',
'Such as compound the long Miseries
of Ciuill Warres'.

335. *deeds*] (i) actions, (ii) legal
instruments, like title-deeds.

he of both] the one of you two. Cf.
Tp., I. ii. 450, 'They are both in
either's pow'rs', and Abbott, 12.

337. *Shall . . . love*] NCS, noting
that this is a broken line, reads 'Shall
have Bianca's love' with F2, suggesting that the metrically disturbing
'my' may have been caught from the
line above.

Is richly furnished with plate and gold,   340
Basins and ewers to lave her dainty hands,
My hangings all of Tyrian tapestry.
In ivory coffers I have stuff'd my crowns,
In cypress chests my arras counterpoints,
Costly apparel, tents, and canopies,   345
Fine linen, Turkey cushions boss'd with pearl,
Valance of Venice gold in needlework,
Pewter and brass, and all things that belongs
To house or housekeeping. Then at my farm
I have a hundred milch-kine to the pail,   350
Six score fat oxen standing in my stalls,
And all things answerable to this portion.
Myself am struck in years, I must confess,

350. pail] *F2;* pale *F.*

340. *plate*] utensils for table or domestic use, originally of silver or gold (*OED, sb.* II. 15 Collective sing.).

341. *lave*] wash.

342. *Tyrian tapestry*] Tyre was famous in classical times for the scarlet or purple dye which was extracted from local shellfish. Shakespeare does not mention Tyre elsewhere, except in *Per.* See Ezekiel, xxvi–xxviii (esp. xxvii. 24), E. H. Sugden, *A Topographical Dictionary &c.* and Jonson, *Catiline,* I. i. 384 (H. & S., v. 447).

344. *arras counterpoints*] counterpanes made of tapestry woven at Arras. These tapestries were more commonly used as wall-hangings (but see Marlowe, *Doctor Faustus (Plays,* ed. Gill, p. 353), II. ii. 115–16, 'I'll not speak another word, unless the ground be perfumed and covered with cloth of arras'). Cf. *Ham.,* III. iv, and Marlowe, *2 Tamburlaine (Plays,* ed. Gill, p. 126), I. ii. 44, 'And cloth of arras hung about the walls'.

345. *tents*] bed-testers or canopies. 'Halliwell quotes Baret's *Alvearie,* 1580, to show that the word is used for "the testorne to hange over a bed"' (Bond).

346. *Turkey cushions*] Turkish trade

with England in tapestries, carpets, cushions, etc., was considerable. See Sugden, *Topographical Dictionary* and cf. *Err.,* IV. i. 104–5.

347. *Valance . . . needlework*] A valance was a border of drapery hanging round the canopy of a bed (*OED, sb.*¹ 2). The singular is here used for the plural. These valances seem to have been adorned with Venetian embroidery in gold thread. For the use of 'Turkey' and 'Venice' as adjectives, see Abbott, 22.

348. *things that belongs*] Abbott, 247. The relative frequently in Shakespeare takes a singular verb, although the antecedent is plural. Cf. *MND,* III. ii. 97, 'With sighs of love that costs the fresh blood dear'.

350. *I . . . pail*] A milch-cow was a cow 'in milk', and 'to the pail' means that the milk went to the dairy, not to calves. Bond quotes North's *Plutarch,* 'Life of Pelopidas' (ed. 1595), p. 323, 'he receiued foure score milch kine to the paile, and neate heardes to keepe them, having need of milke'.

352. *answerable . . . portion*] corresponding to this settlement I am making. 'Answerable' is used 'only thrice in Shakespeare' (Onions). Cf. *Oth.,* I. iii. 345–7.

And if I die tomorrow this is hers,
If whilst I live she will be only mine.   355
Tra. That 'only' came well in. Sir, list to me:
        I am my father's heir and only son.
        If I may have your daughter to my wife,
        I'll leave her houses three or four as good,
        Within rich Pisa walls, as any one   360
        Old Signor Gremio has in Padua,
        Besides two thousand ducats by the year
        Of fruitful land, all which shall be her jointure.
        What, have I pinch'd you, Signor Gremio?
Gre. Two thousand ducats by the year of land!   365
        [*Aside.*] My land amounts not to so much in all.—
        That she shall have, besides an argosy
        That now is lying in Marseilles road.
        What, have I chok'd you with an argosy?
Tra. Gremio, 'tis known my father hath no less   370
        Than three great argosies, besides two galliasses
        And twelve tight galleys. These I will assure her,
        And twice as much whate'er thou off'rest next.
Gre. Nay, I have offer'd all, I have no more,

368. Marseilles] *F2* (Marsellis) *;* Marcellus *F.*   372. tight] *Rowe;* tite *F.*

356. *That . . . in*] Tranio makes great play with the fact that he is his father's only son.

362–3. *Besides . . . land*] Coryat, in 1611, says that 'the Venetian dukat is about four shillings eight pence'. Tranio is offering fertile land which brings in an income of two thousand ducats annually.

363. *jointure*] the estate settled on a woman at marriage to provide for her widowhood (*OED, sb.* 4). Cf. Lyly, *Euphues* (*Works*, ed. Bond, ii. 60), 'I am perswaded, yᵗ my faire daughter shal be wel maryed, for there is none, that will or can demaund a greater ioynter then Beautie'.

364. *pinch'd you*] put you in a tight corner, distressed you (*OED, v.* 7). Cf. Lyly, *Euphues* (*Works*, ed. Bond, i. 230), 'and pinched *Philautus* on the parsons side' (i.e. disappointed him of his wedding).

367. *argosy*] a merchant-vessel of the largest size and burden, especially those of Ragusa and Venice (*OED*). Cf. *Mer.V.*, i. i. 9, and Marlowe, *Doctor Faustus* (*Plays*, ed. Gill, p. 339), i. i. 128, 'From Venice shall they drag huge argosies'.

368. *Marseilles road*] the sheltered anchorage at Marseilles. F's reading, 'Marcellus roade', shows how the name of the port was pronounced in the sixteenth century. See Kökeritz, p. 270.

371. *galliasses*] A galliass was a heavy low-built vessel, larger than a galley (*OED*). Cf. Chapman, *Monsieur D'Olive*, ii. i, 'four great galliasses tost / Upon the wallowing waves'.

372. *tight*] water-tight. Cf. *Tp.*, v, i. 224.

And she can have no more than all I have.   375
If you like me, she shall have me and mine.
Tra. Why, then the maid is mine from all the world
        By your firm promise. Gremio is outvied.
Bap. I must confess your offer is the best,
        And let your father make her the assurance,   380
        She is your own; else, you must pardon me,
        If you should die before him, where's her dower?
Tra. That's but a cavil. He is old, I young.
Gre. And may not young men die as well as old?
Bap. Well, gentlemen,   385
        I am thus resolv'd: on Sunday next you know
        My daughter Katherine is to be married;
        Now, on the Sunday following shall Bianca
        Be bride to you, if you make this assurance;
        If not, to Signor Gremio.   390
        And so I take my leave, and thank you both.
Gre. Adieu, good neighbour.   *Exit* [*Baptista*].
                        Now I fear thee not.
        Sirrah, young gamester, your father were a fool
        To give thee all, and in his waning age
        Set foot under thy table. Tut, a toy!   395
        An old Italian fox is not so kind, my boy.   *Exit.*
Tra. A vengeance on your crafty wither'd hide!
        Yet I have fac'd it with a card of ten.
        'Tis in my head to do my master good.
        I see no reason but suppos'd Lucentio   400
        Must get a father, call'd suppos'd Vincentio.
        And that's a wonder. Fathers commonly
        Do get their children; but in this case of wooing
        A child shall get a sire, if I fail not of my cunning. *Exit.*

403. wooing] *F;* winning *conj. Capell.*

378. *outvied*] out-bidden.
384. *And . . . old*] Tilley, M609,
'Young men may die, old men must
die'. Smith and Wilson adds to Tilley's
examples '1586 La Primaudaye *French
Academy* 205ᵛ That sentence of Plato,
. . . That yong men die very soone, but
that olde men cannot liue long'.
393. *gamester*] gambler, adventurer.
Cf. *Wiv.*, III. i. 35–6.
395. *Set . . . table*] live on your

charity. Cf. Tilley, F572.
398. *Yet . . . ten*] I have brazened
it out. 'Face' was a term in the game
of Primero, in which Knave, Queen
and King each scored ten points and
were the *lowest* cards. Primero was
played in many different ways, and
the exact meaning of Tranio's phrase
is not clear, but see Ross and Rees,
N. & Q. (1966), pp. 403–7.

ACT III

[SCENE I]

Enter LUCENTIO, HORTENSIO, *and* BIANCA.

Luc. Fiddler, forbear. You grow too forward, sir.
   Have you so soon forgot the entertainment
   Her sister Katherine welcom'd you withal?
Hor. But, wrangling pedant, this is
   The patroness of heavenly harmony.   5
   Then give me leave to have prerogative,
   And when in music we have spent an hour,
   Your lecture shall have leisure for as much.
Luc. Preposterous ass, that never read so far
   To know the cause why music was ordain'd!   10
   Was it not to refresh the mind of man
   After his studies or his usual pain?

ACT III
Scene 1

ACT III SCENE 1] *Rowe; Actus Tertia. F.*

F heads this scene '*Actus Tertia.*' though there is no indication where Act II began.

S.D.] Lucentio is disguised as Cambio, and Hortensio as Litio. NCS and other editors suggest that as the scene opens Hortensio is holding Bianca's hand 'to teach her fingering' (II. i. 150) as he taught Katherina, and that this intimacy provokes Lucentio's opening line.

4. *But . . . this is*] The line is in some way incomplete. Various attempts have been made to expand it, but none is more than guesswork. Theobald's proposal to insert 'She is a shrew' at the beginning of the line is as good as any.

6. *prerogative*] precedence (*OED, sb.* 2. b). Cf. *Troil.*, I. iii. 107.

9. *Preposterous*] literally, placing last that which should be first (*OED, a.* 1). See Abbott, p. 14, and cf. Puttenham, *Arte of English Poesie*, ed. Willcock and Walker (1936), p. 170, 'we call it in English prouerbe, the cart before the horse, the Greeks call it *Histeron proteron*, we name it the Preposterous'.

10. *To . . . ordain'd*] Cf. 'Duely consideryng the causes for whiche Matrymonye was ordayned' (*The Boke of Common Prayer* (1552), 'The Fourme of Solemnizacyon of Matrymonye').

12. *usual pain*] normal daily labour. For 'pain' in this sense cf. *MND*, v. i. 80. Bond finds this phrase 'an odd locution', and would prefer to read 'unusual' or 'his manual'.

Then give me leave to read philosophy,
And while I pause serve in your harmony.
Hor. Sirrah, I will not bear these braves of thine.   15
Bian. Why, gentlemen, you do me double wrong
        To strive for that which resteth in my choice.
        I am no breeching scholar in the schools,
        I'll not be tied to hours nor 'pointed times,
        But learn my lessons as I please myself.   20
        And, to cut off all strife, here sit we down.
        Take you your instrument, play you the whiles;
        His lecture will be done ere you have tun'd.
Hor. You'll leave his lecture when I am in tune?
Luc. That will be never. Tune your instrument.   25
Bian. Where left we last?
Luc. Here, madam:
        Hic ibat Simois, hic est Sigeia tellus,
        Hic steterat Priami regia celsa senis.
Bian. Construe them.   30
Luc. *Hic ibat,* as I told you before—*Simois,* I am Lucentio

---

19. 'pointed] *Hanmer;* pointed *F.*   28. *hic*] *Q; hie F.*   28, 32, 41. *Sigeia*]
F2 (subst.); sigeria (l. 32, Sigeria) F.

---

14. *serve in*] serve up (Lucentio dismisses music as a trifle).

15. *braves*] bravadoes, defiances (*OED,* B. 2). Cf. *1H6,* III. ii. 123, and Greene, *Orl. Fur.* (*Plays and Poems,* ed. Collins, I. 229), I. i. 220, 'little brooking these vnfitting braues'.

18. *breeching scholar*] a young scholar still subject to the birch (*OED, vbl. sb.* 2. b). Cf. *Wiv.,* IV. i. 72, 'you must be preeches'. Bond prefers 'of an age to assume breeches', and so generally 'a growing youngster', though examples of this sense are wanting, and the interpretation is unlikely.

21. *cut off*] end. Cf. *John,* II. i. 96.

22. *the whiles*] in the meanwhile (Abbott, 74).

25. *That . . . instrument*] i.e. *you* will never be in a good temper (*OED, sb.* 3. b), so try tuning your lute.

26. *Where . . . last*] From this, and 'as I told you before' in l. 31, it is clear that there must have been at

least one previous lesson. Hortensio makes his first advances at ll. 62 ff., and so Lucentio has an advantage.

28–9. *Hic . . . senis*] 'Here ran the river Simois; here is the Sigeian land [i.e. the plain of Troy]; here stood old Priam's lofty palace' (Ovid, *Heroides,* i. 33–4). Shakespeare obviously knew the *Heroides* (see note to I. ii. 242), and these lines come from the Epistle in which Penelope is imagined as writing to her husband, Ulysses, while surrounded by her unwelcome suitors. All editions of Ovid read 'Hac ibat'.

31–6.] Hosley (*HLQ,* 1963–4) suggests an analogue for this passage in R. W.'s *The Three Lords and Three Ladies of London* (1590), but, as Muir points out (*Sources,* p. 20), the debt could go either way. Bond mentions Middleton's *The Witch,* II. ii (but the play was probably not earlier than 1610), and a passage in Nashe's *Fovre*

> —*hic est*, son unto Vincentio of Pisa—*Sigeia tellus*,
> disguised thus to get your love—*Hic steterat*, and that
> Lucentio that comes a-wooing—*Priami*, is my man
> Tranio—*regia*, bearing my port—*celsa senis*, that we   35
> might beguile the old pantaloon.

Hor. Madam, my instrument's in tune.

Bian. Let's hear. O fie! The treble jars.

Luc. Spit in the hole, man, and tune again.

Bian. Now let me see if I can construe it: *Hic ibat Simois*, I   40
know you not—*hic est Sigeia tellus*, I trust you not—
Hic steterat Priami, take heed he hear us not—*regia*,
presume not—*celsa senis*, despair not.

Hor. Madam, 'tis now in tune.

Luc.   All but the bass.

Hor. The bass is right, 'tis the base knave that jars.   45
[*Aside.*] How fiery and forward our pedant is.

42. steterat] *F2; staterat F.*   46–8.] *assigned to Hort., Rowe; assigned to Luc., F.*
46. S.D.] *Capell; not in F.*

Letters Confuted in *Strange Newse* (1592) (*Works*, ed. McKerrow, rev. Wilson, I. 314), '*Curae leues loquuntur;* he hath but a little cure to look too. *Maiores stupent*, more liuing would make him studie more'. The joke is in the 'mock' translation. In *Shr.* Shakespeare does not play on the two languages, but cf. *H5*, III. iv. On Shakespeare's 'language lessons' see R. C. Simonini, *SQ* (1959), 319–29.

35. *port*] state, social station (Onions, 2). Cf. I. i. 203.

36. *pantaloon*] Gremio. See note to I. i. 47 S.D.

37–9] The lute was notoriously difficult to tune (see *Shakespeare's England*, II. 30). Most commentators take Lucentio's advice 'Spit in the hole' to indicate his ignorance of the instrument, since to spit in the sound-hole 'would not help to tune it' (NCS). But, as Waldo and Herbert point out (*SQ* (1959), 195), the reference is to the treble peg-hole, spitting in which would moisten the peg and make it grip. Lucentio may also be perverting the proverbial 'Spit in your

hands and take better hold' (Tilley, H120–1).

40. *construe*] Here and at l. 30 F reads 'conster', the older form of the word. Both were accented on the first syllable (Kökeritz, p. 335).

46–56.] In F, ll. 46–9 are assigned to Lucentio, 50–1 to Bianca, and 52–6 to Hortensio. This is nonsense, and must have arisen from the use of *Lic.*, or *Lit.*, the shortened form of Hortensio's assumed name in the speech-prefixes. If 'Lic' was written before l. 46 (perhaps as a gloss on 'Hor' above it), it could be mistaken for the speech-prefix 'Luc'. The speech-prefix before l. 49 seems to have been missed, and before l. 50 'Luc' must have been misread as 'Bia' or 'Bian' (quite possible if each is written in miniscule, as NCS argues, p. 102). Then, before l. 52, 'Bia' was misread as 'Lic', and so two consecutive speeches are assigned to Hortensio. The causes of the confusion must be conjectural, but the correct reassignment is obvious. A similar confusion occurs at IV. ii. 4–8.

Now, for my life, the knave doth court my love.
Pedascule, I'll watch you better yet.
Bian. In time I may believe, yet I mistrust.
Luc. Mistrust it not—for, sure, Aeacides   50
Was Ajax, call'd so from his grandfather.
Bian. I must believe my master, else, I promise you,
I should be arguing still upon that doubt.
But let it rest. Now, Litio, to you.
Good master, take it not unkindly, pray,   55
That I have been thus pleasant with you both.
Hor. [*To Lucentio.*] You may go walk, and give me leave a
    while.
My lessons make no music in three parts.
Luc. Are you so formal, sir? Well, I must wait—
[*Aside.*] And watch, withal, for, but I be deceiv'd,   60
Our fine musician groweth amorous.
Hor. Madam, before you touch the instrument
To learn the order of my fingering,
I must begin with rudiments of art,
To teach you gamut in a briefer sort,   65
More pleasant, pithy, and effectual,
Than hath been taught by any of my trade.

49. *Bian.*] *conj. Theobald; no S.H. (so assigned to Luc.) F.*   50. *Luc.*] *conj.*
Theobald; Bian. F.   52. *Bian.*] *conj. Theobald; Hort. F.*   55. master] *F;*
masters *Rowe.*   57. S.D.] *Capell; not in F.*   60. S.D.] *Camb.; not in F.*

48. *Pedascule*] little pedant, a nonce-word created as a diminutive of pedant, and in imitation of Greek διδάσκαλος, 'master'.

50. *Aeacides*] Ajax, son of Telamon, was called Aeacides after his grandfather, Aeacus. Shakespeare might have found this in Ovid, *Met.*, xiii. 25; Bianca looks no farther than the next line of the text she is studying, *Heroides*, i. 35, 'illic Aeacides, illic tendebat Vlixes'.

55–6. *Good . . . both*] All editors from Rowe to Bond emend F's 'master' to 'masters'. But, as Bond points out, 'She is addressing Hortensio, who alone has reason to be displeased; and "pleasant with you both" stretches her apology to cover Lucentio's chaff,

and her laughter at it.'

57. *give me leave*] allow me leisure or opportunity, a polite way of saying 'Please go'. Cf. *Gent.*, III. i. 1.

59. *formal*] punctilious (*OED*, 8). Cf. *R3*, III. i. 82.

60. *but*] unless (Onions, 5).

65. *gamut*] the musical scale. See note to I. ii. 17. The word comes from Greek 'gamma', the alphabet-name for the first or lowest note in the system, plus 'ut', the musical name given by Guido d'Arezzo, who founded the system, to that note. See Grove's *Dictionary*, and *OED*, Gamut, 1 and 2.

briefer sort] quicker way (Onions, sort, sb.[1] 6).

And there it is in writing fairly drawn.
Bian. Why, I am past my gamut long ago.
Hor. Yet read the gamut of Hortensio.   70
Bian. Gamut I am, the ground of all accord—
 A re, to plead Hortensio's passion—
 B mi, Bianca, take him for thy lord—
 C fa ut, that loves with all affection—
 D sol re, one clef, two notes have I—   75
 E la mi, show pity or I die.
 Call you this gamut? Tut, I like it not!
 Old fashions please me best. I am not so nice
 To change true rules for odd inventions.

Enter a Servant.

Serv. Mistress, your father prays you leave your books,   80
 And help to dress your sister's chamber up.

72. *A re*] Q.; *Are* F. 73. *B mi*] Pope; *Beeme* F. 74. *C fa ut*] Q.; *Cfavt* F.
79. change] F2; charge F. odd] Theobald; old F. S.D. Servant] Rowe;
Messenger F. 80. Serv.] Rowe; Nicke. F.

70. *of Hortensio*] Bond suggests that this is 'his first revelation of his disguise, which Bianca has not before penetrated'. It may be so, but in this and the following lines Hortensio does not actually declare his identity, and it is up to the actress playing Bianca how she reacts.

71–6.] Hortensio's letter 'construes' the gamut just as Lucentio had construed Ovid in ll. 31–6. This gamut is a rehearsal of the G or Hard Hexachord in the Guidonian system, covering a declaration of Hortensio's love. The first line seems to offer rich ambiguities: 'Gamut' is the basis of the hexachord just as 'I am' ('sum') is the basis of grammar, and even, perhaps, the name of the Creator (Exodus, iii. 14); 'the ground of all accord' can mean 'the basis of all agreement' and 'the ground-base on which all harmony is reared' (*OED*, Ground, *sb.* 6. c, and Accord, 1). There is no such obvious correspondence in the lines that follow. Ingenious attempts have been made to see

comparisons (see H. C. Miller, in *N. & Q.* (1933), pp. 255–7), but none is convincing.

75. *one . . . notes*] Attempts have been made to find bawdy meanings in these lines. Cf. *Troil.*, v. ii. 10–11. Alternatively, Bond proposes that the 'one clef' is love, and the 'two notes' Hortensio's real and assumed personalities.

78. *nice*] whimsical. Cf. *All's W.*, v. i. 15.

79. *odd inventions*] fantastical new ideas. All modern editors accept Theobald's emendation of F's 'old' to 'odd'.

80.] F gives this line the speech-prefix '*Nicke*', and most commentators, following Steevens, have identified him with Nicholas Tooley, who is named in the list of 'Principal Actors' at the beginning of F. NCS (pp. 116–17) suggests that he also played Biondello and one of Petruchio's servants in Act IV. The evidence, however, is slender.

You know tomorrow is the wedding-day.
Bian. Farewell, sweet masters both, I must be gone.

　　　　　　　　　　　　[*Exeunt Bianca and Servant.*]

Luc. Faith, mistress, then I have no cause to stay.　　[*Exit.*]
Hor. But I have cause to pry into this pedant.　　　　85
　　　Methinks he looks as though he were in love.
　　　Yet if thy thoughts, Bianca, be so humble
　　　To cast thy wandering eyes on every stale,
　　　Seize thee that list. If once I find thee ranging,
　　　Hortensio will be quit with thee by changing.　*Exit.*　90

[SCENE II]

Enter BAPTISTA, GREMIO, TRANIO, KATHERINA, BIANCA,
　　[LUCENTIO] *and others,* Attendants.

Bap. Signor Lucentio, this is the 'pointed day
　　　That Katherine and Petruchio should be married,
　　　And yet we hear not of our son-in-law.
　　　What will be said? What mockery will it be
　　　To want the bridegroom when the priest attends　　5
　　　To speak the ceremonial rites of marriage!
　　　What says Lucentio to this shame of ours?
Kath. No shame but mine. I must forsooth be forc'd
　　　To give my hand, oppos'd against my heart,

---

83. S.D.] *Capell; not in F.*　　84. S.D.] *Rowe; not in F.*　　88–9. stale, . . .
list.] *Capell (subst.);* stale: . . . List, *F.*

Scene II

SCENE II] *Pope; not in F.*　　S.D. *Lucentio*] *Rowe; not in F.*　　1. 'pointed]
Pope; pointed *F.*

88. *stale*] decoy-bird, lure (*OED,*
sb.[3] 1). The image is from falconry;
Hortensio thinks of Bianca as a poor
hawk who will stoop to every lure.

89. *Seize . . . list*] Let anyone have
you.

ranging] (i) straying (used of a
hawk), (ii) being inconstant (*OED,*
v.[1] 7. a, and 8).

Scene II

S.D.] F omits Lucentio from the
list, probably because he does not
speak until l. 136. Baptista's first line
is, of course, addressed to the disguised Tranio.

5. *want*] lack (Onions, 1). Cf. *John,*
IV. i. 99.

Unto a mad-brain rudesby, full of spleen,   10
Who woo'd in haste and means to wed at leisure.
I told you, I, he was a frantic fool,
Hiding his bitter jests in blunt behaviour.
And to be noted for a merry man
He'll woo a thousand, 'point the day of marriage,   15
Make feast, invite friends, and proclaim the banns,
Yet never means to wed where he hath woo'd.
Now must the world point at poor Katherine,
And say 'Lo, there is mad Petruchio's wife,
If it would please him come and marry her.'   20
Tra. Patience, good Katherine, and Baptista too.
Upon my life, Petruchio means but well,
Whatever fortune stays him from his word.
Though he be blunt, I know him passing wise;

13. behaviour.] *F4;* behauiour, *F.*   15. 'point] *Pope;* point *F.*   16. feast,
invite friends,] *Dyce* (feasts)*;* friends, invite, *F;* friends, invite, yes *F2;* friends,
invite them, *Malone;* friends invited, *Grant White.*

10. *rudesby*] ruffian, unmannerly
fellow (from 'rude', plus '-by', a suffix
often used in the 16th and 17th
centuries to coin descriptive personal
appellations; see *OED,* -by. 2). Cf.
Tw.N., IV. i. 50, and Golding's *Ovid,*
v. 722–3, 'This gift of bodie in the
which another would delight,/I
rudesbye was ashamed off'.

spleen] caprice, waywardness
(Onions, 5). Cf. Ind. i. 135 and note;
AYL, IV. i. 192.

11. *Who . . . leisure*] Tilley, H196,
quoting this line. Smith and Wilson,
under the same heading 'Marry in
haste, and repent at leisure', quotes
3H6, IV. i. 18, but not *Shr.*

16. *Make . . . banns*] F reads 'Make
friends, inuite, and proclaime the
banes,' which defies both sense and
metre. Editors from F2 onwards have
sought to emend. F2 proposed 'invite,
yes, and'; Malone suggested 'invite
them, and'; Alexander preferred
'friends invited, and'. NCS and others,
following Dyce, read 'Make feast,
invite friends, and' following the

earlier words of Petruchio 'Provide
the feast, father, and bid the guests'
(II. i. 309). As Sisson says (*New Readings,* I, 164), 'this is indeed the logic
of the process of marriage-making'.
Sisson also suggests emending 'a thousand' in the previous line to 'as
husband', but this has not found
general acceptance.

21–5.] As Hibbard has noted, these
lines come very oddly from Tranio.
He is not Petruchio's friend, and
knows very little about him. They
would be apt and convincing from
Hortensio, and perhaps at some early
stage in the play's history they were
properly assigned to him. Most of
Tranio's other speeches in this scene
are similarly suspect; much of what
he says may have been written for
Hortensio, though the reasons for the
reassignment to Tranio are probably
beyond recovery.

23. *fortune*] accident, chance. Cf.
Mer.V., v. i. 44.

stays] keeps (Onions, 3).

24. *passing*] very.

Though he be merry, yet withal he's honest.   25
Kath. Would Katherine had never seen him though.
> *Exit weeping [followed by Bianca and Attendants].*
Bap. Go, girl, I cannot blame thee now to weep,
    For such an injury would vex a saint,
    Much more a shrew of thy impatient humour.

Enter BIONDELLO.

Bion. Master, master, news! And such old news as you   30
    never heard of.
Bap. Is it new and old too? How may that be?
Bion. Why, is it not news to hear of Petruchio's coming?
Bap. Is he come?
Bion. Why, no, sir.   35
Bap. What then?
Bion. He is coming.
Bap. When will he be here?
Bion. When he stands where I am and sees you there.
Tra. But say, what to thine old news?   40
Bion. Why, Petruchio is coming in a new hat and an old

---

26. S.D. *followed . . . Attendants*] *After Capell; not in* F.   28. saint] *F2; very*
saint *F.*   29. thy] *F2; not in* F.   30. news! And such old] *Collier;* newes,
and such *F;* news, old news, and such *Capell.*   33. hear] *Q;* heard *F.*

---

25. *merry*] facetious, 'pleasant'
(Onions, 3). Cf. *Tim.*, III. ii. 36.
    26. S.D.] F gives only '*Exit weeping*'.
The expansion is necessary to allow
the bridal train to leave the stage.
    27. *to weep*] for weeping (Abbott,
356).
    28. *vex a saint*] Cf. Tilley, S28,
which, however, does not cite this
line; the earliest example given is
1619, from Beaumont and Fletcher's
A King and No King. F reads 'a very
saint', which is an obvious error.
    29. *Much . . . humour*] F reads 'of
impatient', but 'thy' is supplied by F2.
Clearly, some monosyllable has been
omitted in F, and F2's reading makes
the best available sense.
    30. *such old news*] Again, F reads
'such newes', but Baptista's comment
in the next line makes it clear that the

word 'old' is required here. Biondello
offers the word in its sense of 'plenti-
ful, abundant' (*OED, a.* 6; cf. *Ado*,
v. ii. 83); Baptista takes it up in its
modern sense. The presence of three
small errors in consecutive lines in the
text of F at this point suggests a lapse
of concentration on the compositor's
part, or a difficult or defective copy.
    33. *hear*] F reads 'heard'. Final e
and final d are easily confused in
Secretary hand.
    40. *what to*] what of (Onions, 8).
    41–61.] For the description of
Petruchio's dress, cf. Nashe's account
of Greediness and Dame Niggardize
in *Pierce Penilesse* (*Works*, ed.
McKerrow, rev. Wilson, I. 166–7,
and quoted in NCS, p. 156). With
the picture of his horse, cf. *Ven.*, 289–
324 (the good points of a horse), and

jerkin; a pair of old breeches thrice turned; a pair of
boots that have been candle-cases, one buckled,
another laced; an old rusty sword ta'en out of the
town armoury, with a broken hilt, and chapeless;   45
with two broken points; his horse hipped—with an
old mothy saddle and stirrups of no kindred—
besides, possessed with the glanders and like to mose

46. hipped] *Hanmer (subst.); hip'd F.*

Lyly, *Mother Bombie (Works,* ed. Bond,
III. 214), IV. ii. 207 ff. (the bad points).
The standard works on horsemanship
and farriery in Shakespeare's day
were Thomas Blundeville's *The Fower
chiefyst offices belongyng to Horseman-
shippe* (1565–6), and the many works
of Gervase Markham. Almost all
the diseases mentioned in this passage are discussed in Markham's
A discource of horsmanshippe (1593),
and later editions; see also his
Cauelarice (1607), and *Maister-peece*
(1610). Petruchio's horse receives
detailed consideration in Madden,
Diary, pp. 304–6, and *Shakespeare's
England,* II. 423–6. Bond's notes on
this passage, also, are detailed and
extensive.

42. *jerkin*] short outer coat or jacket
(other than the doublet, as is shown
by *Gent.,* II. iv. 19–20, '*Val.* I quote it
in your jerkin./*Thu.* My jerkin is
a doublet').

thrice turned] turned inside out three
times (to conceal wear).

43. *boots . . . candle-cases*] boots too
old for wearing, that have been used
to keep candle-ends in. Cf. *OED,*
Candle, *sb.* 7.

45. *chapeless*] without the chape, i.e
the metal plate on the scabbard covering the point of the sword (*OED,*
Chape, *sb.* 2). Cf. *All's W.,* IV. iii.
135–6.

46. *points*] tagged laces, for attach-
ing the hose to the doublet. Cf *1H4,*
II. iv. 207–8, 'Their points being
broken . . . Down fell their hose' (the
points here are the points of swords);

Tw.N., I. v. 21–3 (where 'points'
means 'matters').

46–8. *his . . . besides*] F reads 'his
horse hip'd with an olde mothy saddle,
and stirrops of no kindred: besides',
which is nonsense. NCS transposes
'with an old mothy saddle, and stirrups of no kindred' to follow after
'two broken points', on the hypothesis that the transcriber omitted the
line accidentally, added it later in the
margin, and the compositor inserted
it incorrectly. Subsequent editors have
preferred Sisson's solution (*New Readings,* I. 165), which simply involves
repunctuating the F text so that everything between 'with' and 'kindred' is
a parenthesis.

46. *hipped*] 'A horse was said to be
hipped when his hip-bone was dislocated so that he halted much and
trailed his legs' (*Shakespeare's England,*
II. 424). See *OED,* Hipped, *a.*[1] 3.

47. *of no kindred*] that do not match.

48. *the glanders*] 'a contagious disease in horses, the chief symptoms of
which are swellings beneath the jaw
and discharge of mucous matter from
the nostrils' (*OED,* Glander, 2, quoting Dekker, *Witch of Edmonton,* IV. i,
'My Horse this morning runs most
pitiously of the glaunders'). Markham
(quoted in *Shakespeare's England,* II.
424) disagreed, and called such in-
flammation the strangle, and the
glanders he defined as 'a Running
Imposthume, ingendred either by
cold, or by Famine'.

48–9. *mose in the chine*] No one
knows what this means. The verb

in the chine, troubled with the lampass, infected
with the fashions, full of windgalls, sped with   50
spavins, rayed with the yellows, past cure of the
fives, stark spoiled with the staggers, begnawn with

50. fashions] *F; farcin Hanmer.*

'mose' is not known outside this passage, and *OED* suggests that it is a corruption of 'Mourn'. Under Mourn, *v.*², *OED* gives 'A perversion of the French name for glanders', noting that it occurs only in phrases like 'Mourn of the chine'. Markham's *Maister-peece* (ch. 42) connects the two complaints as successive stages of one disease: 'this consumption proceeds from a cold, which afterwards grows to a poze, then to a glaunders, and lastly to this mourning of the chine.' He confines the symptoms of this last stage to a discharge from the nostrils, 'dark, thinne, reddish, with little streakes of blood in it'. Thus, Biondello seems to be saying that the horse is suffering from the glanders, and is likely soon to display that disease's terminal symptom. Madden (*Diary*, pp. 305–6) suggests that many of the words in this 'catalogue of unsoundnesses' differ from the accepted terms of farriery because Shakespeare did not, like Jonson, learn them from books, but from blacksmiths and in the stables. Hence, 'mose' might be a local, unrecorded, variant of 'mourn'. It might equally be a misprint. All the possible meanings of 'chine' are discussed by Hilda M. Hulme (*Explorations*, pp. 126–30). Here, it is probably an alternative name for the disease (*OED*, *sb.*² 5), which has become fossilized in the 'mourning' phrase.

49. *lampass*] 'a disease incident to horses, consisting in a swelling of the fleshy lining of the roof of the mouth behind the front teeth' (*OED*, *sb.*¹).

50. *fashions*] farcy, or farcin, 'a disease of animals, especially of horses, closely allied to glanders' (*OED*, Farcy, *sb.*). Cf. Greene, *Looking Glasse* (*Plays and Poems*, ed. Collins, I. 152), I. ii. 230 ff.: 'For let a Horse take a cold, or be troubled with the bots, and we straight giue him a potion or a purgation, in such phisicall maner that he mends straight: if he haue outward diseases, as the spauin, splent, ring-bone, wind-gall or fashion, or, sir, a galled backe, we let him blood and clap a plaister to him with a pestilence.'

windgalls] 'a soft tumour on either side of a horse's leg just above the fetlock, caused by distension of the synovial bursa' (*OED*).

50–1. *sped with spavins*] ruined by swellings of the leg-joints. There is a wet and a dry spavin. Cf. *H8*, I. iii. 12–13.

51. *rayed*] soiled, defiled; a variant form of Berayed (*OED*, *v.*² 5). Cf. IV. i. 3.

the yellows] jaundice (*OED*, Yellows, I. 1). The symptoms in horses are a yellow colouring of the eyes, lips and nostrils, with sweating of ears and flank, faintness, and refusal to eat.

52. *fives*] a swelling of the parotid glands in horses; the strangles. The full form of the word is 'avives', which came into English through French and Spanish from an Arabic original (see *OED*, Avives, and Fives). The aphetic English form 'vives' seems to have been the normal use in Elizabethan farriery. Madden (*Diary*, p. 306) writes 'No one but an ignorant smith, or one bred in a stable, would speak of "the fives". If he had even a smattering of the book-learning of farriery, he would have known that the "vives"

the bots, swayed in the back and shoulder-shotten,
near-legged before, and with a half-cheeked bit
and a headstall of sheep's leather, which, being   55
restrained to keep him from stumbling, hath been
often burst and new-repaired with knots; one girth

53. swayed] *Hanmer* (*subst.*)*;* Waid F.   54. near-legged] *hyphened, Rowe;*
unhyphened (neere leg'd), *F.*   half-cheeked] *Hanmer* (*subst.*)*;* halfe-chekt F.
57. new-repaired] *Walker;* now repaired F.

are "certaine kernels growing under
the horse's eare. . . . The Italians call
them vivole".'

stark spoiled] completely ruined.

the staggers] 'a name for various
diseases affecting domestic animals, of
which a staggering gait is a symptom'
(*OED*, *sb.*[1] 2). Markham's *Maister-
peece* (quoted by Bond) describes it as
'a dizzy madnesse of the braine . . .
from surfeit of meat, surfeit of trauell,
or from corruption of blood', accompanied by 'staggering and reeling of
the horse, and beating of his head
against the walles'.

begnawn with] gnawed at by. Cf. *R3,*
I. iii. 222.

53. *the bots*] A bot, or bott, is,
strictly speaking, the name of a
parasitical worm or maggot; now
restricted to the larvae of flies of the
genus *Oestrus*. But the phrase 'the
botts' came to be used for the disease
caused by these parasites. Cf. *1H4,*
II. i. 9–10, 'that is the next way to give
poor jades the bots'.

swayed . . . back] 'Of a horse: Having
a depression in the spinal column,
caused by strain' (*OED*, Swayed, *ppl.
a.* 1). Bond quotes Markham (*Maister-
peece*, ii. c. 46): 'A Horse is said to be
swayed in the backe, when . . . he hath
taken an extreame wrinch in the
lower part of his backe below his
short ribbes . . . whereof are a con-
tinuall reeling and rowling of the
horses hinder parts in his going.' F
reads 'Waid', but the existence, well
attested, of the phrase 'swayed in the
back' makes Hanmer's emendation
universally acceptable.

shoulder-shotten] 'having a strained or

dislocated shoulder' (*OED*, Shoulder,
sb. 9. c).

54. *near-legged before*] 'knock-kneed
in the front legs' is Hibbard's gloss,
and it is probably the best available.
OED (Near-legged) gives 'Going near
with the (fore) legs', but quotes only
this line from *Shr.* in support. By his
'nere' Madden (*Diary*, p. 305) understands 'never', suggesting that near-
legged' conveys no distinct meaning,
while 'ne'er-legged' plainly signifies
what would be called in stable-
language 'gone before': the "ne'er-
legged" horse is bound to stumble,
even without the additional infirmities
enumerated in the text.' NCS intends,
by 'near-legged', the sense of standing
with the fore-legs close together, and
adds (p. 157), 'As this is a virtue in a
horse, it is clear that what the author
intended to write was "near-legged
behind" '. This is a lame solution.

half-cheeked] 'applied to a bit in
which the bridle is attached halfway
up the cheek or side-piece, thus giving
insufficient control over the horse's
mouth' (Onions). See also *Shakespeare's
England*, II. 421, for a slightly different
interpretation (with illustrations).
Madden (*Diary*, p. 308, n. 1) finds the
term obscure.

55. *headstall*] 'the part of a bridle or
halter that fits round the head' (*OED*).

sheep's leather] less strong than the
pigskin or cowhide which was normally used.

56. *restrained*] drawn tightly (*OED,
v.* 6). Cf. *2H4*, I. i. 176.

57. *new-repaired*] Bond and others
accept F's text, arguing that 'hath
been' is construed with both 'burst'

six times pieced, and a woman's crupper of velure,
which hath two letters for her name fairly set down
in studs, and here and there pieced with pack-   60
thread.

Bap. Who comes with him?

Bion. O sir, his lackey, for all the world caparisoned like
the horse; with a linen stock on one leg, and a kersey
boot-hose on the other, gartered with a red and blue   65
list; an old hat, and the humour of forty fancies
pricked in't for a feather; a monster, a very monster
in apparel, and not like a Christian footboy or a
gentleman's lackey.

Tra. 'Tis some odd humour pricks him to this fashion.   70
Yet oftentimes he goes but mean-apparell'd.

and 'repaired'. This is perfectly possible, and receives some support from the syntax of ll. 55–7, where 'being restrained' and 'hath been' are both dependent on the relative pronoun 'which'. But Walker's emendation (*Crit. Exam.*, II. 214) gives a less contorted sense, makes clearer the fact that the 'repairing' has been done not once but many times, and could easily be explained as a misreading of the manuscript copy, since o and e can be much alike in Secretary hand.

girth] the band of leather or cloth going round a horse's belly and tightened to hold the saddle in place (*OED, sb.*[1] 1).

58. *pieced*] mended, repaired. Cf. *Ant.*, I. v. 45–6, 'I will piece/Her opulent throne with kingdoms'.

crupper] leather strap which passes in a loop from the saddle round the horse's tail to prevent the saddle from slipping. Cf. IV. i. 73.

velure] velvet. In the heavy riding-gear used in Shakespeare's day, a lady's crupper might be covered with velvet and mounted with her initials in silver or brass studs.

60. *pieced*] The piecing, or mending, with pack-thread would apply to the velvet of the crupper, not to the lettering.

64. *stock*] stocking.

kersey] coarse woollen cloth. Cf. *Meas.*, I. ii. 34.

65. *boot-hose*] a long over-stocking which covers the leg like a jack-boot. Cf. Beaumont and Fletcher, *The Knight of the Burning Pestle*, IV. ii, 'The maid/That wash'd my boot-hose'.

66. *list*] a strip of cloth or other fabric (*OED, sb.*[3] 3).

the . . . fancies] 'some ballad or drollery' (Warburton); 'a collection of short poems such as were called fancies' (Steevens); 'a parcel of forty ribbons tied together instead of a feather' (Halliwell); 'some fantastical ornament comprising the humour of forty fancies' (Malone). No one knows what the phrase means, or what it alludes to. Cf. *2H4*, III. ii. 313–16; Lyly, *Sapho and Phao* (*Works*, ed. Bond. II. 414), v. iii. 10–11, 'with my penne to write a fancie'; Peacham, *Worth of a Penny* (1641) (quoted by Malone and by Bond), 'a hat without a band . . . only it wears a weather-beaten fancy for fashion-sake'.

67. *pricked*] fastened with a pin (*OED, v.* 19).

70. *odd humour*] strange fancy.

pricks] urges, incites (*OED, v.* 10). Cf. *Gent.*, III. i. 8.

Bap. I am glad he's come, howsoe'er he comes.

Bion. Why, sir, he comes not.

Bap. Didst thou not say he comes?

Bion. Who? That Petruchio came?   75

Bap. Ay, that Petruchio came.

Bion. No, sir. I say his horse comes, with him on his back.

Bap. Why, that's all one.

Bion. Nay, by Saint Jamy,
         I hold you a penny,   80
         A horse and a man
         Is more than one,
         And yet not many.

Enter PETRUCHIO *and* GRUMIO.

Pet. Come, where be these gallants? Who's at home?

Bap. You are welcome, sir.   85

Pet. And yet I come not well.

Bap. And yet you halt not.

Tra. Not so well apparell'd as I wish you were.

Pet. Were it not better I should rush in thus?
        But where is Kate? Where is my lovely bride?   90
        How does my father? Gentles, methinks you frown.
        And wherefore gaze this goodly company,

79–83.] *as verse, Collier (after Rowe); as prose, F.*   85–6.] *F; as verse, Capell.*
89. not] *Keightley; not in F.*

79–83. *Nay . . . many*] F prints as prose. Rowe gives it as two lines of verse, Collier (and subsequent editors) as five. Bond adds 'No doubt a fragment of some lost ballad'. The reference in l. 79 is probably to St James of Compostella, whose shrine was one of the great objects of pilgrimage in the Middle Ages (an ironic comment on Petruchio's arrival).

80. *hold you*] wager you, bet you (*OED*, v. 13).

83. *many*] NCS notes 'with a quibble upon "meiny" ', presumably in the sense of a retinue or company (see *OED*, Meinie, 2 and 3). This may

be so, though it is not mentioned in Kökeritz.

85–7. *You . . . not*] word-play. Petruchio, noticing the look of displeasure on Baptista's face, suggests (ironically and questioningly) that he has arrived at an inopportune moment. Baptista takes up 'come not well' as meaning 'do not walk soundly', and comments that he does not limp.

89. *Were . . . thus*] F's reading makes sense of a kind, and Bond retains it. Most editors, however, prefer to improve both meaning and metre by following Keightley and reading 'Were it not better'. As NCS points

As if they saw some wondrous monument,
Some comet, or unusual prodigy?

Bap. Why, sir, you know this is your wedding-day.   95
First were we sad, fearing you would not come,
Now sadder that you come so unprovided.
Fie, doff this habit, shame to your estate,
An eyesore to our solemn festival!

Tra. And tell us what occasion of import   100
Hath all so long detain'd you from your wife
And sent you hither so unlike yourself.

Pet. Tedious it were to tell, and harsh to hear.
Sufficeth I am come to keep my word,
Though in some part enforced to digress,   105
Which at more leisure I will so excuse
As you shall well be satisfied withal.
But where is Kate? I stay too long from her.
The morning wears, 'tis time we were at church.

Tra. See not your bride in these unreverent robes,   110
Go to my chamber, put on clothes of mine.

Pet. Not I, believe me. Thus I'll visit her.

Bap. But thus, I trust, you will not marry her.

Pet. Good sooth, even thus. Therefore ha' done with words;
To me she's married, not unto my clothes.   115
Could I repair what she will wear in me

out (p. 158), 'this text is full of little omissions'.

93. *monument*] portent (*OED*, *sb.* 3.b). Shakespeare does not use the word in this sense elsewhere.

94. *comet*] A comet was regarded as a portent of disaster. Cf. *Caes.*, II. ii. 30–1.

prodigy] omen (*OED*, 1). Cf. *1H4*, v. i. 19–21.

98. *estate*] rank, social status.

101. *all so long*] 'All' used intensively was frequently prefixed to other adverbs of degree, like 'so'. See Abbott, 28; cf. *2H4*, v. ii. 23–4, 'our argument/Is all too heavy to admit much talk'.

104. *Sufficeth*] it is enough that. See Abbott, 297; cf. I. i. 247.

105. *digress*] (i) go out of my way, (ii) deviate from my promise. Bond suggests that Petruchio is probably referring to his intended absence from the 'feast' which he himself suggested. See II. i. 309.

109. *wears*] is passing (*OED*, *v.*[1] 19). Cf. *Wiv.*, v. i. 7, 'Away, I say; time wears'.

110. *unreverent*] disrespectful. Cf. *John*, I. i. 227.

115. *To . . . clothes*] Tilley, S451, 'Silk and satin make not a gentleman' —one of a group of proverbs on the general theme of 'Apparel makes (or does not make) the man'.

116. *wear*] wear out, a bawdy allusion. Bond discreetly adds 'perhaps of patience and purse, as well as body'.

As I can change these poor accoutrements,
'Twere well for Kate and better for myself.
But what a fool am I to chat with you,
When I should bid good morrow to my bride,   120
And seal the title with a lovely kiss.

Exeunt [Petruchio and Grumio].

Tra. He hath some meaning in his mad attire.
We will persuade him, be it possible,
To put on better ere he go to church.

Bap. I'll after him and see the event of this.   125

Exeunt [Baptista, Gremio, Biondello, Attendants].

Tra. But, sir, to love concerneth us to add
Her father's liking, which to bring to pass,
As I before imparted to your worship,
I am to get a man—whate'er he be
It skills not much, we'll fit him to our turn—   130
And he shall be Vincentio of Pisa,
And make assurance here in Padua
Of greater sums than I have promised.

---

121. S.D.] *After Dyce; Exit. F.*   125. S.D.] *After Camb.; Exit. F.*   126. sir,
to love] *Sisson;* sir, Loue *F;* to her love *Capell.*   128. I] *Pope; not in F.*

---

121. *lovely*] loving. This sense of the word is not found elsewhere in Shakespeare's plays, but cf. *Pilgr.*, IV. 3. It is common in Lyly, as in *Endimion* (*Works*, ed. Bond, III. 78), v. iii. 242–3, 'Corsites casteth still a louely looke towards you'.

122–4. *He . . . church*] Hibbard and others suggest that these lines were written originally for Hortensio, since he, not Tranio, is Petruchio's close friend, and might 'persuade' him. They also imply that the speaker is about to follow Petruchio off-stage, but Tranio stays on. The best explanation of this and other oddities in the following lines is that a piece of the original text has been cut. Possibly the scene ended after l. 125, and a new scene began with dialogue between Hortensio and Lucentio. Tranio's speech beginning at l. 126 certainly looks like the reply to some-

thing (perhaps Lucentio's account of his success with Bianca).

126. *But . . . love*] F's reading makes no sense. Capell proposed 'But to her love', which makes good sense, but requires the assumption that the transcriber or compositor made two errors. It is simpler to assume that one or other simply omitted the word 'to', which is quite consistent with previous habit in this scene (see notes to ll. 28, 29, 30, above).

concerneth] it concerns (impersonal use, Abbott, 297).

128. *As I before*] F reads 'As before' (another example of a word omitted).

130. *skills not*] does not matter (*OED, v.*[1] 2. b). Cf. *Tw.N.*, v. i. 280; Lyly, *Euphues* (*Works*, ed. Bond, II. 151), 'it skilled not how long things were a doing, but how well they were done'.

So shall you quietly enjoy your hope
And marry sweet Bianca with consent.   135
Luc. Were it not that my fellow schoolmaster
Doth watch Bianca's steps so narrowly,
'Twere good methinks to steal our marriage,
Which once perform'd, let all the world say no,
I'll keep mine own despite of all the world.   140
Tra. That by degrees we mean to look into,
And watch our vantage in this business.
We'll overreach the greybeard Gremio,
The narrow-prying father Minola,
The quaint musician, amorous Litio;   145
All for my master's sake, Lucentio.

Enter GREMIO.

Signor Gremio, came you from the church?
Gre. As willingly as e'er I came from school.
Tra. And is the bride and bridegroom coming home?
Gre. A bridegroom, say you? 'Tis a groom indeed,   150
A grumbling groom, and that the girl shall find.
Tra. Curster than she? Why, 'tis impossible.
Gre. Why, he's a devil, a devil, a very fiend.
Tra. Why, she's a devil, a devil, the devil's dam.
Gre. Tut! She's a lamb, a dove, a fool to him.   155

144. narrow-prying] *hyphened, Pope; unhyphened, F.*   151. grumbling] *F2;*
grumlling *F.*

138. *steal our marriage*] marry
secretly. Cf. *Rom.*, v. iii. 232, 'their
stol'n marriage-day'.

142. *vantage*] opportunity (Onions,
2). Cf. *Gent.*, I. iii. 82.

145. *quaint*] skilled, clever, ingenious (*OED*, *a.* 1). Cf. IV. iii. 102;
2H6, III. ii. 274.

146. S.D.] Only 21 lines separate
Baptista's exit to go to the wedding
and Gremio's entry with a detailed
report of it. This adds to the evidence
that the dialogue between Tranio and
Lucentio may have been cut.

148. *As . . . school*] Tilley, W398.

149. *is*] Shakespeare frequently
uses the singular form of the verb

when the subject is two singular nouns.
Cf. *Cym.*, III. vi. 21, 'Plenty and peace
breeds cowards'; see Abbott, 333–9,
esp. 336. The construction is echoed at
IV. i. 15, 'Is my master and his wife
coming'.

150. *a groom indeed*] i.e. as rough as
a servingman (*OED*, *sb.*[1] 3 and 6).
Cf. IV. i. 112.

151. *A . . . find*] Gremio's old-
fashioned diction (here and elsewhere)
is reminiscent of Old and Middle
English alliterative metres.

154. *the devil's dam*] See note to
I. i. 105.

155. *fool*] frequently used by Shakespeare as a term of endearment or

I'll tell you, Sir Lucentio, when the priest
Should ask if Katherine should be his wife,
'Ay, by gogs-wouns,' quoth he, and swore so loud
That all amaz'd the priest let fall the book,
And as he stoop'd again to take it up,   160
The mad-brain'd bridegroom took him such a cuff
That down fell priest and book, and book and priest.
'Now take them up,' quoth he, 'if any list.'
Tra. What said the wench when he rose up again?
Gre. Trembled and shook. For why, he stamp'd and swore 165
As if the vicar meant to cozen him.
But after many ceremonies done
He calls for wine. 'A health!' quoth he, as it
He had been aboard, carousing to his mates
After a storm; quaff'd off the muscadel,   170

---

164. rose up] *F2;* rose *F;* arose *Reed.*   165–81.] *as verse, Steevens (after F2)*
as prose, F.

pity. Cf. *Gent.*, iv. iv. 89. Onions
(sb.[1] 1) notes that the phrase 'a fool
to' (which he glosses as 'in every way
inferior to') is not pre-Shakespearean.
Hibbard, with somewhat different
emphasis, glosses 'a gentle innocent'.

156. *Sir Lucentio*] In Shakespeare's
day 'Sir' was widely applied to a
variety of people: 'Sir King' (*Tp.*,
v. i. 106), 'sir boy' (*Ado*, v. i. 83), 'sir
priest' and 'sir knight' (*Tw.N.*, iii. iv.
259–60). Hibbard notes that
foreigners belonging to the gentry
were often addressed as 'Sir', and
Lucentio, because he comes from Pisa,
would be regarded as a foreigner. Cf.
iv. ii. 106.

157. *Should ask*] came to ask.

158. *by gogs-wouns*] by Gods'
wounds, a common oath, though not
found elsewhere in Shakespeare.

160. *again . . . up*] to pick it up
again.

163. *Now . . . list*] It is possible
that Petruchio is inviting anyone who
cares to do so to pick up the priest and
his book. It is more likely (see l. 166,
and iv. iii. 154 ff.) that he purports to
suspect the priest of fumbling

with the bride's underwear. Hibbard
points out that some plausibility is
lent to the suspicion by the Elizabethan marriage-custom in which,
after the ceremony, the young men
rushed forward to pull the ribbons off
the bride's dress and to remove her
garter ribbons, 'this sometimes occurring even before she had left the altar'
(*Shakespeare's England*, ii. 146).

164. *rose up*] Some editors prefer
'arose' to 'rose up', and either reading
will correct F's defective metre.

165–81. *Trembled . . . play*] printed
as prose in F. NCS suggests that this is
possibly because the lines were
originally crowded into the foot or
margin of a foolscap page.

165. *For why*] on account of which,
for which cause (*OED*, Forwhy, *adv.*
and *conj.*, A. 3).

166. *cozen*] cheat (by doing something that would invalidate the
marriage). See note to l. 163 above,
and *OED*, Cozen, *v.* 1.

170. *muscadel*] a strong sweet wine
made from the muscat or similar
grape (*OED*, Muscatel, 1). 'At the
conclusion of the service a cup of

And threw the sops all in the sexton's face,
Having no other reason
But that his beard grew thin and hungerly
And seem'd to ask him sops as he was drinking.
This done, he took the bride about the neck,   175
And kiss'd her lips with such a clamorous smack
That at the parting all the church did echo.
And I, seeing this, came thence for very shame,
And after me, I know, the rout is coming.
Such a mad marriage never was before.   180
Hark, hark! I hear the minstrels play.   *Music plays.*

Enter PETRUCHIO, KATHERINA, BIANCA, BAPTISTA,
HORTENSIO [*with* GRUMIO *and* Attendants].

Pet. Gentlemen and friends, I thank you for your pains.
I know you think to dine with me today,
And have prepar'd great store of wedding cheer,
But so it is, my haste doth call me hence,   185
And therefore here I mean to take my leave.
Bap. Is't possible you will away tonight?
Pet. I must away today before night come.
Make it no wonder. If you knew my business,
You would entreat me rather go than stay.   190
And honest company, I thank you all
That have beheld me give away myself
To this most patient, sweet, and virtuous wife.
Dine with my father, drink a health to me,
For I must hence, and farewell to you all.   195

181. S.D. *with Grumio and Attendants*] *After Capell; not in F.*

muscadel with cakes or sops in it was drunk by the bride, the bridegroom, and the company' (*Shakespeare's England*, II. 147), which also quotes Armin's comedy *The History of the Two Maids of More-clacke* (1609), I. i: 'The Muskadine stayes for the bride at Church,/The Priest and himens cerimonies tend/To make them man and wife.'

173. *hungerly*] sparsely. *OED* (Hungerly, *a.*) records only the sense 'Hungry-looking; having a hungry,

starved or famished look', though it quotes this line among its examples. In Shakespeare's other uses of the word (*Tim.*, I. i. 255, *Oth.*, III. iv. 106) it means 'greedily, hungrily' (*OED*, Hungerly, *adv.*).

179. *rout*] crowd of guests (Onions, 2). The sense of 'disorderly flight' is not pre-Elizabethan.

181. *Hark . . . play*] Metrically this line is one foot short. It may be that a word has been omitted.

183. *think*] expect.

Tra. Let us entreat you stay till after dinner.

Pet. It may not be.

Gre.   Let me entreat you.

Pet. It cannot be.

Kath.   Let me entreat you.

Pet. I am content.

Kath.   Are you content to stay?

Pet. I am content you shall entreat me stay;   200

    But yet not stay, entreat me how you can.

Kath. Now if you love me, stay.

Pet.   Grumio, my horse.

Gru. Ay, sir, they be ready; the oats have eaten the

    horses.

Kath. Nay then,   205

    Do what thou canst, I will not go today,

    No, nor tomorrow, not till I please myself.

    The door is open, sir, there lies your way,

    You may be jogging whiles your boots are green.

    For me, I'll not be gone till I please myself.   210

    'Tis like you'll prove a jolly surly groom,

    That take it on you at the first so roundly.

---

197. *Gre.*] *F2; Gra. F.*   197, 198. you] *F;* you, sir *Hanmer;* you stay *Steevens.*

202. *horse*] '*horse* plural was in general use down to 17th c.' (*OED*, Horse, *sb.* 1. b). The same form in singular and plural is found in similar words, like sheep, swine, neat, deer.

203–4. *the . . . horses*] i.e. the horses are full of oats and therefore ready for a journey. The inversion suggests they have had more oats than they could eat. NCS suggests that Grumio may have pronounced 'oats' as 'aits' (a 16th-century variant) to produce a pun 'the aits have aten the horses', though such a possibility is not mentioned in Kökeritz. The phrase sounds proverbial, but it is not listed in Tilley. Smith and Wilson records 'Horse that will not carry saddle must have no oats' and 'A horse will not void oats', but the examples are much later than Shakespeare.

208. *The . . . way*] Tilley, D556. Cf. *Tw.N.*, I. v. 190.

209. *You . . . green*] Tilley, B536. Neither Tilley nor Smith and Wilson offers a pre-Shakespearean example of this proverb. 'Green' here means fresh (Onions, 4). Cf. *Rom.*, IV. iii. 42.

211. *jolly*] Most editors gloss as 'arrogant, overbearing', presumably in the sense of *OED*, *a.* and *adv.* II. 6. *OED*, however, cites the line under B. *adv.* 2, 'Qualifying an adj. or adv.; orig. appreciatively, then ironically, with intensive force: Extremely, very'. This fits the context well, and *OED*'s examples show it to be a well-attested sense in Shakespeare's time. This sense is not found elsewhere in Shakespeare, but there is perhaps a hint of it in *R3*, IV. iii. 43.

212. *roundly*] (i) completely, thor-

Pet. O Kate, content thee, prithee be not angry.
Kath. I will be angry; what hast thou to do?
    Father, be quiet; he shall stay my leisure.   215
Gre. Ay, marry, sir, now it begins to work.
Kath. Gentlemen, forward to the bridal dinner.
    I see a woman may be made a fool
    If she had not a spirit to resist.
Pet. They shall go forward, Kate, at thy command.   220
    Obey the bride, you that attend on her.
    Go to the feast, revel and domineer,
    Carouse full measure to her maidenhead,
    Be mad and merry, or go hang yourselves.
    But for my bonny Kate, she must with me.   225
    Nay, look not big, nor stamp, nor stare, nor fret;
    I will be master of what is mine own.
    She is my goods, my chattels, she is my house,
    My household stuff, my field, my barn,
    My horse, my ox, my ass, my any thing,   230
    And here she stands. Touch her whoever dare!
    I'll bring mine action on the proudest he

229. barn,] *F;* barn, my stable, *Capell;* barn, my grange, *conj. Walker.*

oughly, (ii) plainly, bluntly (*OED,*
adv. 2 and 3). Cf. note to I. ii. 58.

214. *what . . . do?*] What business is
it of yours? Cf. I. ii. 224; *Wiv.,* III. iii.
136–7, 'Why, what have you to do
whither they bear it?'

215. *stay my leisure*] Cf. IV. iii. 59 n.

216. *marry*] Originally the name of
the Blessed Virgin Mary used as an
oath or an invocation, it came to mean
no more than 'indeed, to be sure' (cf.
Err., II. ii. 101). As Gremio uses the
word here it is subtly ironic.

222. *domineer*] revel, roister, feast
riotously (*OED, v.* 2). Cf. Nashe,
Pierce Penilesse (*Works,* ed. McKerrow,
rev. Wilson, I. 166), 'hee can neither
traffique with the Mercers and Tailers
as he was wont, nor dominere in
Tauernes as he ought'.

225. *for*] as for.

226. *Nay . . . fret*] This line is
addressed to the whole company on
stage, who are obviously doing nothing

of the sort. It is clearly what Katherina
herself is doing, and Petruchio affects
not to notice.

stare] gaze in amazement. NCS
glosses as 'swagger, behave in an overbearing manner', but *OED* does not
record this sense, the nearest being *v.*
3. a, 'To open the eyes wide in mad-
ness or fury; to glare'. Cf. *Wiv.,* V. v.
160 (Arden line-numbering, ed.
Oliver) and note.

230. *My . . . thing*] This echoes the
tenth commandment (Exodus, xx.
17). Petruchio is accusing the company of 'coveting' Katherina. Bond
quotes from *A Knack to Know a Knave*
(1594): 'My house? why, 'tis my
goods, my wyf, my land, my horse, my
ass, or anything that is his.'

232. *bring mine action on*] take legal
proceedings against.

he] commonly used for 'man'
(Abbott, 224).

That stops my way in Padua. Grumio,
Draw forth thy weapon, we are beset with thieves,
Rescue thy mistress if thou be a man.   235
Fear not, sweet wench, they shall not touch thee, Kate.
I'll buckler thee against a million.

Exeunt Petruchio, Katherina [and Grumio].

Bap. Nay, let them go, a couple of quiet ones.

Gre. Went they not quickly, I should die with laughing.

Tra. Of all mad matches never was the like.   240

Luc. Mistress, what's your opinion of your sister?

Bian. That being mad herself, she's madly mated.

Gre. I warrant him, Petruchio is Kated.

Bap. Neighbours and friends, though bride and bridegroom
        wants
      For to supply the places at the table,   245
      You know there wants no junkets at the feast.
      Lucentio, you shall supply the bridegroom's place,
      And let Bianca take her sister's room.

Tra. Shall sweet Bianca practise how to bride it?

Bap. She shall, Lucentio. Come, gentlemen, let's go.   *Exeunt.*

237. S.D. *Petruchio, Katherina [and Grumio].] Capell (and Grumio)*; *P. Ka. F.*

237. *buckler*] shield, defend. Cf.
2H6, III. ii. 216; *3H6*, III. iii. 99
(Shakespeare's only other uses).

239. *Went they not*] if they had not
gone.

243. *Kated*] has caught the 'Kate'
(as if it were the name of an illness).
Cf. *Ado*, I. i. 73–5, 'If he have caught
the Benedick, it will cost him a
thousand pound ere 'a be cured'.

244. *wants*] are lacking (Abbott,
297).

246. *junkets*] sweetmeats, delicacies
(*OED, sb.* 3). The word does not occur
elsewhere in Shakespeare.

248. *room*] place. Cf. *John*, III. iv.
93.

249. *bride it*] play the bride. Cf.
Wint., IV. iv. 441 ('queen it'); *Meas.*
III. ii. 89 ('dukes it').

[ACT IV]

[SCENE I]

Enter GRUMIO.

Gru. Fie, fie on all tired jades, on all mad masters, and all
foul ways! Was ever man so beaten? Was ever man
so rayed? Was ever man so weary? I am sent before
to make a fire, and they are coming after to warm
them. Now, were I not a little pot and soon hot, my   5
very lips might freeze to my teeth, my tongue to the
roof of my mouth, my heart in my belly, ere I should
come by a fire to thaw me. But I with blowing the
fire shall warm myself, for, considering the weather,
a taller man than I will take cold. Holla, ho! Curtis!   10

Enter CURTIS.

Curt. Who is that calls so coldly?

ACT IV

Scene 1

ACT IV SCENE I] *Pope; not in F.*   3. rayed] *Johnson (subst.); raide F;* 'wray'd
Capell.

F gives no act- or scene-division
here, and begins '*Actus Quartus. Scena
Prima*' where we begin IV. iii. But
Pope was surely right to begin Act IV
here, since the move to Petruchio's
house in the country is the first real
change of place since the play proper
began.

   3. *rayed*] dirtied. Cf. III. ii. 51.
Bond notes the four occurrences in
Spenser (*FQ*, II. i. 40; III. viii. 32;
VI. v. 23; *Visions of Bellay*, st. xii, l. 13),
and Nashe, *Summer's Last Will* (*Works*,
ed. McKerrow, rev. Wilson, III. 290),
'Let there be a fewe rushes laide in the
place where *Back-winter* shall tumble,
for feare of raying his cloathes'.

   5. *a . . . hot*] Tilley, P497, quoting
'1670 Ray, p. 115: Little persons are
commonly cholerick'. Grumio is
referring to his small stature: cf. ll.
10, 23, 25 below.

   8–9. *blowing the fire*] Tilley, C460,
'Let them that be acold blow at the
Coal'.

   10. *taller*] Onions quotes this line as
an example of 'tall' in the sense of
'goodly, fine, proper', comparing IV.
iv. 17, and *MND*, v. i. 143. But
Grumio's principal point must be his
own lack of inches.

   Curtis] 'Curtis . . . possesses a
strangely English-sounding name for a
steward of a country house near

239

Gru. A piece of ice. If thou doubt it, thou mayst slide
from my shoulder to my heel with no greater a run
but my head and my neck. A fire, good Curtis.

Curt. Is my master and his wife coming, Grumio?   15

Gru. O ay, Curtis, ay—and therefore fire, fire, cast on no
water.

Curt. Is she so hot a shrew as she's reported?

Gru. She was, good Curtis, before this frost. But thou
know'st winter tames man, woman, and beast; for it   20
hath tamed my old master, and my new mistress,
and myself, fellow Curtis.

Curt. Away, you three-inch fool! I am no beast.

Gru. Am I but three inches? Why, thy horn is a foot, and
so long am I at the least. But wilt thou make a fire, or   25
shall I complain on thee to our mistress, whose
hand, she being now at hand, thou shalt soon feel, to
thy cold comfort, for being slow in thy hot office?

22. myself] *F;* thyself *Hanmer (conj. Warburton).*   23. *Curt.*] *Q; Gru. F.*
24. thy] *F;* my *Theobald.*

Verona, bandying jests with a
Grumio. When, however, we dis-
cover that one Curtis was a minor
actor in the King's company, who
took small parts in *The Two Noble
Kinsmen* (1613), the origin of the
character in *The Shrew* finds at least a
possible explanation' (NCS, p. 118).

16–17. *fire . . . water*] a reference to
the well-known catch, which is found
in several variant forms: 'Scotland's
burning, Scotland's burning,/See
yonder! See yonder!/Fire, fire! Fire
fire!/Cast on water! Cast on water!'
It is not in any of the printed collec-
tions of Ravenscroft (*Pammelia*, 1609;
Deuteromilia, 1609; *Melismata*, 1611),
but occurs as early as *c.* 1580 in a MS.
in King's College, Cambridge, which
also contains 'Jack boy, how boy,
news' (cf. IV. i. 36). See Jill Vlasto,
'An Elizabethan Anthology of
Rounds', *Musical Quarterly* (1954),
pp. 222–34.

18. *hot*] Several senses are possible:
(i) of a hot humour—in the physio-

logical sense (*OED, a.* 4); (ii) angry,
violent (*OED,* 6. b)—cf. *Err.,* I. ii. 47,
'She is so hot because the meat is
cold'; (iii) intense, keen (*OED,* 7,
intensive).

20. *winter . . . beast*] Tilley, A64,
'Age (Winter) and wedlock tame both
man and beast'.

22. *myself*] Hanmer suggests 'thyself', to account for Curtis's reply. But
it is the 'fellow' which Curtis takes up.

23. *three-inch*] tiny, diminutive. Cf.
l. 5.

I . . . beast] By naming himself third,
and calling Curtis 'fellow', Grumio
has equated him with the 'beast' of
l. 20.

24–5. *Am . . . least*] Grumio asserts
that he is big enough to have made
Curtis a cuckold. The word 'three-
inch' in l. 23 was offered as an insult
to Grumio's height, but he here takes
it up in another sense.

28. *cold comfort*] Tilley, C542,
quoting '1571 Golding, *Psalms* x 14
. . . : We receive but cold comfort of

Curt. I prithee, good Grumio, tell me how goes the
world?   30
Gru. A cold world, Curtis, in every office but thine; and
therefore fire. Do thy duty, and have thy duty, for
my master and mistress are almost frozen to death.
Curt. There's fire ready, and therefore, good Grumio,
the news.   35
Gru. Why, 'Jack, boy, ho, boy!' and as much news as
wilt thou.
Curt. Come, you are so full of cony-catching.
Gru. Why, therefore, fire, for I have caught extreme
cold. Where's the cook? Is supper ready, the house   40
trimmed, rushes strewed, cobwebs swept, the

36. 'Jack . . . boy!'] *Warburton;* Iacke . . . boy, *F.*   37. wilt thou] *F;* thou
wilt *F2.*

whatsoever the scripture speaketh
concerning Gods power and justice,
onlesse euery of us apply the same to
himselfe according as need that
require'. Cf. *John,* v. vii. 42.

32. *Do . . . thy duty*] 'Evidently
proverbial' says Bond, but not recorded in either Tilley or Smith and
Wilson. The sense is akin to that of
'the labourer is worthy of his hire'.
For 'duty' in the sense of 'what is due
to you' see *OED,* Duty, 2, quoting
Tindale, Matthew xx. 14, 'Take that
which is thy duty' (AV, 'Take that
thine is'); cf. Lyly, *Euphues* (*Works,* ed.
Bond, I. 301), 'those that haue com-
mitted periurie and retained the
duetie of the hirelinges'.

36. *'Jack, boy, ho, boy!'*] The
beginning of a catch, the words and
music of which first appear in
Ravenscroft's *Pammelia,* the first
printed book of English catches (cf.
ll. 16–17 and note, above). The words
are: 'Jacke boy, ho boy, Newes:/
The cat is in the well/Let us sing now
for her knell/Ding dong, ding dong,
bell.' It is, of course, suggested to
Grumio by the word 'news' in l. 35,
but, as NCS points out, possibly the
reference to the cat might link the
catch in the minds of the audience

with Kate the shrew.

37. *wilt thou*] Bond, NCS, and some
other editions emend to 'thou wilt',
following F2. F's reading might be a
transposition error (though they are
not common in this text), but the
meaning is the same in either case,
and *de minimis non curat lex.*

38. *cony-catching*] cheating, duping,
knavery (*OED, vbl. sb.*). A cony is a
rabbit. Cf. v. i. 90–1; *Wiv.,* I. i. 113–
14. Greene's *Conny-Catching* pam-
phlets (1591–2) seem to have given a
literary vogue to this slang term. Bond
quotes Florio's *Montaigne* (1603), ch.
xxx, 'those that gull and conicatch us
with the assurance of an extra
ordinarie facultie'. Curtis is referring
to Grumio's fondness for catches.

39. *Why, therefore, fire*] Well, let's
have a fire to cook the cony. Grumio
goes back to the original meaning of
cony—'rabbit'. Cf. *AYL,* III. ii. 317.

41. *rushes strewed*] The strewing of
fresh rushes on the floor was part of
the normal preparation for receiving
a guest. Cf. *Shakespeare's England,* II.
123; *2H4,* v. v. 1; *Rom.,* I. iv. 36; Lyly,
Sapho and Phao (*Works,* ed. Bond, II.
391), II. iv. 97–8, 'straungers haue
greene rushes, when daily guests are
not worth a rushe'.

servingmen in their new fustian, their white
stockings, and every officer his wedding-garment
on? Be the Jacks fair within, the Jills fair without,
the carpets laid, and everything in order?   45

Curt. All ready; and therefore, I pray thee, news.

Gru. First know my horse is tired, my master and
mistress fallen out.

Curt. How?

Gru. Out of their saddles into the dirt, and thereby hangs   50
a tale.

Curt. Let's ha't, good Grumio.

Gru. Lend thine ear.

Curt. Here.

Gru. There.   [*Strikes him.*]   55

Curt. This 'tis to feel a tale, not to hear a tale.

Gru. And therefore 'tis called a sensible tale; and this
cuff was but to knock at your ear and beseech
listening. Now I begin. *Imprimis*, we came down a
foul hill, my master riding behind my mistress—   60

Curt. Both of one horse?

Gru. What's that to thee?

Curt. Why, a horse.

Gru. Tell thou the tale. But hadst thou not crossed me,
thou shouldst have heard how her horse fell, and she   65
under her horse; thou shouldst have heard in how

---

42. their white] *F3*; the white *F.*   55. S.D.] *Rowe; not in F.*   56. 'tis] *F;* is
Rowe.

---

42. *fustian*] a kind of coarse cloth
made of cotton and flax (*OED*, A.
sb. 1). Not used in this original sense
elsewhere in Shakespeare.

44. *Jacks . . . without*] word-play.
'Jacks' were (i) servingmen, (ii)
leather drinking-vessels (*OED*, *sb.²*
2). 'Jills' were (i) maid-servants, (ii)
vessels (usually metal) holding a gill
of liquid (*OED*, Gill, *sb.³* 2). Perry
quotes Steevens: 'The *jacks*, being of
leather, could not be made to appear
beautiful on the outside, but were
very apt to contract foulness within;
whereas the *jills*, being of metal, were
expected to be kept bright externally,

and were not liable to dirt on the inside, like the leather.' Jack and Jill
were, of course, proverbially associated. Cf. Tilley, J1, J6.

45. *carpets laid*] Carpets were sometimes laid on the floor (cf. *Tw.N.*,
III. iv. 225), but were more commonly
used to cover chests and tables
(*Shakespeare's England*, II. 128).

50–1. *thereby . . . tale*] Tilley, T48.

57. *sensible*] (i) capable of being
felt, (ii) easily understood, effective,
striking (*OED*, *a.* 1 and 5).

59. *Imprimis*] first.

61. *of*] on (Abbott, 175). Cf.
Mer.V., II. ii. 86–90.

miry a place, how she was bemoiled, how he left her
with the horse upon her, how he beat me because
her horse stumbled, how she waded through the dirt
to pluck him off me, how he swore, how she prayed   70
that never prayed before, how I cried, how the
horses ran away, how her bridle was burst, how I
lost my crupper, with many things of worthy
memory, which now shall die in oblivion, and thou
return unexperienced to thy grave.   75

Curt. By this reckoning he is more shrew than she.

Gru. Ay, and that thou and the proudest of you all shall
find when he comes home. But what talk I of this?
Call forth Nathaniel, Joseph, Nicholas, Philip,
Walter, Sugarsop, and the rest. Let their heads be   80
slickly combed, their blue coats brushed, and their
garters of an indifferent knit. Let them curtsy with

---

67. *bemoiled*] covered with dirt and
mire (*OED*, Bemoil, *v.*, quoting *Shr.*
as its earliest instance, and only one
other, dated 1636). The word is not
found elsewhere in Shakespeare.

70–1. *how she . . . before*] Cf. *The
True Chronicle History of King Leir*
(Bullough, VII. 394), sc. 24. After the
King of Gallia has taken an oath to
reinstate Leir the usually comic
Mumford kneels and says 'Let me
pray to, that never pray'd before'.
King Leir was not published until 1605.
Muir notes (*King Lear*, Arden edn, p.
xxiv) that 'a *king leare* was performed
at the Rose Theatre by the combined
Queen's and Sussex's men during an
unsuccessful season early in April
1594'. If this is the same play as the
1605 *King Leir* it is quite possible that
Shakespeare saw it, in or about 1594,
and that there is a debt (one way or
the other) between *Leir* and *Shr.*

72. *burst*] broken. Cf. Ind. i. 6;
III. ii. 57.

76. *shrew*] The word could be
applied to either sex (*OED*, *sb.²* 1).

78. *what*] why (Abbott, 253). Cf.
Tit., I. i. 189.

80. *Sugarsop*] an odd name in the

list, and not recorded elsewhere as a
personal name (see Stokes, *Dictionary*).
A sugarsop was a dish composed of
steeped slices of bread, sweetened and
sometimes spiced.

81. *slickly*] sleekly, smoothly (*OED*,
adv. 1, quoting only *Shr.*).

blue coats] the servants' uniform.
'Servants in good families wore
doublets of shorter waist and rather
longer skirt than their masters. . . . A
shade of blue was very popular for
liveries' (*Shakespeare's England*, II. 112).
Cf. *1H6*, I. iii. 46–7. Cf. note to I. i.
207.

82. *indifferent knit*] in matching
style. Cf. *Tw.N.*, I. v. 232, 'two lips
indifferent red'. Bond proposed
'moderately handsome, in colour or
pattern, *e.g.* with bright threads in
them'; Hibbard suggests 'of a reasonable pattern, not too showy'; NCS
glosses 'indifferent' as 'ordinary,
usual, correct', and this receives some
support from *Tim.*, I. i. 33, *Ham.*, II. ii.
226, but all three interpretations may
safely be rejected. Johnson explained
that the garters were to be 'not
different', i.e. fellows, and this seems
to fit the demands of the context best.

their left legs, and not presume to touch a hair of my
master's horse-tail till they kiss their hands. Are
they all ready?   85

Curt. They are.

Gru. Call them forth.

Curt. Do you hear, ho? You must meet my master to
countenance my mistress.

Gru. Why, she hath a face of her own.   90

Curt. Who knows not that?

Gru. Thou, it seems, that calls for company to countenance her.

Curt. I call them forth to credit her.

Gru. Why, she comes to borrow nothing of them.   95

Enter four or five Servingmen.

95. S.D.] *F (after l. 94).*

Grumio is ensuring that the servants
are well turned out, and he would be
less likely to worry about quality of
material than about the possibility of
someone appearing in garters that
were not a pair. 'Indifferent' can
mean 'not different in character . . .
equal, even; identical, the same'
(*OED, a.*[1] 9, quoting '1584 R. Scot
Disc. Witchcr. v. ix . . . It is indifferent to saie in the English toong;
She is a witch; or, She is a wise
woman'). 'Knit' means 'the style or
stitch in which anything is knitted'
(*OED, sb.* 1, quoting *Shr.*).

82–3. *curtsy . . . legs*] The exact
sense is not clear. There are several
ways of making a curtsy, though all
involve bending one or both legs and
lowering the body. *OED* quotes '1583
HOLLYBAND *Campo di Fior* 57 Put of
thy cappe boye   Make a fine curtesie,
Bowe thy right knee . . . As it hath
bene taught thee', and Bond quotes a
letter of 1586 to the effect that the
prominence of the right leg expressed
defiance. The most obvious sense of
Grumio's words is that the servants
should bend the left leg at the knee,
but it may be that he intends an
obeisance in which the right leg is

withdrawn and bent, leaving the left
leg forward. The spelling here is
'curtsie', but at many places in F it is
'cursie', and this probably indicates
Shakespeare's pronunciation.

84. *kiss their hands*] To kiss one's
own hands was a mark of respect. Cf.
AYL, III. ii. 45–6.

89. *countenance*] encounter, greet.

92. *calls*] Grammar requires
'call'st', but see Abbott, 340, for
occasions on which Shakespeare
alters grammatical endings 'for
euphony'. Bond, however, regards
this instance as a simple mistake 'made
easier by "that" as subject'. Hibbard
notes that 'Shakespeare, who wrote
his words to be spoken, not read,
often avoids the "-est" form'. There
is, however, no particular difficulty of
a vocal kind in pronouncing 'call'st
for'.

94. *credit*] honour, do credit to
(*OED, v.* 5, quoting *Shr.* as its earliest
example). Grumio takes up the word
in its sense of 'provide credit for'
(*OED, v.* 3. a).

95. S.D.] 'Four or five' looks like
an authorial proposal, rather than
one originating in the theatre. NCS
points out that the names given at

Nath. Welcome home, Grumio.

Phil. How now, Grumio.

Jos. What, Grumio.

Nich. Fellow Grumio.

Nath. How now, old lad.   100

Gru. Welcome, you. How now, you. What, you. Fellow,
  you. And thus much for greeting. Now, my spruce
  companions, is all ready, and all things neat?

Nath. All things is ready. How near is our master?

Gru. E'en at hand, alighted by this. And therefore be not   105
  —Cock's passion, silence! I hear my master.

    Enter PETRUCHIO *and* KATHERINA.

Pet. Where be these knaves? What, no man at door
  To hold my stirrup nor to take my horse?
  Where is Nathaniel, Gregory, Philip?

All Serv. Here, here sir, here sir.   110

Pet. Here sir, here sir, here sir, here sir!
  You logger-headed and unpolish'd grooms!
  What, no attendance? No regard? No duty?
  Where is the foolish knave I sent before?

Gru. Here sir, as foolish as I was before.   115

Pet. You peasant swain! You whoreson malt-horse drudge!
  Did I not bid thee meet me in the park,

---

107. door] *F; the door Capell.* 116. peasant swain] *Rowe;* pezant, swain *F.*

ll. 79–80 are not quite the same as
those at ll. 119–23, and neither is
identical with the speech-prefixes
here.

 104. *things is ready*] singular verb
and plural subject. See Abbott, 333,
who does not quote this line, but
suggests that occasionally this may be
intended as a sign of low breeding,
and cites *MND*, III. i. 75.

 106. *Cock's passion*] God's passion!
A common oath. Cf. *All's W.*, v. ii.
39–40.

 107. *man at door*] so F, but some
editors from Capell onwards read
'man at the door' to regularize the
metre. NCS sees this as another
example of the omission of small

words which seems to be a habit of
the compositor or transcriber.

 112. *logger-headed*] thick-headed,
stupid (*OED, a.* 1, quoting *Shr.* as its
earliest example).

 114. *Where . . . before*] Tilley, F488.

 116. *peasant*] rascal. The word is
generally used contemptuously in
Shakespeare. Cf. *Gent.*, IV. iv. 39–40,
'How now, you whoreson peasant';
Ham., II. ii. 543.

 malt-horse] a heavy horse, used by
maltsters to grind malt by working a
treadmill. Cf. *Err.*, III. i. 32; Jonson,
Every Man in his Humour (H. & S.,
III. 211), I. iii. 164–5, 'no more judgement than a malt-horse'.

And bring along these rascal knaves with thee?
Gru. Nathaniel's coat, sir, was not fully made,
And Gabriel's pumps were all unpink'd i' th' heel;   120
There was no link to colour Peter's hat,
And Walter's dagger was not come from sheathing.
There were none fine but Adam, Rafe, and Gregory,
The rest were ragged, old, and beggarly;
Yet, as they are, here are they come to meet you.   125
Pet. Go, rascals, go, and fetch my supper in.

Exeunt Servingmen.

[*Sings.*] Where is the life that late I led?
Where are those—
Sit down, Kate, and welcome. Food, food, food, food!

Enter Servants *with supper.*

126. S.D.] *Theobald (subst.); Ex. Ser. F.*   127. S.D.] *Theobald; not in F.*
129. Food . . . food!] *NCS;* Soud . . . soud. *F.*

119–25. *Nathaniel's . . . you*]
Grumio, who usually speaks prose,
uses blank verse here. The servants'
names again differ from those we have
heard earlier, and Grumio's excuses
for their unpreparedness are at odds
with Curtis's insistence that they are
'all ready', though this inconsistency
is probably a deliberate piece of comic
business to show Grumio's inventive-
ness in 'thinking on his feet'.

120. *unpink'd . . . heel*] To 'pink' is to
pierce with small holes, often for
decoration or to attach ornaments
(*OED, v.*[1] 1 and 3). Grumio seems to
be suggesting either that the pumps
were not completed or that the
decoration had become frayed or
worn. Bond compares *H8*, v. iv. 48–9.

121. *link*] torch. The smoke from a
'link' or pitch torch (or sometimes the
burnt-out material of the torch itself)
was used for restoring the blackness of
an old hat. Bond quotes Greene's
Mihil Mumchance, 'selling old hats
found upon dung-hills, instead of
newe, blackt over with the smoake of
an old linke'.

127–8. *Where . . . those*—] F reads
'Where is the life that late I led?/

Where are those?' The first line has
been identified as the first line of an
old ballad (now lost), and the second
probably continues it. Hence, all
editors since Theobald include a
S.D. indicating that Petruchio 'sings'.
The song would be particularly appropriate to the newly-married man.
Ritson mentions a song in the 1578
anthology *A Gorgious Gallery* 'to the
tune of Where is the life that late I
led'; and there is a 'replie' to it in one
of the pieces in Clement Robinson's
Handefull of Pleasant Delites (1584).
The opening words are quoted by
Pistol, *2H4*, v. iii. 139.

129. *Food . . . food!*] F's 'Soud, soud,
soud, soud', has given rise to a
multitude of interpretations, Malone
even suggesting that it was an
exclamation meant to express heat
and fatigue (surprising in view of
Grumio's earlier complaints of the
cold, and a tribute to Curtis's fire).
Onions yields to despair, glossing
'soud' as 'interjection of doubtful
import'. But the context makes it
clear that Petruchio wants food, and
here he calls for it. The two forms
'food' and 'soud' could easily be con-

Why, when, I say? Nay, good sweet Kate, be merry.   130
Off with my boots, you rogues! You villains, when?
[*Sings.*]   It was the friar of orders grey,
              As he forth walked on his way—
Out, you rogue! You pluck my foot awry.
Take that, and mend the plucking off the other.   135
                                              [*Strikes him.*]
Be merry, Kate. Some water here. What ho!

                Enter One *with water.*

Where's my spaniel Troilus? Sirrah, get you hence,
And bid my cousin Ferdinand come hither.
One, Kate, that you must kiss and be acquainted with.
Where are my slippers? Shall I have some water?   140
Come, Kate, and wash, and welcome heartily.
You whoreson villain, will you let it fall?
                                            [*Strikes Servant.*]

132. S.D.] *Rowe; not in F.*   135. off] *Rowe; of F.*   S.D.] *Rowe; not in F.*
142. S.D.] *Capell (strikes him); not in F.*

fused in manuscript, but the problem remains as to what the compositor who misread 'food' in his copy thought he was setting up. *OED* records 'soud' only as a variant spelling of 'sold' (*sb.*[1], *v.*[1], *v.*[2]) and as a Scottish variant of 'should'; it is unlikely that these would be words familiar to the compositor. Nevertheless, it is clear that Shakespeare intended us to read 'food', and this emendation has the support of Sisson, NCS, Hibbard, and most modern editors. Hulme (*Explorations*) argues ingeniously but unconvincingly for 'sond', meaning 'a serving of food, a course'.

131. *when*] an exclamation of impatience (Onions, 1). Cf. *R2*, i. i. 162; *Caes.*, ii. i. 5.

132–3. *It . . . way*] a bawdy song. See P. J. Croft, 'The "Friar of Order Gray" and the Nun', *RES*, xxxii (1981), 1–16.

135. *mend the*] make a better job of (Onions, 8). Cf. *LLL*, v. ii. 328–9.

136. S.D.] Bond, and some other editors, postpone the S.D. (which occurs at this point in F) until after Petruchio calls for water for the second time, l. 140). But this is to miss the point. The service in Petruchio's house is prompt, and it is Petruchio himself who deliberately refuses to accept that it is satisfactory. Washing the hands at table before a meal was customary when the fingers assisted knife and spoon in eating (see *Shakespeare's England*, ii. 133). Bond provides an illustration from Florio's *Second Frutes*, 1591: '*C*. The meate is coming, let us sit downe. *S*. I would wash first.—What ho, bring us some water to wash our hands.— Give me a faire, cleane and white towel.'

137. *Troilus*] possibly so named as a type of faithfulness. Cf. Stokes (*Dictionary*) and *Lr*, iii. vi. 62 ('Tray').

138. *my cousin Ferdinand*] F gives no 'Exit' for any servant at this point, and Ferdinand never appears.

Kath. Patience, I pray you, 'twas a fault unwilling.

Pet. A whoreson beetle-headed, flap-ear'd knave!
       Come, Kate, sit down, I know you have a stomach.   145
       Will you give thanks, sweet Kate, or else shall I?
       What's this? Mutton?

First Serv.   Ay.

Pet.   Who brought it?

Peter.   I.

Pet. 'Tis burnt, and so is all the meat.
       What dogs are these! Where is the rascal cook?
       How durst you, villains, bring it from the dresser   150
       And serve it thus to me that love it not?
       There, take it to you, trenchers, cups, and all.
                         [*He throws the food and dishes at them.*]
       You heedless joltheads and unmanner'd slaves!
       What, do you grumble? I'll be with you straight.
                                                    [*Exeunt Servants.*]

Kath. I pray you, husband, be not so disquiet.   155
       The meat was well, if you were so contented.

Pet. I tell thee, Kate, 'twas burnt and dried away,
       And I expressly am forbid to touch it,
       For it engenders choler, planteth anger;

---

152. S.D.] *Rowe (subst.); not in F.*   154. S.D.] *Dyce; not in F.*

---

144. *beetle-headed*]   thick-headed,
stupid (*OED, sb.*[1] 3, quoting *Shr.*). A
'beetle' is a heavy wooden mallet. Cf.
Lyly, *Midas* (*Works*, ed. Bond, III.
121), I. ii. 66, 'Thou hast a beetle
head!'

flap-ear'd] having pendulous, flap-
ping ears (*OED, sb.* 10).

150. *dresser*] 'A sideboard or table
in a kitchen on which food is or was
dressed; formerly also, a table in a
dining-room or hall, from which
dishes were served, or on which plate
was displayed' (*OED*, Dresser[1], 1,
quoting *Shr.*). The servants brought
supper in at l. 129, and it is clearly
ready on the table at l. 147. The
interim could easily be taken up with
laying and serving, and there is no
need to assume the presence of a

'dresser' in the hall. Petruchio is
referring to the 'table in a kitchen'.

152. *trenchers*] wooden plates (*OED*,
2). Cf. *Rom.*, I. v. 2-3.

153. *joltheads*]   blockheads.   Cf.
Gent., III. i. 285 (the etymology of
'jolt' is obscure: see *OED, v. Note*).

unmanner'd slaves] Cf. *R3*, I. ii. 39.

154. S.D.] No S.D. in F, but the
exit is required (i) because of Petruchio's threat 'I'll be with you straight'
(cf. *MND*, III. ii. 403), and (ii)
because of F's S.D. 'Enter seruants
seuerally' at l. 165.

155. *disquiet*] restless, uneasy, dis-
turbed (*OED, a.*, quoting *Shr.*).

159. *it engenders choler*] Over-cooked
meat was believed to produce an
excess of the choleric humour, which
stimulated anger. Cf. *Err.*, II. ii. 55-66,

And better 'twere that both of us did fast,   160
Since, of ourselves, ourselves are choleric,
Than feed it with such over-roasted flesh.
Be patient, tomorrow 't shall be mended,
And for this night we'll fast for company.   164
Come, I will bring thee to thy bridal chamber.   *Exeunt.*

Enter Servants *severally*.

Nath. Peter, didst ever see the like?
Peter. He kills her in her own humour.

Enter CURTIS.

Gru. Where is he?
Curt. In her chamber,
Making a sermon of continency to her,   170
And rails, and swears, and rates, that she, poor soul,
Knows not which way to stand, to look, to speak,
And sits as one new risen from a dream.
Away, away, for he is coming hither.   [*Exeunt.*]

Enter PETRUCHIO.

167. S.D.] *Capell; after l. 168, F.   Curtis*] *Curtis a Seruant F.*   171–4.] *as verse,*
Pope; as prose, F.   174. S.D.] Pope; not in F.

where Dromio begs his master not to
eat dry, unbasted meat 'Lest it make
you choleric, and purchase me another dry basting'.

161. *of ourselves*] by nature (Abbott,
20).

164. *for company*] together; by way
of sociableness (Onions, 1).

165. S.D. *severally*] one by one,
singly. Cf. *Troil.*, IV. v. 274.

167. *He . . . humour*] He masters her
ill-temper by his own greater ill-
temper. For 'kill' in the sense of
'suppress' see *OED*, *v.* 4.

S.D.] F reads '*Enter Curtis a Seruant*'
after l. 168. NCS notes: 'Considering
that Curtis has been on for most of the
scene the F description "a Seruant" is
oddly superfluous', and suggests that,
in some earlier state of the play, this
may have been Curtis's first entrance,
and that the prose dialogue between

Grumio and Curtis at ll. 11 ff. was
added later. It is significant that
Curtis is not mentioned by Petruchio
when he himself enters (l. 106),
although he mentions three other
servants by name and Curtis is
obviously an important figure in the
household (cf. F's S.D. at IV. iv. 18).
It is impossible on the available
evidence to conjecture the details of
the original scene, but there does seem
to have been some sort of revision or
rearrangement.

170. *Making . . . her*] giving her a
lecture on the virtues of restraint and
moderation.

171. *rates*] chides, scolds (Onions,
*vb.*²). Cf. I. i. 160 and note.

173. *And . . . dream*] This line would
have an additional resonance and
relevance if Sly were still thought of as
present and sleeping.

Pet. Thus have I politicly begun my reign,   175
    And 'tis my hope to end successfully.
    My falcon now is sharp and passing empty,
    And till she stoop she must not be full-gorg'd,
    For then she never looks upon her lure.
    Another way I have to man my haggard,   180
    To make her come and know her keeper's call,
    That is, to watch her, as we watch these kites

175–98. *Thus . . . show*] Petruchio's soliloquy is central to the play. In it he describes openly to the audience his plan to subdue and train Katherina precisely as a falconer tames a wild bird. All the technical details of 'taming' in falconry are described in *Shakespeare's England*, II. 351–9. Hibbard quotes an illustrative passage from Gervase Markham's *Country Contentments* (1615) (fourth edn, London, 1631, 36–7): 'All hawks generally are manned after one manner, that is to say, by watching and keeping them from sleep, by a continual carrying of them upon your fist, and by a most familiar stroking and playing with them, with the wing of a dead fowl or such like, and by often gazing and looking of them in the face, with a loving and gentle countenance, and so making them acquainted with the man.' Cf., for both strategy and assured tone, Prince Hal's soliloquy, *1H4*, I. ii. 188–210.

175. *politicly*] prudently, shrewdly, in a statesmanlike way (*OED, adv.*, quoting '1603 Knolles *Hist. Turks* 255 The death of Mahomet had been politiquely concealed and fortie daies'). Cf. *2H6*, III. i. 341–2.

177. *sharp*] famished (*OED, a.* and *sb.*[1] 4. f). Cf. *Ven.*, 55, 'Even as an empty eagle, sharp by fast'.

passing] extremely.

178. *stoop*] to descend swiftly on to the prey, to swoop; also to fly to the lure (*OED, v.* 6). The stoop is 'when a Hawke being vpon her wings at the height of her pitch, bendeth violentlie

downe to sticke the fowle or any other pray' (Simon Latham, *Lathams Falconry*). Cf. Madden, *Diary*, pp. 202–3, for another description. There is also a pun on stoop in the sense of 'submit, yield obedience' (*OED*, 2. a).

full-gorg'd] allowed to eat her fill (*OED*, 12. b). Cf. *Lucr.*, 694, 'the full-fed hound or gorged hawk'.

179. *lure*] the apparatus used by a falconer to recall his bird. It could be a leather frame, or a bunch of feathers, or a sham bird, on the end of a cord, but pieces of meat were attached to it and these attracted the bird, which was reclaimed while it fed. Cf. *Ven.*, 1027, 'As falcons to the lure away she flies'.

180. *man my haggard*] tame my wild hawk, accustom her to the presence of men. Tilley, T298, 'In time all haggard hawks will stoop to lure' (with examples from Lyly, Watson and Kyd). Exact definitions of the haggard vary slightly from one Elizabethan falconer to another, but generally speaking it was a wild hawk caught when fully moulted at least once, which was therefore accustomed to prey for itself (as opposed to the eyas, a hawk taken from the nest and reared by hand). Cf. *Ado*, III. i. 36.

182. *watch her*] keep her watching, keep her awake (*OED, v.* 16). 'Sometimes all does not go well, and she must be brought to her bearings by fatigue. . . . She must be watched or kept awake at night till by sheer weariness she settles down into tameness and docility' (*Shakespeare's*

That bate and beat and will not be obedient.
She ate no meat today, nor none shall eat;
Last night she slept not, nor tonight she shall not.   185
As with the meat, some undeserved fault
I'll find about the making of the bed,
And here I'll fling the pillow, there the bolster,
This way the coverlet, another way the sheets.
Ay, and amid this hurly I intend   190
That all is done in reverend care of her.
And in conclusion she shall watch all night,
And if she chance to nod I'll rail and brawl,
And with the clamour keep her still awake.
This is a way to kill a wife with kindness,   195
And thus I'll curb her mad and headstrong humour.
He that knows better how to tame a shrew,
Now let him speak: 'tis charity to show.   *Exit.*

England, II. 357). Cf. *Oth.*, III. iii. 23; *Troil.*, III. ii. 43.

these kites] those falcons. Shakespeare often uses 'these' to denote some topical or well-known person. Cf. *Rom.*, I. i. 228. 'Kite' was a general word for falcon (*OED*, *sb.* 1. b). NCS suggests a possible pun on Kate/Kite.

183. *bate and beat*] flutter and flap the wings. Cf. *1H4*, IV. i. 99.

185. *Last . . . slept not*] It is not clear how Petruchio could know this, since no night has passed since the wedding, unless it was spent on the journey. So presumably this is what Shakespeare intends us to understand.

190. *hurly*] commotion, uproar, tumult, strife (*OED*, Hurly[1], quoting *Shr.* as its earliest example).

intend] pretend, assert, maintain (*OED*, *v.* 22, quoting *Shr.*; Onions, 3). Cf. *Lucr.*, 120–1; *R3*, III. v. 8; *Ado*, II. ii. 33.

194. *still*] constantly. Cf. *Ham.*, IV. vii. 116.

195. *to . . . kindness*] Tilley, K51; Smith and Wilson, p. 423 (with a number of additional examples from

the 16th century). A common phrase for mistaken indulgence, and the title of Heywood's *A Woman Killed with Kindness* (1607), though we need not assume any connection between that play and *Shr.* The phrase usually meant harming someone by excessive care—cf. Tilley, A264, 'The ape kills her young with kindness (by clipping)' and Lyly, *Love's Metamorphosis* (*Works*, ed. Bond, III. 232), IV. ii. 74—but here it has some of the sense of 'to give her a taste of her own medicine'.

197. *shrew*] The rhyme with 'show' indicates the pronunciation 'shrow'. Kökeritz (p. 211) notes 'Shakespeare rhymes *shrew(s)*, often spelt *shrow*, with o's, show, so, woe'. Cf. v. ii. 28, 189.

198. *Now . . . speak*] 'Therefore if any man can shew any iust cause, why they may not lawfully be ioined together: let him now speake, or els hereafter for euer holde hys peace' (*The Boke of Common Prayer* (1552), 'The Fourme of Solemnizacyon of Matrymonye').

charity to show] to show public spirit (Hibbard).

[SCENE II]

Enter TRANIO *and* HORTENSIO.

Tra. Is't possible, friend Litio, that Mistress Bianca
    Doth fancy any other but Lucentio?
    I tell you, sir, she bears me fair in hand.
Hor. Sir, to satisfy you in what I have said,
    Stand by and mark the manner of his teaching.   5

Enter BIANCA [*and* LUCENTIO].

Luc. Now, mistress, profit you in what you read?
Bian. What, master, read you? First resolve me that.
Luc. I read that I profess, *The Art to Love*.
Bian. And may you prove, sir, master of your art.
Luc. While you, sweet dear, prove mistress of my heart.   10

Scene II

SCENE II] *Steevens; not in F.*   1. Litio] *Pelican (throughout scene)*; *Lisio F.*
4. *Hor.*] *F2; Luc. F.*   5. S.D. *and Lucentio*] *Rowe; not in F.*   6. *Luc.*] *F2;
Hor. F.*   7. What . . . First] *Theobald;* What Master reade you first, *F.*
8. *Luc.*] *F2; Hor. F.*   read . . . profess,] *Rowe;* ready . . . profuse *F* (read *F4*).
10. prove] *F2;* ptoue *F.*

1–5. *Is't . . . teaching*] NCS suggests
that this 'looks like adapter's patch-
work'. Ll. 1 and 4 are prose, while the
rest of the scene is verse.

3. *bears . . . hand*] Bond examined
all *OED*'s examples of the phrase 'to
bear in hand', and concluded that
'The majority of instances quoted
have some sense of falsity in accusation', but, on checking the
occurrences of the phrase in Shakespeare, he found that 'the notion of
deceit is due to the other words with
which it is used'. For this line in *Shr.*
he proposed a sense 'only of continu-
ance in one tone or treatment,
specified by "fair"'. The line certainly could mean 'she always treats
me favourably'. Hibbard, on the
other hand, glosses as 'she deceives me
in a very convincing fashion' (influenced, presumably, by the extra-
Shakespearean usage). Yet at *Meas.*,
I. iv. 50–2, *Ado*, IV. i. 302–3, *Mac.*,

III. i. 78–80, and *Ham.*, II. ii. 65–7, the
context and general sense is one of
deception, and the phrase means
something akin to 'carried me along'
or 'took me in', so that Hibbard's
gloss is to be preferred.

4–8.] F assigns these lines incorrectly, giving 4–5 to Lucentio
(before he is on stage), 6 to Hortensio,
7 (correctly) to Bianca, and 8 to
Hortensio. The confusion (and the
failure to mark Lucentio's entry after
l. 6) is probably due to the presence in
the speech-prefixes in the copy of
'Lic' or 'Lit' (short for Hortensio's
name when disguised). See note to
III. i. 46–56.

4. *satisfy you in*] convince you of
(*OED*, v. 7). Cf. *Cym.*, III. v. 93.

8. *that I profess*] what I practise
(Onions, 3).

The . . . Love] Ovid, *Ars Amatoria*.
Cf. Lyly, *Mother Bombie* (*Works*, ed.
Bond, III. 181), I. iii. 130–44.

Hor. Quick proceeders, marry! Now tell me, I pray,
  You that durst swear that your mistress Bianca
  Lov'd none in the world so well as Lucentio.
Tra. O despiteful love, unconstant womankind!
  I tell thee, Litio, this is wonderful.   15
Hor. Mistake no more, I am not Litio,
  Nor a musician as I seem to be,
  But one that scorn to live in this disguise,
  For such a one as leaves a gentleman
  And makes a god of such a cullion.   20
  Know, sir, that I am call'd Hortensio.
Tra. Signor Hortensio, I have often heard
  Of your entire affection to Bianca,
  And since mine eyes are witness of her lightness,
  I will with you, if you be so contented,   25
  Forswear Bianca and her love for ever.
Hor. See how they kiss and court! Signor Lucentio,
  Here is my hand, and here I firmly vow
  Never to woo her more, but do forswear her,
  As one unworthy all the former favours   30
  That I have fondly flatter'd her withal.
Tra. And here I take the like unfeigned oath,
  Never to marry with her though she would entreat.
  Fie on her! See how beastly she doth court him.
Hor. Would all the world but he had quite forsworn!   35
  For me, that I may surely keep mine oath,

13. none] *Rowe;* me *F.*   29. to] *F2;* ro *F.*   31. her] *F3;* them *F.*
35. forsworn!] *Capell;* forsworn *F.*   36. oath,] *Rowe;* oath *F.*

11. *Quick proceeders*] apt scholars
(with a pun on 'to proceed' in the
sense of to advance from the degree of
BA to a higher degree: *OED, v.* 4).
The word-play begins with 'master of
your art' in l. 9.
  15. *wonderful*] incredible. Cf. *Tw.N.,*
v. i. 217.
  18. *scorn*] The verb is agreeing with
'I' in the previous line, not with its
antecedent 'that'.
  20. *cullion*] base or vile fellow,
rascal (cf. *2H6,* i. iii. 38). The word
originally meant 'testicle' as in
Chaucer, *Pardoner's Tale,* 624, 'I wolde

I hadde thy coillons in myn hond'.
  23. *entire*] unfeigned, sincere
(Onions, 2).
  31. *her*] F's 'them' makes no sense
and was corrected as early as F3. The
two forms are not difficult to confuse
in Secretary hand.
  34. *beastly*] like an animal. Cf. *Ant.,*
I. v. 50; *Cym.,* v. iii. 27.
  35. *Would . . . forsworn*] i.e. would
that she had only one lover in the
whole world. In this piece of spite it
does not occur to Hortensio that
Bianca could ever think of marrying
this supposed servant.

I will be married to a wealthy widow
Ere three days pass, which hath as long lov'd me
As I have lov'd this proud disdainful haggard.
And so farewell, Signor Lucentio.   40
Kindness in women, not their beauteous looks,
Shall win my love; and so I take my leave,
In resolution as I swore before.   [*Exit.*]

Tra. Mistress Bianca, bless you with such grace
As 'longeth to a lover's blessed case!   45
Nay, I have ta'en you napping, gentle love,
And have forsworn you with Hortensio.

Bian. Tranio, you jest. But have you both forsworn me?

Tra. Mistress, we have.

Luc.   Then we are rid of Litio.

Tra. I' faith, he'll have a lusty widow now,   50
That shall be woo'd and wedded in a day.

Bian. God give him joy.

Tra. Ay, and he'll tame her.

Bian.   He says so, Tranio.

Tra. Faith, he is gone unto the taming-school.

Bian. The taming-school? What, is there such a place?   55

Tra. Ay, mistress, and Petruchio is the master,
That teacheth tricks eleven and twenty long,

43. S.D.] *Rowe; not in F.*   45. 'longeth] *Hanmer;* longeth *F.*   53. Tranio] *F;* Tranio? *Riverside.*

37. *a wealthy widow*] This character, who has never been mentioned in the play so far, comes in too opportunely, and suggests to most editors and commentators further evidence that the part of Hortensio has undergone revision.

38. *which*] Shakespeare often interchanges 'which' and 'who' (Abbott, 265). Cf. *3H6*, III. iii. 81–2.

39 *haggard*] See note to IV. i. 180.

41–2. *Kindness . . . love*] Tilley, B175, 'Beauty without goodness is worth nothing'. Cf. Spenser, *FQ*, III. i. 48.

43. *In resolution*] firmly determined. Cf. *Troil.*, II. ii. 191.

46. *ta'en you napping*] surprised you, caught you (presumably, here, em-

bracing): *OED*, $v.^1$ b, meaning 'to catch asleep'. Cf. Tilley, N36–7, quoting Lyly, *Mother Bombie* (*Works*, ed. Bond, III. 212), IV. ii. 152–3, '*Accius* and *Silena* courted one another; their fathers toke them napping'; *LLL*, IV. iii. 125–6.

51. *woo'd and wedded*] See note to I. i. 144.

53–8. *Ay . . . tongue*] Here Tranio displays knowledge of Hortensio's plans and actions which he is nowhere given in the extant text. This need not necessarily suggest revision.

53. *He says so*] Tilley, T89.

57. *eleven . . . long*] just right, exactly suitable. The reference is to the card game of Thirty-one (or Trente-et-un, or Trentuno), where

To tame a shrew and charm her chattering tongue.

Enter BIONDELLO.

Bion. O master, master, I have watch'd so long
       That I am dog-weary, but at last I spied   60
       An ancient angel coming down the hill
       Will serve the turn.
Tra.   What is he, Biondello?
Bion. Master, a mercatante, or a pedant,
       I know not what; but formal in apparel,
       In gait and countenance surely like a father.   65
Luc. And what of him, Tranio?
Tra. If he be credulous and trust my tale,
       I'll make him glad to seem Vincentio,
       And give assurance to Baptista Minola
       As if he were the right Vincentio.   70
       Take in your love, and then let me alone.
                          [*Exeunt Lucentio and Bianca.*]

Enter a PEDANT.

63. mercatante] *Capell;* Marcantant *F.*   65. countenance] *F2;* eountenan ce *F.*
surely] *F;* surly *F2.*   71. Take] *F2; Par.* Take *F.*   in] *Theobald;* me *F.*
S.D.] *Rowe; not in F.*

the object was to get a hand of
exactly 31 points. See note to I. ii.
32–3.

60. *dog-weary*] tired out, dog-tired.
Cf. Tilley, D441, and *OED, a.,*
quoting *Shr.* as its earliest example.

61. *ancient angel*] 'a fellow of th'old,
sound, honest, and worthie stampe'
(Cotgrave, s.v. Angelot). An 'angel'
was (i) a ministering spirit, divine
messenger (*OED,* 1; cf. *Err.,* IV. iii.
51–2), (ii) a gold coin, having as its
device the archangel Michael (*OED,*
6; cf. *2H4,* I. ii. 156–8; *Wiv.,* I. iii. 50).

63. *mercatante*] F's 'Marcantant',
must be Biondello's corruption of the
Italian. Most editors correct in the
interests of metre. Cf. I. i. 25.

pedant] schoolmaster, teacher or
tutor (as at III. i. 4 ff.). Cf. *LLL,* III. i.
167; *Tw.N.,* III. ii. 70; Florio's
Montaigne (1603), I. xxiv, 'I have in

my youth oftentimes beene vexed to
see a Pedant brought in, in most of
Italian comedies, for a vice or sport-
maker'. Furnivall noted Shakespeare's
tendency to laugh at schoolmasters in
his early work; e.g. Holofernes in
LLL, Pinch in *Err.*

65. *surely*] The context requires
'surely' in the sense of 'certainly'.
Ff2–4 read 'surly', which Bond
accepts, though noting that 'surly' is
a variant spelling of 'surely' in the
16th century.

71. *Take . . . alone*] F reads 'Take
me' and gives this line the speech-
heading '*Par.*'. NCS suggests that
'Par' stands for a player's name 'which
was written in the margin of the
prompt-book opposite to the stage-
direction to indicate the actor of the
Pedant's part, and was then mistaken
for a prefix to the previous line', and

Ped. God save you, sir.

Tra.   And you, sir. You are welcome.
     Travel you far on, or are you at the farthest?

Ped. Sir, at the farthest for a week or two,
     But then up farther, and as far as Rome,   75
     And so to Tripoli, if God lend me life.

Tra. What countryman, I pray?

Ped.   Of Mantua.

Tra. Of Mantua, sir? Marry, God forbid!
     And come to Padua, careless of your life?

Ped. My life, sir? How, I pray? For that goes hard.   80

Tra. 'Tis death for any one in Mantua
     To come to Padua. Know you not the cause?
     Your ships are stay'd at Venice, and the Duke,
     For private quarrel 'twixt your Duke and him,
     Hath publish'd and proclaim'd it openly.   85
     'Tis marvel, but that you are but newly come,
     You might have heard it else proclaim'd about.

---

73. far] *F* (farre); farrer *Hibbard.*   86. but newly] *F;* newly *Collier.*

proposes William Parr who acted with the Admiral's Men in 1602, and may be the Parr mentioned in Henslowe's *Diary* in 1598. F's 'Take me' makes no sense, and 'me' and 'inne' are easily confused in manuscript. Cf. II. i. 323 and note.

let me alone] you can depend on me. Cf. *Tw.N.*, III. iv. 174.

73. *far*] F reads 'farre', which is a common spelling of 'far' (cf. *Ham.*, II. ii. 188, Q2 and F) but which Hibbard (p. 224) takes as a form of the regular comparative 'farrer' (farther), quoting in support F's reading at *Wint.*, IV. iv. 423, 'Farre then Deucalion off'. In the example from *Wint.* the comparative is essential; here, either positive or comparative will do, and I have preferred the positive.

77. *What countryman*] Where do you come from? To what neighbourhood do you belong? Cf. *Tw.N.*, v. i. 223.

80. *that goes hard*] that's serious.

Cf. IV. iv. 104; *Gent.*, IV. iv. 2; *Mer.V.*, III. ii. 292.

81–7. *'Tis . . . about*] This story is very like the one in *Err.*, I. i. 16–20; Shakespeare may have borrowed from his own play.

83. *stay'd*] detained, held up (*OED*, *v.*[1] 20). Mantua, like Padua (see note to I. i. 42), may have been thought of as a port, though in other plays (e.g. *Rom.*) Shakespeare does not mention it as such (see Sugden, *Topographical Dictionary*). But northern Italy was a network of canals: see note to I. i. 42.

86–7. *'Tis . . . about*] Hibbard (p. 225) points out that two grammatical constructions are involved here. Tranio starts to say something like ' 'Tis marvel that you heard it not', but alters his expression in mid-sentence, as people often do in speech, and says 'Were it not for the fact that you have only just arrived you would have heard it proclaimed publicly'.

86. *are but newly*] Some editors (e.g.

SC. II] THE TAMING OF THE SHREW 257

Ped. Alas, sir, it is worse for me than so!
  For I have bills for money by exchange
  From Florence, and must here deliver them.   90
Tra. Well, sir, to do you courtesy,
  This will I do, and this I will advise you:
  First tell me, have you ever been at Pisa?
Ped. Ay, sir, in Pisa have I often been,
  Pisa renowned for grave citizens.   95
Tra. Among them know you one Vincentio?
Ped. I know him not, but I have heard of him,
  A merchant of incomparable wealth.
Tra. He is my father, sir, and sooth to say,
  In countenance somewhat doth resemble you.   100
Bion. [*Aside.*] As much as an apple doth an oyster, and
  all one.
Tra. To save your life in this extremity,
  This favour will I do you for his sake,
  And think it not the worst of all your fortunes   105
  That you are like to Sir Vincentio:
  His name and credit shall you undertake,
  And in my house you shall be friendly lodg'd.
  Look that you take upon you as you should.
  You understand me, sir. So shall you stay   110
  Till you have done your business in the city.
  If this be courtesy, sir, accept of it.
Ped. O sir, I do, and will repute you ever
  The patron of my life and liberty.
Tra. Then go with me to make the matter good.   115
  This, by the way, I let you understand;

101. S.D.] *Rowe; not in F.*

NCS, Hibbard) omit 'but', NCS
suggesting that it is 'a careless
repetition of the "but" earlier in the
line'.
 89. *bills . . . exchange*] promissory
notes. Cf. *Wiv.*, I. i. 9.
 95. *Pisa . . . citizens*] a repetition of
I. i. 10.
 101. *As . . . oyster*] Tilley, A291.
Smith and Wilson adds earlier
examples, including '1532 More *Wks.*
(1557) 724 No more lyke then an

apple to an oyster'.
 102. *all one*] no difference. Cf.
Tw.N., I. v. 121–2.
 107. *credit*] standing, reputation
(*OED, sb.* 5). Cf. *Err.*, IV. i. 68.
 undertake] assume, take on (*OED, v.*
4). Cf. *R2*, II. ii. 145–6.
 109. *take upon you*] play your part,
or, perhaps, 'assume lofty airs'
(Onions, 5; cf. *1H6*, I. ii. 71).
 113. *repute*] think of, value (*OED,
v.* 4). Cf. *Gent.*, II. vii. 59.

My father is here look'd for every day
To pass assurance of a dower in marriage
'Twixt me and one Baptista's daughter here.
In all these circumstances I'll instruct you.   120
Go with me to clothe you as becomes you.   *Exeunt.*

SCENE III

Enter KATHERINA *and* GRUMIO.

Gru. No, no, forsooth, I dare not for my life.
Kath. The more my wrong, the more his spite appears.
    What, did he marry me to famish me?
    Beggars that come unto my father's door
    Upon entreaty have a present alms,   5
    If not, elsewhere they meet with charity.
    But I, who never knew how to entreat,
    Nor never needed that I should entreat,
    Am starv'd for meat, giddy for lack of sleep,
    With oaths kept waking, and with brawling fed.   10
    And that which spites me more than all these wants,
    He does it under name of perfect love,
    As who should say, if I should sleep or eat,
    'Twere deadly sickness or else present death.
    I prithee go and get me some repast,   15
    I care not what, so it be wholesome food.
Gru. What say you to a neat's foot?

121. me] *F;* me, sir, *F2.*

Scene III

SCENE III] *Steevens; Actus Quartus. Scena Prima. F.*   S.D. *Enter*] *Q ;* Entor *F.*

117. *look'd for*] expected. Cf. *Tw.N.,*
III. ii. 24.
118. *pass assurance*] promise, guarantee. Cf. II. i. 336; *3H6,* IV. i.
141.
121. *Go . . . you*] This line is metrically irregular. F2 emends to 'Go with
me, sir', which some editors follow.

Scene III

F reads '*Actus Quartus. Scena Prima.*'
See headnote to IV. i.

2. *The . . . wrong*] the greater the
injustice I suffer.
5. *Upon . . . alms*] are given charity
as soon as they ask.
present] instant, immediate. Cf.
Wiv., IV. vi. 55.
9. *meat*] food generally (*OED, sb.* 1).
11. *spites*] irritates, mortifies (*OED,
v.* 3).
13. *As . . . say*] as if to say.
17. *neat's foot*] ox-foot, or calf's
foot. A 'neat' was 'an animal of the

Kath. 'Tis passing good, I prithee let me have it.
Gru. I fear it is too choleric a meat.
  How say you to a fat tripe finely broil'd?   20
Kath. I like it well. Good Grumio, fetch it me.
Gru. I cannot tell, I fear 'tis choleric.
  What say you to a piece of beef and mustard?
Kath. A dish that I do love to feed upon.
Gru. Ay, but the mustard is too hot a little.   25
Kath. Why then, the beef, and let the mustard rest.
Gru. Nay then, I will not. You shall have the mustard,
  Or else you get no beef of Grumio.
Kath. Then both, or one, or anything thou wilt.
Gru. Why then, the mustard without the beef.   30
Kath. Go, get thee gone, thou false deluding slave, *Beats him.*
  That feed'st me with the very name of meat.
  Sorrow on thee and all the pack of you
  That triumph thus upon my misery!
  Go, get thee gone, I say.   35

   Enter PETRUCHIO *and* HORTENSIO, *with meat.*

19. choleric] *F; phlegmaticke F2.*

ox-kind' (*OED, sb.* 1). Cf. *1H4*, II. iv.
238, 'you dried neat's-tongue'.
 19. *choleric*] causing bile (Onions,
1), and therefore anger. There seems
no good reason for the alteration, in
Ff2–4, of F1's 'cholericke' to 'phlegmaticke'.
 20. *fat tripe*] 'either the rumen
(paunch), or the reticulum, of the
stomach of a sheep or other ruminant;
the latter, called "honeycomb tripe"
being the best' (Bond). Tripe may be
cooked in several ways, and is pale in
colour: cf. *2H4*, v. iv. 9–10, 'thou
damn'd tripe-visag'd rascal'. Tripe
and onions is still a popular dish in the
north of England.
 broil'd] cooked over the coals,
grilled (*OED, v.*[1] 2).
 23. *beef*] 'in a cholerike stomacke,
beefe is better digested then a chickens
legge, for as much as in a hot stomacke
fine meates bee shortly adust and
corrupted. Contrariwise, in a cold

fleumatike stomacke grosse meate
abideth long undigested' (*Castell of
Health* (1595), quoted by Bond from
Halliwell). Cf. *MND*, III. i. 179.
 32. *very name*] mere name, name
only (*OED, a.* 9. b). Cf. *Gent.*, II. iv.
138; *Ham.*, III. iv. 137; *Cym.*, II. iv.
9.
 35. S.D.] Bond and NCS point out
the corresponding S.D. in *A Shrew*
(Bullough, p. 92), sc. x, '*Enter
Ferando with a peece of meate uppon his
daggers point and Polidor with him*',
suggesting that this may embody the
stage-tradition, and echo the famous
scene between Tamburlaine and
Bajazeth in Marlowe's *1 Tamburlaine*,
IV. iv (*Plays*, ed. Gill, p. 101). This
may be so, but there is nothing in F's
text of the lines which follow l. 35 to
suggest that it must be so, and the
reference to 'this dish' (l. 44) makes it
more likely that the meat is brought
on in the usual way.

Pet. How fares my Kate? What, sweeting, all amort?
Hor. Mistress, what cheer?
Kath.   Faith, as cold as can be.
Pet. Pluck up thy spirits, look cheerfully upon me.
   Here, love, thou seest how diligent I am
   To dress thy meat myself and bring it thee.   40
   I am sure, sweet Kate, this kindness merits thanks.
   What, not a word? Nay then, thou lov'st it not,
   And all my pains is sorted to no proof.
   Here, take away this dish.
Kath.   I pray you, let it stand.
Pet. The poorest service is repaid with thanks,   45
   And so shall mine before you touch the meat.
Kath. I thank you, sir.
Hor. Signor Petruchio, fie! You are to blame.
   Come, Mistress Kate, I'll bear you company.

---

36. *sweeting*] darling, sweetheart (*OED*, Sweeting¹, quoting *Shr.*). Bond notes 'properly, a sweet apple', but *OED* gives no example of this sense before 1530, while the sense of 'darling' is attested as early as 'a 1300'. Shakespeare alludes to the 'sweet apple' in *Rom.*, II. iv. 77–8, but cf. *Tw.N.*, II. iii. 41; *1H6*, III. iii. 21; *Oth.*, II. iii. 244.

all amort] sick to death, dispirited, from French *à la mort* (*OED*, Alamort, 2, quoting *Shr.*). Cf. *1H6*, III. ii. 124; Lyly, *Midas* (*Works*, ed. Bond, III. 155), v. ii. 99–100, '*Pet.* How now, *Motto*, what all a mort?/*Motto.* I am as melancholy as a cat.' See also Abbott, 24.

37. *what cheer?*] how are you? 'Cheer' originally meant 'face, expression, countenance' (*OED*, *sb.* 1 and 2). Katherina's reply takes up the word in its sense of 'provisions, viands, food' (*OED*, 6), with obvious reference to the food she has been denied.

38. *Pluck . . . spirits*] Tilley, H323. Cf. Marlowe, *Dido* (*Plays*, ed. Gill, p. 9), I. i. 149, 'Pluck up your hearts,

since Fate still rests our friend'.

43. *pains*] labour, trouble (plural for singular; cf. *Gent.*, I. i. 125, 'here is for your pains').

sorted to no proof] comes to nothing. 'Sort' means 'lead to, issue in' (*OED*, *v.*¹ 7. b, quoting '1598 Florio To Rdr. b ij, Let . . . the reapers of the fruites iudge betwixt vs whose paines hath sorted to best perfection'). 'Proof' means 'result, issue, fulfilment' (*OED*, *sb.* 7). Cf. *2H4*, IV. iii. 91; *Gent.*, I. iii. 63; Greene, *Friar Bacon and Friar Bungay* (*Plays and Poems*, ed. Collins, II. 64), IV. i. (l. 1643), 'His seuen yeares practise sorteth to ill end'.

46. *mine before*] Grammar requires 'mine be before', but the ellipse of the verb 'be' is common in Shakespeare. Several editors have been tempted to emend to 'mine be, 'fore', but none has actually done so.

48. *to blame*] too much at fault. 'To' was commonly used for 'too', and 'blame' was often considered an adjective. See Abbott, 73; cf. *Rom.*, III. v. 169; *1H4*, III. i. 177, 'In faith, my lord, you are too wilful-blame'.

Pet. [*Aside.*] Eat it up all, Hortensio, if thou lov'st me.—   50
Much good do it unto thy gentle heart.
Kate, eat apace. And now, my honey love,
We will return unto thy father's house,
And revel it as bravely as the best,
With silken coats and caps, and golden rings,   55
With ruffs and cuffs and farthingales and things,
With scarfs and fans, and double change of bravery,
With amber bracelets, beads, and all this knavery.
What, hast thou din'd? The tailor stays thy leisure,
To deck thy body with his ruffling treasure.   60

Enter TAILOR.

Come, tailor, let us see these ornaments.
Lay forth the gown.

Enter HABERDASHER.

What news with you, sir?
Hab. Here is the cap your worship did bespeak.
Pet. Why, this was moulded on a porringer!

50. S.D.] *Theobald; not in F.*   62. S.D.] *in l. 62, Dyce; after l. 61, F.*
63. *Hab.*] *Rowe; Fel. F.*

54. *bravely*] splendidly, finely (*OED,
adv.* 2).

56. *farthingales*] hooped petticoats,
making the skirt of a dress stand out.
Cf. *Gent.*, II. vii. 51, 'What compass
will you wear your farthingale'.

and things] Cf. II. i. 316.

57. *bravery*] finery, fine clothes
(*OED*, 3. b). Cf. Spenser, *Mother
Hubberds Tale*, 608, 'all the brauerie
that eye may see'.

58. *amber bracelets*] 'Bracelets were
composed of ornamental gold links,
enamelled and jewelled, rows of
pearls or beads of amber . . . coral,
agates, and bugles. . . . They were always worn outside the sleeve, which
came down to the wrist' (*Shakespeare's
England*, II. 117). Cf. *Wint.*, IV. iv.
219.

knavery] tricks of dress or adornment
(*OED*, 2. b, quoting *Shr.*).

59. *stays thy leisure*] awaits your
convenience. Cf. III. ii. 215.

60. *ruffling*] Bond and Hibbard
gloss as 'gay, swaggering' (*OED, v.*[2]
2), but *OED* cites this line under
Ruffling, *ppl. a.*[1] 1, 'Forming, or rising
in, ruffles'. We need not choose between these senses: both are present.

63. *Here . . . bespeak*] F gives this
line the speech-prefix '*Fel.*'. This cannot be an abbreviation for any name
in the Folio's list of actors, and Bond
suggests that it is a shortened form of
'Fellow' (though without saying what
that would mean). NCS (p. 118)
proposes William Felle, 'who though
not known as a player appears in
Henslowe's *Diary* under the year 1599
as William Bird's "man" ', though
admitting that 'The identification is a
hazardous one'.

bespeak] order.

64. *porringer*] basin from which soft
or liquid food is eaten (Onions). Cf.
H8, v. iv. 46–9, 'There was a haberdasher's wife of small wit near him,

A velvet dish! Fie, fie! 'Tis lewd and filthy.   65
Why, 'tis a cockle or a walnut-shell,
A knack, a toy, a trick, a baby's cap.
Away with it! Come, let me have a bigger.
Kath. I'll have no bigger. This doth fit the time,
And gentlewomen wear such caps as these.   70
Pet. When you are gentle, you shall have one too,
And not till then.
Hor. [*Aside.*]   That will not be in haste.
Kath. Why, sir, I trust I may have leave to speak,
And speak I will. I am no child, no babe.
Your betters have endur'd me say my mind,   75
And if you cannot, best you stop your ears.
My tongue will tell the anger of my heart,
Or else my heart concealing it will break,
And rather than it shall, I will be free
Even to the uttermost, as I please, in words.   80
Pet. Why, thou say'st true. It is a paltry cap,
A custard-coffin, a bauble, a silken pie.

---

72. S.D.] *Hanmer; not in F.*   81. a] *Q; not in F.*   82. custard-coffin] *hyphened, Warburton; unhyphened, F.*

that rail'd upon me till her pink'd porringer fell off her head'.

65. *lewd and filthy*] 'Elizabethan equivalent of "cheap and nasty"' (Hibbard).

66. *cockle*] cockleshell. Cf. *Per.*, IV. iv. 2.

67. *knack*] trifle, knick-knack. Cf. *MND*, I. i. 34, and Brooks's note in the Arden edn.

toy] insignificant ornament (Onions, 1). Cf. *Wint.*, IV. iv. 313, 'Any toys for your head'.

trick] trifle, knack, toy (Onions, 5). Cf. *Ham.*, IV. iv. 61.

69–70. *I'll . . . these*] Macquoid, in *Shakespeare's England* (II. 97), quotes Van Meteren (1575) writing on the English custom in women's headgear: 'Married women only wear a hat both in the street and in the house; those unmarried go without a hat, although ladies of distinction have lately learnt

to cover their faces with silken masks or vizards, and feathers.'

69. *fit the time*] suit the fashion (Onions, 3; cf. *Wiv.*, II. i. 144).

75. *endur'd me say*] suffered me to speak.

76. *best you*] you would do best to.

77–8. *My . . . break*] one of the great commonplaces of the age; cf. *Mac.*, IV. iii. 209–10; Ford, *The Broken Heart*, V. iii. 75; Tourneur, *The Revenger's Tragedy*, I. iv. 23–4. All derive ultimately from Seneca, *Hippolytus*, II. iii. 607, 'Curae leves loquuntur, ingentes stupent' (light troubles speak; immense troubles are silent). See also Tilley, G449; Smith and Wilson, s.v. 'Grief pent up'.

81. *is a paltry*] F reads 'is paltrie'. See note to III. ii. 30.

82. *custard-coffin*] the crust around a 'custard'. A custard was formerly 'a kind of open pie containing pieces of

I love thee well in that thou lik'st it not.
Kath. Love me or love me not, I like the cap,
    And it I will have, or I will have none.   85
Pet. Thy gown? Why, ay. Come, tailor, let us see't.
                                    [*Exit Haberdasher.*]
    O mercy, God! What masquing stuff is here?
    What's this? A sleeve? 'Tis like a demi-cannon.
    What, up and down, carv'd like an apple tart?
    Here's snip and nip and cut and slish and slash,   90
    Like to a censer in a barber's shop.

86. gown?] *Rowe;* gowne, *F.*   S.D.] *Camb. (after l. 85); not in F.*   88. like
a] *Q;* like *F.*   91. censer] *Rowe;* Censor *F.*

meat or fruit covered with a preparation of broth or milk, thickened with
eggs, sweetened, and seasoned with
spices, etc.' (*OED*). NCS glosses as
'custard-pie', but this obscures the
point: the cap surrounds Katherina's
face as the pie-case surrounds the
custard. Cf. *Tit.*, v. ii. 189, 'And of the
paste a coffin I will rear'.
    86. *Thy gown*] Perhaps Petruchio
deliberately mishears 'have none' in
the previous line as 'my gown',
though 'none' was usually pronounced
as 'known' now is (Kökeritz, p. 121).
    S.D.] F marks no 'Exit' for the
Haberdasher, but he has no further
business in this scene and this line
seems the most opportune moment for
him to leave the stage. The Shakespearean Folios and Quartos not in-
frequently fail to provide 'Exits' for
characters, but this is not surprising
since an actor can usually be trusted
to get himself off the stage. Prompt-
books and theatre manuscripts are,
naturally, more concerned with
making sure he gets on. Cf. *AYL* (ed.
Agnes Latham, Arden edn, p. xv).
    87. *masquing stuff*] clothing fit for
masques. Masques were noted for
their symbolic and extravagant
costumes. See Orgel, *The Jonsonian
Masque* (1965); Orgel and Strong,
Inigo Jones: the Theatre of the Stuart

Court (1973), 2 vols.
    88. *like a demi-cannon*] F reads 'like
demi cannon'. See note to l. 81, above.
A demi-cannon was a large gun of
about 6½ inches bore (see *Shakespeare's
England*, i. 159). The 'sleeve' in this
line is described in *Shakespeare's
England*, ii. 95: 'by the year 1580 a
large leg-of-mutton sleeve had become fashionable, padded and
stiffened with embroidery, and often
profusely sewn with jewels.' Petruchio
attacks these details in the next three
lines.
    91. *censer*] This is usually explained
as 'fumigator; brazier with perforated
cover to emit the smoke of burning
perfumes' (Bond), though *OED* gives
no examples of this, quoting this line
from *Shr.* under Censer, *sb.*[1] 1. b and
stating 'commentators are not agreed
as to what exactly is referred to'.
Shakespeare uses the word twice only:
here, and at *2H4*, v. iv. 19–20, 'you
thin man in a censer', and neither
sheds light on the other. The use of
such fumigators in barbers' shops is
not well attested. Perry states that 'in
addition to sweetening the atmosphere
they were used to warm water and dry
cloths' (p. 113), but cites no authority.
F reads 'Censor', but no sense of the
word in that spelling is appropriate
here.

Why, what a devil's name, tailor, call'st thou this?

Hor. [*Aside.*] I see she's like to have neither cap nor gown.

Tai. You bid me make it orderly and well,
According to the fashion and the time.   95

Pet. Marry, and did. But if you be remember'd,
I did not bid you mar it to the time.
Go, hop me over every kennel home,
For you shall hop without my custom, sir.
I'll none of it. Hence, make your best of it.   100

Kath. I never saw a better-fashion'd gown,
More quaint, more pleasing, nor more commendable.
Belike you mean to make a puppet of me.

Pet. Why, true, he means to make a puppet of thee.

Tai. She says your worship means to make a puppet of   105
her.

Pet. O monstrous arrogance! Thou liest, thou thread,
thou thimble,
Thou yard, three-quarters, half-yard, quarter, nail,
Thou flea, thou nit, thou winter-cricket thou!   110

---

93. S.D.] *Theobald; not in F.*   109. yard,] *F2;* yard *F.*   110. winter-cricket]
hyphened, *Capell;* unhyphened, *F.*

---

92. *what . . . name*] in the name of
the devil. Some editors emend to
'i' devil's name'.

96. *Marry, and did*] Indeed, I did.
'Marry' is a contraction of 'By Mary',
a common oath. For the ellipsis of the
pronoun subject see Abbott, 400; cf.
Tw.N., v. i. 188, 'That's all one; has
hurt me'.

98. *hop . . . kennel*] hop over every
gutter. For this dative use of 'me' see
Abbott, 220. A 'kennel' was a channel
or surface-drain in a street (*OED,
sb.²*).

99. *hop without*] lose. Cf. *2H6*, i. iii.
135, 'hop without thy head'.

100. *make . . . it*] do with it what
you will.

102. *quaint*] skilfully made, pretty,
dainty (*OED, a.* 4). Cf. III. ii. 145;
Wiv., IV. vi. 41; Spenser, *FQ*, IV. x.
22.

commendable] normally, in Shake-

speare, accented on the first syllable.
But see *Mer.V.*, I. i. 111.

103–4. *Belike . . . thee*] Cf. *A Shrew*
(Bullough, p. 95), xiii. 11–13: 'KATE
The fashion is good inough: belike
you,/Meane to make a foole of me./
FERAN. Why true he meanes to
make a foole of thee . . .' *A Shrew*
echoes *Shr.* closely and frequently in
this scene.

105–9. *She . . . nail*] The invective
strains the metre. F prints as five
lines; there is no way of reassembling
them into regular pentameters, and
any arrangement is arbitrary.

109. *nail*] one-sixteenth of a yard
(2¼ inches), a measure of length for
cloth (*OED, sb.* 12). Cf. Lyly, *Midas*
(*Works*, ed. Bond, III. 157), v. ii. 173,
'They be halfe a yeard broad, and a
nayle'.

110. *nit*] either 'the egg of a louse'
or 'a gnat, or small fly' (*OED, sb.* 1

Brav'd in mine own house with a skein of thread?
Away, thou rag, thou quantity, thou remnant,
Or I shall so bemete thee with thy yard
As thou shalt think on prating whilst thou liv'st.
I tell thee, I, that thou hast marr'd her gown.   115

Tai. Your worship is deceiv'd; the gown is made
Just as my master had direction.
Grumio gave order how it should be done.

Gru. I gave him no order, I gave him the stuff.

Tai. But how did you desire it should be made?   120

Gru. Marry, sir, with needle and thread.

Tai. But did you not request to have it cut?

Gru. Thou hast faced many things.

Tai. I have.

Gru. Face not me. Thou hast braved many men, brave   125
not me. I will neither be faced nor braved. I say unto

and b). *OED* quotes *Shr.* under 2,
'Applied to persons in contempt or
jest'. Cf. *LLL*, IV. i. 141 (Shakespeare's
only other use of the word); Nashe,
The Terrors of the Night (*Works*, ed.
McKerrow, rev. Wilson, I. 349),
'Vpon a haire they will sit like a nit'.

winter-cricket] *OED* quotes *Shr.*
under Winter, *sb.*[1] 3, but no other
reference is recorded. There seems no
reason why the cricket (in winter or
any other season) should be the climax
of this list of diminutives. The series of
insults about the Tailor's size led NCS
to suggest that the part was played by
a boy (pp. 119, 167), or the reference
may be to the peculiar appearance of
John Sincklo (see note to Ind. i. 86).
Hibbard points out that 'Petruchio is
practising the rhetorical art of
diminution, encouraged, no doubt,
by the common proverb "Nine tailors
make a man"'. The two proposals
are not mutually exclusive.

111. *Brav'd*] defied (*OED*, *v.* 1).
Cf. *John*, IV. iii. 87; *Lucr.*, 40.

with] by (Abbott, 193).

112. *rag*] scrap of material. But cf.
Tim., IV. iii. 270–1, 'If thou wilt curse
thy father, that poor rag,/Must be
thy subject'.

quantity] fragment (*OED*, 8. b,
quoting *Shr.*). Cf. *John*, v. iv. 23; *2H4*,
v. i. 61.

113. *bemete*] (not found elsewhere in
Shakespeare) measure. *OED* records
one previous example, in King
Alfred's *Orosius* (*c.* 893), but suggests
that Shakespeare's use is an independent re-formation of the word. Here it
collects punning references to 'beat'
and 'mete out' (punishment). The
'yard' is the 'mete-yard' (cf. l. 150),
a stick used by tailors to measure
cloth.

114. *As . . . liv'st*] that you will not
forget your prating for the rest of your
life. 'Think on' means 'remember,
bear in mind' (Onions, think[1], 1). Cf.
All's W., III. ii. 46.

123. *faced*] (i) trimmed with braid
or velvet (*OED*, *v.* 12; cf. *1H4*, v. i.
74), (ii) braved, bullied (*OED*, *v.* 2;
cf. *H5*, III. ii. 34).

125–6. *Face . . . braved*] Cf. *A Shrew*
(Bullough, p. 96), xiii. 34–9. Hickson
(*N & Q*, 30 March, 1850) was the
first to note that the version in *A
Shrew* is best explained as a debased
version of the text represented in F.
See Appendix I.

125. *braved*] (i) made splendid,

thee, I bid thy master cut out the gown, but I did
not bid him cut it to pieces. Ergo, thou liest.

Tai. Why, here is the note of the fashion to testify.

Pet. Read it.   130

Gru. The note lies in's throat if he say I said so.

Tai. [*Reads.*] 'Imprimis, a loose-bodied gown.'

Gru. Master, if ever I said loose-bodied gown, sew me in
the skirts of it, and beat me to death with a bottom
of brown thread. I said a gown.   135

Pet. Proceed.

Tai. 'With a small compassed cape.'

Gru. I confess the cape.

Tai. 'With a trunk sleeve.'

Gru. I confess two sleeves.   140

Tai. 'The sleeves curiously cut.'

Pet. Ay, there's the villainy.

---

132. S.D.] *Capell; not in F.*

---

adorned (*OED*, *v.* 5; cf. I. ii. 216 S.D.;
R3, v. iii. 279), (ii) defied, challenged
(*OED*, *v.* 1; cf. IV. iii. 111 and note).

128. *Ergo*] therefore.

131. *The . . . throat*] word-play. The
phrase means either 'the memoran-
dum is untruthful' or 'the words in the
tailor's mouth are untrue'. For 'note'
in the second sense see *OED*, *sb.*² 5.
See also Tilley, T268.

132. *loose-bodied   gown*]   loosely
fitting dress. But the loose-bodied
gown was the usual wear of loose
women. See Marston, *Scourge of
Villanie* (*Poems*, ed. Davenport, p.
145), II. vii, 'Her loose-hanging
gowne/For her loose lying body';
Dryden, *1 Conquest of Granada*,
Epilogue, 'And oft the lacquey, or the
brawny clown,/Gets what is hid in
the loose-bodied gown'.

134. *bottom*] bobbin or core on
which the thread was wound (*OED*,
15). Cf. Raleigh, *History of the World*
(1614), II. 367, 'He received from her

[Ariadne] a bottome of thred'. Nick
Bottom the weaver in *MND* is named
after it.

137. *compassed*] cut so as to fall in a
circle (*OED*, *ppl. a.* 3). Cf. *Ven.*, 272,
'his compass'd crest'; *Troil.*, I. ii. 106–
7, 'the compass'd window' (mean-
ing the bay-window).

139. *a trunk sleeve*] a large wide
sleeve. See note to l. 88, above.

140. *confess two sleeves*] See Tilley,
T18, 'The Tailor must cut three
sleeves for every woman's gown'.
Hulme (*Explorations*) suggests that by
emphasizing the word 'two' Grumio
makes covert allusion to the well-
known proverb: 'Petruchio complains
that   the   tailor   is   incompetent;
Grumio hints that all tailors, given
the chance, are something worse' (p.
47). Other proverbs associate tailors
with cheating their clients: cf. Tilley,
T18–25.

141. *curiously*] delicately, elaborately, painstakingly. Cf. *Ado*, v. i. 152.

Gru. Error i' th' bill, sir, error i' th' bill! I commanded
    the sleeves should be cut out, and sewed up again;
    and that I'll prove upon thee, though thy little   145
    finger be armed in a thimble.

Tai. This is true that I say; and I had thee in place
    where, thou shouldst know it.

Gru. I am for thee straight. Take thou the bill, give me
    thy mete-yard, and spare not me.   150

Hor. God-a-mercy, Grumio, then he shall have no odds.

Pet. Well sir, in brief, the gown is not for me.

Gru. You are i' th' right, sir, 'tis for my mistress.

Pet. Go, take it up unto thy master's use.

Gru. Villain, not for thy life! Take up my mistress' gown   155
    for thy master's use!

Pet. Why sir, what's your conceit in that?

Gru. O sir, the conceit is deeper than you think for. Take
    up my mistress' gown to his master's use! O fie, fie,
    fie!   160

Pet. [*Aside.*] Hortensio, say thou wilt see the tailor paid.—
    Go take it hence, be gone, and say no more.

Hor. [*Aside.*] Tailor, I'll pay thee for thy gown tomorrow.

---

148. where,] *Q; where F.*   161, 163. S.D.] *Rowe; not in F.*

---

143. *bill*] (i) the 'note' referred to at l. 129, (ii) a bill of indictment, an accusation (*OED, sb.*³ 4).

145. *prove upon thee*] establish in single combat against you. The allusion is to the practice of trial by combat. Cf. *R2*, IV. i. 47.

147–8. *in place where*] in a suitable place. Cf. Lyly, *Mother Bombie* (*Works*, ed. Bond, III. 178), I. iii. 25–6, 'wert thou in place where, I would teach thee to cog'.

149. *I . . . straight*] I am ready for you here and now. Cf. *Tw.N.*, III. iv. 302.

bill] (i) the 'note' of l. 129, (ii) a weapon, a kind of pike, used by soldiers and watchmen (*OED, sb.*¹ 2 and 3). The pun is common in Shakespeare. For examples in *AYL*,

2H6, Ado, and *Tim.*, see Kökeritz, p. 95.

150. *mete-yard*] tailor's measuring rod. See note to l. 113, above.

151. *he . . . odds*] he will not be the favourite (cf. *Wint.*, v. i. 207), with a pun on 'odds' in the sense of the scraps of material left over from making a garment, which the tailor regarded as his perquisites (*OED,* Odd, 8).

154–9. *Go . . . use!*] Cf. *A Shrew* (Bullough, p. 96), xiii. 44–9.

154. *Go . . . use*] Take it away, and let your master make of it what use he can. The punning which follows is like that at III. ii. 163: see note.

157. *conceit*] meaning, idea, innuendo. Cf. *LLL*, II. i. 72.

158. *think for*] imagine, expect (*OED, v.*² 12. d, quoting *Shr.*).

Take no unkindness of his hasty words.   164
Away, I say, commend me to thy master.   *Exit Tailor.*
Pet. Well, come, my Kate, we will unto your father's
Even in these honest mean habiliments.
Our purses shall be proud, our garments poor,
For 'tis the mind that makes the body rich,
And as the sun breaks through the darkest clouds,   170
So honour peereth in the meanest habit.
What, is the jay more precious than the lark
Because his feathers are more beautiful?
Or is the adder better than the eel
Because his painted skin contents the eye?   175
O no, good Kate; neither art thou the worse
For this poor furniture and mean array.
If thou account'st it shame, lay it on me.
And therefore frolic. We will hence forthwith,
To feast and sport us at thy father's house.   180

172. What,] *Theobald (after Pope)*; What *F.*   178. account'st] *Rowe*;
accountedst *F.*   me.] *F4*; me, *F.*

164. *no unkindness of*] no offence at.
Cf. *Wiv.*, I. i. 178.

167. *Even . . . habiliments*] verbatim
in *A Shrew* (Bullough, p. 96). Cf.
Gent., IV. i. 13, 'My riches are these
poor habiliments'.

169. *'tis . . . rich*] not recorded as a
proverb, though many proverbs are
like it. See Tilley, S668, 'The Soul
needs few things, the body many', and
the cross-references listed for this proverb in Smith and Wilson. Cf. *Ham.*,
II. ii. 248–50, 'for there is nothing
either good or bad, but thinking
makes it so'; Spenser, *An Hymne in
Honovr of Beavtie*, 132–3, 'For of the
soule the bodie forme doth take:/
For soule is forme, and doth the bodie
make'.

170. *And . . . clouds*] Bond quotes the
prose tract *The History of Patient
Grisel* (1619, but probably originally
printed before 1590): 'sit downe till
the dinner is done, and bid the company welcome in this poore attire; for
the sun will break through slender

clouds, and vertue shine in base array.'

171. *peereth*] The precise sense is not
certain. From *c.* 1590 'peer' could
mean 'to look narrowly', 'to peep out',
'to come in sight' (it was a variant
spelling of 'pear' meaning 'appear'),
and 'to make to appear' (*OED, v.* 2,
which does *not* quote *Shr.*). All these
senses are recorded in Shakespeare. In
the present instance the context
strongly suggests some such paraphrase as 'So honour peeps out
through the holes in the most ragged
clothes'. Cf. *1H4*, v. i. 1–2, 'How
bloodily the sun begins to peer/
Above yon busky hill!'

172. *What, is*] F reads 'What is',
which Bond accepts, glossing 'What'
as 'how'. See Abbott, 253. But the
grammatical form of ll. 172–5
suggests that 'What' is an interroga-
tive exclamation.

175. *painted*] 'adorned with bright
or varied colouring' (*OED, ppl. a.* 3).

177. *furniture*] equipment, outfit,
dress (*OED, 2, quoting Shr.*).

[*To Grumio.*] Go call my men, and let us straight to him;
And bring our horses unto Long-lane end,
There will we mount, and thither walk on foot.
Let's see, I think 'tis now some seven o'clock,
And well we may come there by dinner-time.   185
Kath. I dare assure you, sir, 'tis almost two,
And 'twill be supper-time ere you come there.
Pet. It shall be seven ere I go to horse.
Look what I speak, or do, or think to do,
You are still crossing it. Sirs, let 't alone,   190
I will not go today, and ere I do,
It shall be what o'clock I say it is.
Hor. Why, so this gallant will command the sun.   [*Exeunt.*]

[SCENE IV]

Enter TRANIO, *and the* PEDANT *dressed like Vincentio.*

Tra. Sir, this is the house. Please it you that I call?
Ped. Ay, what else? And but I be deceiv'd
Signor Baptista may remember me

181. S.D.] *Hibbard; not in F.*   193. S.D.] *Rowe; not in F.*

Scene IV

SCENE IV] *Steevens; not in F.*   1. Sir] *Theobald; Sirs F.*

181. S.D.] There is no S.D. in F, but, as Hibbard points out, Petruchio would never give orders of the kind that follow to Katherina.

184. *some*] about (Onions, 2; Abbott, 21).

185. *dinner-time*] between eleven o'clock and noon. See *Shakespeare's England*, II. 134; cf. *Err.*, I. ii. 44–5.

187. *supper-time*] 'Supper was taken about 5.30' (*Shakespeare's England*, II. 134).

189. *Look what*] whatever (Onions, look, 3). Cf. *Sonn.*, xxxvii. 13, 'Look what is best, that best I wish in thee'. See Mark Eccles, 'Shakespeare's use of *Look How* and similar idioms', *JEGP* (1943), pp. 386–400.

190. *still crossing*] always thwarting. Cf. IV. v. 10.

Scene IV

S.D.] Tranio is still disguised as Lucentio. For the Pedant's appearance see note to l. 18, below.

1. *Please it*] The subjunctive here 'represents our modern "may it please?" and expresses a modest doubt' (Abbott, 361).

2. *what else?*] of course, certainly. Cf. *Cor.*, IV. vi. 149; Lyly, *Midas* (*Works*, ed. Bond, III. 152), V. ii. 21.

but] unless (Onions, 5; Abbott, 120). Cf. *Cym.*, V. v. 41.

3. *may remember me*] This is a fake reminiscence, made only to show that

Near twenty years ago in Genoa,
Where we were lodgers at the Pegasus.   5
Tra. 'Tis well, and hold your own, in any case,
        With such austerity as 'longeth to a father.
Ped. I warrant you.

Enter BIONDELLO.

                But sir, here comes your boy.
'Twere good he were school'd.
Tra. Fear you not him. Sirrah Biondello,   10
        Now do your duty thoroughly, I advise you.
        Imagine 'twere the right Vincentio.
Bion. Tut, fear not me.
Tra. But hast thou done thy errand to Baptista?
Bion. I told him that your father was at Venice,   15
        And that you look'd for him this day in Padua.
Tra. Th'art a tall fellow. Hold thee that to drink.
        Here comes Baptista. Set your countenance, sir.

Enter BAPTISTA *and* LUCENTIO.

4. Genoa,] *Theobald; Genoa.* F.   5. Where] *Theobald; Tra.* Where F.
6. *Tra.* 'Tis] *Theobald; Tis* F.   7. 'longeth] *Hanmer;* longeth F.   8. S.D.]
in l. 8, NCS; after l. 7, F.   18. S.D. Lucentio.] *Pope; Lucentio: Pedant booted/and
bare headed.* F.

the Pedant can play his assumed part.
Since he never met the true Vincentio
(IV. ii. 97) he could not know of any
such meeting with Baptista.

   5. *Where . . . Pegasus*] F prints this
as the first line of Tranio's speech, the
result, probably, of faulty alignment
of the speech-prefix in the manuscript.
NCS quotes Greg: 'Nothing is com-
moner in play-books than bad
aligning of speakers' names, which
were often supplied after the text was
written.' Bond and Hibbard are
attracted by the idea that F may be
correct, showing Tranio filling out
the Pedant's invention. This seems
unlikely.

   Pegasus] the arms of the Middle
Temple, and a popular inn-sign in
Shakespeare's London. Bond quotes
2 Returne from Parnassus, I. ii, 'Meete

me an houre hence at the signe of the
Pegasus in Cheapside'.

   9. *school'd*] instructed in his part,
told how to act (*OED, v.*[1] 5, quoting
Shr.). Cf. Spenser, *Shepheardes Calender*,
May, 227, 'So schooled the Gate her
wanton sonne'.

   16. *look'd for*] expected (as at
IV. ii. 117).

   17. *tall*] goodly, fine (Onions, 1).
Cf. IV. i. 10; *MND*, v. i. 143.

   Hold . . . drink] Take that, and buy
yourself a drink (Onions, hold, B. 8).
Cf. *R3*, III. ii. 108.

   18. S.D.] F reads 'Enter Baptista and
Lucentio: Pedant booted and bare headed.'
The Pedant has been on stage for 18
lines, and was carefully described at
the start of the scene as '*dressed like
Vincentio*'. It seems likely that the
scene originally opened at this point

Signor Baptista, you are happily met.—
Sir, this is the gentleman I told you of.   20
I pray you stand good father to me now,
Give me Bianca for my patrimony.
Ped. Soft, son.
    Sir, by your leave, having come to Padua
To gather in some debts, my son Lucentio   25
Made me acquainted with a weighty cause
Of love between your daughter and himself.
And, for the good report I hear of you,
And for the love he beareth to your daughter,
And she to him, to stay him not too long,   30
I am content, in a good father's care,
To have him match'd; and, if you please to like
No worse than I, upon some agreement
Me shall you find ready and willing
With one consent to have her so bestow'd.   35
For curious I cannot be with you,
Signor Baptista, of whom I hear so well.
Bap. Sir, pardon me in what I have to say.
    Your plainness and your shortness please me well.
Right true it is your son Lucentio here   40
Doth love my daughter, and she loveth him,
Or both dissemble deeply their affections.
And therefore if you say no more than this,
That like a father you will deal with him,
And pass my daughter a sufficient dower,   45

23-4.] *two lines, Hanmer; one line,* F.   34. ready and] *F;* most ready and
most *F2.*

and with this S.D., which has only
been partially corrected by the
excision of Tranio's name. The
Pedant is 'booted and bare headed'
because he is arriving from a journey
and greeting Baptista courteously.
    21. *stand good father*] possibly a
punning reference here in (i) be a good
parent, and (ii) stand as god-father.
    24. *having come*] I having come (the
subject of the sentence is the Pedant,
not Lucentio). The omission of the
noun or pronoun on which a participle

depends is not uncommon in Shakespeare. See Abbott, 378; Hibbard
compares *Caes.,* v. i. 79-80.
    30. *stay*] delay.
    35. *bestow'd*] given in marriage
(*OED, v.* 4). Cf. *AYL,* v. iv. 7.
    36. *curious*] over-particular, nigg-
ling (*OED, a.* 10, quoting '1535
Coverdale *Job* xxxv. 15 Nether hath
he pleasure in curious and depe in-
quisicions'). Cf. *All's W.,* i. ii. 20.
    45. *pass*] settle upon, hand over to
(*OED, v.* 46, quoting *Shr.*).

The match is made, and all is done,
Your son shall have my daughter with consent.

Tra. I thank you, sir. Where then do you know best
We be affied and such assurance ta'en
As shall with either part's agreement stand?   50

Bap. Not in my house, Lucentio, for you know
Pitchers have ears, and I have many servants.
Besides, old Gremio is hearkening still,
And happily we might be interrupted.

Tra. Then at my lodging, and it like you.   55
There doth my father lie; and there this night
We'll pass the business privately and well.
Send for your daughter by your servant here.
My boy shall fetch the scrivener presently.
The worst is this, that at so slender warning   60
You are like to have a thin and slender pittance.

Bap. It likes me well. Cambio, hie you home,
And bid Bianca make her ready straight.
And, if you will, tell what hath happened:
Lucentio's father is arriv'd in Padua,   65
And how she's like to be Lucentio's wife. [*Exit Lucentio.*]

Bion. I pray the gods she may with all my heart.

62–3. It . . . home,/And . . . straight.] *Pope;* It . . . well:/*Cambio* . . . straight: F.
64. happened:] *Capell (subst.);* hapned F.   66. S.D.] *Camb.; not in* F.

49. *affied*] affianced, betrothed, en-
gaged. This formal betrothal ceremony before witnesses was almost as
binding as the marriage ceremony
itself. See E. Schanzer, *Sh.S.*, 13
(1960), 81–9, and *AYL* (ed. Agnes
Latham, Arden edn, Appendix B).
When accompanied by the legal
settlement, as it is here, it was also
known as 'assurance' (*OED*, 2). Cf.
Lyly, *Euphues* (*Works*, ed. Bond, I.
228): 'I cannot but smile to heare,
that a marriage should bee solem-
nized, where neuer was any mention
of assuringe, and that the woeing
should bee a day after the weddinge.'
52. *Pitchers have ears*] Tilley, P363.
The pun is on the handles of water-
jugs or drinking-vessels. Cf. *R3*, II. iv.
37.

53. *hearkening still*] constantly on the
watch (Onions, 2, 'peculiar to Eliz.
and Caroline times').
54. *happily*] haply, by chance (the
words were interchangeable). Cf.
Tw.N., IV. ii. 51 (where F reads
'happily' and the context requires
'haply').
55. *and it like you*] if you prefer.
57. *pass*] transact, carry through
its stages (*OED, v.* 45, quoting
Shr.).
58. *your servant*] Lucentio, who, as
Cambio the schoolmaster, was presented as servant to Baptista at II. i.
79 ff. NCS and Hibbard add a S.D.
to show that Tranio winks at Lucentio
(as required by l. 74, below).
59. *My boy*] Biondello.

Tra. Dally not with the gods, but get thee gone.

Exit [Biondello].

Enter PETER *[a servingman].*

Signor Baptista, shall I lead the way?
Welcome. One mess is like to be your cheer.   70
Come sir, we will better it in Pisa.

Bap. I follow you.   *Exeunt.*

Enter LUCENTIO *and* BIONDELLO.

Bion. Cambio.

Luc.   What sayest thou, Biondello?

Bion. You saw my master wink and laugh upon you?

Luc. Biondello, what of that?   75

Bion. Faith, nothing. But 'has left me here behind to ex-
        pound the meaning or moral of his signs and tokens.

Luc. I pray thee moralize them.

Bion. Then thus: Baptista is safe, talking with the
        deceiving father of a deceitful son.   80

Luc. And what of him?

Bion. His daughter is to be brought by you to the supper.

Luc. And then?

Bion. The old priest at Saint Luke's church is at your
        command at all hours.   85

Luc. And what of all this?

Bion. I cannot tell, except they are busied about a
        counterfeit assurance. Take you assurance of her,

---

68. S.D. *Exit [Biondello].] Camb.; Exit. F (after l. 67).   a servingman] Hibbard;
not in F.   76. 'has] Hanmer (h'as); has F.   87. except] F2; expect F.

68. S.D.] F reads 'Enter Peter.' but
gives him nothing to say. Bond was
the first to suggest that he is 'some
servant come to warn Tranio that his
meal is ready', and NCS (p. 118)
believes that it is an actor's name and
connects him with Peter, Petruchio's
servant in IV. i. No one has identified
the actor. The proposal fits the facts,
but makes for an unnecessary and unconvincing piece of stage business.
Perhaps some piece of text has been

cut.
    70. *mess*] dish (Onions, 1). Cf. *Lr*,
I. i. 116.
    78. *moralize*] explain, interpret
(*OED*, *v*. 1). Cf. *AYL*, II. i. 44; *R3*,
III. i. 83.
    88. *counterfeit assurance*] the legal
settlement referred to at l. 49, above.
The word 'assurance' occurs more
frequently in *Shr.* than in any other
Shakespeare play.

cum privilegio ad imprimendum solum. To th' church!
Take the priest, clerk, and some sufficient honest   90
witnesses.
If this be not that you look for, I have no more to say,
But bid Bianca farewell for ever and a day.

Luc. Hear'st thou, Biondello—

Bion. I cannot tarry. I knew a wench married in an after-   95
noon as she went to the garden for parsley to stuff a
rabbit. And so may you, sir; and so adieu, sir. My
master hath appointed me to go to Saint Luke's, to
bid the priest be ready to come against you come
with your appendix.   *Exit.* 100

Luc. I may and will, if she be so contented.
She will be pleas'd, then wherefore should I doubt?
Hap what hap may, I'll roundly go about her:
It shall go hard if Cambio go without her.   *Exit.*

---

89. *privilegio . . . solum*] *F2; preuilegio ad Impremendum solem F.*   church!]
Rann (church;)*; Church F.*   102. doubt?] *F* (doubt:)*; doubt her? Pope.*

---

89. *cum . . . solum*] an inscription often found on the title-pages of sixteenth- and seventeenth-century books. Strictly, it means 'with the privilege for printing only' but it came to be understood as 'with the sole right to print'. It indicated that the publisher had received special licence or patent, for life or for a fixed term, to print books in a certain category (e.g. in 1559 R. Tottell received a licence to print books on common law). See Chambers, *ES*, III. 159; Greg, *SFF*, p. 70. Biondello is referring to the exclusive rights conferred by marriage, and punning on 'imprimendum' in its sense of 'pressing upon'.

90. *sufficient*] substantial, well-to-do, of adequate means or wealth (*OED*, 4, quoting *Shr.*). Cf. *2H4*, III. ii. 94;

Mer.V., I. iii. 17. Hibbard glosses 'some sufficient' as 'enough, the right number required by law', but this is not convincing.

93. *for . . . day*] Tilley, D74, and earlier examples in Smith and Wilson.

99. *against you come*] in preparation for your coming.

100. *appendix*] probably Biondello means 'appendage' and refers to Bianca, though the word 'appendix' neatly rounds off the 'printing' jest of l. 89. NCS prefers to think that Biondello means 'attendant' and compares Nashe, *Unfortunate Traveller* (*Works*, ed. McKerrow, rev. Wilson, II. 209), 'a certain kind of an appendix or page'—but this leaves Lucentio's next speech without point.

103. *Hap . . . may*] Tilley, C529.

[SCENE V]

Enter PETRUCHIO, KATHERINA, HORTENSIO [*and* Servants].

Pet. Come on, a God's name, once more toward our father's.
　Good Lord, how bright and goodly shines the moon!
Kath. The moon? The sun! It is not moonlight now.
Pet. I say it is the moon that shines so bright.
Kath. I know it is the sun that shines so bright.　　　　　5
Pet. Now by my mother's son, and that's myself,
　It shall be moon, or star, or what I list,
　Or e'er I journey to your father's house.—
　[*To Servants.*] Go on, and fetch our horses back again.—
　Evermore cross'd and cross'd, nothing but cross'd.　　10
Hor. Say as he says, or we shall never go.
Kath. Forward, I pray, since we have come so far,
　And be it moon, or sun, or what you please.
　And if you please to call it a rush-candle,
　Henceforth I vow it shall be so for me.　　　　　　　15
Pet. I say it is the moon.
Kath. 　　　　　　　I know it is the moon.
Pet. Nay, then you lie. It is the blessed sun.
Kath. Then, God be blest, it is the blessed sun.
　But sun it is not, when you say it is not,
　And the moon changes even as your mind.　　　　　20
　What you will have it nam'd, even that it is,
　And so it shall be so for Katherine.

Scene v

SCENE v] *Steevens; not in F.*　　S.D. *Hortensio*] *Q ; Hortentio F.*　　*and Servants*]
Camb.; not in F.　　9. S.D.] *Hibbard; not in F.*　　18. is] *Q ; in F.*　　22. be so]
F; be, so, *Rowe;* be, sir *Capell.*

This scene takes place somewhere
on the road between Petruchio's
house and Padua. The fact that the
horses have gone on before (l. 9) suggests that they are walking up a hill.

7. *list*] please, choose.

14. *rush-candle*] a candle of feeble
power made by dipping the pith of a
rush in tallow or other grease. It is not
mentioned elsewhere by Shakespeare,
but cf. Nashe, *Preface to Sidney's
'Astrophel and Stella'* (*Works*, ed.

McKerrow, rev. Wilson, III. 330),
'Put out your rush candles, you Poets
and Rimers'.

20. *And . . . mind*] Tilley, M1111.

22. *And . . . Katherine*] so F. Editors
from Rowe to Bond have felt a need to
add punctuation after 'be', to make
two phrases, and Capell went so far
as to emend the second 'so' to 'sir'.
But F makes perfect sense as it stands,
and shows Katherine reiterating her
vow that 'it shall be so' (l. 15).

Hor. Petruchio, go thy ways, the field is won.

Pet. Well forward, forward. Thus the bowl should run,
    And not unluckily against the bias.   25
    But soft, company is coming here.

                    Enter VINCENTIO.

[*To Vincentio.*] Good morrow, gentle mistress, where
        away?
    Tell me, sweet Kate, and tell me truly too,
    Hast thou beheld a fresher gentlewoman?
    Such war of white and red within her cheeks!   30
    What stars do spangle heaven with such beauty
    As those two eyes become that heavenly face?
    Fair lovely maid, once more good day to thee.
    Sweet Kate, embrace her for her beauty's sake.   34

Hor. A will make the man mad, to make the woman of him.

Kath. Young budding virgin, fair, and fresh, and sweet,
    Whither away, or where is thy abode?
    Happy the parents of so fair a child,

26. *company*] *F;* what company *Steevens.*   27. S.D.] *Rowe; not in F.*   35. the
woman] *F;* a woman *F2.*   37. where] *F2;* whether *F.*

23. *go thy ways*] carry on. The old
genitive of 'way' survived in certain
adverbial expressions like 'go your
ways' and 'come your ways'. Onions
compares German 'geht Eures Weges!'
Cf. *All's W.*, IV. v. 50; *Ham.*, III. i. 129.

25. *against the bias*] against its
natural inclination. One side of a
bowl, in the game of bowls, is weighted,
which gives it a natural curving path.
Cf. *Tw.N.*, v. i. 251–2.

29. *fresher*] more youthful, healthy,
blooming (*OED, a. adv.* and *sb.*[1] 9. b,
quoting *Shr.*).

30. *war . . . cheeks*] a commonplace.
Cf. *Lucr.*, 71–2; *Ven.*, 345–6.

31–2. *What . . . face*] Cf. *Sonn.*,
cxxxii. 7–9: 'Nor that full star that
ushers in the even/Doth half that
glory to the sober west,/As those two
mourning eyes become thy face.'

35. *the woman*] so F. F2 and most
editors read 'a woman'. I follow
Hibbard (p. 234), who argues, 'The

allusion is, however, to the theatre,
where the part of the woman was
played by a boy. Petruchio, says
Hortensio, is assigning the old man
the woman's role in the little play he
is staging.' Cf. *Cor.*, II. ii. 93–5: 'In that
day's feats,/When he might act the
woman in the scene,/He proved best
man i' th' field . . .' There is a similar
complexity of reference in *Ant.*, v. ii.
219, 'Some squeaking Cleopatra boy
my greatness'.

37. *Whither . . . where*] F reads
'Whether . . . whether'. NCS notes
that this is 'Probably a case of incorrect expansion by the compositor,
"where" being a contracted form of
"whether"'. Kökeritz (p. 321) says
'Intervocalic [ð] has disappeared
in monosyllabic *whether*' and records
spellings 'whe'r', 'wher' and 'where'.

38–40. *Happy . . . bedfellow*] from
Golding's *Ovid*, iv. 392–7: 'right
happie folke are they,/By whome

Happier the man whom favourable stars
Allots thee for his lovely bedfellow.   40
Pet. Why, how now, Kate, I hope thou art not mad.
This is a man, old, wrinkled, faded, wither'd,
And not a maiden, as thou say'st he is.
Kath. Pardon, old father, my mistaking eyes,
That have been so bedazzled with the sun   45
That everything I look on seemeth green.
Now I perceive thou art a reverend father.
Pardon, I pray thee, for my mad mistaking.
Pet. Do, good old grandsire, and withal make known
Which way thou travellest: if along with us,   50
We shall be joyful of thy company.
Vin. Fair sir, and you my merry mistress,
That with your strange encounter much amaz'd me,
My name is call'd Vincentio, my dwelling Pisa,
And bound I am to Padua, there to visit   55
A son of mine, which long I have not seen.
Pet. What is his name?
Vin.   Lucentio, gentle sir.
Pet. Happily met; the happier for thy son.
And now by law, as well as reverend age,
I may entitle thee my loving father.   60
The sister to my wife, this gentlewoman,
Thy son by this hath married. Wonder not,

40. Allots] *Q; A* lots *F;* Allot *Pope.*

thou camste into this worlde, right
happy is (I say)/Thy mother and thy
sister too (if any bee:) good hap/
That woman had that was thy Nurce
and gave thy mouth hir pap./But
farre above all other, far more blist
than these is shee/Whome thou
vouchsafest for thy wife and bedfellow for too bee.' Bond notes that
Ovid took it from *Odyssey*, vi. 154-9.

40. *Allots*] the old form of the third
person plural (Abbott, 333). F reads
'A lots', which Pope corrected to
'Allot', thus obscuring the original
form.

46. *green*] (i) green in colour, (ii)
fresh, young (*OED, a.* and *sb.* 7). Cf.

Troil., II. iii. 248; *Pilgr.*, iv. 2; *Tim.*,
IV. i. 7.

52. *mistress*] trisyllabic.

53. *encounter*] mode of address,
behaviour (*OED, sb.* 3, quoting *Shr.*).
Cf. *Ham.*, v. ii. 186; *Wint.*, III. ii. 47.

60. *father*] the word was 'col-
loquially extended to include a father-
in-law, stepfather, or one who adopts
another as his child' (*OED, sb.* 1. e,
quoting several examples from Shakespeare, though none earlier).

61-2. *The . . . married*] Petruchio
cannot know this because it has not
yet happened. Hortensio does not
contradict him, and, indeed, confirms the account at l. 73. Hortensio

Nor be not griev'd, she is of good esteem,
Her dowry wealthy, and of worthy birth;
Beside, so qualified as may beseem   65
The spouse of any noble gentleman.
Let me embrace with old Vincentio,
And wander we to see thy honest son,
Who will of thy arrival be full joyous.

Vin. But is this true, or is it else your pleasure,   70
Like pleasant travellers, to break a jest
Upon the company you overtake?

Hor. I do assure thee, father, so it is.

Pet. Come, go along and see the truth hereof,
For our first merriment hath made thee jealous.   75

                              Exeunt [all but Hortensio].

Hor. Well, Petruchio, this has put me in heart.
Have to my widow! And if she be froward,
Then hast thou taught Hortensio to be untoward.   *Exit.*

75. S.D. *all but Hortensio*] *Warburton; not in F.*   77. be] *F2; not in F.*

should have remembered that Lucentio (i.e. Tranio) has joined with him in forswearing Bianca for ever (IV. ii). These inconsistencies pass quite unnoticed in the theatre, and need not be taken as evidence of revision. Shakespeare often leaves just such loose ends.

65. *so qualified*] of such qualities.

Cf. *Wint.*, II. i. 113.
    beseem] befit.
    71. *break a jest*] play a practical joke (Onions, 2). Cf. *Troil.*, I. iii. 148.
    75. *jealous*] suspicious (Onions, 2). Cf. *Gent.*, III. i. 28.
    78. *untoward*] intractable, unruly, perverse (*OED, a.* 2). Cf. *John*, I. i. 243.

[ACT V]

[SCENE I]

Enter BIONDELLO, LUCENTIO, *and* BIANCA. GREMIO
is out before.

Bion. Softly and swiftly, sir, for the priest is ready.
Luc. I fly, Biondello. But they may chance to need thee
at home, therefore leave us.   *Exit* [*with Bianca*].
Bion. Nay, faith, I'll see the church a your back, and

ACT V

Scene 1

ACT V SCENE 1] *Theobald; not in F.*   S.D. *Bianca*] *Q ; Bianea F.*   3. *with*
Bianca] *This edn; not in F.*

F marks no act- or scene-division here, reserving '*Actus Quintus*' for what all modern editors call Act v, scene ii. But Act v begins better at this point since here the action moves from the country to Padua, where it remains for the rest of the play.

S.D.] Lucentio is no longer disguised as Cambio. The direction 'Gremio is out before' is unique in Elizabethan and Jacobean dramatic texts. It seems to mean that Gremio enters before the others, and Greg (*SFF*, pp. 125–6) includes it in a group of stage-directions under the comment: 'Often the grouping of characters is indicated, particularly in entries from opposite directions.' Greg adds later (p. 213), 'Gremio comes on first and the others enter to him'. Hibbard agrees, adding that the S.D. 'has all the appearance of an afterthought', but see Allardyce Nicoll, 'Passing over the Stage' (*Sh.S.*, 12 (1959), 47–55). Professor Nicoll, in a private letter, suggested that 'Gremio is out before' may be 'an

early version of this stock S.D., meaning that Gremio strolls in by himself, and during this stroll encounters the others'. The text gives no reason why Gremio should be 'out before', or here at all. His last encounter with Lucentio/Cambio was in 1. ii, when he employed him as his go-between with Bianca. Perhaps this gives point to l. 6.

4. *I'll . . . back*] The precise meaning is uncertain. Biondello's general sense is 'I'll see you married', and Hibbard glosses 'I'll see the church at your back'. But *OED* does not record 'a' as a variant spelling of 'at', nor (under 'a') does it give any convincing examples of 'a' used in that positional sense which would be necessary to justify Hibbard's gloss. But 'a' commonly means 'on' (*OED*, A, *prep.*[1]) and Bond glosses 'on your back, over you, *i.e.* see you into the church', adding that l. 36 precludes the more natural sense 'at your back'. If we accept that the line means 'I'll see the church on your back', Bion-

then come back to my master's as soon as I can. [*Exit.*]   5
Gre. I marvel Cambio comes not all this while.

Enter PETRUCHIO, KATHERINA, VINCENTIO, GRUMIO,
with Attendants.

Pet. Sir, here's the door, this is Lucentio's house.
  My father's bears more toward the market-place.
  Thither must I, and here I leave you, sir.
Vin. You shall not choose but drink before you go.   10
  I think I shall command your welcome here,
  And by all likelihood some cheer is toward.   *Knocks.*
Gre. They're busy within. You were best knock louder.

PEDANT *looks out of the window.*

Ped. What's he that knocks as he would beat down the
  gate?   15
Vin. Is Signor Lucentio within, sir?
Ped. He's within, sir, but not to be spoken withal.
Vin. What if a man bring him a hundred pound or two
  to make merry withal?

5. master's] *Capell;* mistris *F.*   S.D.] *This edn; not in F; Exeunt Lucentio,
Bianca and Biondello/Rowe.*

dello is saying either (i) I'll conduct
you to the church and take you inside,
or (ii) I'll come with you to your
wedding and see you yoked in holy
wedlock.

5. *master's*] F reads 'mistris' but all
editors now accept Capell's emendation. The error probably arises from
the abbreviation 'Mrs' in the copy.
Cf. l. 47, below, and I. ii. 18.

8. *bears*] lies. The basic sense is
nautical (*OED*, *v.*[1] 39, quoting *Shr.*).

12. *toward*] in preparation, about
to take place. Cf. *MND*, III. i. 70.

13. S.D.] Cf. *Supposes* (Bullough, p.
139), IV. iii, '*Dalio commeth to the
wyndowe, and there maketh them answere*',
where the reception of the hero's true
father is close to this scene in *Shr.* It is
now generally agreed that 'the
window' means some point on the
upper stage level. Cf. Marlowe,

Doctor Faustus (*Plays*, ed. Gill, p. 367),
IV. i. 23 S.D., '*Enter* Benvolio *above at a
window in his nightcap, buttoning*'. The
Pedant's 'window' was probably *above*
one or other of the doors giving access
to the main stage through the façade
of the tiring-house (probably one of
these doors represents the entrance to
Lucentio's house, and the other,
Baptista's). We know there was 'a
gallery over the stage', and it seems
most likely that this scene makes use
of it. See Chambers, *ES*, III. 58, 94;
Southern, *Sh.S.*, 12 (1959), 22–34,
especially Plates II and III (cf. the
'De Witt' drawing of the Swan
Theatre, reproduced in Hodges, *The
Globe Restored* (1953), Plate 7); Latter,
Sh.S., 28 (1959), 125–35.

19. *withal*] with (Onions, 3; Abbott,
196). Cf. *Err.*, V. i. 268.

Ped. Keep your hundred pounds to yourself. He shall   20
      need none so long as I live.

Pet. Nay, I told you your son was well beloved in Padua.
      Do you hear, sir? To leave frivolous circumstances,
      I pray you tell Signor Lucentio that his father is
      come from Pisa, and is here at the door to speak with   25
      him.

Ped. Thou liest. His father is come from Mantua, and
      here looking out at the window.

Vin. Art thou his father?

Ped. Ay, sir, so his mother says, if I may believe her.   30

Pet. [*To Vincentio.*] Why, how now, gentleman! Why,
      this is flat knavery, to take upon you another man's
      name.

Ped. Lay hands on the villain. I believe a means to cozen
      somebody in this city under my countenance.   35

Enter BIONDELLO.

Bion. I have seen them in the church together. God send
      'em good shipping! But who is here? Mine old

27. Mantua] *Malone;* Padua *F;* to Padua *Pope.*   and] *F;* and is *Dyce.*
31. S.D.] *Capell;* not in *F.*

23. *frivolous   circumstances*] trivial
matters. Cf. *1H6,* iv. i. 112.
   27. *Mantua*] F reads 'Padua', which
the Globe editors justify on the
grounds that 'the Pedant has been
staying some time in Padua, and that
is all he means'. This is not convincing.
If 'Mantua' stood in the copy it might
well be misread as 'Padua', since the
initial capital letters can be similar in
Secretary   hand   (see   McKerrow,
Introduction to Bibliography (1928), p.
349), and the joke is better if the
Pedant forgets, at this point, that the
real Vincentio is from Pisa, and gives
the name of the place he himself has
come from. NCS notes that Shakespearean texts are prone to confuse
the names of these Italian cities (cf.
Gent., ii. v. i; iii. i. 81; v. iv. 130).
   27–8. *and here*] Dyce's emendation
'and is here' is adopted by NCS (pp.

97, 174) on the grounds that F's text
of *Shr.* is characterized by the omission
or addition of small words.
   30. *his mother says*] Tilley, M1193,
'Ask the Mother if the child be like
his father', quoting seven examples in
Shakespeare.
   32. *flat*] absolute, downright (*OED,*
a. 6).
   35. *under   my   countenance*] in   my
person, by pretending to be me. Cf.
l. 115, below; i. i. 228.
   36–7. *God ... shipping*] not recorded
in Tilley or Smith and Wilson, but
OED (Shipping, *vbl. sb.* 3. b) says
'God send you good shipping!' was used
proverbially   in   the   sixteenth   and
seventeenth centuries as a wish for
success in any venture', and quotes
Shr. together with Nashe, *Unfortunate*
Traveller (*Works,* ed. McKerrow, rev.
Wilson, ii. 222), sig. B4, 'Gone he is;

master Vincentio! Now we are undone and brought
to nothing.

Vin. [*To Biondello.*] Come hither, crack-hemp.   40

Bion. I hope I may choose, sir.

Vin. Come hither, you rogue. What, have you forgot
me?

Bion. Forgot you? No, sir. I could not forget you, for I
never saw you before in all my life.   45

Vin. What, you notorious villain, didst thou never see
thy master's father, Vincentio?

Bion. What, my old worshipful old master? Yes, marry,
sir. See where he looks out of the window.

Vin. Is't so, indeed?   *He beats Biondello.*   50

Bion. Help, help, help! Here's a madman will murder
me.   [*Exit.*]

Ped. Help, son! Help, Signor Baptista! [*Exit from the window.*]

Pet. Prithee, Kate, let's stand aside and see the end of
this controversy.   55

Enter PEDANT *with* Servants,
BAPTISTA, TRANIO.

Tra. Sir, what are you that offer to beat my servant?

Vin. What am I, sir? Nay, what are you, sir? O immor-
tal gods! O fine villain! A silken doublet, a velvet

---

38. brought] *Q;* brough *F.*   40. S.D.] *Rowe (seeing Biondello); not in F.*
47. master's] *F2;* Mistris *F.*   52. S.D.] *Capell; not in F.*   53. S.D.]
Hibbard; not in F; Exit above/Capell.   55. S.D. *Pedant] F; Pedant below,*
Capell.

God send him good shipping to
Wapping'. The phrase also occurs in
Kyd's *Soliman and Perseda* (ed. Boas,
p. 214), IV. ii. 79, and the anonymous
Club Law (1599–1600), ed. Moore
Smith (1907), ll. 46–7.

40. *crack-hemp*] one likely to strain
the hangman's rope, a gallows-bird.
The word is peculiar to Shakespeare
and found only here. The more usual
term was 'crack-halter', which *OED*
cites first in *Supposes* (Bullough, p.
120), I. iv, 'You cracke halter, if I
catche you by the eares, I shall make
you answere me directly'. This is a

possible link between the two plays.

41. *I . . . choose*] I hope I may have
some choice in that matter (*OED, v.*
4. b). Cf. *Mer.V.*, I. ii. 42–3.

47. *master's*] see note to l. 5, above.

52. S.D.] No exit for Biondello is
marked in F, but Biondello must go
out to tell Lucentio and Bianca what
has happened. Similarly, after l. 53,
no exit is marked for the Pedant, but
he must be given time to leave the
window before his entry on the
main acting level after l. 55.

56. *offer*] venture (Onions, 2). Cf.
Wint., IV. iv. 767.

hose, a scarlet cloak, and a copatain hat! O, I am
undone, I am undone! While I play the good hus-   60
band at home, my son and my servant spend all at
the university.

Tra. How now, what's the matter?

Bap. What, is the man lunatic?

Tra. Sir, you seem a sober ancient gentleman by your   65
habit, but your words show you a madman. Why,
sir, what 'cerns it you if I wear pearl and gold? I
thank my good father, I am able to maintain it.

Vin. Thy father? O villain! He is a sail-maker in
Bergamo.   70

Bap. You mistake, sir, you mistake, sir. Pray, what do
you think is his name?

Vin. His name? As if I knew not his name! I have
brought him up ever since he was three years old,
and his name is Tranio.   75

Ped. Away, away, mad ass! His name is Lucentio, and
he is mine only son, and heir to the lands of me,
Signor Vincentio.

66. madman] *Rowe;* mad man *F.*   67. 'cerns] *Collier;* cernes *F.*   75. Tranio]
F2; Tronio *F.*

59. *copatain hat*] 'a high-crowned
hat in the form of a sugar-loaf' (*OED*,
quoting *Shr.* as its only example). It is
apparently the same as 'Copintank',
of which *OED* gives a number of
examples with a wide variety of
spellings. The etymology is obscure.

60–1. *good husband*] economical
manager (Onions, 2). Cf. *Meas.*, III. ii.
65; *H8*, III. ii. 142.

67. *'cerns*] short for 'concerns'
(*OED* records only this example of the
abbreviated form). NCS points out
that the contraction seems pointless in
a piece of prose, and suggests that it
'forms part of a fossil line of verse—
"What 'cerns it you, if I wear pearl
and gold?" ' Such so-called fossils are
not difficult to find. In this same
speech we have 'you seem a sober
ancient gentleman', but it is difficult
to imagine why any 'reviser' should

find it necessary to reduce original
verse lines to prose and do it so imperfectly. The present example sounds
more like a quotation.

68. *maintain*] bear the expense of,
afford (*OED*, *v.* 8. c, quoting *Shr.*).

70. *Bergamo*] about 120 miles west
of Padua, and not much mentioned in
Elizabethan literature (see Sugden,
Topographical Dictionary). It is possible,
as Bond suggests, that Shakespeare
conceived it as a port, but it has never
been famous for sail-making. It lies
between lakes Iseo and Como, and
this may have given rise to a small
local trade, but Shakespeare is not
likely to have known this. He never
refers to Bergamo elsewhere, but see
MND, v. i. 344, 'Bergomask'.

73–4. *I . . . old*] Bond notes how
close this is to *Supposes* (Bullough, p.
144), IV. viii, 'he whome I brought up

Vin. Lucentio? O, he hath murdered his master! Lay
    hold on him, I charge you, in the Duke's name. O,   80
    my son, my son! Tell me, thou villain, where is my
    son Lucentio?

Tra. Call forth an officer.

[*Enter an* OFFICER.]

Carry this mad knave to the gaol. Father Baptista, I
    charge you see that he be forthcoming.   85

Vin. Carry me to the gaol?

Gre. Stay, officer. He shall not go to prison.

Bap. Talk not, Signor Gremio. I say he shall go to
    prison.

Gre. Take heed, Signor Baptista, lest you be cony-   90
    catched in this business. I dare swear this is the right
    Vincentio.

Ped. Swear, if thou dar'st.

Gre. Nay, I dare not swear it.

Tra. Then thou wert best say that I am not Lucentio.   95

Gre. Yes, I know thee to be Signor Lucentio.

Bap. Away with the dotard, to the gaol with him!

Vin. Thus strangers may be haled and abused. O
    monstrous villain!

Enter BIONDELLO, LUCENTIO, *and* BIANCA.

Bion. O, we are spoiled, and yonder he is. Deny him,   100
    forswear him, or else we are all undone.

Luc. (*Kneels.*) Pardon, sweet father.

---

83. S.D.] *Capell (subst.); not in F.*   98. haled] *F3* (hal'd); haild *F.*
99. S.D. *Bianca*] *Q ; Biancu F.*

of a childe, yea and cherished him as
if he had bene mine owne, doth nowe
utterly denie to knowe me'.

    79. *O . . . master*] 'Out and alas, he
whom I sent hither with my son to be
his servaunt, and to give attendance
on him, hath eyther cut his throate, or
by some evill meanes made him away'
(*Supposes*, IV. viii, Bullough, p. 145).
In the first edition (1575) there is a
marginal note at this point: 'A

shrewde suppose.'
    85. *forthcoming*] 'ready to appear or
to be produced when required, e.g. in
court' (Onions). Cf. *2H6*, I. iv. 53;
II. i. 174.
    90–1. *cony-catched*] cheated, de-
ceived. See note to IV. i. 38.
    97. *Away . . . him*] It may be, as
Bond suggests, that the first half of this
line refers to Gremio and the second
half to Vincentio.

Vin.   Lives my sweet son?
   Exeunt Biondello, Tranio and Pedant, as fast as may be.
Bian. Pardon, dear father.
Bap.   How hast thou offended?
  Where is Lucentio?
Luc.   Here's Lucentio,
  Right son to the right Vincentio,   105
  That have by marriage made thy daughter mine,
  While counterfeit supposes blear'd thine eyne.
Gre. Here's packing, with a witness, to deceive us all.
Vin. Where is that damned villain Tranio,
  That fac'd and brav'd me in this matter so?   110
Bap. Why, tell me, is not this my Cambio?
Bian. Cambio is chang'd into Lucentio.
Luc. Love wrought these miracles. Bianca's love
  Made me exchange my state with Tranio,
  While he did bear my countenance in the town,   115
  And happily I have arriv'd at the last
  Unto the wished haven of my bliss.
  What Tranio did, myself enforc'd him to;
  Then pardon him, sweet father, for my sake.
Vin. I'll slit the villain's nose that would have sent me to   120
  the gaol.
Bap. But do you hear, sir? Have you married my

102. *Exeunt . . . be.*] *F (after l. 101).*

102. S.D.] Cf. *Err.*, IV. iv. 144, 'Exeunt omnes, as fast as may be, frighted'. NCS cites this among evidence to show that the same hand was responsible for the stage-directions in *Err.* and *Shr.* (p. 100). But see *Rom.* (Q1), II. vi. 15 (Arden edn numbering), 'Enter Juliet somewhat fast', and Gibbons's discussion (Arden edn, p. 11).
107. *While . . . eyne*] while deceitful suppositions confused you (*OED*, Suppose, *sb.* 1). This line obviously refers to Gascoigne's *Supposes*. For the phrase 'blear'd thine eyne' Bond compares Chaucer, *Manciple's Tale*, 148, and Golding's translation of

Caesar, sig. L4, 6, 'to the intent to bleare his enemies eyes with the suspicion of fearefulness'. Onions notes that the archaic plural 'eyne' is used in Shakespeare eleven times in rhyme, and three times where rhyme is not required.
108. *packing*] plotting. (*OED*, *vbl. sb.*²). Cf. *Lr*, III. i. 26 (and Muir's note in the Arden edn); *Cym.*, III. v. 82; *Ant.*, IV. xiv. 19.
with a witness] and no mistake, with a vengeance (*OED*, *sb.* 14, quoting *Shr.*). The line shows that Gremio has been hoodwinked as well.
110. *fac'd and brav'd*] See notes to IV. iii. 111, 123, 125.

daughter without asking my good will?

Vin. Fear not, Baptista, we will content you, go to. But I
    will in, to be revenged for this villainy.   *Exit.*   125
Bap. And I, to sound the depth of this knavery.   *Exit.*
Luc. Look not pale, Bianca; thy father will not frown.

                          Exeunt [Lucentio and Bianca].

Gre. My cake is dough, but I'll in among the rest,
    Out of hope of all, but my share of the feast.   [*Exit.*]
Kath. Husband, let's follow to see the end of this ado.   130
Pet. First kiss me, Kate, and we will.
Kath. What, in the midst of the street?
Pet. What, art thou ashamed of me?
Kath. No, sir, God forbid; but ashamed to kiss.   134
Pet. Why, then, let's home again. Come, sirrah, let's away.
Kath. Nay, I will give thee a kiss. Now pray thee, love, stay.
Pet. Is not this well? Come, my sweet Kate.

    Better once than never, for never too late.   *Exeunt.*

---

127. S.D. *Lucentio and Bianca*] *Capell; not in F.*   129. S.D.] *Rowe; not in F.*
134. No] *Q;* Mo *F.*   138. once] *F;* late *Hanmer.*

124. *go to*] don't worry. Onions says 'used to express disapprobation, remonstrance, protest, or derisive incredulity', but here it is simple reassurance.

128. *My . . . dough*] Tilley, C12. See note to I. i. 108.

129. *Out . . . all*] with no hope of anything. Cf. *Tp.*, III. iii. 11.

130–8.] This dialogue between Katherina and Petruchio, when they are alone on the stage (apart from their servants), is extremely important in any attempt to interpret the tone of Katherina's speech of submission in v. ii. Here, for the first time, there seems to be affection between the two, and the kiss seems a genuine expression of love. It is *possible* to play the lines as yet another example of Petruchio imposing his will on his unwilling wife, but to do so is to fly in the face of Shakespeare's obvious intention.

138. *Better . . . late*] Petruchio combines two proverbs: Tilley, L85, 'Better late than never', and M875, 'It is never too late to mend'.

SCENE II

Enter BAPTISTA, VINCENTIO, GREMIO, *the* PEDANT, LUCENTIO *and* BIANCA, [PETRUCHIO *and* KATHERINA, HORTENSIO] *and* WIDOW; *the* Servingmen, *with* TRANIO, BIONDELLO, GRUMIO, *bringing in a banquet.*

Luc. At last, though long, our jarring notes agree,
  And time it is, when raging war is done,
  To smile at scapes and perils overblown.
  My fair Bianca, bid my father welcome,

Scene II

SCENE II] *Steevens; Actus Quintus. F.*   S.D. *Petruchio . . . Hortensio*] *Rowe*
(subst.); not in F.   *and . . . Grumio,*] *This edn; Tranio, Biondello Grumio, and*
Widdow: The Seruingmen with Tranio F.   2. done] *Rowe;* come *F.*

F heads this scene '*Actus Quintus.*', though, like the previous scene, it takes place in Padua, inside Lucentio's house. All editors since Theobald have preferred to consider this scene and its predecessor as forming the fifth Act.

S.D.] F reads '*Enter Baptista, Vincentio, Gremio, the Pedant, Lucentio, and Bianca. Tranio, Biondello Grumio, and Widdow: The Seruingmen with Tranio bringing in a Banquet.*' The repetition of Tranio suggested to NCS that the last part of the S.D. was a later addition, and in several ways it is unsatisfactory. Petruchio, Katherina and Hortensio are not mentioned at all (though Petruchio is the second person to speak), but there is a rudimentary processional order: the older generation precede the host and hostess, then follow Tranio, Biondello and Grumio in roughly their order of importance here, but the Widow is utterly anomalous. It is tempting to conjecture that the words '*Petruchio, Katherina, Hortensio*' came before '*and Widdow*'; this would get the right people on stage, but in an improper processional order,

masters following servants. F's direction, as it stands, would be impossible in the theatre.

banquet] a course of sweetmeats, fruit and wine, served as a continuation of the principal meal (*OED, sb.*[1] 3). Cf. *Rom.*, I. v. 120; *Tim.*, I. ii. 149.

1. *long*] after a long time (Onions, adj.[1]).

our jarring notes agree] a general remark, but Lucentio may direct it lightly towards Hortensio, as a reminiscence of their cultural combat in III. i.

2. *done*] F's 'come' is clearly wrong. NCS suggests unconvincingly (p. 103) that the error is more likely due to mishearing than misreading, but Sisson (*New Readings*, I. 166) finds it 'a plausible graphic confusion' and adds that 'Heywood offers instances'.

3. *scapes*] escapes (Onions, I). Cf. *Oth.*, I. iii. 136.

overblown] blown over, that have passed away (*OED, ppl. a.*[1] 1, quoting *Shr.*). Cf. *2H6*, I. iii. 150, 'my choler being overblown'.

4–10. *My . . . cheer*] Lucentio provides the 'banquet' at his house, to which he and his bride welcome the

While I with self-same kindness welcome thine.   5
Brother Petruchio, sister Katherina,
And thou, Hortensio, with thy loving widow,
Feast with the best, and welcome to my house.
My banquet is to close our stomachs up
After our great good cheer. Pray you, sit down,   10
For now we sit to chat as well as eat.
Pet. Nothing but sit and sit, and eat and eat!
Bap. Padua affords this kindness, son Petruchio.
Pet. Padua affords nothing but what is kind.
Hor. For both our sakes I would that word were true.   15
Pet. Now, for my life, Hortensio fears his widow.
Wid. Then never trust me if I be afeard.
Pet. You are very sensible, and yet you miss my sense.
    I mean Hortensio is afeard of you.
Wid. He that is giddy thinks the world turns round.   20
Pet. Roundly replied.
Kath.   Mistress, how mean you that?
Wid. Thus I conceive by him.
Pet. Conceives by me! How likes Hortensio that?
Hor. My widow says thus she conceives her tale.
Pet. Very well mended. Kiss him for that, good widow.   25
Kath. 'He that is giddy thinks the world turns round'—
    I pray you tell me what you meant by that.

wedding party, after the wedding feast ('our great good cheer') which would have taken place at Baptista's.

5. *kindness*] (i) affection, good will (*OED*, 5), (ii) kinship, natural affection arising from this (*OED*, 1). Cf. *Ham.*, I. ii. 65.

8. *with*] on (Abbott, 193). Cf. *LLL.*, I. i. 281; *R2*, III. ii. 175.

9. *close . . . up*] provide the finale to our feast, with a subsidiary sense of 'put an end to our quarrelling'. Cf. IV. i. 145. Bond mentions a phrase found at the end of old lists of dinner-dishes: 'and cheese to close up the stomach'.

16. *fears*] (i) is afraid of (*OED*, v. 5), (ii) frightens (*OED*, v. 1). Petruchio uses the word in the first sense,

the Widow understands it in the second.

18. *sensible*] endowed with good sense; intelligent, reasonable, judicious (*OED*, a. 14). Cf. *Wiv.*, II. i. 131; *2H4*, I. ii. 187.

20. *He . . . round*] Tilley, W870.

21. *Roundly*] plainly, outspokenly, frankly (*OED*, adv. 3), though possibly the sense of 'fluently, glibly' (*OED*, 6) is present. Cf. *R2*, II. i. 122.

22. *Thus . . . him*] That is what I imagine his condition to be. 'Conceive' is used in the common sense of 'understand' (Onions, 1; cf. *Wiv.*, I. i. 222), but the phrase is strained to provide the *double entendre* of following line.

24. *conceives her tale*] understands her remark, interprets her statement.

Wid. Your husband, being troubled with a shrew,
  Measures my husband's sorrow by his woe.
  And now you know my meaning.   30
Kath. A very mean meaning.
Wid.   Right, I mean you.
Kath. And I am mean, indeed, respecting you.
Pet. To her, Kate!
Hor. To her, widow!
Pet. A hundred marks, my Kate does put her down.   35
Hor. That's my office.
Pet. Spoke like an officer. Ha' to thee, lad. *Drinks to Hortensio.*
Bap. How likes Gremio these quick-witted folks?
Gre. Believe me, sir, they butt together well.

37. thee,] *F2 (comma, Theobald)*; the *F*.

28. *shrew*] pronounced 'shrow' to rhyme with 'woe'. Kökeritz, p. 211. Cf. IV. i. 197; l. 189, below.

32. *And . . . you*] It is difficult to know precisely what Katherina intends here. The line could mean 'And I demean myself in paying you any attention' (*OED*, Mean, *a.*1 2), or, if said with sarcasm, 'And I am an inferior creature, of course, in comparison with you'. But 'mean' has other meanings, and NCS and Hibbard prefer the sense of 'moderate, close to the average' (*OED, a.*2 6), so that Hibbard glosses 'I am moderate in behaviour by comparison with you'. But see Hulme (*Explorations*), pp. 123 and 249, for discussion of *Mer.V.*, III. v. 68 (Globe, III. v. 82), where 'meane it' (the reading of F) has the sense of 'to live chastely' (a sense found also at *1H6*, I. ii. 121). *OED* cites two contemporary examples (*a.*2 5. c (b)) of the sense 'said of the married state as contrasted with continence on the one hand and unchastity on the other', and it may be that Katherina, in her choice of this word, is implying that she is a respectable married woman, a follower of holy and godly matrons, where her adversary is a remarried widow, a type conventionally sus-

pected of lustful proclivities (see C. Leech, *John Webster* (1951), pp. 69 ff.; Chapman, *The Widow's Tears*, ed. Smeak (1966), pp. xiii ff., where the contemporary importance of this idea is discussed). The tone of this line is important, since it is Katherina's last utterance before she leaves the stage, not to reappear until summoned by Petruchio to make her formal act of submission. In her dialogue with the Widow she is clearly 'spoiling for a fight', but in this line she wins the bout with a remark which is all the more deadly for being richly ambiguous.

35. *put her down*] (i) defeat her, (ii) have sexual intercourse with her—the sense Hortensio takes up in the following line. Cf. *Ado*, II. i. 252–6.

37. *Ha' to thee, lad*] F's 'ha to the lad' is corrected as early as F2, and is supported by the S.D. in F '*Drinkes to Hortensio.*' Cf. I. i. 139; IV. v. 77.

39. *butt together*] F reads 'But together', and editors from Rowe to Capell (1768) emended to 'butt Heads together', to prepare for Bianca's retort. This is unnecessary. The use of the head is implied in the act of butting (*OED, v.*1 1). Gremio's general sense is an analogy between repartee and the playful butting of

Bian. Head and butt! An hasty-witted body   40
    Would say your head and butt were head and horn.
Vin. Ay, mistress bride, hath that awaken'd you?
Bian. Ay, but not frighted me, therefore I'll sleep again.
Pet. Nay, that you shall not. Since you have begun,
    Have at you for a bitter jest or two.   45
Bian. Am I your bird? I mean to shift my bush,
    And then pursue me as you draw your bow.
    You are welcome all.

                Exeunt Bianca [and Katherina and Widow].
Pet. She hath prevented me. Here, Signor Tranio,
    This bird you aim'd at, though you hit her not;   50
    Therefore a health to all that shot and miss'd.
Tra. O sir, Lucentio slipp'd me like his greyhound,
    Which runs himself, and catches for his master.
Pet. A good swift simile, but something currish.

40. butt!] *Rowe (subst.); But F.*   45. bitter] *Capell (conj. Theobald); better F.*
48. S.D. *and Katherina and Widow] Rowe (subst.); not in F.*

young cattle. Cf. *LLL*, v. ii. 251–2.
But a subsidiary sense may also be
intended; the word-play here is
complex. *OED* (Butt, *v.*² 3) quotes
'1581 Savile *Agric.* (1622) 188 The
neerest [Britons] to France likewise
resemble the French . . . because . . .
that in countries butting together the
same aspects of the heauens doe yeeld
the same complexions of bodies',
where 'butting' is a form of 'abutting'
or 'adjoining', and this would fit
Gremio's sense.

40. *Head and butt*] head and tail.
Butt here means 'buttock' (*OED*, *sb.*³
3).

41. *butt*] (i) horn, (ii) buttock.

horn] (i) symbol of cuckoldry, (ii)
phallus. The central point of Bianca's
witticism is that a quick-witted
person might say that Gremio was a
cuckold, but the other senses of 'butt'
and 'horn' make a related interpretation.

45. *bitter jest or two*] All modern
editors accept the emendation 'bitter',
which means 'shrewd, or sharp' without any necessary sense of ill-nature

(*OED*, *a.* 7). Cf. *Lr*, I. iv. 135, 'A
bitter fool!', which Muir (Arden edn)
glosses 'sarcastic'.

46–7. *Am . . . bow*] Elizabethan
fowlers used a variety of weapons,
including the stone-bow or birding-
bow (which resembled a hand-
catapult), as well as the shot-gun, the
decoy, the stalking-horse, and the
springe. The bow required a sitting
target, and if the bird moved from one
bush to another the fowler would have
to pursue it. Cf. *Ado*, II. iii. 86–7;
Shakespeare's England, II. 369–72;
Madden, *Diary*, pp. 206–7.

49. *prevented*] (i) anticipated
(Onions, 2), (ii) escaped from
(Onions, 3).

Signor Tranio] NCS notes 'This title
sits oddly upon the son of a "sail-
maker in Bergamo"'.

52. *slipp'd*] unleashed. Cf. Madden,
Diary, pp. 173–4; *1H4*, I. iii. 278; *H5*,
III. i. 31; *Cor.*, I. vi. 38.

54. *swift*] quick-witted. Cf. *AYL*,
v. iv. 60.

currish] Cf. *Gent.*, IV. iv. 45–7,
'Marry, she says your dog was a cur,

Tra. 'Tis well, sir, that you hunted for yourself.   55
  'Tis thought your deer does hold you at a bay.
Bap. O, O, Petruchio! Tranio hits you now.
Luc. I thank thee for that gird, good Tranio.
Hor. Confess, confess, hath he not hit you here?
Pet. A has a little gall'd me, I confess;   60
  And as the jest did glance away from me,
  'Tis ten to one it maim'd you two outright.
Bap. Now, in good sadness, son Petruchio,
  I think thou hast the veriest shrew of all.
Pet. Well, I say no. And therefore for assurance   65
  Let's each one send unto his wife,
  And he whose wife is most obedient,
  To come at first when he doth send for her,
  Shall win the wager which we will propose.
Hor. Content. What's the wager?
Luc.   Twenty crowns.   70
Pet. Twenty crowns?
  I'll venture so much of my hawk or hound,
  But twenty times so much upon my wife.
Luc. A hundred then.
Hor.   Content.
Pet.   A match! 'Tis done.

---

62. two] *Rowe;* too *F.*   outright] *F3;* out right *F.*   65. for] *F2;* sir *F.*

---

and tells you currish thanks is good enough for such a present'.

56. *'Tis . . . bay*] A stag is said to be 'at bay' when it turns on the hounds and defends itself at close quarters (*OED*, Bay, *sb.*⁴ 4). Tranio puns on 'deer' and 'dear'.

58. *gird*] taunt, biting remark. Cf. *2H4*, I. ii. 6; Lyly, *Euphues* (*Works*, ed. Bond, II. 68), 'so many nips, such bitter girdes, such disdainfull glickes'.

60. *gall'd me*] made me sore (*OED*, *v.*¹ 1). Hibbard glosses 'scratched me, given me a surface wound', but *OED* records no such sense, the nearest being *v.*¹ 5, 'To harrass or annoy in warfare (esp. with arrows or shot)'.

Other examples in Shakespeare support a meaning like 'wounded, hurt'. Cf. *Tit.*, IV. iii. 71; *John*, IV. iii. 94–5; *H8*, III. ii. 207.

61. *glance away from*] ricocheted off. Cf. *Wiv.*, V. v. 223.

63. *in good sadness*] seriously. (*OED*, 2. b). Cf. *Wiv.*, III. v. 109; *Rom.*, I. i. 197; *Ven.*, 807.

65. *therefore for assurance*] so, to increase confidence or certainty, to put the matter to the test (Onions, 3; cf. *MND*, III. i. 20; *Tp.*, V. i. 108). F reads 'therefore sir assurance', but the error is corrected in F2. The two forms could be easily confused in manuscript.

Hor. Who shall begin? 75
Luc. That will I.
    Go, Biondello, bid your mistress come to me.
Bion. I go. *Exit.*
Bap. Son, I'll be your half Bianca comes.
Luc. I'll have no halves. I'll bear it all myself. 80

             Enter BIONDELLO.

    How now, what news?
Bion.   Sir, my mistress sends you word
    That she is busy and she cannot come.
Pet. How? She's busy, and she cannot come?
    Is that an answer?
Gre.   Ay, and a kind one too.
    Pray God, sir, your wife send you not a worse. 85
Pet. I hope better.
Hor. Sirrah Biondello, go and entreat my wife
    To come to me forthwith. *Exit Biondello.*
Pet.   O ho, entreat her!
    Nay, then she must needs come.
Hor.   I am afraid, sir,
    Do what you can, yours will not be entreated. 90

             Enter BIONDELLO.

    Now, where's my wife?
Bion. She says you have some goodly jest in hand.

83–9. How . . . come.] *as verse, Rowe; as prose, F.*   90. S.D.] *Capell; after* can, *l. 90, F.*

75–6. *That . . . Go*] F's reading 'That will I./Goe *Biondello*' is metrically unsatisfactory, but I do not follow Hibbard in emending.

79. *be your half*] go half-shares with you in the gamble that. A 'half' is 'one of two partners or co-sharers' (*OED, sb.* 5, quoting *Shr.*). Cf. *LLL*, v. ii. 249.

80. *have no halves*] There may have been a pun or jingle here, but the pronunciation of 'half' and 'halves' is not certain and was probably various (Kökeritz, 184, 310).

83. *How?*] What? (an elliptical

form of 'How is it?' or 'How say you?' —*OED, adv.* 4). Cf. *Meas.*, ii. i. 68; *Gent.*, ii. iv. 22.

She's] F prints ll. 83–4 as prose, and yet retains the contracted form 'she's', where the uncontracted form would create a regular blank-verse line. Much of the dialogue in this part of the scene has these loose verse-rhythms.

86. *I hope better*] I have better expectations. Cf. *Tw.N.*, iii. iv. 161, 'my hope is better'. NCS notes that 'By placing a comma after "hope" editors have made "better" refer to

She will not come. She bids you come to her.

Pet. Worse and worse, she will not come! O vile,
     Intolerable, not to be endur'd!   95
     Sirrah Grumio, go to your mistress,
     Say I command her come to me.   *Exit* [*Grumio*].

Hor. I know her answer.

Pet.   What?

Hor.   She will not.

Pet. The fouler fortune mine, and there an end.

Enter KATHERINA.

Bap. Now, by my holidame, here comes Katherina.   100

Kath. What is your will, sir, that you send for me?

Pet. Where is your sister, and Hortensio's wife?

Kath. They sit conferring by the parlour fire.

Pet. Go fetch them hither. If they deny to come,
     Swinge me them soundly forth unto their husbands. 105
     Away, I say, and bring them hither straight.
                              [*Exit Katherina.*]

Luc. Here is a wonder, if you talk of a wonder.

Hor. And so it is. I wonder what it bodes.

97. *Grumio*] *Rowe; not in F.*   106. S.D.] *Rowe (subst.); not in F.*

"answer", and thus given a hesitating note to Petruchio's calm assurance'. There is no need to do so.

94. *Worse . . . vile*] Abbott, 485, notes that monosyllables containing a vowel followed by 'r' are often prolonged, and quotes this line as if the first word were a metrical foot in itself (though he counts the second 'worse' as a monosyllable). But see note to l. 83, above, and cf. the metre of l. 96, below.

99. *there an end*] that's that. Cf. *Gent.*, I. iii. 65; *R2*, V. i. 69; *Mac.*, III. iv. 80.

100. *by my holidame*] F reads 'by my hollidam'. *OED* allows 'Hollidam(e) -dome' only as variant spellings of 'Halidom', noting that 'the substitution of *-dam*, *-dame*, in the suffix was app. due to popular etymology, the word being taken to denote "Our Lady" '. From an original meaning of 'holiness, sanctity', halidom came to mean 'a holy thing, a holy relic; anything regarded as sacred' (*OED*, 3), and 'by my halidom' meant 'by all that I hold sacred'. If F readings are to be trusted, Shakespeare's other uses of the phrase (*Gent.*, IV. ii. 131, 'hallidome'; *Rom.*, I. iii. 44, 'holydam'; *H8*, V. i. 116, 'Holydame') suggest that he may have been the victim of popular etymology.

103. *conferring*] conversing, talking together (*OED*, *v.* 6, quoting *Shr.*). Cf. *Gent.*, II. iv. 115.

104. *deny*] refuse (Onions, 1). Cf. II. i. 179.

105. *Swinge*] whip, thrash (*OED*, *v.*1 1, quoting *Shr.*). Cf. *John*, II. i. 288.

107. *wonder*] miracle. Cf. *Err.*, III. ii. 30.

Pet. Marry, peace it bodes, and love, and quiet life,
   An awful rule, and right supremacy,   110
   And, to be short, what not that's sweet and happy.
Bap. Now fair befall thee, good Petruchio!
   The wager thou hast won, and I will add
   Unto their losses twenty thousand crowns,
   Another dowry to another daughter,   115
   For she is chang'd, as she had never been.
Pet. Nay, I will win my wager better yet,
   And show more sign of her obedience,
   Her new-built virtue and obedience.

            Enter KATHERINA, BIANCA, *and* WIDOW.

   See where she comes, and brings your froward wives
   As prisoners to her womanly persuasion.   121
   Katherine, that cap of yours becomes you not.
   Off with that bauble, throw it under foot.   [*She obeys.*]
Wid. Lord, let me never have a cause to sigh
   Till I be brought to such a silly pass.   125
Bian. Fie, what a foolish duty call you this?
Luc. I would your duty were as foolish too.
   The wisdom of your duty, fair Bianca,
   Hath cost me a hundred crowns since supper-time.
Bian. The more fool you for laying on my duty.   130

123. S.D.] *Hibbard; not in F; She pulls off her cap, and throws it down/Rowe.*
129. a] *Capell;* fiue *F;* an *Rowe.*

110. *awful*] commanding reverential fear or profound respect (Onions, 1). Cf. *2H6*, v. i. 98.

119. *obedience*] Most editors follow F, but suspect that this is not the word Shakespeare intended. NCS states, 'The word has been caught by the compositor's eye from the previous line and substituted for another'. This may well be so, but if it is, the original word is beyond recovery.

123. S.D.] no S.D. in F, but most editors since Rowe have added one.

129. *a hundred crowns*] F's 'fiue hundred crownes' contradicts what Lucentio seems to say about the wager at l. 74. The best explanation is Sisson's (*New Readings,* I. 167), who argues that the copy for F probably read 'Hath cost me a hundr crownes' and the compositor misread 'a' as 'v', the roman numeral for five, and expanded it. This is probably right. But it is just possible to defend F's reading: Lucentio (l. 70) originally proposed a wager of twenty crowns, Petruchio avers that he would bet twenty times as much on his wife (400 crowns), and if one takes Lucentio's 'A hundred then' as 'I'll raise you a hundred' the total is exactly five hundred crowns.

130. *laying*] wagering.

Pet. Katherine, I charge thee, tell these headstrong women
      What duty they do owe their lords and husbands.
Wid. Come, come, you're mocking. We will have no telling.
Pet. Come on, I say, and first begin with her.
Wid. She shall not.   135
Pet. I say she shall. And first begin with her.
Kath. Fie, fie! Unknit that threatening unkind brow,
      And dart not scornful glances from those eyes,
      To wound thy lord, thy king, thy governor.
      It blots thy beauty as frosts do bite the meads,   140
      Confounds thy fame as whirlwinds shake fair buds,
      And in no sense is meet or amiable.
      A woman mov'd is like a fountain troubled,
      Muddy, ill-seeming, thick, bereft of beauty,
      And while it is so, none so dry or thirsty   145
      Will deign to sip or touch one drop of it.
      Thy husband is thy lord, thy life, thy keeper,
      Thy head, thy sovereign; one that cares for thee,
      And for thy maintenance; commits his body

131–2.] *as verse, Rowe; as prose, F.*   133. *you're*] *F3;* your *F.*
149. maintenance;] *F* (maintenance.)*; * maintenance *Camb.*

131–2. *Katherine . . . husbands*] prose
in F.

137–80.] Katherina's famous
speech has been interpreted in many
ways, and its tone is crucial to the
meaning of the play. See Intro.,
pp. 144–9.

138. *And . . . eyes*] The scornful
darts shot from a mistress's eyes form
one of the great commonplace images
of Elizabethan poetry. Cf. *Ven.*, 196.

140. *blots*] tarnishes, stains, sullies
(*OED, v.*[1] 3. a, quoting *Shr.*), i.e. your
frown tarnishes your beauty as frosts
bite the meadows.

141. *Confounds thy fame*] destroys
your reputation.

      shake fair buds] shake the young
buds off the trees. Cf. *Sonn.*, xviii. 3;
Cym., III. iii. 60–4.

143. *mov'd*] exasperated, stirred to
anger. Cf. *Rom.*, I. i. 86.

      a fountain troubled] Cf. the very

similar image Achilles uses in *Troil.*,
III. iii. 303–8.

144. *ill-seeming*] of unpleasant
appearance (not found elsewhere in
Shakespeare; *OED* records no other
example.)

145. *none so dry*] Abbott, 281
(Relatival Constructions).

147. *Thy . . . lord*] Genesis, iii. 16;
Ephesians, v. 22; 1 Peter, iii. 1.

149. *maintenance; commits*] F reads
'maintenance. Commits'. Many
editors (including Bond and NCS)
read 'maintenance commits', thus
creating the sense that the husband
'commits his body to painful labour'
in order to maintain his wife. There is
no need to alter the punctuation of F
so violently, since, as Sisson points out
(*New Readings*, I. 167), 'The contrast,
after *maintenance*, is between the
husband's labour and dangers abroad
and the wife's safety at home'.

To painful labour both by sea and land,   150
To watch the night in storms, the day in cold,
Whilst thou liest warm at home, secure and safe;
And craves no other tribute at thy hands
But love, fair looks, and true obedience;
Too little payment for so great a debt.   155
Such duty as the subject owes the prince
Even such a woman oweth to her husband.
And when she is froward, peevish, sullen, sour,
And not obedient to his honest will,
What is she but a foul contending rebel,   160
And graceless traitor to her loving lord?
I am asham'd that women are so simple
To offer war where they should kneel for peace,
Or seek for rule, supremacy, and sway,
When they are bound to serve, love, and obey.   165
Why are our bodies soft, and weak, and smooth,
Unapt to toil and trouble in the world,
But that our soft conditions and our hearts
Should well agree with our external parts?
Come, come, you froward and unable worms,   170
My mind hath been as big as one of yours,
My heart as great, my reason haply more,
To bandy word for word and frown for frown.
But now I see our lances are but straws,
Our strength as weak, our weakness past compare,   175

---

150. *painful*] toilsome, laborious (*OED*, *a.* 3). Cf. *LLL*, ii. i. 23; *H5*, iv. iii. 111.

151. *watch*] be on watch through.

160. *contending*] antagonistic, warlike. Cf. *Ven.*, 82.

161. *graceless*] probably the dominant sense here is 'ungrateful, wanting a sense of propriety' (cf. i. ii. 268), but the word carried theological overtones, and its primary sense was 'not in a state of grace, unregenerate' (*OED*, *a.* 1).

165. *serve, love, and obey*] 'Wylte thou obey him, and serue him, loue,

honor, and kepe him, in sickenes and in health?' (*The Boke of Common Prayer* (1552), 'The Fourme of Solemnizacyon of Matrymonye').

167. *Unapt*] unfitted. Cf. *Lucr.*, 695.

168. *conditions*] qualities, characteristics (Onions, 6). Cf. *Gent.*, iii. i. 275; *H5*, iv. i. 106.

170. *unable*] weak, impotent (*OED*, *a.* 2). Cf. *H5*, v. ii. 366; *Lr*, i. i. 59.

173. *bandy*] toss to and fro, like a ball at tennis. Cf. *3H6*, i. iv. 49, 'I will not bandy with thee word for word'.

175. *as weak*] i.e. as weak as straws.

That seeming to be most which we indeed least are.
Then vail your stomachs, for it is no boot,
And place your hands below your husband's foot.
In token of which duty, if he please,
My hand is ready, may it do him ease.   180
Pet. Why, there's a wench! Come on, and kiss me, Kate.
Luc. Well, go thy ways, old lad, for thou shalt ha't.
Vin. 'Tis a good hearing, when children are toward.
Luc. But a harsh hearing, when women are froward.
Pet. Come, Kate, we'll to bed.   185
We three are married, but you two are sped.
[*To Lucentio.*] 'Twas I won the wager, though you hit the
white,

187. S.D.] *Malone; not in F.*

176. *seeming . . . are*] seeming to be
in the highest degree what in fact we
are in the least degree. This twelve-
syllable line rhymes with the previous
line which is an ordinary iambic
pentameter. Abbott (497) scans it as:
That séeming | to be móst | which wé |
indéed | least áre, but it runs far
more easily and convincingly as an
alexandrine.

177. *vail your stomachs*] abase your
pride (*OED*, Vail, *v.*² 4a, quoting
Marlowe, *Jew of Malta*, v. ii, 'Now
vaile your pride you captiue Chris-
tians'). Cf. *2H4*, I. i. 129; *Cor.*, III. i. 98.
it is no boot] there is no help for it.

178. *And . . . foot*] This may allude
to some traditional act of allegiance or
submission (cf. Sir Toby in *Tw.N.*,
II. v. 168, 'Wilt thou set thy foot o'
my neck?', which itself may recall the
Emperor's submission to the Pope at
Canossa, regularly cast in the teeth
of Roman Catholics by sixteenth-
and seventeenth-century Protestants).
Such actions are recorded as far back
as the Old English poem *The
Wanderer*: 'And, dreaming, he clasps
his dear lord again,/Head on knee,
hand on knee, loyally laying,/
Pledging his liege as in days long
past' (40–2, trans. C. W. Kennedy),

but no precise origin for Katherina's
symbolic offer has been proposed.

182. *thou shalt ha't*] The phrase is
required for a rhyme with 'Kate', but
its meaning is not clear. It may refer
to the money Petruchio has won from
Lucentio, but Bond proposes a more
general sense, 'you shall carry the
prize, have your wish', and quotes T.
Heywood's *Wise Woman of Hogsdon*
(1638), IV. iv, 'Go thy ways, for thou
shalt ha't'.

183. *a good hearing*] a thing good to
hear.
toward] willing, compliant, docile
(*OED*, *a.* 4). The opposite of 'froward'.

186. *sped*] done for. Cf. *Rom.*, III. i.
88. Petruchio's point is that he,
Lucentio and Hortensio are all
married, but Lucentio and Hortensio
have been defeated already by their
wives.

187. *the white*] a term in archery.
'There were three chief methods of
shooting, Prick, or Clout, Butt, and
Roving. Prick or Clout shooting was
carried on at from 160 to 240 yards,
the mark being 18 inches in diameter,
made of canvas stuffed with straw,
and having a small white circle
painted on it, in the centre of which
was a wooden peg; to "hit the white"

And being a winner, God give you good night!
                    Exeunt Petruchio [and Katherina].
Hor. Now go thy ways, thou hast tam'd a curst shrew.
Luc. 'Tis a wonder, by your leave, she will be tam'd so.   190
                                            [Exeunt.]

188. S.D. *and Katherina*] *Rowe (subst.); not in F.*   190. S.D.] *Rowe; not in F.*

meant to hit the white mark . . . to "cleave the pin" to strike the peg' (*Shakespeare's England*, II. 380). Petruchio has 'cleaved the pin', while Lucentio has done the next best thing (there is also the pun on the name Bianca, Italian for white).

188. *being a winner*] 'alluding to the natural wish of successful gamesters to leave the table before their luck turns' (Bond).

189. *shrew*] F spells 'Shrow', indicating the pronunciation and the rhyme with the final 'so'. See note to IV. i. 197; l. 28, above.

APPENDIX I

Evidence to establish the relationship of *The Shrew* and *A Shrew*, from Samuel Hickson, 'The Taming of The Shrew', *N&Q* (30 March 1850), pp. 345–7.

The first passage I take is from Act IV. Sc. 3.

> *Grumio* Thou hast fac'd many *things*?
> *Tailor* I have.
> *Gru.* Face not me: thou hast brav'd many men; brave not me. I will neither be fac'd nor brav'd.

In this passage there is a play upon the terms 'fac'd' and 'brav'd'. In the tailor's sense, 'things' may be 'fac'd' and 'men' may be 'brav'd'; and, by means of this play, the tailor is entrapped into an answer. The imitator, having probably seen the play represented, has carried away the words, but by transposing them, and with the change of one expression—'men' for 'things' —has lost the spirit: there is a pun no longer. He might have played upon 'brav'd', but there he does not wait for the tailor's answer; and 'fac'd', as he has it, can be understood but in one sense, and the tailor's admission becomes meaningless. The passage is as follows:

> *Saudre* Dost thou hear, tailor? thou hast brav'd many men: brave not me. Th'ast fac'd many men.
> *Tailor* Well, Sir?
> *Saudre* Face not me: I'll neither be fac'd nor brav'd at thy hands, I can tell thee.

A little before, in the same scene, Grumio says, 'Master, if ever I said loose-bodied gown, sew me in the skirts of it, and beat me to death with a bottom of brown thread'. I am almost tempted to ask if passages such as this be not evidence sufficient. In the *Taming of a Shrew*, with the variation of 'sew me in a *seam*' for 'sew me in *the skirts of it*', the passage is also to be found; but who can doubt the whole of this scene to be by Shakspeare, rather than by the author of such scenes, intended to be comic, as one referred to in my last communication (no. 15, p. 227, numbered 7), and

shown to be identical with one in *Doctor Faustus*? I will just remark, too, that the best appreciation of the spirit of the passage,
which, one would think, should point out the author, is shown in
the expression, 'sew me in the *skirts of it*', which has meaning,
whereas the variation has none. A little earlier, still in the same
scene, the following bit of dialogue occurs:

> *Kath.* I'll have no bigger; this doth fit the time,
>   And gentlewomen wear such caps as these.
> *Pet.* When you are gentle, you shall have one too, and not
>   till then.

Katharine's use of the term 'gentlewomen' suggests here
Petruchio's 'gentle'. In the other play the reply is evidently
imitated, but with the absence of the suggestive cue:

> For I will home again unto my father's house.
> *Ferando* I, when y'are meeke and gentle, but not before.

Petruchio, having dispatched the tailor and haberbasher,
proceeds—

> Well, come my Kate: we will unto your father's,
> Even in these honest mean habiliments;
> Our purses shall be proud, our garments poor;

throughout continuing to urge the vanity of outward appearance,
in reference to the 'ruffs and cuffs, and farthingales and things',
which he had promised her, and with which the phrase 'honest
mean habiliments' is used in contrast. The sufficiency *to the mind*
of these,

> For 'tis the mind that makes the body rich,

is the very pith and purpose of the speech. Commencing in nearly
the same words, the imitator entirely mistakes this, in stating the
object of clothing to be to 'shrowd us from the winter's rage';
which is, nevertheless, true enough, though completely beside the
purpose. In Act II. Sc.1, Petruchio says,

> Say that she frown; I'll say she looks as clear
> As morning roses newly wash'd with dew.

Here is perfect consistency: the clearness of the 'morning *roses*',
arising from their being 'wash'd with dew'; at all events, the
quality being heightened by the circumstance. In a passage of the
so-called 'older' play, the duke is addressed by Kate as 'fair,
lovely lady', &c.

> As glorious as the morning wash'd with dew.

As the morning does not derive its glory from the circumstance of its being 'wash'd with dew', and as it is not a peculiarly apposite comparison, I conclude that here, too, as in other instances, the sound alone has caught the ear of the imitator.

In Act v. Sc. 2, Katharine says,

> Then vail your stomachs; for it is no boot;
> And place your hand below your husband's foot;
> In token of which duty, if he please,
> My hand is ready: may it do him ease.

Though Shakspeare was, in general, a most correct and careful writer, that he sometimes wrote hastily it would be vain to deny. In the third line of the foregoing extract, the meaning clearly is, 'as which token of duty'; and it is the performance of this 'token of duty' which Katharine hopes may 'do him ease'. The imitator, as usual, has caught something of the words of the original, which he has laboured to reproduce at a most unusual sacrifice of grammar and sense; the following passage appearing to represent that the wives, by laying their hands under their husbands' feet— no reference being made to the act as a token of duty—in some unexplained manner, 'might procure them ease'.

> Layir   hands under their feet to tread,
> If t¹   we might procure their ease,
> A   ¹ent, I'll first begin
>   nder my husband's feet.

O   done. Shakspeare has imparted
a   is play, exemplified, among
                                       following words as—

                                    st] I may.

                                 fine array.

                              ngales and things.

                           habit was Shakspeare's. In
Ac   that would thoroughly woo her,
wed ۱   the house of her'. The sequence
here is ۱   it observe the change: in Ferando's
first interv   ne says,

> My n.   eet Kate, doth say I am the man
> Must we and bed and *marrie* bonnie Kate.

In the last scene, Petruchio says,

> Come, Kate, we'll to bed:
> We three are married, but you two are sped.

Ferando has it thus:

> 'Tis Kate and I am wed, and you are sped:
> And so, farewell, for we will to our bed.

Is it not evident that Shakspeare chose the word 'sped' as a rhyme to 'bed', and that the imitator, in endeavouring to recollect the jingle, has not only spoiled the rhyme, but missed the fact that all 'three' were 'married', notwithstanding that 'two' were 'sped'?

It is not in the nature of such things that instances should be either numerous or very glaring; but it will be perceived that in all of the foregoing, the purpose, and sometimes even the meaning, is intelligible only in the form in which we find it in Shakspeare. I have not urged all that I might, even in this branch of the question; but respect for your space makes me pause.

APPENDIX II

THE SLY SCENES IN *A SHREW*

After scenes i and ii (corresponding to the Induction in *The Shrew*) *A Shrew* has four Sly 'interludes' and an Epilogue. Pope inserted these into his text of Shakespeare's play, and I include them because I believe they are witnesses to similar passages which originally stood in *The Shrew* (see pp. 39–45). The text is quoted from *Narrative and Dramatic Sources of Shakespeare*, ed. Bullough, vol. I.

1. *A Shrew*, v. 187–94.
The contact between *A Shrew* and *The Shrew* is very distant in this part of the play, and so it is not possible to say exactly where in Shakespeare's play this interruption would come. Hibbard (Penguin edn, p. 157) suggests the end of II.i, but it would arise equally well at the end of I.ii:

Then Slie speakes

SLIE   *Sim*, when will the foole come againe?
LORD   Heele come againe my Lord anon.
SLIE   Gis some more drinke here, souns wheres
The Tapster, here *Sim* eate some of these things.
LORD   So I doo my Lord.
SLIE   Here *Sim*, I drinke to thee.
LORD   My Lord heere comes the plaiers againe,
SLIE   O brave, heers two fine gentlewomen.

2. *A Shrew*, xiv. 78–xv. I.
This corresponds to the end of IV.iv and the opening of IV.v in *The Shrew*, when Lucentio has gone off to marry Bianca, and Katherina and Petruchio enter to dispute about 'the sun and the moon':

SLIE   *Sim* must they be married now?
LORD   I my Lord.

303

[Scene xv]

Enter Ferando and Kate and Sander

SLIE   Looke *Sim* the foole is come againe now.

3. *A Shrew*, xvi. 45–54.
In *A Shrew* the Duke of Cestus has just ordered that the impostors
Phylotus and Valeria should be sent to prison, and there follows
the stage-direction: '*Phylotus and Valeria runnes away | Then Slie
speakes*'. This corresponds to the stage-direction at v.i. 101,
'*Exeunt Biondello, Tranio and Pedant, as fast as may be*':

Phylotus and Valeria runnes away
Then Slie speakes

SLIE   I say wele have no sending to prison.
LORD   My Lord this is but the play, theyre but in jest.
SLIE   I tell thee *Sim* wele have no sending,
To prison thats flat: why *Sim* am not I *Don Christo Vary*?
Therefore I say they shall not go to prison.
LORD   No more they shall not my Lord,
They be run away.
SLIE   Are they run away *Sim*? thats well,
Then gis some more drinke, and let them play againe.
LORD   Here my Lord.

Slie drinkes and then falls asleepe

4. *A Shrew*, xvi. 127–33.
There is no trace of this in *The Shrew*, but it obviously belongs
between v.i and v.ii:

Exeunt Omnes
Slie sleepes

LORD   Whose within there? come hither sirs my Lords
Asleepe againe: go take him easily up,
And put him in his one apparell againe,
And lay him in the place where we did find him,
Just underneath the alehouse side below,
But see you wake him not in any case.
BOY   It shall be don my Lord come helpe to beare him
hence.

5. Epilogue. *A Shrew*, xix (after the end of v.ii in *The Shrew*):

[*Scene xix*]

Then enter two bearing of Slie in his
Owne apparrell againe, and leaves him
Where they found him, and then goes out

Then enter the Tapster

TAPSTER   Now that the darkesome night is overpast,
And dawning day apeares in cristall sky,
Now must I hast abroad: but soft whose this?
What *Slie* oh wondrous hath he laine here allnight,
Ile wake him, I thinke he's starved by this,
But that his belly was so stuft with ale,
What how *Slie*, Awake for shame.

SLIE   *Sim* gis some more wine: whats all the
Plaiers gon: am not I a Lord?

TAPSTER   A Lord with a murrin: come art thou dronken
      still?

SLIE   Whose this? *Tapster*, oh Lord sirra, I have had
The bravest dreame to night, that ever thou
Hardest in all thy life.

TAPSTER   I marry but you had best get you home,
For your wife will course you for dreming here to night,

SLIE   Will she? I know now how to tame a shrew,
I dreamt upon it all this night till now,
And thou hast wakt me out of the best dreame
That ever I had in my life, but Ile to my
Wife presently and tame her too
And if she anger me.

TAPSTER   Nay tarry *Slie* for Ile go home with thee,
And heare the rest that thou hast dreamt to night.

Exeunt Omnes

FINIS

APPENDIX III

A SOURCE AND ANALOGUES

1. Extracts from Gascoigne's *Supposes*
2. Grimeston's translation of Goulart
3. 'The Wife Wrapt in Wether's Skin'

Apart from Gascoigne's *Supposes* there are no direct 'sources' for *The Shrew* or, at least, none which has survived in documentary form. *Supposes* is reprinted in full in *Narrative and Dramatic Sources of Shakespeare*, ed. Bullough, vol. I, pp. 111–58, and the brief extracts below illustrate some points of contact between the two plays.

Grimeston's translation of Goulart (also reprinted in Bullough, op. cit., vol. I, pp. 109–10) is one of a large number of analogues to the Sly story, beginning as early as *The Arabian Nights*. The story is well known in the folklore of many countries (see p. 76).

The ballad of 'The Wife Wrapt in Wether's Skin' is an example of Aarne–Thompson Type 901, and it shows the differences between the extant versions of the folk-tale and the Katherina–Petruchio plot in *The Shrew*. The point of contact is the 'displacement' of the shrew's punishment on to someone or something else (cf. *The Shrew*, IV.i. 107ff.). I quote the ballad, with the editor's commentary, from Child's *English and Scottish Ballads*, where the different versions illustrate the variety of the surviving texts.

1. (a) *Supposes*, Actus ii. Scena i; cf. *The Shrew*, IV.ii. 59 ff.

ERO. Well harken a while then: this morning I tooke my horse and rode into the fieldes to solace my self, and as I passed the foorde beyonde *S. Anthonies* gate, I met at the foote of the hill a gentleman riding with two or three men: and as me thought by his habite and his lookes, he should be none of the wisest. He saluted me, and I him: I asked him from whence he came, and whither he would? he answered that he had come from *Venice*, then from *Padua*, nowe was going to *Ferrara*, and so to his countrey, whiche is *Scienna*: As soone as I knewe him to be a *Scenese*, sodenly lifting up mine eyes, (as it were with an admiration) I sayd unto him, are you a *Scenese*, and come to *Farrara*? why not, sayde he: quoth I, (halfe and more with a trembling voyce) know you the daunger that should ensue if you be knowne in *Ferrara* to be a *Scenese*? he more than halfe amased, desired me earnestly to tell him what I ment.

(b) *Supposes*, Actus iiii. Scena i.

EROSTRATO faines.

What shall I doe? Alas what remedie shall I finde for my ruefull estate? what escape, or what excuse may I now devise to shifte over our subtile supposes? for though to this day I have usurped the name of my maister, and that without checke or controll of any man, now shal I be openly discyphred, and that in the sight of every man: now shal it openly be knowen, whether I be *Erostrato* the gentleman, or *Dulipo* the servaunt. We have hitherto played our parts in abusing others: but nowe commeth the man that wil not be abused, the right *Philogano* the right father of the right *Erostrato*: going to seke *Pasiphilo*, and hearing that he was at the water gate, beholde I espied my fellowe *Litio*, and by and by my olde maister *Philogano* setting forth his first step on land: I to fuge and away hither as fast as I could to bring word to the right *Erostrato*, of his right father *Philogano*, that to so sodaine a mishap some subtile shift might be upon the sodaine devised. But what can be imagined to serve the turne, although we had [a] monethes respite to beate oure braines about it, since we are commonly knowen, at the least supposed in this towne, he for *Dulipo*, a slave & servant to *Damon*, & I for *Erostrato* a gentleman & a student? But beholde, runne *Crapine* to yonder olde woman before she get within the doores, & desire hir to call out *Dulipo*: but heare you? if she aske who would speake with him, saye thy selfe and none other.

(c) *Supposes*, Actus v. Scena decima.

CLEANDER PHILOGANO. DAMON. EROSTRATO.
PASIPHILO. POLINESTA. NEVOLA.
and other servaunts.

[CLE.] We are come unto you sir, to turne you[r] sorowe into joy and gladnesse: the sorow, we meane, that of force you have sustained since this mishappe of late fallen in your house. But be you of good comforte sir, and assure your selfe, that this yong man which youthfully and not maliciously hath commited this amorous offence, is verie well able (with consent of this worthie man his father) to make you sufficient amendes: being borne in *Cathanea* of *Sicilia*, of a noble house, no way inferiour unto you, and of wealth (by the reporte of suche as knowe it) farre exceeding that of yours.

PHI.   And I here in proper person, doe presente unto you sir, not onely my assured frendship and brotherhoode, but do earnestly desire you to accepte my poore childe (though unworthy) as your sonne in lawe: and for recompence of the injurie he hath done you, I proffer my whole lands in dower to your daughter: yea and more would, if more I might.

CLE.   And I sir, who have hitherto so earnestly desired your daughter in marriage, doe now willingly yelde up and quite claime to this yong man, who both for his yeares and for the love he beareth hir, is most meetest to be hir husband. For wher I was desirous of a wife by whom I might have yssue, to leave that litle which god hath sent me: now have I litle neede, that (thankes be to god) have founde my deerely beloved sonne, whom I loste of a childe at the siege of *Otranto*.

DA.   Worthy gentleman, your friendship, your alliaunce, and the nobilitie of your birthe are suche, as I have muche more cause to desire them of you than you to request of me that which is already graunted. Therfore I gladly, and willingly receive the same, and thinke my selfe moste happie now of all my life past, that I have gotten so toward a sonne in lawe to my selfe, and so worthye a father in lawe to my daughter: yea and muche the greater is my contentation, since this worthie gentleman maister *Cleander*, doth holde himselfe satisfied. And now behold your sonne.

ERO.   O father.

PAS.   Beholde the naturall love of the childe to the father: for inwarde joye he cannot pronounce one worde, in steade wherof he sendeth sobbes and teares to tell the effect of his inward in[t]ention. But why doe you abide here abrode? wil it please you to goe into the house sir?

DA.   *Pasiphilo* hath saide well: will it please you to goe in sir?

NE.   Here I have brought you sir, bothe fetters & boltes.

DA.   Away with them now.

NE.   Yea, but what shal I doe with them?

DA.   Marie I will tell thee *Nevola*: to make a righte ende of our supposes, lay one of those boltes in the fire, and make thee a suppositorie as long as mine arme, God save the sample. Nobles and gentlemen, if you suppose that our supposes have given you sufficient cause of delighte, shewe some token, whereby we may suppose you are content.

Et plauserunt.

FINIS

2. From S. Goulart, *Thrésor d'histoires admirables et mémorables,* trs. Edward Grimeston (1607), pp. 587–9 (Bullough, vol. 1, pp. 109–10):

Vanity of the World as represented in State

Philip called the good Duke of Bourgondy, in the memory of our ancestors, being at Bruxells with his Court and walking one night after supper through the streets, accompanied with some of his favorits: he found lying upon the stones a certaine Artisan that was very dronke, and that slept soundly. It pleased the Prince in this Artisan to make triall of the vanity of our life, whereof he had before discoursed with his familiar friends. Hee therfore caused this sleeper to be taken up and carried into his Pallace: hee commands him to bee layed in one of the richest beds, a riche Night-cap to bee given him, his foule shirt to bee taken off, and to have an other put on him of fine Holland: when as this Dronkard had digested his Wine, and began to awake: behold there comes about his bed, Pages and Groomes of the Dukes Chamber, who draw the Curteines, make many courtesies, and being bare-headed, aske him if it please him to rise, and what apparell it would please him to put on that day. They bring him rich apparrell. The new Monsieur amazed at such curtesie, and doubting whether he dreampt or waked, suffered himselfe to be drest, and led out of the Chamber. There came Noblemen which saluted him with all honour, and conduct him to the Masse, where with great ceremonie they give him the Booke of the Gospell, and the Pixe to Kisse, as they did usually unto the Duke: from the Masse they bring him backe unto the Pallace: hee washes his hands, and sittes downe at the Table well furnished. After dinner, the great Chamberlaine commandes Cardes, to be brought with a great summe of money. This Duke in Imagination playes with the chiefe of the Court. Then they carrie him to walke in the Gardein, and to hunt the Hare and to Hawke. They bring him back unto the Pallace, where hee sups in state. Candles beeing light, the Musitions begin to play, and the Tables taken away, the Gentlemen and Gentle-women fell to dancing, then they played a pleasant Comedie, after which followed a Banket, whereas they had presently store of Ipocras and precious Wine, with all sorts of confitures, to this Prince of the new Impression, so as he was drunke, & fell soundlie a sleepe. Here-upon the Duke commanded that hee should bee disrobed of all his riche attire. Hee was put into his olde ragges and carried into the same place, where he had been found the night before, where hee spent that night. Being awake in the morning, hee began to remember what had happened before, hee knewe not whether it were true in deede, or a dreame that had troubled his braine. But in the end, after many discourses, hee concluds that all was but a dreame that had happened unto him, and so entertained his wife, his Children and his neighbors, without any other apprehension. This Historie put mee in minde of that which Seneca sayth in the ende of his 59 letter to Lucilius. No man, saies he, can rejoyce and content himselfe, if he be not nobly minded, just and temperate. What then? Are the wicked deprived of all joye? they are glad as the Lions that have found their prey. Being full of wine and luxury, having spent the night in gourmandise, when as pleasures poored into this vessell of the bodie (beeing to little to containe so much) beganne to foame out, these miserable wretches crie with him of whome Virgill speakes,

> Thou knowest, how in the midest of pastimes false & vaine,
> We cast and past our latest night of paine.

The dissolute spend the night, yea the last night in false joyes. O man, this stately usage of the above named Artisan, is like unto a dreame that passeth. And his goodly day, and the years of a wicked life differ nothing but in more and lesse. He slept foure and twenty houres, other wicked men some-times foure and twenty thousands of houres. It is a little or a great dreame: and nothing more.

3. 'The Wife Wrapt in Wether's Skin', *English and Scottish Popular Ballads*, Francis James Child (1966), vol. v, pp. 104–6.

A (a) 'Sweet Robin', Jamieson's Popular Ballads, 1, 319. (b) Macmath MS., p. 100, three stanzas.
B 'Robin he's gane to the wude', Harris MS., fol. 26 b.

C 'The Cooper of Fife', Whitelaw, The Book of Scottish Song,
p. 333.
D Jamieson-Brown MS., Appendix, p. iii.
E Jamieson's Popular Ballads, I, 324.

JAMIESON cites the first two stanzas of A (a) in a letter of
inquiry to *The Scots Magazine*, October 1803, p. 700, and the first
half of D (with alterations) in his preface, Popular Ballads, I, 320.
The ballad, he says, is very popular all over Scotland.

Robin has married a wife of too high kin to bake or brew, wash
or wring. He strips off a wether's skin and lays it on her back, or
prins her in it. He dares not beat her, for her proud kin, but he
may beat the wether's skin, and does. This makes an ill wife good.

A fragment in Herd's MSS, I, 105, II, 161, belongs, if not to
this ballad, at least to one in which an attempt is made to tame
a shrew by castigation.

> 'Now tak a cud in ilka hand
>   And bace[1] her up and doun, man,
>
> And she'll be an o the best wives
>   That ever took the town, man.'

>   *   *   *

> And Jammie's turnd him round about,
>   He's done a manly feat:
> 'Get up, get up, ye dirty slut,
>   And gie to me my meat.'

>   *   *   *

> 'Say't oer again, say't oer again,
>   Ye thief, that I may hear ye;
> I'se gar ye dance upon a peat,
>   Gin I sall cum but near ye.'

The story of the ballad was in all likelihood traditionally
derived from the good old tale of the wife lapped in Morrel's
skin.[2] Here a husband, who has put up with a great deal from an

---

1. *Bace* in the second copy, rightly, that is, *bash*, beat; *bare* in the first (probably mistranscribed).

2. A merry jeste of a shrewde and curste wyfe lapped in Morrelles skin for
her good behauyour. Imprinted at London in Fleetestreete, beneath the
Conduite, at the signe of Saint John Euangelist, by H. Jackson; without date,
but earlier than 1575, since the book was in Captain Cox's library. Reprinted
in Utterson's *Select Pieces of Early Popular Poetry*, 1825, II, 169; *The Old Taming
of the Shrew*, edited by T. Amyot for the Shakespeare Society, 1844, p. 53;
W. C. Hazlitt's *Early Popular Poetry*, IV, 179.

excessively restive wife, flays his old horse Morrell and salts the hide, takes the shrew down cellar, and, after a sharp contest for mastery, beats her with birchen rods till she swoons, then wraps her in the salted hide: by which process the woman is perfectly reformed.[1]

A (a)[2]

Jamieson's *Popular Ballads*, I, 319. 'From the recitation of a friend of the editor's in Morayshire.'

> 1 She wadna bake, she wadna brew,
>   Hollin, green hollin
> For spoiling o her comely hue.
>   Bend your bow, Robin
>
> 2 She wadna wash, she wadna wring,
> For spoiling o her gay goud ring.
>
> 3 Robin he's gane to the fald
> And catched a weather by the spauld.
>
> 4 And he has killed his weather black
> And laid the skin upon her back.

1. These passages are worth noting:

> She can carde, she can spin,
> She can thresh and she can fan.   (v. 419f.)
>
> In euery hand a rod he gate
> And layd vpon her a right good pace.   (v. 955f.)
>
> Where art thou, wife? shall I haue any meate?
>   (v. 839.)

(Compare Herd's fragments with the last two, and with 903–10.)

2. A. (a.) The refrain, altered by Jamieson, has been restored from his preface. Five stanzas added by him at the end have been dropped. (b) From the recitation of Miss Agnes Macmath, 29 April 1893; learned by her from her mother, who had it from *her* mother, Janet Spark, Kirkcudbrightshire.

> 2. She could na wash and she coud na wring,
>   Hey, Wullie Wyliecot, noo, noo, noo
> For the spoiling o her gay gold ring.
> Wi my Hey, Wullie Wyliecot, tangie
>   dooble,
> That robes in the rassiecot, noo, noo, noo
> (*Refrain perhaps corrupt.*)
>
> 3. He's gane oot unto the fauld,
> He's catched a wather by the spaul.
>
> 5. 'I darena thrash ye, for yer kin,
> But I may thrash my ain wather-skin.'

5 'I darena pay you, for your kin,
   But I can pay my weather's skin.

6 'I darena pay my lady's back,
   But I can pay my weather black.'

7 'O Robin, Robin, lat me be,
   And I'll a good wife be to thee.

8 'It's I will wash, and I will wring,
   And never mind my gay goud ring.

9 'It's I will bake, and I will brew,
   And never mind my comely hue.

10 'And gin ye thinkna that eneugh,
    I'se tak the goad and I'se ca the pleugh.

11 'Gin ye ca for mair whan that is doon,
    I'll sit i the neuk and I'll dight your shoon.'

B

Harris MS., fol. 26 b, No. 25, from Miss Harris.

1 Robin he's gane to the wast,
      Hollin, green hollin
   He's waled a wife amang the warst.
      Bend your bows, Robin

2 She could neither bake nor brew,
   For spoilin o her bonnie hue.

3 She could neither spin nor caird,
   But fill the cup, an sair the laird.

4 She could neither wash nor wring,
   For spoilin o her gay goud ring.

5 Robin's sworn by the rude
   That he wald mak an ill wife gude.

6 Robin he's gaun to the fauld,
   An taen his blaik [wither] by the spauld.

7 He's taen aff his wither's skin
   An he has preened his ain wife in.

8 'I daurna beat my wife, for a' her kin,
   But I may beat my wither's skin.'

9 'I can baith bake an brew;
What care I for my bonnie hue?

10 'I can baith wash an wring;
What care I for my gay gowd ring?

11 'I can baith spin an caird;
Lat onybodie sair the laird.'

12 Robin's sworn by the rude
That he has made an ill wife gude.

C

Whitelaw's *Book of Scottish Song*, p. 333.

1 There was a wee cooper who lived in Fife,
  Nickity, nackity, noo, noo, noo
And he has gotten a gentle wife.
  Hey Willie Wallacky, how John Dougall,
  Alane, quo Rushety, roue, roue, roue

2 She wadna bake, nor she wadna brew,
For the spoiling o her comely hue.

3 She wadna card, nor she wadna spin,
For the shaming o her gentle kin.

4 She wadna wash, nor she wadna wring,
For the spoiling o her gouden ring.

5 The cooper's awa to his woo-pack
And has laid a sheep-skin on his wife's back.

6 'It's I'll no thrash ye, for your proud kin,
But I will thrash my ain sheep-skin.'

7 'Oh, I will bake, and I will brew,
And never mair think on my comely hue.

8 'Oh, I will card, and I will spin,
And never mair think on my gentle kin.

9 'Oh, I will wash, and I will wring,
And never mair think on my gouden ring.'

10 A' ye wha hae gotten a gentle wife
Send ye for the wee cooper o Fife.

D

Jamieson-Brown MS., Appendix, p. iii, letter of R. Scott to Jamieson, 9 June 1805.

1 There livd a laird down into Fife,
    Riftly, raftly, now, now, now
An he has married a bonny young wife.
    Hey Jock Simpleton, Jenny['s] white petticoat,
    Robin a Rashes, now, now, now

2 He courted her and he brought her hame,
    An thought she would prove a thrifty dame.

3 She could neither spin nor caird,
    But sit in her chair and dawt the laird.

4 She wadna bake and she wadna brew,
    An a' was for spoiling her delicate hue.

5 She wadna wash nor wad she wring,
    For spoiling o her gay goud ring.

6 But he has taen him to his sheep-fauld,
    An taen the best weather by the spauld.

7 Aff o the weather he took the skin,
    An rowt his bonny lady in.

8 'I dare na thump you, for your proud kin,
    But well sall I lay to my ain weather's skin.'

*   *   *

E

Jamieson's Popular Ballads, I, 324.

1 There lives a landart laird in Fife,
    And he has married a dandily wife.

2 She wadna shape, nor yet wad she sew,
    But sit wi her cummers and fill hersell fu.

3 She wadna spin, nor yet wad she card,
    But she wad sit and crack wi the laird.

4 He is down to his sheep-fald
    And cleekit a weather by the back-spald.

5 He's whirpled aff the gude weather's-skin
  And wrappit the dandily lady therein.

6 'I darena pay you, for your gentle kin,
  But weel I may skelp my weather's-skin.'

*   *   *